Cape Verde Islands

the Bradt Travel Guide

Aisling Irwin
Colum Wilson
Updated by
Siân Pritchard-Jones & Bob Gibbons

edition
3

www.bradtguides.com

Bradt Travel Guides Ltd, UK
The Globe Pequot Press Inc, USA

Cape Verde Islands

Don't miss...

Hiking
Plantations, Santo Antão
(CN) page 223

Beaches
Fishing boats, Tarrafal, Santiago
(CN) page 142

Landscapes
Gom Gom, Santiago
(CN) pages 146–51

Ribeiras
Fontainhas, Santo Antão
(CN) page 237

Pico de Fogo
(CN) page 173

above Windsurfing at Ponta Preta, Sal
(LC) page 86

main Coast of Santo Antão
(SPJ) page 233

above **Fishing boats at sunset,
Mindelo, São Vicente**
(CN) pages 207–15

centre **Beach at
Tarrafal, Santiago**
(CN) page 142

below **Playtime,
Santa Maria, Sal**
(CN) pages 90–7

above **Mindelo, São Vicente**
(CN) pages 207–15

centre **Pressing sugarcane for distilling *grogue*, Santo Antão**
(CN) pages 232–3

below **Copper kettle for distilling *grogue*, Santo Antão**
(CN) pages 232–3

above **View of Fogo from Santiago** (CN) page 162

centre **Saltpans, Pedra de Lume** (CN) page 97

below **Saltpans, Pedra de Lume** (CN) page 97

Authors

AUTHORS

Colum Wilson and Aisling Irwin are husband and wife. Aisling is a journalist and writer, specialising in the environment, the developing world and science. Colum is a relief worker. They have also written *In Quest of Livingstone: a Journey to the Four Fountains*, about their journey retracing the last footsteps of the explorer.

UPDATERS

Siân Pritchard-Jones and Bob Gibbons

Siân Pritchard-Jones and Bob Gibbons were both born in the UK but met in Kashmir. Since then they have been leading and organising treks in the Alps, Nepal and the Sahara. In 2004, they took their rather ancient Land Rover from England to Cape Town, after which they wrote the fourth edition of the Bradt guide *Africa Overland*. Visiting the Maldives to update that guidebook could hardly have presented a greater contrast, and the Cape Verde Islands was another follow-up.

Third edition March 2006
Reprinted December 2006
First published 1998

Bradt Travel Guides Ltd
www.bradtguides.com
23 High Street, Chalfont St Peter, Bucks SL9 9QE, England
Published in the USA by The Globe Pequot Press Inc,
246 Goose Lane, PO Box 480, Guilford, Connecticut 06437-0480

British Library Cataloguing in Publication Data
A catalogue record for this book is available from the British Library

ISBN-10: 1 84162 102 1
ISBN-13: 978 1 84162 102 9

Photographs
Front cover: Colum Wilson (CW)
Back cover: Fishing boats, Santiago (CN)
Title cover: Plantations, Santo Antão (CN), Girl, Fogo (CN), Sailing, Sal (CN)
Text: Christian Nowak (CN); Luis Conto, GPF (LC); Colum Wilson (CW); Siân
Pritchard-Jones & Bob Gibbons (SPJ)

Illustrations Carole Vincer
Maps Steve Munns, Alan Whitaker

Typeset from the author's disc by Wakewing, High Wycombe
Printed and bound in Italy by Legoprint SpA, Trento

PUBLISHER'S FOREWORD

The first Bradt travel guide was written in 1974 by George and Hilary Bradt on a river barge floating down a tributary of the Amazon. In the 1980s and '90s the focus shifted away from hiking to broader-based guides covering new destinations – usually the first to be published about these places. In the 21st century Bradt continues to publish such ground-breaking guides, as well as others to established holiday destinations, incorporating in-depth information on culture and natural history with the nuts and bolts of where to stay and what to see.

Bradt authors support responsible travel, and provide advice not only on minimum impact but also on how to give something back through local charities. In this way a true synergy is achieved between the traveller and local communities.

* * *

When we commissioned the first edition of this guide in 1997 it seemed an almost impossibly obscure destination. The authors struggled to get around the remote archipelago and the concept of a guidebook to these islands puzzled many of the Cape Verdeans they spoke to. But once the book was published, the visitors started coming: first the windsurfers and other watersports enthusiasts arrived after word got around that this was one of the best regions in the world for their hobby; they were followed by the hikers and outdoors people lured by the remote, volcanic interior; and finally there came those seeking a second home on an island with guaranteed sunshine. It's a pleasure to be able to give these disparate visitors the information they require.

Happy travelling!

Hilary Bradt

Hilary Bradt

23 High Street, Chalfont St Peter, Bucks SL9 9QE, England
℡ 01753 893444 f 01753 892333
e info@bradtguides.com
www.bradtguides.com

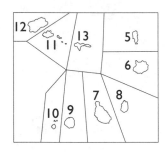

Contents

LIST OF MAPS

Acknowledgements

First and second editions

We are grateful for the help given to us by Promex, in particular Aida Duarte Silva and Isabel Duarte; the national airline TACV; Ron Hughes and Vicky Parnaby of Cape Verde Travel, who specialise in making things possible; and to Barbara Stahler, head of the US peace corps mission.

Particular thanks to Hannah Cruttenden, Simon Day and Jonathan Grepne, who gave a lot of help with the first edition. For the second edition we are very grateful for the time and enthusiasm of Steven Maddocks and Gabi Woolf in Praia; of Keith West in Mindelo; and of Alex Hirtle in Assomada.

Those who have deepened our perspective on the islands include Prof Richard Lobban of Rhode Island College; Daniel Pereira, historian and adviser to the prime minister and historian, Jorge Sousa Brito, rector of the new Jean Piaget University; and Joachim Tavares and John Fernandes for insight into Brava. Also, António Canuto, British honorary consul; Ray Almeida; Traudi Coli; Dr Anibal Lopes da Silva; and Peter and Jill Delgado.

Our understanding of science and conservation issues has been helped greatly by Pedro Lopez for turtles; Beatrice Jann for whales; Emitério Ramos, for forest issues in Santo Antão; Frederick Wenzel, a whale expert; Teresa Leyens, working to conserve Fogo crater; and Dr Peter Wirtz, who specialises in the marine biology of Cape Verde.

Robert Pemberton and Erica Jolly brought useful insights, as did Piran Johnson, Peter Darracott, François Guy, Derek Risebrow and Luigi Zanini.

Several Peace Corps volunteers gave up time to help, for which we are very grateful. Special thanks to Willie Ruzzo on Santo Antão, Tiffany Ko on Boavista, Barry Collins on Santiago and Stephen Murphy on São Nicolau.

Third edition

Without the help of the national airline TACV, the research would not have been possible, and we thank them for their exciting and nearly always punctual flights. Ron Hughes and Lisa Newlove at Cape Verde Travel in the UK also offered indispensable assistance, both before and after the trip.

Many thanks for their great hospitality to the Pousada Belavista in São Filipe, Fogo; Jorge Xavier at the Hotel Pestana Trópico in Praia, Santiago; Virgilio Graça at the Mindel Hotel in Mindelo, São Vicente; and Sophie Marcellesi at the Hotel Morabeza in Santa Maria, Sal.

Thanks also to Agnelo Vieira de Andrade of Dja'r Fogo Travel for his company, good safe driving on the crater roads, enlightening conversation and superb homegrown lemon grass tea. Patrick – we will never forget your mouth-watering chocolate mousse at the crater hotel Pousada Pedra Brabo in Fogo! In Boavista, thanks to Emmeline and Leonardo of ATC Scooters and Quads in Sal Rei. To Xisto Almeida in Praia, thanks for helping us to extricate our passports from the police station and obtain our visa extensions.

On Santiago we are particularly grateful to Gerhard and Sibylle Schellmann, who run a trekking tour company there, for their updates concerning the central and northern zones of the island, and for their updates to the Brava chapter.

Special thanks to Harry Wilson and Michael Turner of the Drake Exploration Society, whose magazine is *The Drake Broadside*, for their help and information concerning Drake's visits to the Cape Verde Islands.

Finally, thanks to Unotour in Santa Maria, one of the few local sources of current information, and to Isabel Duarte, who still works at the Praia Promex office, now referred to as the Agencia de Promoção de Investimentos.

Islands lost
in the midst of the sea
forgotten
in an angle of the World
– where the waves
cradle
abuse
embrace ...

Jorge Barbosa, poet of Cape Verde, in Basil Davidson's
The Fortunate Isles, Hutchinson, 1989

Introduction

The flight to the island of Maio was full. As the tiny propeller plane bounced over Atlantic air currents, I was the only passenger to gaze out with a lick of fear at the mighty mid ocean below. Inside the plane everyone else seemed to have forgotten the sea. All was exuberance, chatter and a roaring laughter. The passengers were young men in polished shoes, expensive trousers and heavy gold jewellery. They spoke in a Creole that was too rapid for me to grasp and I wondered what interest Maio – flat, dry and quiet even by Cape Verdean standards – could hold for them.

A few days later I was being driven through the north of Maio, mesmerised by its endless stony red plains where the goats seem to eat rock and the people eat goats. I reached a village – a single street of dust, two rows of parched, single-storey houses, a few skeletal dogs. 'This is Alcatraz,' the driver said.

The street was quiet apart from a few of the ragged, wide-eyed children who populate the poorer half of the world. Some of the houses were nothing more than bare concrete carcasses while others were painted in greens and pinks and blues and even had glass in their windows.

From the front door of one of the smarter houses a family appeared. I crossed the street and said in Portuguese: 'Do you mind if I take a photo of this place?'

'Not at all,' the man replied in perfect English. 'But don't you remember me? I was on the flight here the other day.'

My perception jolted and suddenly I saw the urbane passenger, representative of a richer world, gold still gleaming at his neck. And then my world altered again and I saw a destitute village, forgotten even within Cape Verde. He must have noticed my perplexity: 'I live in Holland,' he explained. 'I work on the ships … I've come back to see my wife and children.' The woman at his side, uncomprehending, scooped a child on to her hip.

'How long have you been away?' I asked.

'Three years.'

'That's hard.'

'Yes,' he replied and then he leant a little towards me, his hands pressing at the low wall in front of his house. 'But we Cape Verdeans – we have hard lives.'

That is one of the paradoxes of Cape Verde. There is a widespread cosmopolitanism that dates from centuries ago, but it lives side by side with poverty and isolation. For generations the young men have gone abroad – to the USA, to Europe, to the African mainland – because the land cannot sustain them, because their families need money. Back at home their relatives mourn not just the loss of their own sons and husbands but the painful emigrations of generations before. They mourn the peculiar lot of the Cape Verdean, stranded on outcrops in the Atlantic, abused over the centuries not just by the waves but by many nations. They mourn in a particularly beautiful way which I first discovered on Fogo, the volcano island.

I was clinging to the bench in the back of a small truck as it jolted up and down the steep cobbled roads of the old Portuguese town of São Filipe. Every so often the vehicle would halt in front of a house, the driver would shout a greeting and a man would appear in the doorway clutching a violin or some other instrument and scramble in beside me.

Soon we had gathered the band back together and we careered up into the foothills of Fogo's dark volcano till we reached the house of Joaquim, a blind musician. Inside his white-painted, two-roomed home the men dragged chairs and benches together and I sat in a far corner as the violins made their awakening screeches and the guitars were tuned. Then the music began: sweet melodies and melancholy harmonies. The music was so sad, it was as if the sorrow of generations had erupted in the house.

The Cape Verdeans express through their *mornas* the sorrow of sons lost to the wider world, droughts, famines and relatives drowned at sea. Their music is exquisite, an Atlantic art form with influences from the four continents that surround it. But soon the sadness was done with and the music changed to the lively strains of a *funana*. Now we were celebrating ... what, I wondered? I knew the answer, though. We were celebrating the same notion that had just made us cry – *Caboverdeanidade*, the essence of Cape Verde.

I absorbed it all in the dim room with its rough furniture and garish crocheted ornaments. Later I stepped outside where the sun was dissolving into the ocean. As I watched, the music still playing behind me, I thought: this is the reason to visit Cape Verde. There are fine mountains, wildernesses of desert dunes and warm waters. But what makes Cape Verde take hold of your heart is that rare moment, that flush of empathy, when you begin to understand what they mean by *sodade*.

Introduction to the third edition
Sîan Pritchard-Jones and Bob Gibbons

Our first contact with anyone from the Cape Verde Islands was with an expatriate family working in the tiny Swiss alpine village of Trient. The children had never been to their ancestral homeland, being born in Portugal, the old colonial ruler of the islands. This is the story of many Cape Verdeans today, for the islands are harsh and dry, supporting little life, yet having a uniquely stark beauty of their own.

Expatriates send back remittances or return themselves to build superb homes, which often double as *residencials* and *pensãos*. The number of tourist developments is also increasing rapidly, with building sites aplenty. Because of this, the country does not appear poor on the surface. Nevertheless, there are few natural resources and a distinct lack of water, so most food and goods have to be imported.

Each of the islands has its own qualities; none is like any of the others. Tourism at the moment can basically be split into two main categories: beach and watersports on the eastern islands, and mountain trekking in the western isles. Both of these are equally valid reasons to visit the country and both will help to develop prosperity for the people. The music, full of emotion, is an added bonus for all visitors.

Travelling around Cape Verde to update this book was for us a profoundly different experience, and we hope that readers of this new edition will feel equally inspired to visit these remote islands for themselves.

Part One

The Country

Grey-headed kingfisher

CAPE VERDE ARCHIPELAGO AT A GLANCE

Islands Santa Luzia (uninhabited), Santo Antão, São Vicente, São Nicolau, Sal, Boavista, Maio, Santiago, Fogo, Brava

Location Atlantic Ocean, approximately 1,000km southwest of the Canary Islands, and 460km from the Senegalese coast

Size Ten islands varying from 35km^2 (Santa Luzia) to 990km2 (Santiago), spread over an east–west band of 370km of ocean

Status Independent republic

Government African Party for Independence of Cape Verde or PAIVC

Population 418,244 (2005)

Life expectancy 70.5 years

Capital Praia, on Santiago (population around 117,000)

Economy Tourism an increasing earner; bananas most important export

Language Officially Portuguese, commonly Creole

Religion Roman Catholic

Currency Cape Verdean escudo (CVE, written as $, after the numeral)

Exchange rate US$1 = 92.12$, £1 = 162.26$, 1 = 110.25$ (January 2006)

International telephone code +238

Time GMT –1

Electricity supply 220 volts AC, 50Hz. Round, European two-pin sockets

Flag Horizontal yellow and green rectangles, joined to vertical red rectangle with star and clam emblem

Public holidays 1 January, 20 January, 1 May, 5 July, 15 August, 12 September, 1 November, 25 December. See also page 52.

Helmeted guinea fowl (galinha de guinea)

Perspective

HISTORY

White lives in big house
Mulato lives in shop
Black lives in hut
Sancho lives in mountain:
But a day will come
When Sancho turn all upside down:
Horribly grimacing
Tail curled up
Sancho drag black from hut
Black drag mulato from shop
Mulato drag white from big house
White run to mountain and there he fall

A *batuque* of Santa Caterina, published in the magazine *Claridade* (1948)
Translated by Basil Davidson, *The Fortunate Isles* (Hutchinson, 1989)

When the first island of Cape Verde erupted from the ocean hundreds of kilometres from the African coast, the archipelago's fate was sealed. For, overwhelmingly, the islands' unique and often tragic history has been the result of their position. Their history is one of use and abuse by nationalities from the four corners of the Atlantic. The world has changed around them and has found fleeting uses for them: they have served until they are exhausted and then they have been forgotten until another convulsion in world affairs has produced a new use for them.

The archipelago's story is a sad one but it has a happy, or at least a hopeful, ending. For now the Cape Verdeans have their own identity, proclaim their own culture and, most importantly, govern themselves. For the first time they can act strategically. At the same time the outside world has changed and has found new uses for Cape Verde: white beaches to serve the interests of mass tourism, abundant fish when other seas are severely depleted. Whether the archipelago will be able to exploit these riches for itself, or whether the 21st century will be just another chapter in which it is sucked dry and thrown away, it is too early to tell.

Rocks appear and life arrives

According to local lore, when God was satisfied with Creation, and brushed his hands together, the crumbs that fell unnoticed from his fingers into the sea formed Cape Verde.

The geological explanation for their existence is just as seductive. Under the plates of the Earth's crust lie 'hot spots' of bubbling magma, one of which is several hundred kilometres west of Senegal. Every so often, when the conditions of heat and pressure are right, this hot spot has erupted as a volcano, leaving an island in the Atlantic to mark where it has been. In this way, some fifteen million years ago, the island of Sal was created. It was a mountainous pile of rock which has since been the victim of the ocean winds and has eroded away to become flat and brown.

The hot spot erupted every few millions of years to make another pimple on the Atlantic. Today it is still putting the final touches to youthful Fogo, which lies in the southwest. The island is 100,000 years old. One senses that brooding Fogo gazes east towards Sal preparing to spend the next ten million years weathering down to a similar fate.

Somehow, plant life found Cape Verde, carried there on winds from mainland Africa or by the ocean itself. Over such a distance there was only a tiny chance of such a voyage culminating in life reaching the islands – but millions of seeds over millions of years transformed that chance to a certainty. Once they had arrived they were cut off from their relatives and evolved into new species, as island life does.

Next came aquatic life. Washed into the Cape Verdean shallows by accident, many species remained to evolve their own identity in the same way as the plants. Other, more ocean-going species, such as turtles, have found the islands a useful stopping point. The story of the birds is much the same.

Legend shrouds the tales of the first humans to arrive at the islands. They may have been Phoenician sea captains who landed there and left no trace except for some enigmatic inscriptions on a rock that survive until the present day. In 445BC the Phoenican captain Hanno sailed from Cadiz and reported that he passed some small islands which scholars now believe may have been Cape Verde. He named them Hesperias. Once Hanno wrote that he had seen a large volcano off the west African coast: perhaps it was Fogo. West African sailors, too, may have reached Cape Verde in their sea-going canoes, but they left no trace.

And so the islands lay, effectively undiscovered, until the middle of the 15th century. The reason for their elusiveness is also the very reason why, when they were discovered, they were to prove so useful. For they lie below the latitude of the Canary Islands, a region into which any ship that dared to venture would never return. Myths surrounded the fate of the ships from the north that vanished beyond the Canaries but their disappearance has a simple explanation. The prevailing northeasterly wind drove them south but then, like a one-way valve, blocked their return.

In the 15th century this barrier to human ambition fell. The rig was invented, and allowed mariners to harness the wind so they could sail against as well as before it. It was one of the most significant of all inventions, enabling humans to emerge from their home continents and link every region of the globe. The west coast of Africa was now a prize for whichever nation could reach it first, and it was inevitable that the Portuguese, with the skills and vision of Prince Henry the Navigator behind them, would win.

Several famous mariners pushed ever further south in the 1460s and more than one claimed to have discovered Cape Verde. The debate will probably never be resolved. Perhaps it was the Venetian, Cadamosto, who claimed to have sighted the islands first in 1456. More likely, it was the Genoese António de Noli who may have stumbled on them in 1455 or in 1461. Some reports say he was accompanied by the Portuguese Diogo Gomes.

Whatever the truth is, all the islands were discovered between 1455 and 1461 and the credit generally goes to de Noli and to Gomes, for discovering Santiago and the other leeward isles. Diogo Afonso discovered the windward islands of Santo Antão, São Vicente and São Nicolau. The archipelago was named Cape Verde, not because it was verdant, but after the green butt of Senegal that lies across the sea.

It is hard to understand now the value of such a discovery. Venturing over the seas with only the capricious wind for power, with no facility for measuring longitude and with limited water and food that would swiftly rot or be eaten, the cry of 'land ahoy' could mean the difference between life and death.

The Portuguese realised that the islands could be of immense strategic power. And so colonisation began in 1462 when a small group of Portuguese, Spanish and Genoese settled on the most promising island, Santiago. The southern half was allotted to de Noli, who set up in Ribeira Grande on the south coast. The northern half fell to Afonso, who began much less successfully in the northwest.

Lisbon wanted to entice talented men to live on the islands and develop them, so Cape Verde was awarded a valuable advantage over other Portuguese colonies. Settlers were given exclusive trading rights along the creeks and shores of the west African coast between Senegal and Sierra Leone. These rivers thus became known as the Rivers of Cape Verde, later to be known as the Rivers of Guinea.

At this time the Atlantic was dotted with Portuguese and Spanish ships making prolific discoveries in the Americas, Africa and beyond Africa's southern tip, as far as India and China. It was the beginning of the expansion of Europe, the spread of its civilisation around the globe and unprecedented mass migration. Over the next 300 years Europeans would emigrate to North and South America and Africa. Africans would fill the Americas, mainly as slaves. The Portuguese and Spanish had begun nothing less than a global redistribution of races, animals and plants and the beginnings of modern mass trade. Meanwhile, the few resources of Cape Verde were put to use, and trading began that would supply the Portuguese Crown with income for centuries.

From rock to trading post: the 1500s

The first desire of the colonisers of Santiago was to plant and reap, for which they wanted the services of an unpaid labour force. They found what they wanted on the mainland coast of Africa: slaves. Over the next century these captives from the great tribes of west Africa arrived in their thousands, and were soon put to work growing food and cotton in the valleys. By 1582, there were 13,700 slaves labouring on Santiago and Fogo under a regime of 100 white men.

The settlers released goats on to the uninhabited islands where they devoured the scrub pasture and provided meat, hides, butter, milk and cheese, and some cattle were farmed. But barren Cape Verde would never provide enough food for prosperity. Wealth generation was to come from two other activities: resupply of ships, and the slave trade.

Cape Verde lies at the Atlantic crossroads, not just because of its position in relation to the land masses of the Americas, Europe and Africa, but because of where it lies in relation to the north Atlantic wind patterns and to ocean currents. Both factors drew America-bound ships towards the archipelago. Increasingly, in the latter part of the 16th century, the Portuguese who stopped there were on their way to open up the treasure of Brazil. The Spanish were ferrying goods and people to and from the vast new empire they were creating in South America.

In 1580, Spain and Portugal united to create an Iberian empire with three powerful realms, the spice empire of the east, the sugar empire of the south Atlantic, and the silver empire of Spanish America. Iberian vessels often found it useful to stop at Cape Verde for beverages and victuals, for ship repair and for nautical supplies.

Thus, throughout the 1500s, ship supply was the islands' great function, and the most basic commodities of water and food were its speciality. They charged a high price for fresh water and sold maize, beans and dried or salted goat meat.

They also exported horses, donkeys, cattle and goat hides. Cape Verde's other commodity lay in sparkling white lakes on the three flat islands to the east: salt, and enough, it seemed, to supply mankind in perpetuity.

Once there were sufficient slaves working on the islands, the Portuguese looked west for new markets. They were in a unique position to sell slaves for labour in South American colonies and so the archipelago became a warehouse for human merchandise.

For slave merchants who would otherwise have had to visit the African coast, Cape Verde was an expensive market but a sanitised one. Forays to the mainland could be dangerous and lengthy. Ships were often delayed, sometimes for months. Payment methods were elaborate: tribal leaders often demanded a multiplicity of items, iron bars, cloth, brandy, guns, knives, ribbons and beads. In addition, the land was rife with disease and the creeks and rivers of the coast were tricky to navigate. If a ship became stranded on the shore the local people would claim it for their own.

There were other advantages in shopping for slaves in Cape Verde. The negroes had been 'seasoned'. The sickly, unfit and obstinate had been weeded out or had died. Those who remained had given up hope of escape. They had also learned a few Portuguese words so they would understand orders, and they had been baptised. The Portuguese Church argued that a baptised slave was luckier than a free African because the former had achieved the chance of a place in heaven.

Thousands of slaves were Fula. They were victims of Gabu, a tributary kingdom to the Mandingo Empire of Mali. Gabu, founded in the mid 13th century, stretched through most of today's northeastern Guinea-Bissau. Its people were warriors and their battles generated many of the slaves who were then traded in the coast.

Alongside the business of slavery grew trade in other goods from the African coast: ivory, wax, hides, gum, amber, musk, honey and gold dust. Cape Verde took them and became a depot where these products were exchanged for goods coveted by wealthy Africans, Venetian beads and wine from Europe, for example; silver from Spanish America; cloves and coral from the East. Cape Verde itself supplied the African coast with raw cotton, cloth, salted goat meat, horses and cattle.

The important islands in those first years were Santiago, where the settlers built a capital in the green valley of Ribeira Grande; Fogo, a live but fertile volcano; and the lonely salt island of Maio. Ribeira Grande was the first city built by Europeans in the tropics and became one of the highest-yielding cities of the Portuguese kingdom. Visitors praised its comforts and in 1533 it was elevated from the rank of *vila* to *cidade*. In 1556, the Bishop of Cape Verde, whose jurisdiction extended to the mainland, began building his cathedral there, and in 1570 the king agreed to the founding of a seminary. All was optimism and prosperity.

Cape Verde mustered few home-produced goods with one major exception: cotton. It was grown by slaves who then wove it into cloth of the finest quality, which was marketed along the west African coast and in Brazil. Its skilful patterns became outstandingly popular amongst Africans and the cloth rose to be the chief currency for trading (see *Culture*, page 23). This gave Cape Verde a continuing hold on the slave trade even when competition appeared from other nations. English and French ships were forced to stop at the archipelago to obtain cloth for barter on the mainland.

Another trade was in the dye-yielding lichen orchil, which was collected in mountainous areas and transformed into a potion of vivid blue.

Thus, positioned between the Old World, Africa and South America, slicing taxes from every import and export, and with a monopoly on trade with the mainland, Cape Verde had become a viable community, with the slave trade its fundamental market and Portugal reaping as much as it could.

During this period the botanical colonisation of the islands was completed as well. As a traffic junction, Cape Verde received plants from everywhere, particularly maize from Brazil, which became a staple, and cassava, which was later planted on the African mainland.

The Atlantic grows busier: the 1600s

Driving the defenders before them they entered the City almost without resistance, where they sacked houses and destroyed them. The authorities fled to the hills and the English, carrying away their spoil, departed to Cartagena and San Domingo.

Contemporary account of the sacking of Ribeira Grande

As the 1600s began, rival nations appeared on the seas. The French, English and Dutch spilled into the Atlantic, and aggression on the ocean became more than the sporadic acts of piracy and smuggling that had characterised the second half of the previous century. Cape Verde became increasingly vulnerable to attack and Portugal foresaw this, responding in 1587 by appointing a governor-general for the islands who was directly responsible to the Crown for Cape Verde and the Guinea coast.

Now France, England and Holland were becoming serious forces in the Atlantic, making their discoveries mainly in North America. As they began to make settlements in their new lands they, too, started to look for slaves. Business across the Atlantic multiplied as the desire for sugar, slaves, salt and fish sent trading ships in a perpetual circle between the four continents.

As international affairs fluctuated so, too, did Cape Verdean fortunes. They fell for a while when the Dutch seized Portuguese slaving sources in west Africa. They were sacked and plundered by nations who were at odds with Spain or Portugal. Their fortunes rose after 1640 when Portugal achieved independence from Spain.

Overall, though, the archipelago still made money because the demand for slaves was rising. It was at its peak for Cape Verde during the 1600s and 1700s. Numbers are uncertain, partly because many slaves were not measured in whole 'units'. A 15–25-year-old was a *peca*'s worth. A 30-year-old in good health was two-thirds of a *peca*. Records are poor but it has been estimated that 3,000 slaves a year left the Cape Verdes in 1609 and 1610, although these were probably peak years. These slaves earned Cape Verde about £6,500 in import taxes and £1,300 in export taxes over the two years. Nearly three-quarters of the revenue the Portuguese Crown received from Cape Verde was from the slave trade.

The question that exercised the people of the archipelago was why much of its profit should go straight back to Lisbon. It was part of a wider question: what was the purpose of Cape Verde? If it was merely an overseas warehouse then the Portuguese were entitled to shift headquarters elsewhere or neglect to invest if it failed to make enough profit. But Cape Verde was now a place that some called home and they were trying to make a living there in spite of increasingly tight controls from the Crown.

During the first 150 years of colonisation, blacks and whites came together to found the Cape Verdean ancestry, and the core of Cape Verde society became remarkably stable. Other Portuguese were reluctant to follow as settlers because the islands were perceived as an arduous posting. In particular, few Portuguese women arrived. The black population was similarly stable, with the shiploads of slaves destined for distant lands mere transient visitors, isolated from the static population of local slaves which after the 1500s was not added to.

Black and white, isolated from the rest of the world by the ocean, developed complex layers of relationships. Interbreeding produced a race of *mestiços* who had nowhere else to call their motherland and who were not to assert their national identity until the 20th century.

Cape Verdean Creole heritage differed from other Creole cultures around the world for several reasons. The Cape Verdeans emerged in an empty place where there had been no indigenous population. They were the descendants of a smaller number of whites than is the case with other Creole cultures and so the European element was never sufficiently strong to have cultural dominance.

It was these 'pre-Cape Verdeans' – whites and, increasingly, people of mixed race governing a large number of slaves – who complained bitterly and frequently about the way Lisbon organised the slave and other trades, and in particular about the rise of the Crown monopolies.

The monopolies

The right to extract slaves from the African coast was awarded by the Crown as a single, monopolistic contract which lasted for six years. The benefit for the Crown was that the contractor paid a lump sum and agreed to supply a few incidentals including slaves for the king, and some money donated to the church.

Whoever bought this slaving right then subcontracted it to smaller enterprises. The Portuguese Crown received customs duties when contractors deposited slaves at Cape Verde, and also export duties from those who bought them. The people of Cape Verde were banned from engaging in other trade with non-Portuguese. This rule was resented and widely flouted.

The islanders began to feel seriously undermined in 1675, when the Crown handed out to various companies a series of crippling monopolistic rights over the west African and Cape Verdean trades. The terms seemed to bypass the role of the archipelago as middleman.

Under the rules of the first monopoly, the contractor possessed the sole right to take international products to the Guinea coast for trading: Cape Verdeans were permitted to trade with only homegrown products such as cloth and salt. Santiago's access to Africa, therefore, was deeply threatened.

Further decrees were issued by Lisbon. Perhaps the most memorable was that of 1687 which banned anyone on Cape Verde from selling cloth to foreigners, under penalty of death.

The second monopoly was granted in 1690 to a newly formed organisation, the Company of the Islands of Cape Verde and Guiné (Companho Nacional de Cabo Verde e Guiné). Even more restrictive conditions were included in the new contract, and two seemed almost guaranteed to ensure that Cape Verde was bypassed in the international slave trade. Firstly, the contractor bought the right to supply the Spanish Indies directly with slaves so he had no need to find someone to buy them on the archipelago. Secondly, the Governor of Cape Verde was put in the pay of the new company so that if he complained about the regime he could be silenced.

By 1700, Cape Verde felt that it had been ousted by the monopoly companies from its role as a slave-trading depot. It was left to concentrate on the more predictable business of victualling the hundred ships a year that called at Santiago for supplies in the second half of the 1600s.

Conflict: the 1700s

The 1700s began with a bang and the War of the Spanish Succession to stop France gaining control of Spain. Fears that the fusion of the two countries would give them too much power over Atlantic possessions were typical of the concerns of other European powers at the time. The century was to be one of territorial expansion to the west of the Atlantic, consolidation, and the rise of the British as the supreme naval force.

Cape Verde would always be prey to the whims of the rest of the world, successful when exploiting the needs of a diversity of countries and unsuccessful when those needs suddenly changed. When Portugal was drawn into the War of Succession, the slave trade with the Spanish Indies came to a sudden end for Cape Verde but also for the monopoly companies.

That war did not finish until 1714 and was the cause of the sack of Santiago in 1712, a disastrous plunder by the French which robbed Ribeira Grande of all its riches. The people of Cape Verde urged Lisbon to liberalise its trade and finally, in 1721, Portugal gave in and relaxed the rules so that the people could trade with whom they wished. Business was reinvigorated. But the central problem remained – Portugal was not prepared to pour money into a string of rocks which could not guarantee much return. The people of the islands were left to live on their wits, thinking only from day to day.

This conflict was behind many of the background problems of the archipelago. Goats chomped inexorably at the fragile vegetation that had taken millions of years to win a hold in the face of Saharan winds. Without sophisticated and long-term management of the land it was inevitable that famine would increasingly afflict the islands. Every century there were one or two more than the century before and, in 1773–76, 44% of the population died.

Lack of investment in proper military protection also led to raids which were a perpetual drain on resources. Like a fleet of sail-less ships the islands were unable to flee marauders of the high seas.

The end of slavery: the 1800s

Towards the end of the 1700s the seeds were sown in America and Europe for convulsions that would end the 300-year-old Atlantic slave trade and transform life for most nations that bordered the Atlantic. The changes were partly intellectual. The Enlightenment grew in Europe, with its faith in rationality and social progress; with it came the concepts of the rights of man and the iniquity of slavery, both of which served to justify the French and American revolutions. After the French Revolution Napoleon's energies were unleashed on the oceans and one of the consequences was that Portugal and Spain were cut off from their colonies in South America. The effect of this was profound. A vacuum arose in 19th-century South America into which grew movements for liberation, followed by the abolition of slavery and, later, the rise of concepts such as African nationalism which would inspire countries such as Cape Verde to fight for independence.

Slavery was disappearing in North America as well, following independence in 1783. America became a land of promise that lured millions of emigrants fleeing starvation or unemployment in other parts of the world. The 1800s became an era of mass global migration.

Cape Verde was buffeted by these 19th-century Atlantic storms. One of the most bitter was the demise of its own slave trading, abolished as a 'business' by the Portuguese in 1854, with private slavery ending in 1876.

During the 19th century the dominance of the sailing ship came to an end, and with it Cape Verde's prime function as a resupplier. But as Santiago suffered there were two other islands where seminal, and profitable, changes were occurring.

SIR FRANCIS DRAKE IN CAPE VERDE

with Harry Wilson and Michael Turner, using background information from
issue 17 of the Drake Broadside journal issued by the Drake Exploration
Society, June 2005, edited by Michael Turner

Sir Francis Drake, seaman, pirate, adventurer or loyal servant of the Crown –
take your own definition – first visited the Cape Verde Islands in 1578. He made
landfall on 28 January close to modern-day Vila do Maio on Maio Island, not far
from the saltpans.

> ...we found a town not far from the water's side, of a great many
> desolate and ruinous houses, with a poor naked chapel...

A further impression of Maio at the time of Drake's visit is gleaned from the
following:

> This island yields other great commodities, as well as herds of goats,
> infinite store of wild hens, and salt without labour, only the gathering
> it together excepted, which continually in a marvellous quantity is
> increased upon by the sands by the flowing of the sea...

That the island's climate has changed in the last 550 years is not in doubt, yet
what is seen today remains all too familiar, in a less isolated way.

> We found good water in diverse places, but so far off the road that
> we could not with any reasonable pains enjoy it.

from Penzer, World Encompassed

Drake stayed only two days, departing for Santiago on 30 January. A modern-day
visitor will probably stay no longer, unless he or she is travelling to the ends of the
earth, seeking solitude on desolate isolated beaches away from all humanity, or
seeking to make gains in exporting its finest salt. Some of Drake's men are
believed to have marched inland as far as Figuera Horta, but other than observing
valleys of fruits within the low hills, his brief sojourn is of little other interest.

From various information and descriptions, Drake is believed to have landed
on Santiago, close to modern-day Praia Baixo and its bay. Drake observed
Cidade Velha before continuing on towards Brazil:

> South west from Saint Iago, in 14 deg. 30mins, about 12 leagues
> distant, yet by reason of the height, seeming not about 3 leagues, lay

The first was São Vicente. It has a perfect and generous natural harbour, perhaps
the safest place to pause in the entire eastern Atlantic. Other than that it is a sterile
pile of stones and so it had been of little interest in previous centuries.

This deep harbour was just the place for the new steam ships born of the
Industrial Revolution to stop and reload with coal on their journeys along the
Atlantic shipping lanes. The British, riding the crest of the invention of the steam
engine, flocked to São Vicente to set up coaling stations. Mindelo, its capital, grew
at an astonishing rate.

The second island where epochal events were taking place was a tiny one: Brava.
It was at this insignificant dot at the end of the archipelago that whaling ships from
New England began to stop and pick up eager crews of young men. The ships
offered the possibility of passage to America and in this way Cape Verdeans joined
the mass migration to the New World.

> another island, called by the Portugalls, Fogo, the burning land or fiery
> furnace, in which rises a steep upright hill…within the bowels where of
> is a consuming fire,…the fire showeth itself but four times an hour…

from Penzer, World Encompassed

Passing swiftly on, Drake sailed to Brava (no waiting around for a ferry in those days!). In fact Drake needed to replenish his water supplies before crossing the ocean to landfall on the Brazilian coast:

> From the banks into the sea do run in many places the silver streams
> of sweet and wholesome water, which with boat or pinnaces may be
> easily taken in.

from Penzer, World Encompassed

A brief exploration of the island revealed a single inhabitant, a hermit who fled from the scene until the motley crew had departed for South America.

Drake returned to Cape Verde in November 1585. This time he anchored close to Ribeira Grande, now called Cidade Velha. From descriptions and drawings produced by Baptista Boazio, an Italian cartographer sailing with Drake on this voyage, it would appear that little has changed in this historic settlement. Around 1,500 people lived in the town at the time, and Drake's total forces numbered 2,300 men. During Drake's visit the town was nominally under a Spanish governor with a Portuguese bishop, a brief legacy of the political situation in the Iberian Peninsula at the time.

Finding all the inhabitants of Cidade Velha had fled, Drake ordered his men to head inland to São Domingo.

> This part of the island is the most pleasant and richest of all the rest,
> abounding with stores of fruits, having a fair and pleasant river running
> by the bishop's house.

Leicester Journal

Here too the people had dispersed, so, finding little plunder of value, Drake's men torched the village and set off for Porto Praia. About 500 people dwelt in Praia at the time. Drake again fired the town and left the islands for the West Indies.

Fever decimated his crews from that time on, a divine retribution perhaps for his actions?

They went on emigrating throughout the century and on into the next. In the first 20 years of the 1900s, 19,000 Cape Verdeans set up new homes there. Many of them still regarded the archipelago as their home, which would eventually bring great economic benefit to Cape Verde.

The structure of Cape Verdean society changed in the 19th century as homegrown slavery disappeared. In 1834, a rough count yielded 52,000 free or freed men and women, and 4,000 slaves. Yet for most people the 1870s declaration that, finally, slavery was to end, did not mean a better life, for slaves had to serve further years of forced labour which were to continue in various guises until well into the following century. Another social change occurred as Cape Verde became a place of exile for Portuguese convicts, from thieves to political dissidents. Between 1802 and 1882, according to the English historian Basil Davidson, nearly 2,500 such *degredados* arrived at the islands: 'They were at once absorbed into a population increasingly homogeneous in its culture and way of life, if notably various in the colours of its skin.'

Portugal ruled by skin colour. A census of 1856 listed 17 distinctions ranging from various shades of 'very dark' to 'almost white'. Many lighter Cape Verdeans clung to their rank and despised the darker ones.

Suffering: the beginning of the 1900s

The 20th century began with a very different Cape Verde. The cinder heap of São Vicente, not fertile Santiago, was its chief commercial centre. São Vicente attracted a hopeless migration of the desperate from other islands in search of work. But the island had virtually no natural resources and was incapable of sustaining a rural peasant population. So when the shipping business dipped, as it did from time to time, the consequences of drought became increasingly shocking. Some 17,000 died in 1921. In 1922, the Santiago journal *A Verdade* reported:

> 1921 was horrific ... yet now follows this of 1922, equally horrific but with the addition that people have spent all they possess, whether in clothes or land, livestock or trinkets, and today are in the last stage of poverty, while emigration is carrying away all whom the steamers can embark.

The rains came in the end. In the 1930s they were plentiful and the archipelago turned green. Emigrants, fleeing the Depression in the USA, returned to live with their families. But it did not last, and hunger returned in the early 1940s.

Outside the archipelago World War II began. On the islands, anti-Portuguese sentiment surged when Lisbon decided to garrison over 6,000 men amongst the islands' starving population. It is possible that Portugal feared that the British or the Germans were planning to seize the archipelago, and their fears were justified. Winston Churchill had well-developed plans to invade Cape Verde but called them off at the last minute. The matter of who controlled the islands was still of interest to the world.

Peace came in 1945 but for the Cape Verdeans the worst drought they were ever to face was looming. Some 30,000 people died. The hunger was exacerbated by the return of the emigrant Americans a few years before: they swelled the numbers and decreased the remittances.

This hideous cycle of drought and famine raises the question: could it have been avoided? After all, Cape Verdeans do not die of hunger today. The answer is still obscure but it seems certain that an important ingredient of the famines was the way the land was owned and run. It was a system which discouraged peasants from planning more than a season ahead.

Agriculture was mired in a system of inheritance which split land with each generation until people farmed it in splinters in an inefficient way. Land that was not subject to this system was owned in great swathes by a small number of men who rented it out in patches a year at a time. The peasants who farmed this land had no incentive to improve it: they knew that the extra yield would be taken as rent.

So, at a time when the people could have been producing income for the islands by cultivating cash crops such as coffee for export, agriculture stagnated. This, combined with the dwindling of tree cover, imposed deep poverty. Cape Verde was becoming an increasingly unsustainable place. Population control was left to the crude device of starvation.

People escaped not just to America but also to work on other Portuguese islands. They left for São Tomé and Príncipe in their tens of thousands: 24,000 Cape Verdeans worked there between 1902 and 1922; 34,000 laboured there from

1950–70. In this way these *contratados* escaped starvation, though some said the labourers returned more emaciated than when they left.

Soon Cape Verde's only lingering use, as a coaling station, seemed to be vanishing as well; oil was replacing coal as the fuel for the high seas and, as a result, few ships needed to pause there. When they did stop, resupply with oil was an easier, smaller business than loading coal. There was no need to maintain great companies with armies of staff on the crescent of rock halfway to South America. The world had dumped Cape Verde.

Revolt

Ideas of independence began to grow in the minds of 20th-century Cape Verdeans as a result of several world events. The consequences of their uprising, when it eventually came, were momentous. It was probably the first time in Cape Verde's history that the rocks made a splash of their own, and the ripples spread far. For it was Cape Verdeans, unique in Portuguese Africa because of their education and cosmopolitanism, who led the ferment in other Portuguese African colonies. This in turn weakened Portugal and was the direct cause of the unseating of its fascist dictatorship.

One important force arose from the European 'scramble for Africa', which began in the late 1800s and had allocated most of the continent to colonial rule by the early 1900s. When World War I diverted the colonists' attention, resistance to colonial rule gathered pace, giving rise to the growing feeling that European reins could be thrown away. Cape Verde, unusual in having been subjugated for long centuries rather than mere decades, absorbed these ideas as they emerged in other European colonies.

Allied to this was the rise of communism, which leaked into Africa and gave structure to undirected stirrings of antagonism amongst the people towards their rulers.

Another factor was necessary, however, for Cape Verdeans to begin to assimilate these ideas: they needed to hear about them and they needed to be educated enough to understand them. This impetus came, ironically, from the beneficence of Lisbon. Portugal had acknowledged the peculiarity of its Cape Verde colony and recognised its *mestiço* population as closer to its own than were the natives of mainland Africa. As a result, Cape Verdeans were granted a form of Portuguese citizenship, although it is unclear how this benefited most of them. The archipelago was also the intellectual centre of the Portuguese African colonies, with a secondary school which attracted pupils from the mainland, and a seminary.

There arose a small group of urbane, mixed-race Cape Verdeans whom the Portuguese employed as middlemen. They were halfway between black and white and so they could more easily administer the people of Portuguese Guinea, Angola, Mozambique and São Tomé, while being an acceptable interface with the true Portuguese. A select group of Cape Verdeans was thus educated, chosen as a literate class of administrators, and sent to work in diverse outposts of empire.

From this group sprang poets and journalists who began to seek to express the nature of Cape Verdeanism. Their political objectives were limited: they prized the privilege of Portuguese citizenship and supported enlightened colonialism, defending the fledgling republic that was born in Portugal in 1910.

Perhaps if the liberalism that accompanied the new Portuguese republic had been allowed to continue, the movement for independence would have come earlier. Perhaps it would have fizzled out. We shall never know, for in 1926 the republic was overthrown by its own military, inaugurating 50 years of fascist dictatorship. Freedom of speech disappeared.

More visible twitchings of nationhood came with the publication of *Claridade*, a journal that called to the nation to realise the essence of 'Cape Verdeanness'. It published the work of some gifted writers in four issues between 1936 and 1941, and in another six after the end of World War II.

For 500 years there had been no such race or culture as the Cape Verdean. There were Portuguese, there were slaves and there were *mestiços*. Yet the Cape Verdeans were there, incipient, infused with the knowledge of their African and European roots, endowed with a musical and poetic culture. *Claridade* helped them to see this – to define as Cape Verdean their laments and their poetry, the way they wore their clothes and their craftsmanship. *Claridade* reminded them that they had their own language: Creole.

It was those members of the educated class who were teenagers in the early 1940s who made the crucial step in the evolution of Cape Verdean thought. They were so angered by the mass of deaths in the droughts of that time that they began to believe that Cape Verde could be better off if it was independent from Portugal.

Amílcar Cabral was just 17, and in his second year at secondary school, when the 1941 famine ravaged the people of Mindelo. His later success in rousing the people of Cape Verde and Portuguese Guinea to rise against the Portuguese, and his effective fighting techniques, have been ascribed by historians to his profound knowledge of these countries and his ability to inspire Africans with a concept of their own nationality.

Born in 1924 of Cape Verdean parents, Cabral grew up in what is today Guinea-Bissau, then Portuguese Guinea, in great poverty, finding the money to attend school from the small profits of his needleworking mother, whom he greatly admired. He had at least 61 brothers and sisters, all sired by his father, Juvenal Cabral. After school he studied agrarian engineering at Lisbon where he graduated with honours. He had a sound colonial career at his feet.

But while he was a student he imbibed from various clandestine sources ideas of communism and liberalism as well as news from revolutionary intellectuals from other African colonies. After graduating, Cabral's career move must have seemed bizarre to outsiders. He buried himself in the backlands of Guinea, an employee of the farming and forestry service, making the first analysis of its agrarian and water resources. During this time he acquired an intimate knowledge of the country's landscape and social structure.

Cabral's battle was not just against the Portuguese. Cape Verdeans themselves accepted assimilation, and the cycles of drought and emigration, as an unavoidable consequence of the land. Cabral formed a tiny nationalist movement in 1954.

He made friends with another product of the Mindelo secondary school, Aristides Pereira, who worked in the posts-and-telegraph office in Guinea. They learned local languages, read literature on uprisings around the world and worked on until Cabral was deported from the country in 1955. The following year, the two formed a tiny party: the PAIGC (Party for the Independence of Guinea and Cape Verde). Other members were educated people with administrative jobs in Portugal, Angola and Guinea. The party pursued peaceful means at first, appealing for better conditions. One of their group, Abilio Duarte, returned to Cape Verde to agitate there amongst the students and the dockers, while Cabral set up a base in Conakry, capital of ex-French Guinea.

The insurrection stumbled forward, manifesting itself publicly through graffiti at first and then through strikes, which inevitably led to sporadic massacres. A wages strike in Portuguese Guinea left 50 shot dead and the rest sentenced to 15 years' hard labour.

Throughout 1959 and 1960 the activists moved around the world, gaining confidence from news of uprisings outside Portuguese Africa while the islands suffered another drought. This time, however, the loss of life was not of disastrous proportions because of a more compassionate governor.

Fighting began in Portuguese Guinea in 1963 and Cape Verdeans made their way to the mainland to join the army. The war lasted for ten years, with the PAIGC, numerically tiny compared with the number of Portuguese troops, employing brilliant guerrilla tactics to lure the enemy into dispersing into numerous garrisons which it could then besiege. Arms from the USSR eventually arrived and by 1972 the PAIGC had control of half of the country, but not the air, where the commanding general, António Spínola, retained supremacy.

Back in Cape Verde, nothing had happened superficially even by 1971. Abilio Duarte worked both at the Mindelo school, transforming the aspirations of the next generation, and amongst the dockers of Mindelo, more open to new ideas than their inland counterparts.

From 1966 a band of 30 of the most talented young men of Cape Verde had been living in Cuba, where they trained for a surprise landing on Santiago and Santo Antão which would begin the war on the archipelago. In fact the landings plan would never be executed, most critically because the group failed to find the transport they needed across the ocean.

It was just as well, because swooping arrests in 1967 eliminated any organised reception the rebels might have hoped for, while the drought of 1968 would have starved any guerrillas trying to survive in the highlands.

So, back on the archipelago, there was no war, just the arrests of increasing numbers of suspected rebels. The peasants were waiting with messianic expectation for Amílcar Cabral to come from Portuguese Guinea and liberate them.

But they would never see him. Tragedy struck on 20 January 1973 when traitors from within the PAIGC's own ranks murdered the 52-year-old Cabral on the mainland, just a few months before the victory in Guinea. Anger at his death shook any stagnation out of the guerrilla ranks and this, together with the arrival of ground-to-air missiles from the USSR, triggered the final offensive which was to bring them victory. Guinea-Bissau became a member of the Organisation of African Unity on 19 November 1973.

Cabral had been right when he prophesied in 1961: 'We for our part are sure that the destruction of Portuguese colonialism is what will destroy Portuguese fascism.' Young officers in the Portuguese army in Guinea became convinced that they would never win their African wars. Portugal was becoming over-burdened, economically and politically, by these African questions. The officers grouped to form the Armed Forces Movement, returning to Portugal to overthrow the dictator, António de Oliveira Salazar, just five months after Guinea's liberation. Independence followed quickly for some other Portuguese colonies, though for Cape Verde it was far from automatic. Spínola, head of the AMF and new leader of Portugal, wanted to hang on to the strategically positioned islands.

The USA was reluctant to help, fearing that an independent Cape Verde would become a Soviet base. Meanwhile all the leading militants on the islands were locked up and the remainder were still on the mainland. All Cape Verde had won was an agreement that it could have its own National Council.

Returning from the mainland war in August 1974, the Cape Verdean heroes were given a rapturous welcome. But they arrived in a country where Portuguese authority was not just intact but working overtime under the orders of Spínola.

There were those on the islands who wanted to remain with Portugal. Intellectuals from the old *Claridade* movement argued that Cape Verde could never be economically viable on its own and should remain associated with someone, Portugal or the United Nations. They supported the words of Eugénio Tavares, the poet:

> For Cape Verde? For these poor and abandoned rocks thrown up in the sea, independence? What sense is there in that? God have pity on thoughtless men!

But most could not bear to remain allied to the country that had caused them so much ill.

Rescue came in the form of the democrats in Portugal who overthrew Spínola and were more receptive to Cape Verdean demands. After a transitional, joint government, a general election was held at the end of June 1975, and the PAIGC became the new government, a National Assembly proclaiming independence for the archipelago on 5 July 1975. The president was Aristides Pereira, secretary general of the PAIGC. Cape Verde and Guinea-Bissau were a joint country.

After independence

Cape Verde was free but it was a wasteland: its resources plundered over centuries, its soil thin and disappearing with every gust of Saharan wind. Drought had come again in 1969 and afflicted the islands for six years. In 1977, the maize and bean harvest was nil. There was no work for wages and exports were almost non-existent. Over half of the islands' imports were of famine food and emigration surged. The shock of suddenly assuming responsibility for such a land must have been acute.

Cape Verde had few advantages but it had one: it was not riven with tribal rivalries. In that sense it began rebuilding from a metaphorical, as well as a literal, bare ground.

Another advantage lay in its good contacts with the outside world. The democrats of Portugal were on friendly terms with Cape Verde, a relationship that continues today.

Help came from many countries: once the USA was convinced that Cape Verde was indeed 'non-aligned' it sent a gift of US$7 million. The World Food Programme despatched thousands of tonnes of maize, and a variety of countries, including Sweden, Holland and the USSR, also sent aid.

Uniquely, the Cape Verdean government insisted that the WFP grain was not handed out as charity but was sold to people who did construction work on water-retention and anti-erosion dykes and on barrages in return for wages.

The government was a socialist one which attracted the interest of the USSR, China and Cuba. There are still strong ties with these countries: Cuba and Russia have been the destination of many Cape Verdean university students, while university links with China are underway. Indeed, the Chinese embassy is the most prestigious building in Praia, and sits opposite Cape Verde's parliament.

Guinea-Bissau, meanwhile, suffered more turbulence than Cape Verde, which led to a coup in 1980 that ruptured the link between the two countries. After that 'The Party', for there was only one, renamed itself the PAICV (Partido Africano de Independência de Cabo Verde).

PAICV had a political monopoly enshrined in the country's constitution and which went unchallenged at first. One person within the party who objected to the lack of democracy, and also to the centralised control of the party and the limits placed on free enterprise, was one Carlos Veiga, who formed the MpD (Movimento para a Democracia) in 1990.

Things moved swiftly and by September 1990 Cape Verde legally became a multi-party state. Elections the following January swept out the PAICV and handed power to Veiga, who was prime minister from 1991 to 2001. A month later the candidate the MpD supported for president, António Manuel Mascarenhas, was elected.

Flagship policies of the government in 1991 were a market economy with less public spending, opening up to foreign investment, and the development of fishing, tourism and service industries. A new national anthem and flag were adopted in September 1992.

A decade later, on 14 January 2001, the PAICV regained control in an overwhelming victory. The people then elected for President Pedro Pires, who had been prime minister of the first government in 1975. More importantly for PAICV, it won in the Legislative Assembly, which is headed by the more powerful position of prime minister. In recent years Cape Verde looked set to be more questioning of the activities of foreign investors, more circumspect towards Portugal and warmer towards Africa, with perhaps some more left-of-centre policies aimed at youth and education. However, it was thought unlikely that there would be a return to the statist policies of the past.

So the islands survive to face a brighter future than ever before. The land now receives the love it needs. The people are trying to demonstrate that the islands' history has been due to incompetence, greed and neglect, not because they are no more than 'bitter bare rocks strung out in mid Atlantic like a crown of thorns floating on the sea'.

GEOGRAPHY

Just a few geographical oddities shape Cape Verde's natural history and economy to a profound degree, a combination of winds and currents that bring heat and cool, dust, dryness and the occasional monsoons. Drought is the key to everything and, as the Cape Verdeans say, 'the best governor is rain'.

Location and size

The Cape Verdes are an arrow-shaped archipelago of ten islands, five islets and various rocks and stacks which poke out of the eastern Atlantic on a band of latitude that runs between Senegal in the east and the Caribbean, 3,600km to the west. They stretch between 14° and 18°N and 22° and 26°W. The archipelago is the furthest south of the groups of islands known to scientists as Macronesia. Others of that group include the Azores and the Canary Islands, but the distance between them is great. The Canaries, off Morocco, are over 1,000km away while the Azores, parallel with Portugal, are at a distance of about 2,500km. The islands are widely spaced. The most easterly is 460km from Senegal and the most westerly is 830km. The largest island is 990km², about twice the size of the Isle of Wight. The smallest is the 35km² pinprick of Santa Luzia. Brava is the smallest inhabited island at 64km². The total land area is 4,033km², scattered over 58,000km² of ocean.

The archipelago is popularly divided into two groups. The *Barlavento*, or windward, islands in the north are Santo Antão, São Vicente, Santa Luzia, São Nicolau, Sal and Boavista. The *Sotavento*, or leeward, islands to the south are Maio, Santiago, Fogo and Brava.

Terrain

A more obvious way of dividing the islands is longitudinally: the easterly islands of Sal, Boavista and Maio are extremely flat, while the rest are mountainous. There is extraordinary variation in heights within Cape Verde: Fogo's peak reaches 2,829m, and you can walk to the top of it, while Boavista musters only a small hill of 390m.

The variation in heights reflects the huge age span of the islands and therefore the time available for erosion to take place. Their geological history is still controversial but the most popular theory estimates the flat ones to be up to 26 million years old, dating from the Miocene era. It has been shown that the central islands of São Nicolau and Maio appeared less than 12 million years ago, in the Pliocene. To the west Fogo and Brava, the youngest, have been around for a mere 100,000 years.

The theory is based on the drift of the African plate, a section of the earth's crust that stretches well beyond the African landmass as far as the middle of the Atlantic. This tectonic plate began a slow drift to the east about 120 million years ago. Underneath it lies a 'hot spot'. As the plate above has drifted, this spot has periodically erupted, poking a series of holes like molehills through the crust.

It is thought that the most eroded volcanoes can no longer be seen, submerged by the Atlantic somewhere between Boavista and the mainland. It is even possible that the basalts of Cap Vert, the Senegal promontory, are remnants of the first eruption of the hot spot into the Atlantic.

But some of the islands are more complicated than that. Not all of the magma that erupted from below actually blasted through to the surface. Some of it became trapped within the crust and cooled there, forming large igneous intrusions. The intrusions swelled up and rose within the forming volcanoes, lifting with them the ancient marine sediments that had been deposited on the ocean floor long before any islands developed. The intrusions and the uplifted sediments remained hidden within the volcanoes for millions of years, but the distance between them and the surface has slowly been shrinking as wind and flash floods have eroded the volcanoes away. Now, like slicing the top from a boiled egg, the sediments are revealed, the yolk within. The result is that the flat land of some islands (Maio in particular) is, very roughly, young volcanic rock around the outside and much older sedimentary rock forming an uplifted ring around the intrusions that are exposed in the heart of the island.

The mountainous islands can be very rugged, sometimes with virtually no flat land. Dunes, both still and wandering, are present mainly in the flat islands, most visibly and beautifully in Boavista where parts feel like true desert.

Climate

Caught in the Sahel zone, Cape Verde is really a marine extension of the Sahara. The northeast tradewind is responsible for much of its climate. It blows down particularly strongly from December to April, carrying so little moisture that only peaks of 600m or more can tease out any rain. The high peaks, particularly on Fogo, Santo Antão and Brava, can spend much of the year with their heads in the clouds.

Added to that wind are two other atmospheric factors. First is the harmattan – dry, hot winds from the Sahara that arrive in a series of blasts from October to June, laden with brown dust which fills the air like smog. The second factor is the southwest monsoon, which brings the longed-for rains between August and October. Often half the year's rainfall can tumble down in a single storm or series of storms. Unfortunately Cape Verde's position is a little too far north for the rains to be guaranteed each year: it lies just above the doldrums, the place where the northeast and southwest tradewinds meet and where there is guaranteed rainfall. The longest recorded time Cape Verde has gone without being watered by the southwest monsoon is 18 years. For 12 years from 1968 there was a similar drought.

In the ocean, the cool stream known as the Canary Current reaches the archipelago from the north and mitigates the heating effect of the northeast tradewind.

Temperature variation on the islands is small – it remains between 22°C and 27°C on Santiago throughout the year. But these figures mask big variations within and between islands. In the desert centre of some of the flat islands it can reach 40°C between July and September, while on the moist peaks of Santo Antão early in the year it can be as cool as 10°C.

Cape Verde's rainfall figures tell a similar strange story. A recurring theme is the wide variation in rainfall even between different slopes of the same island – the northeastern slopes are the wettest. On Fogo for example, the average rainfall over 35 years for the northeastern slope of Monte Velha is 1,190mm, while the average on its leeward side is 167mm. Monte Velha's figures also reveal how suddenly precious rain can deluge an island. In a single month, 20 years ago, 3,000mm of rain fell there. The lower islands, the flat ones, São Vicente and Santa Luzia, receive much less moisture, leaving them almost totally barren.

These chaotic figures can be processed to give mean average rainfalls in the range 10–900mm. Most regions of Cape Verde are classified as arid or semi-arid.

Ecology

Old folk on some of the islands reminisce about the greenery there was during their youth, which may be because of an unusual glut of rain in the 1930s. But Cape Verde suffers terribly from desertification which has three major causes: prolonged droughts, the eroding wind and bad farming techniques including unrestrained munching by goats. Soil erosion is compounded when the rains come; they are generally short and violent and wash topsoil swiftly down the steep slopes and into the sea. The only island with streams that run all through the year is Santo Antão. But the islands are riven with deep dry creeks which can turn to turbulent rivers during the rainy season.

To boost attempts at conservation, the government began a National Parks and Protected Areas Programme in 1988. Theoretically there are, as a result, protected areas and conservation programmes dedicated to birds, plants and sea turtles. The government declared in 1990 that most of the uninhabited islands and islets are nature reserves, only visitable with a permit. However, few people, including senior officials, seem to have heard of this law and you are likely to be laughed at if you try to obtain one. It is illegal to capture turtles between June and February, a law that is increasingly enforced.

SOCIAL GEOGRAPHY
Population

Cape Verde has 418,224 inhabitants (according to the latest figures from 2005) and they range in ethnicity from virtually white to black: about 70% are mixed race, 1% are white. Women outnumber men because of emigration. The lack of men, together with the intermittent returns and lengthy absences, are two of the reasons why marriage, and family units of father, mother and children are unusual. Men typically have children by many women and are often married to none of them; the same applies to women. Responsibility for bringing up children invariably falls to the women, who may be dependent on remittances sent back from abroad by the various fathers.

Population growth is 2% and the government has campaigned hard to bring it down through birth control, including abortion. The Catholic Church has campaigned hard against the latter. Life expectancy is 66 for men and 75 for women. Some 70% of people are literate. In the last census 42% of the population was under 14 years of age, with this figure on an upward trend.

SOCIAL STRUCTURE

Numerous categories defined the different elements of Cape Verde society. *Fidalgos* were the noblemen, representing the king and making money for themselves and for the Crown through a system of royal charters, trade monopolies and land grants. They tended to be Portuguese, though there were some Genoese, Venetians and Spanish. *Capitãos* were military governors appointed by the Crown, with a high degree of local autonomy. *Feitors* were powerful private business agents who had won royal trade monopolies and also represented private mercantile concerns.

The pariahs of the slave trade were the *lançados*. They were, by definition, outcasts, but they were essential middlemen, embedding themselves in the tropical creeks of the west African coast where they channelled the trade in goods and humans. Portuguese, they were often political or religious criminals, and many of them were Jews who had fled the Inquisition. *Lançados* had an ambiguous relationship with the Crown: in theory they complied with royal trade monopolies, but in practice they had a pervasive power that the Crown could not control. They traded with whom they pleased and flouted Portuguese tax and other restrictions. *Ganagogas* were technically Jewish *lançados*, but in practice the term embraced anyone who could speak many local African languages.

Tangamãus were the public interface of the African involvement in the trade, and functioned mainly as translators; the name probably comes from *targuman*, the Arabic for translator. The mercenary bodyguards of the *lançados* and *tangamãus* were the *grumettas*.

Banished from Portugal for criminal or political reasons, *degredados* often became galley slaves in rowing boats. They lived either on Cape Verde or on the African coast, where some became *lançados*. Like the *lançados*, they became an important white ingredient in the founding of the Creole population. *Pretos* were free blacks, while *ladinos* were slaves who had been baptised and given a Latin name.

As slaves escaped or were freed, the peasant population grew. At its core was a group whom the Portuguese despised, as did the later *mestiço* class. These were the *badius*, and they clung to their African culture. They were small-scale farmers generally living in the remote central regions of Santiago. *Parcerias* were colonial partnership share-cropping systems; share-croppers usually gave between a half and two-thirds of the crops they grew to their landowner. *Rendeiros* grew subsistence crops for themselves and worked on other people's land, generally for wages.

Later in the history came *contratados*, contract labourers who worked in São Tomé and Príncipe and also in the United States.

More than half the population lives on Santiago, and of these about 117,000 live in Praia, the capital of Cape Verde. The only other big population centre is Mindelo on São Vicente. The island of Santa Luzia is uninhabited.

Religion

The islands have been Catholic from the beginning and most other denominations have had little chance to win many converts. Some 95% of the nation is ostensibly Catholic, though the priests complain that they have lost their influence. The largest minority, less than 1%, is the Nazarene Church. This is a Protestant grouping introduced to Brava in the early 1900s by emigrants returning from the USA. The Nazarenes collaborated with another group, the Sabbatarians, to build two Protestant churches, and they translated the gospels into Creole, the local language. The islands are seen as fertile recruiting grounds by several groups, including the Church of Jesus Christ of Latter Day Saints (popularly known as the Mormons). The Church claims around 3,000 members in Cape Verde. Jehovah's Witnesses proselytise here as well. The Jews have a fascinating history on Cape Verde, fleeing there to escape persecution (see *Santiago*, page 121).

Government

Cape Verde is a democratic republic with no political prisoners and a clean human rights record. In the military league of nations most likely to go to war, Cape Verde rates 154th out of 156.

The oldest party is the PAICV, which won independence for the country in 1975 and ruled it as a one-party state for many years. The MpD (Movimento para a Democracia), devoted to liberal economic and social reform, won democracy for Cape Verde in 1990 and was elected in 1991 and then again in December 1995. A sliver of the MPD broke away to form the Partido da Convergencia Democratica (PCD) in 1994. In late 2000 the PAICV came to power again. The president is Pedro Pires. The current prime minister is Jose Maria Neves.

Elections are scheduled for February 2006.

Economy

On the United Nations' quality of life index, Cape Verde comes top in west Africa. Its Gross National Product was US$1,245 per head in 2001. Inflation rates for recent years vary from 3.7% in 2001 to 1.2% in 2003. Unemployment is in the order of 25%, although these people are probably occupied for at least some of the time in fishing or farming.

The economy has grown steadily since 1975. It is largely subsistence and the World Bank classifies 14% of the population as very poor, and 30% as poor.

Aid and remittances

The islands have been the recipients of one of the highest amounts of international aid, per capita, in the world (US$270 per person annually in 1997) but this figure was due to fall from 2006 after their upgrading by the United Nations from 'least-developed country' to 'medium-developed country'. A huge percentage of their grain is imported by aid organisations or other governments. Foreign aid money comes principally from Portugal, Germany, the Netherlands, USA and France. Many European countries seem to have adopted a single island. The results are evident everywhere: new harbours and ports, forests of acacia, freshly painted hospitals, schools and town halls.

There are now more Cape Verdeans abroad than at home. Their remittances have in recent years accounted for more than half of the gross domestic product (GDP).

Agriculture

Subsistence agriculture doesn't have a hope of meeting the food needs of the country and at present produces just 10–15% of demand, yet it employs 80% of the population. The soil is good but production is hampered by the lack of water and the legacy of the inefficient land tenure system. 'It is heartbreaking,' says one scientist working there, 'to watch a peasant woman patiently prepare the ground and sow, then wait for months while it doesn't rain, then return to break the ground and sow again.'

Only a tenth of the land, 40,000ha, is suitable for cultivation. Of this, 34,000ha are cultivated and less than a tenth of that is irrigated. Some 90% of the crop is maize and beans which are often grown together. The beans grow up the maize stalks which act as trellises and offer some shade. Other major crops are bananas, sugar cane, sweet potatoes, manioc and cassava. The only significant exported crop is the banana, although other cash crops are coffee, peanuts, castor beans and pineapples. More than half of the total irrigated land grows sugar cane, most of which is used in the production of *grogue*, the local rum.

Historical patterns of ownership have deterred investment and maintenance of agricultural land (see *History*, page 3) but land reform has been very hard to implement. The PAICV attempts in 1981 were so unpopular that the next government reversed them in 1993.

Cajoling water into the soil is the great battle of Cape Verdean agriculture. Apart from reafforestation, the other archipelago-wide project has been the building of catchment dams that will detain rainwater. Drip irrigation, where the water spills out of tiny holes in a pipe, which have been positioned only at the exact places where plants are sown, is spreading.

Even finding enough water to drink is a problem. There are desalination plants on São Vicente and on Santiago, Sal and Boavista. Programmes to drill deep wells have been going for some time and many of the windmills you see are pulling water from the depths of the ground.

A second battle of Cape Verdean agriculture is to recover more land from hostile mountainsides. In *ribeiras* blessed with streams, such as those on Santo Antão, terracing goes to extraordinary heights.

Another major problem is pests, such as the millipede on Santo Antão, which devours potatoes and carrots. Grasshoppers cause devastation on other islands.

There is one goat for every two people on the islands, as well as cattle; pigs snuffle round every village. They forage for scraps, so they cost little and are an important source of meat.

Building the economy

The archipelago is at the centre of one of the last great under-used fishing grounds of the world. Tuna and lobster abound, but at present fishing is a trade of artisans, though there is some export of fish and crustaceans. There are great hopes that shipping services, including repair yards and refrigerated storage, can be improved. The airport is already used as a stopover point for planes crossing the Atlantic.

Tourism

The most likely big growth area of the economy is set to be in the tourism sector. In 2001, the tourism sector contributed about 3.5% of GDP. Following the terrorist attacks of 11 September 2001, some decline in tourism was noted. The main growth is now set to be in the beach sector of the industry, with significant growth in charter-flight traffic. Further income is expected from foreigners able to buy apartments. Figures for tourist arrivals reveal the growth in tourism.

In 1991, there were 19,000 tourist arrivals. By 1999 this had risen to 67,000 and in 2001 there were 161,000 arrivals. After a dip in 2002, the latest figures show tourist arrivals at 178,000.

Tourists from Italy form the largest percentage of visitors, with Portugal the next source of tourists. Germany and France follow and the rest are from a multitude of countries in Europe. The number of visitors from North America and Brazil is likely to rise.

THE CAPE VERDEAN DIASPORA TODAY

Since independence many islanders have emigrated, principally to the USA, the Netherlands, Italy and Portugal. Emigration to the USA in the 20th century has risen and fallen with immigration rules: in 1922, restrictions were introduced and the numbers plunged. The new rules also deterred Cape Verdean Americans from visiting the archipelago in case they were not allowed back into the USA on their return. This divided the two communities for several decades and increased emigration to Europe, South America, and west Africa. The American rules were relaxed in 1966 and Cape Verdeans began to arrive again. Thus there are two groups in the USA today, with significant cultural differences.

More than 30,000 have emigrated to Portugal since the 1968 drought. Italy has up to 10,000 Cape Verdean immigrants, many of whom went to work there as domestics in the 1970s, a route opened up by the Church and which became self-perpetuating.

Senegal and Angola each have tens of thousands of Cape Verdeans. There are emigrants in Luxembourg, France (10,000–15,000) and Holland (8,000–10,000). There are substantial numbers in Argentina and Brazil and in Spain and Sweden. In Britain there are Cape Verdeans in Liverpool, Cardiff, Newcastle and Hull.

In all, there are more Cape Verdeans living outside the archipelago than within it, including 350,000 in the USA.

CULTURE

The faces of Cape Verde are numerous: blue eyes gazing out from above a brown cheek; green eyes below the tight curls of black hair with a wisp of blonde; Chinese eyes set in a black face. Race in Cape Verde is not just Portugal mingled with the Rivers of Guinea, but also Italy and drops of Lebanon, China, Morocco and more. Pirates, sailors and merchants from Spain, France, England, Holland, Brazil and the USA deposited their genes here. Senegambians, Mandingos and Fulas gave variety to the African blood that arrived in the form of slaves.

This disorientation of racial types was regarded for centuries as a bastardisation. Then, in the very late 19th century, when the stirrings of nationalism began, the idea arose that Cape Verde had its own identity, not an unholy mixture but an exciting synthesis. This idea marked the emergence of Creole (*Crioulo*) nationhood. The Cape Verdean people have their own history, the result of a unique combination of social and natural forces.

Language

In the ethnic mosaic of Cape Verdean slave communities, the speaking of tribal languages was actively discouraged. To communicate with each other, slaves were forced to piece together words from Portuguese and a mélange of other sources. It was these fumblings that were the beginnings of the Cape Verdean mother tongue, Creole. It is at root Portuguese, primarily the 15th-century Portuguese of the Algarve, with a simplified grammar. Phonetics, and some words, have been added from some Mandingo and Senegambian languages, members of the large Niger–Congo family of African languages. Creole varies between islands, influenced by the different nationalities that have lived there.

Creole is not fully a written language. There are some small Creole dictionaries but spellings are not always standardised, which can lead to entertaining disputes if

PORTUGUESE AND CREOLE: TWO OLD RIVALS
Steven Maddocks

Portuguese is the official language of Cape Verde. All business is conducted in Portuguese; it is used for correspondence, newspapers, road signs, in fact anything that needs to be written down. But only very rarely will Cape Verdeans speak Portuguese to each other. In the bank, the doctor's surgery, or the barber's, at work or after hours, everyone, be they president or peasant, uses Creole. It is their national language, and the mother tongue of all Cape Verdeans.

Creole (*Crioulo*) is not just a product of Cape Verdean history, it is an index of the Cape Verdean identity. Like the language they speak, Cape Verdeans are a mixture of Portuguese and west African. Cape Verdean Creole has its origins in the pidgin used by Portuguese slave masters to communicate with their slaves, who were brought mainly from Guinea-Bissau. During Portuguese colonial rule it was forbidden to use Creole in public situations. Of course, this law was impossible to enforce, and the use of Creole became an act of defiance against the Portuguese.

Creole is now being used in more and more public situations. The DJs on the very popular Praia FM introduce Creole music in Creole. The tagline for one of the campaigns for the February 2001 presidential election was *Nôs Presidente* – which is Creole for 'Our President'. And yet, despite the fact that many Cape Verdeans feel Portuguese to be an alien and difficult language for them, and despite the fact that the Portuguese of a lot of Cape Verdeans is not particularly good, Creole is perhaps even further now than it was 20 years ago from becoming the official language.

For a start, a lot of people, among them a number of Cape Verdeans, don't consider Creole to be worthy of the name 'language'. It is a dialect of Portuguese, or, as some would have it, badly spoken Portuguese (others counter that French is just a 'dialect' of Latin).

Secondly, Creole is a spoken language only. Written Creole exists, but it is very scarce. A handful of books have been written, among them collections of traditional stories and poems, a grammar, and a structural analysis. Attempts to settle upon a standard way of writing Creole, and more importantly to disseminate Creole texts and get people into the habit of writing Creole, have consistently failed.

The earliest attempt at an alphabet was an 1888 grammar written by António de Paula Brita. This was an etymological version, that is, it was based on Portuguese. The most recent was 1994's Alupec (Unified Alphabet for the Cape Verdean Language). In March 1979 a two-week colloquium was staged in Mindelo, and the international team of linguists proposed an alphabet which is still the most widely used. But the situation remains that, although the vast majority of Cape Verdeans speak Creole with great passion, wit and intelligence, they are totally unaccustomed to, and even incapable of, reading or writing it.

you ask a group of locals to write some words for you. The official language remains Portuguese, the medium of teaching in secondary schools and of formal occasions.

Creole was the language in which Cape Verdean writers began to express themselves, sometimes in order to hide their ideas from Portuguese officials but principally as a way of defining themselves. Poems do not always translate easily.

There are powerful arguments both for and against making Creole the official language. By doing so, Cape Verdeans might finally break the colonial yoke, achieving cultural as well as political independence from Portugal. Thus the language of their folklore, of their poems, stories and songs, might also be the language of their business. The current situation is also very damaging for children in the early years of their life, who lack the opportunity to learn to read the language they speak. There are no children's books in Creole, so they never learn a correspondence between written symbols and the noises they and their mother make. The first language children learn to read or write is not their mother tongue, but a foreign language, learnt in school. Illiteracy is widespread, and if Cape Verdeans want to express their imagination in writing, or conduct any kind of business, they are forced to resort to a foreign language, divorced from the home and the heart.

But, on the other hand, Portuguese is the sixth most commonly spoken language in the world. With it Cape Verdeans have immediate access to 170 million people, plus the possibility of a halting conversation with the world's 266 million Spanish speakers. What use is Creole in the global village?

Officialising Creole would be a mammoth task. It would mean a total overhaul of a whole host of current procedures from the highest levels down. A commission of international linguists would need to be assembled to settle upon an alphabet and a standard form, prepare an official grammar, and develop educational materials for teaching in schools. It would take years. And who would pay?

The most vexed question is that of a standard form. Creole differs greatly from island to island, and even within the islands. The main division is between *Barlavento* and *Sotavento* Creole, and at the heart of this difference is the political rivalry between Praia and São Vicente. People from São Vicente will gladly offer you the opinion that Praia is dirty, polluted, and overcrowded. The people there are 'Africans' and their standards of personal hygiene leave much to be desired. Praia Creole is impossible to understand. *Badius* (people from Santiago) will counter that people from Mindelo walk around with their noses in the air, that they're unfriendly, and that they all wish Cape Verde were still a Portuguese colony. São Vicente Creole is impossible to understand. So tell someone from Mindelo that the standard form of Creole is *Badiu*? Or someone from Praia that he must start speaking and writing São Vicente Creole? You might as well tell a cat that from now on it should bark. But those differences are only superficial. The 1979 colloquium categorically declared that everyone in this country is speaking, structurally, an identical language.

Visitors to Cape Verde will communicate successfully in Portuguese. But if they want to participate in something that is unique to Cape Verde, if they really want to impress, flatter, and entertain Cape Verdeans, if they want to approach Cape Verdeans as friends, they will be richly rewarded by using just a few words of Creole.

Eugénio Tavares of Brava, the legendary writer of *mornas*, was reported by the later luminary Baltasar Lopes to be 'a very mediocre poet in Portuguese but a very good poet in *Crioulo*'.

Above all, Creole is the informal, spoken language that everyone understands. It is the language for sharing the Cape Verdean sentiment, the language of intimacy and feeling. The soul of Cape Verde speaks in Creole.

CLOTH

The slaves on Brava, Santiago and Fogo all wove fine cloth using skills learned on the African mainland. The cloth was in great demand in the 17th century among the upper classes along the rivers of Guinea and it was also worn by the elite as far away as the Gold Coast and Brazil. The deep blues and beautiful patterns of Cape Verdean cloth were superior to what these people could produce themselves but they were familiar, with a west African aesthetic. It became one of the principal currencies underpinning the slave trade, more in demand than European, Indian or African alternatives.

The demand forced English and French slaving vessels that wished to avoid Cape Verde to call there first for rolls of cloth so that they could barter on the coast. In the late 17th century a slave was worth 60 *barafulas*, cloths of standard length and width, which in turn were worth 30 iron bars. In the 18th century Cape Verde exported 6,000 of the 2m-long cloths a year to the mainland.

The cloth was woven on a narrow loom made of cane, sticks and banana leaves, which produced strips never more than 7in wide. Dye was made from *urzella*, a lichen (see *Brava*, page 183), and from the indigo plant. Female slaves pounded the leaves of the latter, pressed them into small loaves, dried them in the sun and then left them to ferment in a pot with water and ashes.

The standard design was a six-banded cloth (*pano*). Within that strict formula there were many variations. *Panos listrados*, for example, were alternating bands of white and indigo. *Panos simples* were simply white. Others interwove silk with the cotton. *Panos de bicho* interwove white, blue and black threads to make intricate geometric designs including the shapes of leopard and snakeskins and also of Portuguese crosses. The most expensive were cloths of a pure deep blue.

The desirability of such cloth continued for hundreds of years, from the 16th until the early 19th centuries. When the wealthy Diogo Ximenes Vargas died in Cape Verde in 1624, his estate consisted chiefly of hoards of the cloth: 1,800 *barafulas* in 45 large rolls and 840 plain white cloths in 21 rolls. Their value was recorded to be £630.

Today *panos* are worn by women either as shawls or as sashes tied just below the waist. They are packed into a hard ball for drumming during the *batuko* dance chants.

For basic words and phrases and hints on pronunciation, see *Appendix 1, Language*.

Literature

The soul of Cape Verde is expressed in poetry, the lyrics of *mornas*, folk stories and novels. The sentiment that dominates is a sorrowful one, known as *sodade*. It is often translated as 'nostalgia', though that word has over-sentimental connotations in English and does not convey the depth of feeling or the unsentimentality of expression. 'Longing' is a better word. *Sodade* is the longing of the emigrant looking across the sea to the motherland; the longing of mothers for their exiled children. Much Cape Verdean poetry focuses on the sea as the bringer of riches, but also of loneliness and sometimes death: 'Oh gold of the sea, you are dearly earned,' wrote Tavares.

The first Cape Verdean poetry arose in the 1890s and did not directly address the Cape Verdean condition. It followed Portuguese patterns with their rigidity of metre and verse. The movement began in São Nicolau, then the intellectual centre of the archipelago. Writers produced a literary annual and a book of poetry. This period, known as the Classical period, lasted until the 1930s. Amongst the writers were a very few who did not remain bound within Portuguese tradition. It was then, for example, that Tavares honed and popularised the art form of the *morna*, a combination of music, dance and poetry that expresses *sodade*. Another rebel, whose militant ideas would not be recognised for decades to come, was Pedro Cardoso, who signed himself 'Afro'. He named his journal *O Manduco* (The Cudgel), and he was the first Cape Verdean to try, albeit in a stumbling way, to articulate ideas such as pan-Africanism and Marxism.

With a clarion call in 1936, the Classical period was shattered and a new literary movement began. *Claridade*, a literary review, was published, addressing head-on the nature of Creole culture and the conditions people endured in the islands. Tales of the lives of Cape Verde appeared in the classic novel *Chiquinho* by Baltasar Lopes. It is a seminal work, one of the first novels from Portuguese Africa, and it was written in Creole.

Essays on Creole culture and language poured from the *Claridosos* in their irregularly published journal whose last edition appeared in 1960. Other leaders were Jorge Barbosa and Manuel Lopes. Barbosa introduced a new style of poetry which he thought reflected better the Cape Verdean character, a looser verse for a freer spirit. His book *Arquipélago*, published in 1935 when he was 33, was his pioneering work. It established the central axis of the Cape Verdean tragedy, the desire to leave while being forced to stay, and the desire to stay while being forced to leave.

More recently, literature has become more militant and artists and writers have turned to Africa for inspiration. Onésimo Silveira has written of the 'force which only the black man knows', and Kaoberdiano Dambara has produced some of the first Cape Verdean poems in the negritude tradition, though these concepts are far less commonly expressed than on mainland Africa.

Some critics believe that Creole is not a sufficiently complex language to be a literary vehicle and that the success of Tavares and Cardoso was an exception. Serious Cape Verdean writers overwhelmingly use Portuguese, albeit the Creole-infused Portuguese of the islands.

Music and dance

Music underpins Cape Verdean life, gives it continuity and draws meaning from collective, often brutal experience. A key element of the Cape Verdean experience is to hear the bitter-sweet *morna* wrought from a collection of guitars and violins in an evening café; or the more lively, escapist strains of the *funana* embellished with the scratchings of some unique percussive instrument. Music-making happens everywhere – in the nightclubs of Mindelo where people dance into the small hours, in restaurants, in people's homes. There are several musical forms that have evolved over the last 500 years. Some are essentially European, some are African and many lie in between the two.

Traditional musical forms

The *morna* and the *coladera* are the principal forms. Obscurity surrounds the origins of the *morna*, but it seems to have emerged in the mid 19th century on the island of Boavista influenced by the *modinha* of Portugal and Brazil (see *Boavista*, page 103). Of all the musical forms, it is the most European and literary; the lyrics are sophisticated expressions of tragedy, the instruments are similar to those played in Portuguese folk music. Technically, the *morna* is a poem set in four-line verses and put to music, but the name is also given to some music without words, and to some distinctive poems without music. The singer performs to the strains of stringed instruments, violins (*rabeças*), guitar-like violas and *cavaquinhos*, which resemble ukeleles. The singer tends to sing a line twice and then another line twice. This double pattern is then repeated.

The *coladera*, or *cola*, is a processional dance performed on festival days on São Vicente and Santo Antão. It has also over the last few decades come to mean a fast, danceable music with singing, influenced by Afro-American music.

More powerful rhythms, with less emphasis on melody, emanate from the *batuko, finaçon, funana* and *tabanka*. These musical forms are more rooted in Africa and arose mainly on Santiago and on Fogo, where defiant, escaped slaves looked for inspiration eastwards in the land of their origins. The slaves were from a diversity of African ethnic backgrounds, so the resulting musical culture was a mixture with a Cape Verdean identity. In these musical forms the singer calls and the rest respond, the harmonies are simple and there is much repetition. The singing is open and coarser in tone and the words are often improvised.

Batuko dancing is the most reminiscent of Africa; the rhythm is often provided by surrogate drums: rolled-up cloth held between the legs and pounded with the hands. It is the music and dance of women in the inland villages of Santiago, who will sit round in a semi-circle and beat the *panos*, all taking different rhythms that layer together into a complex structure. The women sing and a woman dances, slowly at first, with gyrating hips and then faster and faster until there is a climax of the dancing, *panos*-pounding and chanting. Then another woman takes her place. The origins of the *batuko* are obscure. Some trace it back to a time when a slave owner would offer a guest the pick of his female slaves. Others believe it originates from within the women's culture itself – it is a way of coping with the grief of widowhood, or other loss, through a purging frenzy of dancing.

Tabanka is drummed out on conch-shell horns and drums. Again, it comes from Santiago, and it is repetitive, accompanied by women who play percussion on plastic sheets, bags, bottles and their thighs (see *Santiago*, page 141).

If you hear an accordion, you are probably listening to a *funana*. This is energetic, fast, joyful and sensuous – one of the most traditional expressions of resistance to Portuguese domination. Its home, again, is Santiago. The traditional instruments on which it is played are the *gaita*, a type of accordion, and the *ferro*, a stick of iron scraped with a table knife. The *gaita*-player alternates between just two chords and plays a melody on top. Modern musicians have replaced the *gaita* with keyboards or guitar, and the *ferro* with drums. The *funana's* popularity has led to a number of *funana* dance bands.

There are many other musical forms, such as the *mazurka*, imported from Europe and given a new twist. Sadly, some of the most African of instruments that local people used to play have all but disappeared.

The international stage

Cape Verdean music is flourishing. Cesária Evora, barefoot diva with the mellow, unschooled voice, is the figurehead of the *morna* (see *São Vicente*, page 213) who sells albums in hundreds of thousands and is particularly popular in France.

Other musicians are increasingly better known on the international stage. In the 1960s it was Bana, and the Voz di Cabo Verde, who popularised the *morna* in Europe. They were influenced by Latin American and Brazilian rhythms and styles, particularly *cumbia*.

Bands and singers with a long history in the archipelago include Luis Morais, Os Tubaroes and its lead singer Ildo Lobo, Norberto Tavares, Bulimundo and Finaçon. The last three turned the accordion-based *funana* into its high-energy offspring.

Other well-known Cape Verdean musicians are Paulino Vieira, Dany Silva and Tiro Paris. The Mendes brothers, emigrants from Fogo, set up in 1976 and have worked particularly with the *coladera*. They also work with Angolan music, introduced to them by natives of Fogo returning from doing their military service on the mainland.

Commercial Cape Verdean music has often incorporated new ideas from Latin America, and today it is filled with other styles to the extent that purists fear that true Cape Verdean musical culture could vanish. Optimists believe that the Cape Verdean nature, whose essence is to absorb and transform multi-national influences, will ensure that Cape Verdean music remains distinctive and fertile.

For CDs to watch out for, see the box on page 134.

Folklore

Folklore is rich with tales of Sancho, the mischievous monkey who lives in the mountains and causes chaos wherever he goes. He remained in the hills throughout the Portuguese oppression, waiting until it was time to 'turn all upside down', as the poem on page 3 describes. Sancho's threat of confusion is generally a desirable one, a welcome anarchy upsetting those in power. But sometimes Sancho is purely an agent of trouble. He pops up in proverbs, such as the one reminding the lazy or naughty that they will go hungry if they don't till the soil: 'Beans don't grow where monkeys are.'

Another character is Nho Lobo, the lazy wolf, who appears in many cycles of tales in the oral tradition handed down through generations. A Nho Lobo story generally conveys a moral for children.

Speech is also rich in proverbs: 'A scratching chicken will meet its grandmother'; 'A man without a wife is a vase without flowers'; 'A lame goat does not take a siesta'; 'In cooking, eggs show up rotten' and 'They'll pay you to climb up the coconut palm but getting down again, that's your affair.'

Festivals

Traditional festivities are generally Catholic saints' days. They usually begin with church services and include processions, drumming and the eating of specially prepared foods. Many have their own traditions, some of which are described in the island chapters, and most occur in the summer. All the islands celebrate Christmas, Saint John (São João, 24 June) and Carnival (around 16 February).

NATURAL HISTORY

Many species on Cape Verde exist nowhere else in the world – the phenomenon known as endemicity. Unlike other islands such as the Caymans, which were once part of a bigger land mass and carry species left over from the greater continent, life here has arrived by chance. Which species completed the extraordinary journey was a lottery and the winners were a peculiar assortment. In addition, these species have had millions of years of isolation in which to branch out on their own, adapting to suit the oddities of the habitat. The grey-headed kingfisher, *Halcyon leucocephela*, for example, in the absence of much inland water in which to live up to its name, dines on insects instead.

The closest relatives of some of the plants are found in east Africa rather than the west. Scientists think that they were borne here from west Africa, which then itself became so dry that they disappeared from there.

Vegetation

Cape Verde has probably never been profusely covered in greenery. Lack of research and poor early records mean we know little about what it was like before humans arrived. The lower slopes were probably grassy and treeless (steppe) or with low vegetation dotted with trees (savanna). There is a few indigenous trees that still survive, the lovely blue-green, gnarled, flat-topped dragon tree, *Dracaena draco*, fast disappearing except on São Nicolau; the tamarisk palms, known locally as *tamareira* (*Phoenix atlantica*), that fill the lagoons and sunken deserts of Boavista; the ironwood tree and perhaps a species of fig tree and one of acacia.

The indigenous plants are adapted to dryness (with small leaves for example) and are small and sturdy to cope with strong winds.

Over the last 500 years, plants have been introduced from all over the world, and people have tried to cultivate wherever they can. Shrubs and trees have been cleared to make way for arable land. Poor farming techniques and the ubiquitous goat have combined with these forces to oust most of the original vegetation. The result is that, of the 600 species of plant growing in Cape Verde (aside from crops), only a quarter are natural to the islands and about half of those are endemic. Some of the endemic plants are suited only to ranges of crazily small dimensions, as frustrated botanists will tell you (see *Fogo*, page 165).

More recently, people have been making a Herculean effort to plant trees. The roots form a matrix that traps earth so that heavy rain cannot wash it away, and the branches prevent the wind scattering the precious soil. The trees are also supposed to create a moist microclimate. The reafforestation figures are almost unbelievable: about three million new trees are planted each year, or 7,000 a day. The result is pine trees, oaks and sweet chestnuts on the cool peaks of Santo Antão, eucalyptus on the heights of Fogo, and forests of acacia on Maio.

The lower lands have been covered with vast and hopeful swathes of acacias (commonly referred to as *Acacia americana*, though experts will tell you they are in fact South American *Prosopis juliflora*). This planting is controversial. The tree has a prodigious appetite for water, sucking it up through two root systems, one that probes deep into the earth and another that spreads just under the surface and can pick up tiny quantities of rainfall. The soil around the trees is thus so dry it cannot sustain any other growth except briefly, after the rains. Meanwhile there are some fears that the deep root system takes important drinking water. Newer programmes are using different trees, although they do not grow as fast.

The other great ecological rescue plan has been dyke-building to retain storm water; in some places expanses of hillside have been concreted so that water will run off into collecting tanks.

Birds

Cape Verde has a dedicated following of ornithologists and amateur birdwatchers who can be found wedged into crevices high up mountainsides or trying to secure passages with local fishermen across wild stretches of sea to some of the uninhabited islands. Their dedication stems from the fact that Cape Verde abounds in endemics and some of the seabirds living on cliffs around the islands are particularly important. The archipelago lies on the extreme southwestern corner of the Western Palaearctic region and is thus the only place in that region where certain species, mainly African or tropical, can be found to breed regularly.

However, as with the plants, much of the natural birdlife has been wiped out, particularly by hungry locals tempted by succulent seabirds or by fishermen treading on their burrows as they search for shellfish along the beaches.

The most prized birds to discover in the islands include the raso lark (*Alauda razae*) and the magnificent frigatebird (*Fregata magnificens*), both with extraordinarily restricted breeding areas. The Cape Verde petrel (*Pterodroma feae*), or *ngon-ngon* bird, is disappearing fast (see *Fogo*, page 179) and the beautiful white-tailed, red-billed tropicbird (*Phaethon aethereus*) is also plunging in number. More common birds include the colourful grey-headed kingfisher known locally as *passarinha*. It can be found on Santiago, Fogo and Brava, and has a red beak, and orange, black and blue plumage. You will also see plenty of helmeted guineafowl (*Numida meleagris*) on mountain slopes and even the distinctive white Egyptian vultures (*Neophron percnopterus*) at high altitudes. Waders frequent the few lagoons and saltpans, on Sal, Maio, Boavista and Santiago. If you miss the brown booby (*Sula leucogaster*) – known locally as the *alcatraz* – take a look at the 20-escudo piece.

Details of some of these birds are given in the island chapters and some bird books are mentioned in *Further reading*, page 268.

Other fauna

There are no large mammals and no snakes, but several species of bat can be found, and green monkeys inhabit Santiago. There are also many small, brown, endemic reptiles, geckos and skinks. The Cape Verde giant skink (*Macroscincus coctei*) – delicious, sadly – became extinct in the 1940s (see *São Nicolau*, page 257). Many interesting endemic insects and beetles live on the islands and there are collections of them in the Natural History Museum in London.

Marine life

Marine life is more tropical than would be found at the same latitude of mainland Africa, on the coast of Senegal. This is because the archipelago is sufficiently far from the mainland to escape the cold 'winter upwellings', whereby the turning of the globe causes water from deep in the ocean to surface at the coast. This would otherwise decrease the temperature of the 21°C waters to about 10°C.

The water is abundant in undiscovered species, making it an exciting place for biologists to explore. Divers will see a selection of big flamboyant tropical fish such as the spectacularly coloured west African angelfish, tunafish and parrotfish. There are green turtles, yellow-fin tuna, moray eels, marlin, dolphins and groupers (see *Practical information*, page 36). Further from shore are sharks and 17 species of dolphin.

There are no true coral reefs in Cape Verde, but there are small slabs and pinnacles the sizes of tables and chairs. Beautiful cone shells litter the beaches.

Marine turtles are some of the most important species on the islands. Cape Verde is an important staging post for them along their long migratory corridor between America and Africa. Cape Verde is probably one of the most significant breeding sites for them in this part of Africa. The turtles breed all year round, particularly in the summer, and all the islands harbour them, the most important being São Vicente, followed by the flat islands of Sal, Maio and Boavista.

To the north of Cape Verde, turtles die in their thousands as they get caught in the drift nets of fishing boats. Pollution is an even bigger killer. Cape Verde is a refuge for them and, while local people still take eggs and praise the taste of turtle soup, they are aware of increasing pressure not to touch them.

Turtle ethics dictate that you should not go near the creatures and should avoid shining bright lights at them at night. However, if you see a tag on one of them, then you'll make some marine biologist's day if you note the serial number and report it to the national natural history museum in your home country. See the box, page 115, for more on turtles.

Practical Information

PREPARATION

In many practical ways travelling around the islands is a joy, and in general the people are keen to encourage tourism. Culturally there is little corruption and bribery. Bargaining, though it is necessary sometimes, is not widespread. Hassle is trivial compared with many countries on the mainland, while crime is almost exclusively confined to pickpocketing and opportunist swipings. Telephones and faxes work and the main towns have electricity and water without too many interruptions. Hot water is increasingly common in hotels.

The cost of living is high compared with other west African destinations, but if you make a few policy decisions before you go it is possible to see the islands relatively cheaply.

Highlights

You can hike up steep *ribeiras* – normally dry river valleys – on Santo Antão, São Nicolau and Santiago or explore the volcanic craters of Fogo and Brava. Unusually, the locals have been forced by the topography to construct paths and roads over mountain ridges rather than between them. As a result even the most breathtaking and isolated walks can often be done entirely on cobbled paths and some of the best views can be enjoyed from a vehicle.

Watersports are another attraction. Even experts from Hawaii rave about the strength and consistency of the wind and the shapes of the waves (see *Sal*, page 87, and *São Vicente*, page 207). You can rent good- quality equipment, and take lessons, in Sal and Boavista; it's more tricky to do so in São Vicente..

The diving, while not up to the standards of the Red Sea, is fascinating for several reasons: the volcanic underworld, the shipwrecks, and the big fish close to shore. The other excitement is going out with a local fisherman to hunt for supper with a harpoon.

Boat-fishing is another possibility. A trip with local fishermen can net the most spectacular catch, from bright orangey-pink grouper to long coiled moray eels. There is organised game-fishing for tourists on Sal and Boavista and the odd quiet lodge offering fishing on other islands. Wahoo and blue marlin are common.

Sun-seekers are a key target of the government, though real luxury that traditionally accompanies such holidays is available only on Sal, Boavista and Santiago, and to a lesser extent on São Vicente and Maio. Elsewhere the most beautiful beaches are also desolate, miles from the road and with absolutely no facilities. The beaches have little greenery. Also, remote beaches are not necessarily safe ones – so it is important to check locally before you plunge.

Despite the archipelago's fascinating history there is little to see in the form of buildings or museums. The one exception to this is on Santiago, where there are two museums and the old city of Ribeira Grande (Cidade Velha), the first

European city in the tropics, complete with fort, the remains of a cathedral and numerous churches. Most island capitals have southern European architecture and ambience, and some have a faded Portuguese feel to them with narrow cobbled streets, ochre-tiled roofs and abundant flowers in well-tended public gardens. But don't expect to be able to fill more than a day in total with visits to monuments.

Finally, you might want to visit Cape Verde for the music, addictive dancing and sumptuous festivals.

Activities
Hiking
Cape Verde is a superb hiking destination – the vistas from the mountains of Santo Antão or from the depth of its gorges; the lonely slopes of Brava and the stunning interior of the brooding volcano crater of Fogo make for a unique experience. Much of the walking on Cape Verde is on the extraordinary cobbled paths that have been constructed in the most unlikely corners and up the steepest of slopes, making the walking much easier than might be construed from the map.

On Santo Antão the classic walks are up or down the *ribeiras*, taking transport at the beginning or end (see *Santo Antão*, page 223). On Fogo the great challenge is to ascend the Pico, the 2,829m spectacular volcano cone and, for some, to spend the night with the villagers who make their unique home in its shadow. On Brava there are endless walks criss-crossing the steep 'flower' island and you are unlikely to meet any other travellers. São Nicolau is a gentle and quiet island with a hidden, green and mountainous heartland filled with beautiful walks.

Finally, don't overlook the walking on Santiago with its central mountain zone (see page 147 for more details).

Most of the walks require a certain amount of fitness because they are steep. In this book each is rated according to a rough scheme:

1 Easy path with little fitness required.
2 Medium fitness, with some bursts of steep ascent and/or the odd slippery stretch.
3 Prolonged steep walking and/or slippery, uncobbled paths.

While we attempt to make our assessments uniform, it is inevitable that our judgements of time lengths and difficulty are a little partial. Because of this, we have identified the writer of each hike description at the top: CW – fit male, mid-thirties; AI – unfit female, mid-thirties.

One should perhaps consider that a thirty-something, self-confessed unfit female might still be faster than someone approaching the age of receiving a free senior citizen's bus pass. To be fair, it could also be the case that a keen retired walker may also be faster. It should however be borne in mind that the hot dry climate can make any walk considerably longer in duration, so be prepared to add extra hours for this factor.

Guides are easy to find in the crater on Fogo and available, though less easy to track down, on Santo Antão (use one of the agencies listed in that chapter). You may need a guide for walks in Santiago, and are very likely to need one for a potentially dangerous peak like Pico do Santo António. However, there are no 'professional' guides on this island and you may end up worse off than you would be without one, if you rest false hopes in a man who does not know the route. Guides should cost between 1,500$ and 3,000$.

Hikers should be aware that longer routes and some paths can be remote. They should therefore always carry a good supply of emergency food and water. Despite

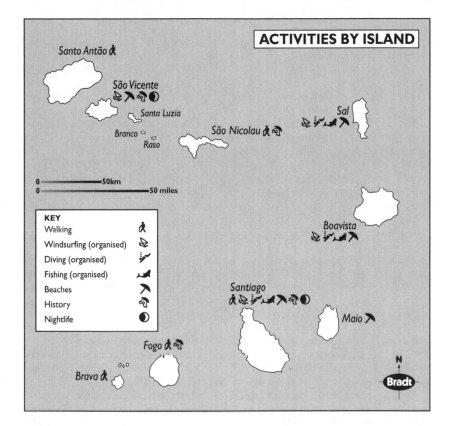

the high daytime temperatures, at night it can be surprisingly cool, and being forced to overnight on a high ridge for any unexpected reason may be unpleasant, if not actually life threatening.

Surfing

Cape Verde has 965km of coastline, spotted with reefs and points, so its potential for surfing is high. The water is warm and the swell from the open Atlantic, during the winter, can be big. It is similar to the Canaries and the Azores in the kind of swell it picks up – but it is warmer. The *Barlavento* islands in the north are in the best position for winter surf, while the *Sotavento* – southern islands – pick up summer, tropical swells and swells from far away in the south Atlantic.

The winter swell season runs from January to March and at this time the average deep swell height is about 1.8m. The swells tend to hit the western coasts of the islands and wrap around into spots heading south. The result is offshore conditions with northeast winds.

The best-known island for surfing is Sal, whose most famous wave is at Ponta Preta – a long, classic right-hand reef with 200m rides. There are also surfing spots on Santiago – Tarrafal, and the coast in the southeast, south of Ponte de Lobo.

Some local expats manage to transport their boards around on the local *aluguer hiaces*, but you will probably need to hire a vehicle. For more information consult *The Surf Report* (see *Further reading*, page 270).

Windsurfing

Cape Verde is a popular destination for windsurfers from Europe to Hawaii, and regularly hosts championships. The two main islands for windsurfing are Boavista and Sal, with São Vicente offering a lot of potential but little as yet in the way of facilities.

Northeast tradewinds blow over Cape Verde consistently from October to June, and from February to June northeast winds often reach very high speeds.

In Sal, windsurfing mainly occurs in Santa Maria, at the southern end of the island, where there are several windsurfing centres. The bay and surrounds are most suitable for intermediate sailors up to advanced wave sailors. At the centre of the 4km, white-sand bay, where the windsurfing centres are, the water is flat and the wind direction ideal for blasting across the waters. Further upwind, at the end of the bay, the swells get bigger and there is plenty of opportunity for wave-riding. In general the Santa Maria wind is cross-shore and, sometimes, cross-offshore. The shorebreak is mild to moderate.

There are other coveted wave spots in Sal, in particular Rife das Tartarugas and Ponta Preta.

On Boavista, the presence of the island of Sal Rei opposite the bay makes for near-perfect conditions for a wide range of abilities and the island is getting international recognition for its windsurfing. The bay is sufficiently protected for beginners – and, though huge, it is shallow – never more than 1?m deep. There is no coral to damage the feet and virtually no current.

The waves vary in size and suit most levels of expertise, according to François Guy, an ex-international champion who runs one of the two windsurfing establishments on Boavista. The biggest waves are greater than those on Sal. All can be reached by windsurfers from the beach beside Sal Rei town. Other windsurfing activities including slaloming up and down the bay and racing around the island of Sal Rei.

In São Vicente, in the bay of Mindelo, the average wind speed between January and June is 16 knots, with gusts of up to 30 knots. Round the coast in São Pedro bay, world windsurfing speed records have been set and the current record is over 40 knots. The wind there, at the southwest corner of the island, is the result of an unusual quirk in the landscape: the long straight valley behind the bay acts as a funnel concentrating the wind – a phenomenon known as the Venturi effect. The result is an unusually steady and strong breeze. However, though there are facilities for guests at the resort hotel in São Pedro, there is otherwise little for the would-be windsurfer. This situation may change in the future. Costs for windsurfing tend to be fairly standard. For sample costs, see under *Boavista*, page 105.

Diving

Ray Almeida

Much of Cape Verde presents an underwater world of massive rock formations, caves, canyons, ledges and sharp wall drop-offs. All of these are home to fish, eel, lobster and in many areas, intensely yellow polyps.

There are brilliantly coloured parrot and trigger fish but in general the fish life is not as colourful, nor the plant life as plentiful and varied as in the Red Sea. But there is something very special: one can observe big fish and large schools of fish relatively close to shore. During the warmer weather it is not uncommon to see metre-long trumpet fish, massive loggerhead or green turtles sometimes a metre across, manta rays up to 3m, the largest balloon fish you will find anywhere and schools of dolphins. Heading from Sal towards the northern coast of Boavista you sometimes see hundreds of big yellow-fin tuna breaking the surface and rocketing skyward like missiles. In March and April humpback and grey whales often appear off shore. There are large schools of barracuda numbering a hundred animals, strawberry-coloured coney grouper and clouds of beautiful reef fish such as the yellow-tailed snapper. Some eels have heads the size of footballs.

There are shipwrecks of all types and vintages. Off Sal there is easy access to three wreck sites at depths of 9–12m.

There are a lot of waves, especially during the winter (November to April), and so divers have to take the chance that conditions will be right. June to September is the best season.

Diving is offered in Sal, Boavista and in the northern town of Tarrafal on Santiago Island. (See also *Sal*, page 87.)

Fishing
Cape Verde offers a variety of opportunities for fishing. There are now several companies, operating mainly out of Sal, Boavista and Santiago, which offer high-sea fishing for blue marlin, wahoo, yellow-fin tuna, shark, white marlin, sailfish and spearfish. Around the archipelago it is possible to join local fishermen on their trips. Often they go out a few hundred metres, drop anchor, and fish for goldfish, grouper and squirrel fish. Some go night-fishing for morays. The locals use harpoons to catch lobster, octopus and parrotfish.

Music
The Cape Verdean music scene is thriving, with an increasing number of bands making the international break and joining the renowned Césaria Evora on the world scene. The music is a blend of African, European and more recently Latin. The traditional African music came with the slaves. When Europeans entered the scene, their string instruments fused with the African sounds. The famous *morna* music with its slower rhythms developed after this. Its themes are those of love, sentimentalism and heart-wrenching emotions for a land left behind or lost.

Back on the archipelago, whose history is the musicians' constant source of inspiration, music is everywhere – in Fogo crater, in every little village, down the *ribeiras* and of course in the cities of Praia and Mindelo. All the differing blends of music have evolved with markedly differing rhythms.

The main rhythms are called *coladera*, *funana* and *mazurka*. The last is particularly common on Santo Antão and São Nicolau and is a dancing rhythm, which expresses warmth and joy. All in all there is an astonishing number of outstandingly talented musicians for such a small group of islands.

To hear the music in a planned way, spend time in Mindelo and Praia (see the relevant island chapters for discussions of venues).

Dancing
Every town has its disco tucked away behind some nondescript wooden door, and nightlife in Praia and Mindelo is vibrant. Clubs don't tend to get going until after midnight.

Music is in general Cape Verdean, interspersed with hip-hop, techno/house and Brazilian samba. You will soon pick up the popular local dance forms. *Possada* is a favourite of Mindelo clubs, danced to zouk music; *funana*, a fast dance done mainly to the strains of the accordion, is a more southern dance form, not really accepted in Mindelo; *cola* (which means 'glue') is a slow and amorous pelvic grind.

Planning an itinerary
To get the most out of Cape Verde, choose carefully the time of year and the islands you wish to visit, as well as picking modes of travel that will suit your purse.

Tourist information

The Cape Verde Tourist Guide, a small booklet, contains a lot of useful information. This can sometimes be obtained at the airport on arrival. See also www.guiadecaboverde.cv, www.guiadecaboverde.com.

Unotur CP 97 Santa Maria, Rua 15 de Agosto, Santa Maria; ⟩ +238 242 1771; f +238 242 1744; e unotur@cvtelecom.cv. A non-profit agency that seeks to promote the Cape Verde Islands and is sponsored by a number of hotels, agencies, car hire, island promoters and real-estate agents. In effect it is the only functioning tourist office and tourism promotion organisation. It produces a large brochure full of useful information.

With the demise of nearly all the CVTS (Cape Verde Tourist Service) offices, there are no longer any other obvious tourist-information centres available on the islands. Hotels and travel agents are the only possible sources of basic information. Promex, the former government tourist-development section in Praia, is no longer producing any current information or maps of the islands. They are now concerned mainly with foreign investors.

The small booklet *Cape Verde Tourist Guide* is issued yearly and is a useful source of current information. It is issued in Portuguese, French, English and Italian. For details contact them at www.guiadecaboverde.cv.

Planning an outline itinerary for an independent tour can be done using this guidebook. The highlights of each island are described in the text. For those unwilling to take on the burdens of self-planning, a list of tour operators is given on pages 40–1.

When to go

Four factors should govern when to visit the islands: temperature, scenery, carnivals and overcrowding.

In January the midday temperature is about 27°C, falling to 20°C at night. This rises through the year until September when the midday temperature is 31°C, dropping to 24°C at night. Temperatures then fall again towards December.

Rains fall between July and October, and can impede hikes up some of the Santo Antão *ribeiras*. The rains release a fur of greenery over many of the barren slopes which dramatically increases their beauty. Harmattan winds blow intermittently between December and March which can disrupt plane schedules, dull photographs and irritate the nose.

Every island has its festivals (see the relevant island chapter for details), but the most famous is the São Vicente Mardi Gras Carnival in February and the music festival on the same island during the August full moon. At Carnival and at Christmas, Cape Verde is deluged with relatives visiting home. International air tickets, internal flights and hotel rooms are gold dust. Taken together, the best time to visit is probably October followed by March.

ANNUAL WEATHER STATISTICS

	Jan	Feb	Mar	Apr	M
Temperature °C day	24	25	25	25	2
Temperature °C night	18	17	18	18	I
Sea temperature °C	21	20	20	20	2
Hours of sunshine	8	9	10	10	I
Days of rain	0	0	0	0	

The chart below indicates the recent average temperatures, rainfall and hours of sun for Cape Verde as a whole.

Where to go

You can select islands to suit your tastes from the map on page 35. For general sightseeing you need three full days for Santo Antão, Fogo and Santiago and two days for each of the other islands. The most- visited islands are Sal, Boavista, Fogo and Santo Antão, with the vast majority of visitors going to Sal. For hiking, the most dramatic options are Fogo and Santo Antão, with Santiago and São Nicolau providing some pleasant hikes as well. Brava is excellent for hiking, but its inaccessibility rules it out for most people. For beach holidays and watersports, Sal is the best equipped with international hotels, windsurfing equipment etc; Boavista is much quieter, though still with good hotels and facilities, and there is some windsurfing on São Vicente. Maio has yet to get really started, but the beginnings of small-scale apartment-style vacationing are stirring. For Cape Verdean music and/or nightlife, São Vicente, followed by Santiago, are the chief islands to visit.

How to see the islands

The simplest and most convenient, as well as the most reliable way to visit the islands is to fly with TACV in their ATR 42-300 aircraft. Anyone with only two weeks should not consider taking any long ferries or other alternatives. The only ferry one should expect to use in a short itinerary is the reliable scheduled ferry service between Mindelo and Santo Antão. Anyone visiting Cape Verde for a month or more should not expect to be able to travel on a budget, as the generally high accommodation costs preclude long stays for budget travellers without local contacts anyway.

Ferries do operate between some of the islands, although schedules are not always strictly adhered to, so it is worth double-checking the sailing times listed throughout the guide. Generally the *Barlavento* runs between Santiago, Brava and Fogo and the *Tarrafal* between São Vicente, São Nicolau and Santiago twice a week, but it would be good to check out the situation on arrival.

Flights cost about £60 (85) per single journey, although there are substantial savings with an airpass (see *Getting there*, page 41). Journeys take between 20 and 50 minutes, and are generally very reliable.

When available, boats cost about £12 (20) per journey. You are unlikely to find a ferry too full to take you, however boats can be delayed for days and journeys are long (typically 14 hours between all but the closest islands). Also, seasickness abounds. The car ferry between Mindelo on São Vicente and Porto Novo on Santo Antão is reliable and efficient.

Budget

Many goods and services are at European prices. Unless proposed ferry services materialise, one should plan a budget utilising the TACV airpass. Once on land it

Jun	Jul	Aug	Sep	Oct	Nov	Dec
27	27	28	30	29	28	27
20	22	23	24	23	22	20
22	23	24	25	25	24	22
8	7	6	8	8	9	8
2	3	3	7	4	1	0

is cheapest to use the local *aluguer* transport, eat at local (as opposed to tourist) restaurants and buy picnic lunches from markets and shops. Chartered taxis, and cars with drivers, are ten times the price of shared local transport, and it is quite expensive to hire guides (about £12–15 or 20–25 per day).

Not including air tickets, two budget travellers would find it hard to avoid spending between them £25 a day (40, US$45, 4,400$). This breaks down into: hotel room 1,500–2,500$; breakfasts for two 500$; picnic lunch 400$; dinner for two 1,200$. A mid-range trip would cost two people a core £45 a day (60, US$70, 6,600$), which assumes you take some taxis, stay in nicer hotels and eat out at lunchtime. For a full-blown holiday with some sort of daily tourist activity, such as diving or car hire, and a smart hotel, expect two people to pay between them £120 a day (170, US$200, 18,700$), which breaks down into: hotel room 8,500$; activity 3,500$; lunch 2,000$; dinner 4,000$. A package trip is likely to be cheaper.

Tour operators

Operators in the UK are unusual. There is a large number of operators in France, Germany and Italy, a few of which are listed below:

UK
Cape Verde Travel 14 Market Pl, Hornsea, East Yorks HU18 1AW; ⟩ 01964 532679; f 01964 536192; e info@capeverdetravel.com; www.capeverdetravel.co.uk. The only operator in the UK that organises a variety of trips to Cape Verde, it can set up anything from 2 weeks' windsurfing in Sal to eco-tourism in Santo Antão. Welcomes orders from outside the UK.
Explore Worldwide Nelson House, 55 Victoria Rd, Farnborough GU14 7PA; ⟩ 0870 333 4001; f 01252 760001; e res@exploreworldwide.com; www.explore.co.uk. Small-group holidays, 14-day tour of the 5 main islands, with the emphasis on hiking in Santo Antão and Fogo.
Strand Leisure Travel 577–579 Fishponds Rd, Bristol BS16 3AF; ⟩ 0870 330 8040; f 0870 330 8041; e holidays@strandtravel.co.uk; www.strandtravel.co.uk

US and Canada
The Adventure Centre 1311 63rd St, Suite 200, Emeryville, CA 94608; ⟩ 0800 227 8747; e tripinfo@adventurecenter.com. Specialises in adventurous trips.
Trek Holidays Canada Toll free ⟩ +1 888 456 3522; *Calgary* ⟩ 403 283 6115; *Vancouver* ⟩ 604 734 1066; *Edmonton* Westcan Treks ⟩ 780 439 0024

Germany
Eden Roc Hörder Str 382, D-58454, Witten; ⟩ 2302 47902; f 2302 48824; e info@eden-roc.de; www.eden-roc.de. Specialises in diving.
Hauser Exkursionen International Marienstr 17, 803331 Munich; ⟩ 8923 50060; f 8929 13714; www.hauser-exkursionen.com. Specialising in trekking, mainly in Santo Antão.
M&M Inselreisen Saargemünderstr 136, 66119, Saarbrücken; ⟩ 6813 98098; f 6813 905060; e info@centertours.com; www.centertours.com
Olimar Reisen Unter Goldschmied 6, 50667, Cologne; ⟩ 2212 05900; f 2212 51591; e service.center@olimar.de; www.olimar.de. A big operator doing mainly package seaside holidays in Sal. Its holidays can be booked from Britain with a credit card.
Studiosus Reisen München Riesstrasse 25, D-80992, Munich; ⟩ 6171 6500; f 6171 652125; e tours@studiosus.com; www.studiosus.de. Takes groups to the 5 major islands, accompanied throughout by a tour guide.
Sun & Fun Sportreisen Franz-Josef-Str 43, D-80801, Munich; ⟩ 8933 8833; f 8934 6644; e marion.henne@sportreisen.de; www.sportreisen.de. Specialising in sport travel such as surfing, windsurfing, kitesurfing and diving.

France
Nomade Aventure www.nomade-aventure.com. A specialist company.
Terres d'Aventure www.terdav.com. A large operator of adventure holidays.

Cape Verde
Alsatour CP 33, Paúl, Santo Antão; ↘ +238 231213, m 925875; f +238 231520;
e alfred@alsatour.de; www.alsatour.de. Specialises in trekking tours in Santo Antão,
particularly those into remote areas, staying with local people. Also organises trips in other
parts of the archipelago, inc sailing.

GETTING THERE
By air
At present all long-haul flights land on Sal. But a new airport with a longer runway
is due to open at any moment in Praia, on Santiago. This will allow long-haul
flights, not just those from the African mainland, to land on Santiago. If flying
from Europe, sit on the right for the best view of the archipelago.

The new airport was due to start operating in November 2005, but owing to
heavy rain and flooding the opening has had to be delayed. When it does eventually
open, the following schedule is planned, but of course may well change, so do
check before you make firm plans.
Lisbon to Santiago Mon, Tue, Thu and Fri 11.00–14.20; returning Mon, Tue, Thu and
Fri 04.00–09.00
Santiago to Paris Fri 03.40–11.50
Santiago to Amsterdam Fri 03.40–14.05

Flights in May 2005 to Sal were as follows:
Amsterdam Thu – flight duration 6¼hrs
Bergamo Sun – flight duration 6hrs
Lisbon Tue/Wed/Sat/Sun – flight duration 3½hrs
Munich Fri – flight duration 6hrs
Paris Mon – flight duration 6½hrs
Dakar Sat – flight duration 1hr
Fortaleza Sat – flight duration 3hrs

From the UK
TACV Book via its ticketing agent Cape Verde Travel (see *Tour operators*, opposite). There are
currently no direct flights from London, though there are plans for these soon, but there are
through-booked flights from UK regional airports via Amsterdam and Paris, with return fares
starting at £460. Cape Verde Travel can also book you on flights departing from the various
European cities below; the cheapest is Lisbon (around £319 return, not inc the UK–Lisbon leg).
TAP Air Portugal ↘ 0870 240 0033; www.tap.pt. Flights from London to Sal via Portugal,
starting at £550 return inc airport tax in low season. It is hard to find good discounts with
travel agents, but you might get £20 off with TAP's own consolidator IATC (↘ +44 020
7581 0722) or Cape Verde Travel (see opposite). TAP currently flies to Cape Verde on
Tue, Wed, Fri, Sat, Sun.
Charter flights to The Gambia and Dakar During the winter (Oct–May) long-haul
charters to Banjul, The Gambia, are available for under £300, and flights to Dakar, Senegal,
cost around £400. For the connecting flight to Cape Verde with TACV, prices vary with the
season, but a typical cost is 26,690$ (249) one way or 25-day return fare 39,530$ (370).
Try Senegambia Travel and the usual high-street travel agents in the UK for charter flights.
Charter flights to Canary Islands There are many flights to Las Palmas; prices vary
hugely with the season – from about £150 upwards. To link with a flight from Las Palmas

to Cape Verde, see *From the Canary Islands*, below. This appears on the surface to be an attractive option, but matching flights is tricky, and you could wait for several days in the Canaries for connecting flights in either direction.

From the rest of Europe

TACV www.tacv.com or www.tacv.aero. Flies direct from France (Paris), the Netherlands (Amsterdam), Switzerland (Zurich), Germany (Munich), Italy (Milan – Malpensa and Bérgamo), and Portugal (Oporto and Lisbon). If your country does not have a TACV office, try the Rotterdam office: Weena 95–97; 3013 CH Rotterdam, Netherlands; ❭ 104 115411; f 104 124998.

TAP Air Portugal www.tap.pt. Connects most major European cities with Lisbon for the onward flight to Cape Verde. Head office in Lisbon: Av da Liberdade, 36-1A, 1200 Lisbon; ❭ 1 323 0500.

Air France www.airfrance.com. Fly to Dakar for connections on Air Senegal or TACV to Cape Verde.

Neos Air www.neosair.it. Operates frequent charters from various cities in Italy: Milan, Verona, Bologna and Rome.

From North America

Some visitors from North America fly to a European capital, then to west Africa and from there to Praia in Cape Verde (for example New York–Paris–Dakar–Praia) but this takes some time and is not recommended.

Sun Travel 598 Warren Av, East Providence, RI; ❭ 401 434 7333. Experienced at getting people to and from Cape Verde on any available airlines, including occasional charters at competitive prices.

South African Airways ❭ 0800 722 9675; www.flysaa.com

TACV ❭ +1 617 47 22227; f 617 47 22521; e dboston@tacv.aero; www.tacv.cv. Flights from Boston to Sal; some may be via Lisbon. Plus, a twice-weekly non-stop scheduled service directly from Boston to the New International Airport in Praia (ADP).

TAP Air Portugal ❭ 617 262 8585; www.tap.pt. Flights from New York and Boston–Lisbon–Sal.

From Africa

Angolan Airlines Stops en route to Europe from Luanda. Their office is in Espargos.

Air Senegal www.air-senegal-international.com. Flights to Praia from Dakar in Senegal with links to Bissau in Guinea-Bissau, and Banjul in The Gambia.

TACV Operates flights to/from Dakar in Senegal, with connections on other carriers to Banjul, Bissau and Conakry. Flights should be in operation from the new airport at Praia on Santiago. Sample fares: 26,687$ one way and 39,527$ return for 25-day validity.

South African Airways ❭ +27 11 978 1111; www.flysaa.com. Daily flights from Johannesburg to Sal; return flights once a week.

From the Canary Islands

TACV One flight a week from Las Palmas to Sal. In the UK, tickets can be bought from Cape Verde Travel (see page 40). TACV office in Gran Canaria at Planta Baja Hall, Aeroporto Gran Canaria, 35230 Las Palmas; ❭ 92 857 9573; f 92 857 9271; e tacvlpa@todoair.com.

Ataman Tours Las Palmas; www.atamantours.com. Tickets might also be available through this agent.

From South America

TACV and **Varig** fly from the Brazilian city of Fortaleza, on the northeast coast of Brazil. From Fortaleza there are connections to São Paulo and other cities in Brazil, as well as to other South American capitals. TACV flies on Saturdays to Brazil. Varig currently flies on Fridays.

TACV: the national airline
The national carrier of the Cape Verde Islands is Transportes Aereo de Cabo Verde, commonly referred to as TACV. It was formed in 1976 with flights to the Canaries and Guinea. In 1985 a route was opened to Lisbon, followed by Boston in the US. These flights gave emigrants better access to their former home. TACV acquired its first Boeing 757 in 1996 and has since expanded to include flights to some major European cities and the Americas.

Those arriving on TACV and TAP, the Portuguese airline, are entitled to an **airpass**. For details concerning TACV's internal flights and their promotional airpass see *Travel within the islands* on page 48.

The airline has offices worldwide, including the following:

Austria Openring 1/e/7a, 1010 Vienna; ☎ 1585 3630; f 1585 3688
Brazil *Fortaleza* Enterprise Turismo Lda, Av Dom Luis 796, Aldeota CEP 60.160.230; f 85 268 1020; e tacv@tacvfortaleza.com.br; *São Paulo* Rua 7 de Abril, 127 4 Andar-Conj 42; ☎ 11 325 788 55; f 11 325 501 52; *Rio de Janeiro* Mindelo Representacocs, Rue Figuiroedo Magalhaes, 286 SI 201 Copacabana; ☎ 21 2548 4649; f 21 2235 0923; e tacv.mindelo@uol.com.br
Canaries Planta Baja Hall, Aeroporto Gran Canaria, 35230 Las Palmas; ☎ 92 857 9573; f 92 857 9271; e tacvlpa@todoair.com
France 101 Rue de Prony, 75017 Paris; ☎ 1 56 79 13 13; f 1 43 80 68 18; e tacv.fr@tacv.aero
The Gambia Banjul International Airport; ☎ 47 27 48; e saulnje@hotmail.com
Germany Landsberger Strasse 155, 80687 Munich; ☎ 89 5525 3333; f 89 5450 6855
Italy Viale L/ Majno 38, 20129 Milano; ☎ 02 29 53 63 10; f 02 20 10 45; e tacv.milano@tacv.aero
Mali Quartier du Fleuve face EDM; ☎ 23 89 69; f 23 89 70; e nasairsa@datatech.net.ml
Netherlands Weena 95-97-3013 CI I Rotterdam; ☎ 10 411 5411, f 10 412 4998, e Rotterdam@tacv.aero
Portugal Av da Liberdade 36. 1A 1250-145 Lisbon; ☎ 21 323 0555/323 0527; f 21 347 8101; e reservaslis@tacv.aero
Senegal 103 Rue Mousse Diop, BP 1636 Dakar; ☎ 821 3968; f 822 8285; e dakar@tacv.aero
Spain C/Christobal Bordiu 22, Local E, 28003 Madrid; ☎ 91 395 2030; f 91 395 2031; e tacvesp@todoair.com
Switzerland Schanzeggstrasse 1, 8002 Zurich; ☎ 1 286 9999; f 1 286 9900
UK c/o Cape Verde Travel, 14 Market Pl, Hornsea, East Yorks HU18 1AW; ☎ 01964 532679; f 01964 536192; e info@capeverdetravel.com; www.capeverdetravel.co.uk
USA 1245 Hancock St, Ste 22, Quincy, Boston, MA 02169; ☎ 617 47 22227; f 617 47 22521; e dboston@tacv.aero

By sea
Ships and cruises
Arriving by sea and watching the Atlantic crags materialise from the ocean is an unusual and uplifting way of reaching the islands. Cape Verde is a shipping nation and so in theory it ought to be possible to do this, but in practice it is not so simple.

A La Carte Cruises Buikslotermeerplein 329, 1025 XE Amsterdam; ☎ 20 492 32 14; f 20 492 32 15; e info@alacartecruises.nl; www.alacartecruises.nl, www.scheepszaken.nl
Arca Verde CP 153, Rua Senador Vera-Cruz, Mindelo, São Vicente; ☎ 321349; f 324963, for information on any links between Cape Verde and the west African coast.
Atlantic Shipping Cape Cod, MA; ☎ 508 672 1870. Sometimes offers sailings from the US to Cape Verde.

Strand Voyages 1 Adam St, London WC2N 6AB; ☎ 020 7766 8220; f 020 7766 8225;
e voyages@strandtravel.co.uk; www.strandtravel.co.uk
Strand Leisure Travel 577–579 Fishponds Rd, Bristol BS16 3AF; ☎ 0870 330 8040;
f 0870 330 8041; e holidays@strandtravel.co.uk; www.strandtravel.co.uk

By yacht

Cape Verde is still an unusual place for yachts to stop, but numbers are increasing, and it is not uncommon to see 20 boats at anchor in Palmeira harbour in Sal, with more at Santa Maria, and others dotting bays around the archipelago.

Apart from visiting the islands for their own sake, the big draw is their convenient position for those about to cross the Atlantic. Pausing in Cape Verde can cut by a week the amount of time that would be spent at sea.

There are three good harbours and these are on the best -resourced islands (Sal, São Vicente and Santiago). The other islands all have reasonable anchorages, but at some the safety or comfort depends on the weather.

Cape Verde is still a long way from competing materialistically with the facilities on the Azores or the Canaries. Boat repair facilities are not too advanced; food is expensive and it can sometimes be hard to find fresh meat and vegetables. Water is available alongside in the three good harbours but otherwise it can be a case of making journeys to the tap. Water is scarce on Cape Verde and much of it comes from desalinisation plants. Overall, it is best to stock up before you arrive so your needs in Cape Verde are as modest as possible.

You do not need a visa unless you are planning to sleep onshore, or to stay for longer than three months. You must enter and clear at every island you visit.

In the island chapters, brief information is given as to anchorages and facilities, which may help you decide whether to make the trip. However, the approaches to many of the islands are tricky and it is best to consult the excellent *Atlantic Islands: Azores, Madeira, Canary and Cape Verde Islands* (see *Further reading*, page 268). The most detailed charts are pre-1975 Portuguese; there are also British Admiralty charts but these have errors, sometimes dangerous ones. The British Admiralty Africa Pilot has lots of useful information about weather, sea conditions and currents. All these can be obtained from Imray, Laurie, Norie and Wilson's aforementioned guide.

To find a crewing place from home, check the classified advertisements in yachting magazines. If you have no experience, expect to pay for your board. To find a place while already abroad, advertise yourself on a notice board in the nearest yacht club (or even in the laundrette or poste restante). Alternatively find out which is the favourite nautical bar near the harbour.

Majorca, Gibraltar and Gran Canaria are the best places to look for passage to Cape Verde. The last has several large marinas in which to search for a place.

Yachts tend to cross the Atlantic late in the year. They leave Britain and Europe from May to August and then leave the Canary Islands and Madeira in November, some then calling at Cape Verde. Other yachts passing through Cape Verde leave from Cape Town in February to April to sail up the Atlantic, reaching the islands sometime before May.

RED TAPE

Every non-Cape Verdean visitor needs a visa unless they are married to, or are the offspring of, a Cape Verdean citizen – in which case they need their marriage or birth certificate.

There is no official visa office in the UK, so visitors have two sensible options. The first is to post your passport, two photos, a copy of your ticket, a completed form and a banker's draft to the embassy in Paris, Brussels or the Netherlands (addresses below), which we found to be expensive and time-consuming. A simpler alternative is to book through a recognised travel agent (such as Cape Verde Travel, see page 40), who will fax a photocopy of your passport to Sal airport, where you can collect the visa on arrival. The cost, at present, is 45, whichever option you choose. Although it is in theory possible to buy a visa on arrival, this is not recommended as your airline may not permit you to board the connecting flight to Cape Verde without such documentation.

Visas are normally valid for 90 days. However, those obtaining a pre-arranged visa may find that they are given only eight days on arrival. This is a common scenario and no cause for alarm. Your plane ticket will act as sufficient evidence of your guaranteed departure from the islands.

If you are worried and decide to contact the authorities, be aware that they may want to retain your passports for a week, and arranging a visa extension may cost you an extra 2,000$ (18). If in doubt try contacting the islands' Honorary Consul, Mr Joao Roberto (*18–20 Stanley Street, Liverpool L1 6AF;* \ *0151 236 0206;* f *0251 255 1314;* e *joao.roberto@capeverdeconsul.com*).

Anyone planning to visit Cape Verde from west Africa should if possible get a visa before leaving Europe, as it may add time and complications to get a visa in African capitals. In The Gambia there is no Cape Verdean representation, so organise a visa before leaving home or fly to Senegal.

Cape Verdean embassies and consulates

Austria Embaixada de Viena; e embaixada@Eunet.at

Belgium Rue Antonie Laborre 30, 1050 Brussels; \ 2 646 9025; f 2 646 3385; e emb.caboverde@skynet.be

Brazil SHIS-QL 06 Conj 04, Casa 15, Lago Sul, Brasilia, DF CEF 71620-045; \ 61 365 3190; f 61 365 3191; e Embcaboverde@rudah.com.br

Canada (consulate) 802 The Queensway, West Suite 103, Etobicoke, Ontario M8Z 1N5; \ 416 252 1082; f 416 252 1092

France Rue Jouffroy D'Abbans, 80, 75017 Paris; \ 1 42 12 73 54; f 1 40 53 04 36; e ambassade-cap-vert@wanadoo.fr

Germany Dorotheenstr 43, D 10117 Berlin; \ 30 2045 0955; f 30 2045 0966; e info@embassy-capeverde.de

Italy Viale Giosué Carducci, 4-1° Interno 3, 00187 Rome; \ 06474 4678/4596; f 06474 4764; e elviofernandes@hotmail.com

Luxembourg 46, R Goethe, L-1637, Luxembourg; \ 2648 0948; f 2648 0949

Netherlands 44 Kninginnegracht, 2514 AD The Hague; \ 70 34 69 623; f 70 34 67 702

Portugal Av do Restelo, 33 1400 Lisbon; \ 1301 9521; f 1301 5308; e emb.caboverde@mail.telepac.pt

Russia Rubliovskoe Chaussé, 26 APT 180, Moscow; \ 095 415 4503; f 095 415 4504; e Pts28/(@1pc.ru

Senegal 3 Av El Hadji Djilly M'baye, BP 11269, Dakar; \ 224285; f 210697; e acvc.sen@metissacana.sn

Spain (consulate) Calle Capitán Haya, 51 Planta 4, Of8 28020 Madrid; \ 1 570 2568; f 1 570 2563; e con.geral_cv@mad.servicom.es

Sweden (consulate) Tellusvägen 16, 135 47 Tyresö, Stockholm; \/f 8 742 29 27, m 70 541 09 47

Switzerland (consulate) Rümelinplatz 14, CH-4001 Basel; \ 61 269 8095; f 61 269 8050; e awg@bluewin.ch

USA 3415 Massachussetts Av NW, Washington, DC 20007; \ 202 965 6820; f 202 965 1207; e ambacvus@sysnet.net or cvesemedo@sysnet.net

Embassies and consulates in Cape Verde

Belgium (consulate) Plateau, Praia; ℃ 261 3892; f 261 6880

Brazil (embassy) Cha D, Agreia, Praia; ℃ 261 5607/0809; f 261 5609; e emb.brasil@cvtel:ecom.cv

Denmark (consulate) Madeira Shipping, Mindelo; ℃ 232 1785; f 232 1726

France (embassy) Prainha, Praia; ℃ 261 5589/5591; f 261 5590; e fransula@cvtel:ecom.cv

Germany (consulate) Achada Santo António, Praia; ℃ 262 3100/3102; f 262 3103; e halmdasociados@cvtel:ecom.cv

Israel (consulate) Mindelo; ℃ 232 3353; f 232 3351

Italy (consulate) Cha D'Areia, Praia; ℣f 261 9343; e italconsulato.cv@katamail.com

Netherlands (consulate) Praia; ℣f 261 2333. Also Rua Thomas Ribeiro, 18 X, Mindelo; ℃ 232 1461; f 232 4957/7333; e consulmindelo@cvtel:ecom.cv

Norway (consulate) Tira-chapéu, Praia; ℃ 262 7555; f 262 7874

Portugal (embassy) Achada Santo António, Praia; ℃ 262 6097/3925; f 262 3036; e emb.portugal@cvtel:ecom.cv

Senegal (embassy) Rua Abilio Macedo, Praia; ℃ 261 5621; f 261 2838; e ambsenecvpraia@cvtel:ecom.cv

Spain (consulate) Prainha, Praia; ℃ 261 4342; f 261 3108

Switzerland (consulate) CP 876, Plateau, Praia; ℣f 261 9868; e c.suisse@cvtel:ecom.cv

Sweden (consulate) Plateau, Praia; ℣f 261 7969; e consulsuede@cvtel:ecom.cv

UK (consulate) CP 4, Mindelo; ℃ 326625; f 232 2584/230 7602; e elisabete.e.soares@cvtel:ecom.cv

USA (embassy) CP 201, Rua Abilio Macedo 6, Plateau, Praia; ℃ 261 5616; f 261 1355; e emb.usa@cvtel:ecom.cv

MONEY

The currency is the escudo, represented by the $ sign at the end of the number, or by the letters CVE. The escudo is officially set to a fixed exchange rate with the euro, currently 1 = 110$. In practice, banks and exchange bureaux/*cambios* vary the rates slightly. Rates are also varied – by as much as 110$ – by hotels charging in local currency. Other exchange rates will vary of course, but a sample at the time of going to press is £1 = 162$; US$1 = 92$. The euro is increasingly accepted in Sal.

Credit cards are accepted at an increasing number of upmarket hotels, but not all of them. MasterCard and Visa are the most widely accepted so far. Visa cards can be used to withdraw funds at Banco Comercial do Atlântico for a minimum charge of 1,000$ with other charges of 0.5% of the amount withdrawn. Rates seem to vary throughout the different islands.

Automated teller machines (ATMs) can be found at the major banks in most island capitals but not all. Those on less-frequented islands may not always be in operation.

Cash is the most easily used form of currency. On arrival at the airport in Sal and, when it opens, Praia, cash is both quickest and simplest.

Travellers' cheques are a safer way to carry money around and the three banks (Banco Comercial do Atlântico, Caixa Económica and Banco Interatlântico) all cash them. However, check the details of fees beforehand because some individual branches make perverse charges – up to 10 per transaction. (Note also that when you change travellers' cheques, if they are not consecutive numbers, you may have to pay a separate fee for each 'break' in the series!) Even cash in the banks and *cambios* can attract a charge of up to 600$. The BCA bank in Ribeira Grande on Santo Antão did not charge commission on cash, but normally charges do apply, so ask before the transaction.

Money transfers can be done very quickly through Western Union to Caixa Económica. High-street banks in the UK will transfer funds to Cape Verdean banks urgently (within two or three days) for a fee of about £20–25.

WHAT TO TAKE

In general take as little as you deem necessary. With generally warm nights, most clothes will dry overnight, so if you are a casual visitor, it's not necessary to be burdened down with too many. Even the more remote island capitals have all the basic necessities. Travelling light with only hand luggage is possible for those not hiking, and becomes a bonus on internal flights, but remember to take blunt-ended scissors and disposable razors.

Very cheap hotels cannot always be guaranteed to have towels, soap, loo paper or a basin plug and, while standards of cleanliness are high even in most budget places, those using a homestay might sometimes be thankful they brought a sheet sleeping bag and a pair of flip-flops for washing. For overnight boat trips, which you may spend on deck, you must have a sleeping bag for warmth.

For the average trip a mosquito net is probably surplus to requirements. The few mosquitoes encountered tend to be an irritant rather than a health menace, for virtually all islands. That said, recommendations regarding malaria do change, and since its effects can be devastating you are advised to seek out the latest information. See the *Health* chapter for further details. Insect repellent can be useful for the evenings.

At cooler times of year you may need a jumper for the evenings, and you will need one for the tops of Fogo and Santo Antão. Hikers are very strongly advised to take walking boots, and definitely sun hats, as paths can be unyielding. Many hikers now take walking poles.

The electricity supply is 220V 50Hz, which is standard in western Europe. The plug is a standard European two-pin type.

A Portuguese dictionary is useful – although a French dictionary can sometimes be more helpful if you speak no Portuguese. French is the second European language on the islands. There is only a few books in English, so take your own reading matter.

Biros are useful presents for children (but see *Begging*, page 58). An ordinary driving licence suffices for car hire.

Maps

The following maps may be useful, particularly for hikers:

Cabo Verde 1:200,000 tourist map published by Karten-Verlag. Cost: about £12. Order through ReiseTraeume; www.reisetraeume.de/kapverden/reisefuehrer/en/bookshop.html. The proprietors, Gerhard and Sibylle Schellmann, speak English, and can provide current maps of the islands and towns of Cape Verde.

Santo Antao 1:50,000 tourist and hiking map; published by Goldstadt Wanderkarte; e info@goldstadtverlag.de; www.bela-vista.net. Cost: about 18–20. Excellent production with many numbered and annotated hikes superimposed, and plenty of photographs on the other side. New edition is awaited.

Santo Antão 1:100,000; *São Nicolau, São Vicente* 1:150,000 tourist map published by Karten-Verlag. 3 maps in one plus a simplified street map of Mindelo and small explanations of each of the 3 islands in 5 languages. May be discontinued, therefore check with ReiseTraeume (above).

Fogo 1:60,000 Attila Bertolan; www.kartenverlag.de. Cost: about 8.

São Vicente, Sal, Santiago 3 separate maps published by Promex, the Cape Verdean tourist promotion board. There is a rudimentary drawing of each island plus street maps of towns

and cities on that island. Cost: 250$ each; buy in Cape Verde. Clipart in Lisbon previously produced towns and island maps for the Promex tourism promotion board, but the latest versions are from 2003.
Mindelo, Nicolau, Sal/Boavista/Maio Goldstadt has new editions.
Cape Verde 1:500,000 produced by International Travel Maps, a Canadian map maker which is a division of ITMB Publishing Ltd. (ISBN number 1 89590 793 4). Contact address; International Travel Maps, 530 West Broadway, Vancouver, BC Canada, V5Z 1E9; ✆ +1 604 879 3621; f +1 604 879 4521; www.itmb.com.
Cabo Verde Sal, Maio, Boavista; Cabo Verde São Vicente, Sta Luzia, São Nicolau, Santo Antão; Santiago, Brava, Fogo 1:100,000 published by Inatur. Satellite photographs of the islands with roads crudely superimposed. They are, nevertheless, still interesting for the satellite images. Available in Cape Verde, where isolated stocks remain.

TRAVEL WITHIN THE ISLANDS
By air
TACV has flights to all the islands except Santo Antão and Brava, ranging in frequency from six times a day, between big hubs, to once a week. You can reach most places you wish to on the day you would like to if you are prepared to fly via a third island. For flight frequencies see island chapters. Flights can fill quickly, especially through the summer, so early booking is essential. There is nothing worse than being stuck on a remote island with an international flight looming in Sal and a TACV employee advising you to turn up on standby every day for the next week.

Even being checked in is not a guarantee of getting on the flight because of overbooking. Sometimes overbooked flights sneak away 15 minutes earlier than stated. Our advice is to be mildly paranoid. The golden rule is to reconfirm your flight 72 hours beforehand: this is absolutely essential to avoid your seat being given to someone else. Make sure all your flights and times are booked as soon as possible; arrive early to beat the crowds; keep watch and be first in the queue to get on the plane; and avoid travelling in large groups.

If you run into problems and are told all flights are full it is worth persisting. Every flight has seats automatically reserved for government employees and, on the lesser islands, for medical emergencies. They regularly become available for standby passengers at the last minute.

Baggage allowance for internal flights is 20kg. You can normally transport a surfboard or a bicycle on TACV's 46-seater ATRs. Flight details appear under island chapters.

TACV airpass
Our experiences of the country's airline Cabo Verde Airlines (TACV) have generally been first rate but others have reported overnight delays at Sal after check in, so keep your toothbrush to hand. Check your ticket details thoroughly as it is time consuming to make alterations on the islands. There is a hidden saving through booking with TACV (or the Portuguese airline TAP) because you become entitled to a substantial discount on inter-island flights in the form of an airpass. The airpass should be booked when you buy your international ticket. A two-flight pass costs US$120, three flights US$150, four flights US$180 and five flights US$205. Subsequent flights are offered at US$20 per sector. These prices were quoted to us by TACV in Cape Verde, but it may not be easy to obtain once in Cape Verde, so check for the current rules about this. It might be more expensive to purchase the pass abroad. The pass is valid for only 21 days. Domestic airport tax is 626$.

For further details about the airpass contact TACV Promotion Department (☎ +238 260 8200; f +238 261 7275; e marketing@tacv.aero).

Cabo Verde Express operates charter day trips, in general from Sal and Boavista to Fogo. For contact details see the island chapters.

By ferry

Ferries do operate between some of the islands, although schedules are not always strictly adhered to, so it is worth double-checking the sailing times listed throughout the guide. When operating, most of the longer ferry crossings take 14–16 hours and the ferries usually spend a full night or day in a harbour before moving on.

There is a national propensity towards seasickness, and it is advisable to keep your bags slightly off the floor and keep an eye on the passengers immediately beside you if you want to escape the results of this. Take food and drink and something warm to wear, particularly for night crossings.

Tarrafal runs between São Vicente, São Nicolau and Santiago twice a week. It has no beds, but is stable and comfortable. It can be overcrowded in summertime.
Barlavento runs between Santiago, Brava and Fogo.
Rincon Unfortunately the catamaran travelling between Sal, Boavista, Santiago, Maio, Fogo and Brava was not running on our return in 2005.

To book, go in advance to the ferry ticket office, often found in the docks. The alternative is to buy from the captain, which is generally more expensive.

Cargo boats

There are sometimes a few travelling between the islands, and the ferry ticket offices sell a few passenger tickets on these for reduced prices – typically about two-thirds of the full price.

There are also sailings aimed at tourists, in motor and sailing boats. By far the most common route is a day trip between Sal and Boavista (see *Sal*, page 86). Fogo Adventures, who mainly operate tours for fishing clients in São Filipe, might take tourists from Fogo to Brava (see *Fogo*, page 167).

By bus

Minibuses, commonly referred to as *hiaces* ('yassers'), and open trucks with seating in the back (*carros*), constitute the public transport, recognisable by the sign '*aluguer*'. They are typical African minibuses, often overloaded with people, chickens and packages and trundling along, often rather fast, with happy-go-lucky music tinkling from a cassette player.

Generally, *aluguers* converge at a point in a town or village which anyone can point out to you; often they drive round town picking up passengers and few leave town before they are full. You shout when you want to get off and you pay after disembarking. *Aluguers* can be flagged down anywhere along the roads. In Cape Verde, unusually for west Africa, many of these vehicles are in very good condition and consequently most of their drivers are careful and reasonably slow.

The great disadvantage for visitors is the times of the *aluguers*. With some exceptions (noted in each chapter), *aluguers* leave outlying villages at 05.00 or 06.00 to take people to town. They then leave town for the outlying villages between 11.00 and mid afternoon. Over and over again tourists pile into the 11.00 *aluguer* only to find they have no way of getting back to town in the evening without chartering a vehicle at great cost.

By taxi

The term taxi refers both to the cars with meters and taxi signs, found in towns, and to public minibuses or trucks that have been chartered by an individual. Chartering costs about ten times the public fare and you may be forced to do it if you want to go somewhere at a different time of day from everyone else. Sometimes the fares can be bargained down and occasionally an opportunist will try to diddle you, but generally prices are fixed – they're just very high. Drivers in general love to be chartered by a tourist so watch out when they tell you there is no more public transport that day – hang around to check and ask around for an *aluguer coletivo*. Tourists often get together to share a chartered minibus, which has the added advantage that they can control the speed of the driver.

Hitchhiking

Cars are likely to pick you up, except in Santiago. Offer the price of the *aluguer* fare if it seems appropriate. In remote areas there may be no traffic all day. Women travelling on their own should always exercise caution when attempting to hitchhike.

Car rental

This is possible through local chain firms on São Vicente, Sal and Santiago and there are tiny firms on some of the other islands. International firms have opened on Sal. For contact details see the relevant island chapters. Book several days ahead if you can and don't expect things to run smoothly – for example, the wrong car might arrive several hours late with no price reduction offered for the inconvenience. In May 2005, petrol was 120$ per litre and diesel was 69$ on the more populated islands, though these prices are likely to have gone up significantly with the worldwide increase in the price of oil since then. An ordinary driving licence is sufficient, plus a deposit of 10,000–20,000$.

Cycling

Keen cyclists do take their bicycles to the archipelago and return having had a good time. Bicycles can be transported between the islands on the larger TACV 46-seater planes. You pay by weight, just as with other baggage. Bicycles may be hired on Sal and are likely to be available shortly on Boavista.

However, there are several caveats about cycling in Cape Verde. Firstly, virtually all roads are cobbled, causing ceaseless, tiring vibrations to the hands as they clutch the handlebars. Secondly, the bulk of roads in Cape Verde are utterly devoid of shade and the constant sunshine can be exhausting. Thirdly, some of the most interesting islands have many stretches that are too steep for cycling – in particular, much of Santo Antão and many roads in Fogo.

ACCOMMODATION

The hotel star-rating system is an inflated one, internal to Cape Verde. The term 'hotel' implies a place of superior quality. The other terms, *pousada*, *pensão* and *residencial*, are interchangeable.

At the bottom of the range there are some very cheap, grubby places that are not intended for tourists. No-one will mention them, they will not be marked, and even the proprietors may discourage you from staying for fear you'll complain about the conditions.

Above this level hotels are almost invariably clean, if basic, and en-suite bathrooms are common. Rooms can vary enormously in quality within the same hotel. In particular the windows of inner rooms often open only on to a central shaft, which makes them dark and noisy. Quite a number of '*residencial*' hotels do not have signs, but this does not bracket them into the 'unusable' category alluded to above. Finding them, though, is not easy.

Hotels are listed in descending order of price and, where useful, have been grouped as upmarket, mid range and budget. Prices also vary considerably with the season, and we have listed some of the bigger hotel variations. Some prices include breakfast ('*con pequeno almoço*' – at its most basic, bread, bananas, a slice of the solid local marmalade and coffee).

Luxury hotels of international standard can be found on Sal, Santiago, São Vicente and Boavista. These are of a standard similar to those of the larger European chains and are increasingly managed by foreign concerns. Many islands have ambitious hotel-building plans.

Rooms in most three-star hotels will have hot water, telephone, fan or air conditioning, and often a fridge and television. Conditions and facilities in hotels listed under 'mid range' may vary considerably. Hotels listed under 'budget' are often very good value, but not always. In this context the term 'budget' does not mean the backpacker's version of 'budget'. Even so-called budget hotels are not cheap in comparison with such places in, say, south Asia.

Virtually all hotels other than those in the budget category have en-suite bathrooms. Increasingly, hotels have hot water, though in some cases it will remain in the pipe system until you have finished your shower. Do not expect hot water in budget or remote hotels.

In Sal and Boavista, and often in Fogo, there is immense pressure on bed space at popular times, so it is advisable to book well ahead for the first two, and a day or two ahead for Fogo.

Hotels open and shut rapidly, so if you are heading for a remote one, check beforehand that you won't be stranded for the night: it happens. Camping is permitted on the beaches, but finding a natural water supply may be difficult.

Living with the people

On the two great hiking islands, Santo Antão and Fogo, local people are increasingly opening up their homes to walkers. In general you sleep in a spare (or hastily vacated) bedroom and are fed your evening meal as well as breakfast the next day. Sometimes local people have built concrete annexes on to their houses to accommodate tourists. A few homestays are starting to provide better facilities. The system has several advantages. It allows trekkers to do more ambitious journeys safe in the knowledge that they have places to stay along the way. It brings locals and visitors into closer contact – you experience a taste of the rural lifestyle while they derive entertainment and cash from you.

But most rural homestays are not for every visitor. Conditions will be basic: perhaps there will be a room without windows, a very old mattress and some sort of shared washing facility without a huge amount of privacy. Although the price will be lower than that of hotels, it may be higher than you expected it to be. This can be because of the high cost of arranging special food for visitors (for example, some homestay hosts in Santo Antão have to spend a day travelling to town and back to purchase food for their guests). For some, a homestay is the high spot of their trip and even a formative experience in their lives; for others it is a disaster from which they can't wait to escape. Crucially, you must be able to lay aside the mindset of the demanding European/American consumer-holidaymaker and become an anthropologist for a while, accepting what is given and taking an interest in everything you are privileged to witness.

Apartment-style accommodation

On Sal, Boavista and even to a limited degree on Maio, new projects are springing up to cater for apartment rental for one week and much longer. Many of these projects anticipate selling apartments to foreigners. Just outside Sal Rei on Boavista are some quite large new complexes aimed at both these markets, and even on Maio there are three such new projects. On Sal, building continues apace around Santa Maria. There is a new complex to the north on the west coast of Sal at Baia de Murdeira, which is a vast apartment-style resort. See the relevant chapters for further details about these options.

PUBLIC HOLIDAYS AND OPENING HOURS

Everything is closed on public holidays and on Sundays, and many shops also close early on Fridays. Opening hours tend to be Mediterranean – that is, Monday–Friday 08.00/08.30–12.00/12.30 and 14.00/14.30–18.00/18.30; Saturday 08.30–12.00. Banks are often shut in the afternoon. Restaurants operate from about 19.00 to 23.00. Nightclubs tend to open at midnight.

Public holidays

1 January	New Year
20 January	National Heroes Day
1 May	Labour Day
5 July	Independence Day
15 August	Nossa Senhora da Graça (Our Lady of Grace)
12 September	Nationality Day
1 November	All Saints Day
25 December	Christmas Day

Mardi Gras and Good Friday are also national holidays.

Festivals

Each island has a calendar of festivals, many of which originated as saints' days and all of which offer a great excuse for music and dancing. The most renowned is the São Vicente Carnival in mid February. Others of particular interest are described in the island chapters.

FOOD AND DRINK

Fish lovers will be in heaven on Cape Verde. The grilled lobster is superb, as are the fresh tuna, octopus and a multitude of other delicacies. Vegetarians who don't eat fish may find only omelette on the menu but can always ask for a plate of rice and beans. A speciality is *cachupa*, a delicious, hearty dish that comes in two varieties: poor-man's *cachupa* (boiled maize, beans, herbs, cassava, sweet potato) and rich-man's *cachupa* (the same but with chicken and other meat). *Cachupa* takes a long time to prepare: some restaurants put a sign in their windows to indicate when they will next be serving it. For the casual visitor it may be quite hard to sample this famous dish. *Cachupa grelhada* is perhaps the most palatable – everything available all fried up together.

A local speciality is jams and semi-dried fruits. These are often served as desserts along with fresh goat's cheese, making a delicious end to the meal.

Most towns will have local eateries where huge platefuls of rice, chips, beans and fish, or of *cachupa*, are served up for 300–500$. They may not be open all day though. Restaurant prices are indexed in the rest of this book by the cost of their cheapest main meat or fish dish. In most places, these start at 500–900$. Lobster tends to be 1,200$ upwards. Tea is typically 50$ a cup.

Food on the streets is fine, if unexciting. There are many women with trays of sweets, monkey-nuts, sugared peanuts and popcorn. Sometimes they will have little *pasteis* (fish pastries). Trays of homemade sweets are ubiquitous. The confectionery is very sugary, and flavours are mainly coconut, peanut and papaya. Here and there ladies fry *moreia* – moray eel. Nice, greasy, very bony – just spit the bones out, the dogs will get them.

Cheap picnic lunches can be bought from supermarkets, markets and from bakeries. These exist in every town but they can be hard to track down. Outside the big towns try to call in at your chosen restaurant about two hours in advance to order your meal: most restaurants prepare just one or two basic dishes to serve all evening because it is too expensive to keep the rest of the menu in readiness without a guaranteed customer.

Many villages have no eating-places, but somewhere there will be a shop – often hard to distinguish from an ordinary house. There you can buy biscuits and drinks. For useful food terms see *Language*, page 261.

Bottled water is widely available and in ordinary shops is cheap (70$ for a 1.5-litre bottle); prices are inflated at hotels (up to 180$). Some of the wine brewed on Fogo Island is distinctive and very quaffable and can be found for sale around the archipelago. There are three principal beers: Coral, which is a new domestic brand, and two brands imported from Portugal; the maltier Superbock and Sagres. Costs are typically 100$ for local beer and 250$ for imported brands.

'The Coral in the one-litre deposit bottle is popularly called "Titanic". When mixed with the sweet limonade of Ceris with its clear, lemon taste, it makes a good shandy or *panache*, much better than a combination of Superbock and Sprite. Aqua Tonica de Ceris (locally bottled) tastes much better than the Coca-Cola Schweppes.'

The drink that Cape Verdeans literally live and die for is *grogue*. It is locally produced (see *Santo Antão*, pages 232–3) and abundantly available – in any dwelling carrying a sign above its door prohibiting children under 18 from entering.

NB On quieter islands such as Maio and Sao Nicolau, food shops and restaurants may open erratically and only for short periods. To avoid hours of hunger, always have provisions with you.

Cost of day-to-day groceries

water 1l	70–100$; 5l 253–250$
fruit juice	70–100$
tinned tomatoes	180–200$
mayonnaise tube	85–100$
bread roll/baguette	10–30$
yoghurt	25–50$
cornflakes	130$ plus
chocolate bar	80$
margarine	85$
cheese triangles	115–125$
banana	15–20$ each
spam meat tinned	135$
cigarettes	400$

SHOPPING

The island capitals are well stocked and it is easy to buy items such as hair conditioner, razors, sanitary towels (but rarely tampons – see below), camera film, Imodium and painkillers. Shopping outside the towns is almost non-existent. The most colourful market is in Assomada, on Santiago, a flavour of mainland Africa. Most island capitals have some sort of fruit and vegetable market though the only one of touristic interest is on the Plateau in Praia, Santiago. Local crafts can be bought in Mindelo, in São Vicente, where there have been revivals of skills such as the weaving of cloth and baskets. Baskets and clay figures can also be bought in São Domingo on Santiago. For excellent souvenirs of the islands, buy bottles of *grogue* (available in any small shop in a town), Fogo wine and coffee beans, little bags of the abundant local sweets, and CDs of Cape Verdean music (in Mindelo, Praia and the airport duty-free shop). A CD costs around 2,100$.

Note that for women it is better to bring tampons from home. On Santiago you can buy them in Praia in a few supermarkets and occasionally in Chinese shops. Sometimes they can be found in some pharmacies, but this cannot be relied upon. On the smaller islands they can be hard or impossible to find, since there is often only a small shop selling medication. So, considering the small weight and bulk involved, it is much better to come prepared!

The cost of a haircut ranges from 250$ for men to 750$ for women.

COMMUNICATIONS
Internet
There are internet cafés in all the island capitals now. Connections are in general pretty fast, and the cost varies, but is generally about 200$ per hour, 50$ for ten minutes and 100$ for 30 minutes. The cafés can be popular and it may be necessary to go in and book ahead.

Telephone
Telephone calls abroad are made most cheaply from post offices and CV Telecom offices, which have phone booths where you make your call and pay afterwards. Use booths for short calls. Alternatively, buy telephone cards at the post office and make calls from public telephones – this can be frustrating, however, as so many such phones are out of order. Telephone cards cost 750$ or 1,000$. Many of the mid–top-range hotels have telephones in the bedrooms. Mobile phones are ubiquitous and many subscribers can use their mobile phones throughout Cape Verde.

If you expect to make a lot of international calls from Cape Verde, look out for the special telephone SIM cards valued at 500$ and 1,000$. For further details call **Telefacil** on 125.

For directory services and yellow pages, see the telephone book website www.paginasamarelas.cv or Cabo Verde telecom at www.nave.cv.

The international telephone code for Cape Verde is 238.

Post office
Cape Verde post offices are well equipped and it is possible to transfer money, send and receive faxes, make phone calls and often make photocopies there. Opening times vary considerably but tend to be Monday–Friday 08.00–12.00 and 14.00–18.00.

Post is reliable to the more important islands, but can take weeks to the others. Most addresses in Cape Verde require a PO box, or *caixa postal* number, prefixed with 'CP'. Follow this with the name of the town and then the name of the island.

Radio and TV
Local television is provided by **TNCV** (12.00–midnight), which sometimes broadcasts English-language films. A wide range of satellite channels is now

available. These include, as well as all the film channels, BBC, CNN, RAI, French and German stations, Portuguese of course and even Brazilian soap operas. Voice of America, RDP and BBC (Portuguese and English versions) are rebroadcast on FM radio. Radio Cape Verde has an office in the cultural centre in Mindelo.

LANGUAGE

Everyone speaks *Crioulo*, an Africanised Creole Portuguese. Portuguese (the official language) is spoken fluently by most townspeople but is not well understood in outlying villages – some people do not speak it at all. Everything official and everything written is in Portuguese. The most common second European language is French, spoken widely by officials, with English third. If you are struggling then keep asking people if they speak English or French (*fale inglês?, fale francês? – fowle eenglaysh?, fowle frensaysh?*). It's astonishing how often such a speaker can be found even in the remotest village. For words and phrases and a discussion of Creole see *Language*, page 264.

CRIME

Although Cape Verde remains a peaceful place with a very low incidence of crime, theft is increasing as a direct consequence of tourism. It is most common in Mindelo and Praia, as well as isolated spots on Sal. In Sao Vicente, tourists regularly fall victim to gangs of bag-snatchers. In Mindelo this kind of robbery seems common and blends with aggressive begging which occurs mostly on the waterfront (young men who may throw a stone at you if you fail to hand over money), and on the Amílcar Cabral square (children who follow you until you retreat into a hotel, asking for money but also trying to take it from your pocket). In Praia the speciality theft venue remains Sucupira market, where pickpocketing is common. In Sal it remains Buracona, on the west coast, where the theme is to hide behind a rock and break into cars once their drivers have gone for a walk.

Follow the usual rules. Carry a purse in an inside pocket; when paying, don't open a purse stacked with cash. Keep valuables hidden in money belts, or leave them in the hotel safe where possible. If you are a victim, make a fuss so that people come to your aid. Also, it is irresponsible not to report it to the police, who are striving to fight crime (also, if you are to claim on your travel insurance you must have a police report).

CULTURAL SENSITIVITIES

Tourism is a new business for Cape Verde and if it grows in the way it is envisioned then thousands of local people will suddenly be witnessing, intimately, the riches of foreigners.

Cape Verde has a history of cosmopolitanism; people know about the outside world because their sons and brothers live there. Nevertheless, tourism always brings with it crime, envy, loss of dignity, hassle and some despoiling of nature. It also remains to be seen what impact the opening of some islands to foreign ownership of apartments will have on local people. Indirectly such apparent new beneficial influences may also affect the cost of food and services, where locals and foreigners are buying what currently limited supplies are to be found in shops. In some more isolated areas less frequented by tourists, like Maio and São Nicolau, and indeed even in Mindelo, some local people are apparently not that pleased by the presence of outside visitors. A certain isolated island mentality is evident in a small minority of people. The following points may be worth considering in your approach to local people.

PHOTOGRAPHIC TIPS
Ariadne Van Zandbergen
Equipment
Although with some thought and an eye for composition you can take reasonable photos with a 'point-and-shoot' camera, you need an SLR camera if you are at all serious about photography. Modern SLRs tend to be very clever, with automatic programmes for almost every possible situation, but remember that these programmes are limited in the sense that the camera cannot think, but only make calculations. Every starting amateur photographer should read a photographic manual for beginners and get to grips with such basics as the relationship between aperture and shutter speed.

Always buy the best lens you can afford. The lens determines the quality of your photo more than the camera body. Fixed fast lenses are ideal, but very costly. Zoom lenses are easier to change composition without changing lenses the whole time. If you carry only one lens, a 28–70mm (digital 17–55mm) or similar zoom should be ideal. For a second lens, a lightweight 80–200mm or 70–300mm (digital 55–200mm) or similar will be excellent for candid shots and varying your composition. Wildlife photography will be very frustrating if you don't have at least a 300mm lens. For a small loss of quality, tele-converters are a cheap and compact way to increase magnification: a 300 lens with a 1.4x converter becomes 420mm, and with a 2x it becomes 600mm. Note, however, that 1.4x and 2x tele-converters reduce the speed of your lens by 1.4 and 2 stops respectively.

For wildlife photography from a safari vehicle, a solid beanbag, which you can make yourself very cheaply, will be necessary to avoid blurred images, and is more useful than a tripod. A clamp with a tripod head screwed on to it can be attached to the vehicle as well. Modern dedicated flash units are easy to use; aside from the obvious need to flash when you photograph at night, you can improve a lot of photos in difficult 'high contrast' or very dull light with some fill-in flash. It pays to have a proper flash unit as opposed to a built-in camera flash.

Digital/film
Digital photography is now the preference of most amateur and professional photographers, with the resolution of digital cameras improving the whole time. For ordinary prints a 6 megapixel camera is fine. For better results and the possibility to enlarge images and for professional reproduction, higher resolution is available up to 16 megapixels.

Memory space is important. The number of pictures you can fit on a memory card depends on the quality you choose. Calculate in advance how many pictures you can fit on a card and either take enough cards to last for your trip, or take a storage drive on to which you can download the content. A laptop gives the advantage that you can see your pictures properly at the end of each day and edit and delete rejects, but a storage device is lighter and less bulky. These drives come in different capacities up to 80GB.

Dress codes
Although attitudes in Cape Verde are generally fairly relaxed, it is nonetheless appropriate to dress more conservatively when visiting towns and when trekking in the countryside. You are more likely to have a better interaction with local people.

Bear in mind that digital camera batteries, computers and other storage devices need charging, so make sure you have all the chargers, cables and converters with you. Most hotels have charging points, but do enquire about this in advance. When camping you might have to rely on charging from the car battery; a spare battery is invaluable.

If you are shooting film, 100 to 200 ISO print film and 50 to 100 ISO slide film are ideal. Low ISO film is slow but fine grained and gives the best colour saturation, but will need more light, so support in the form of a tripod or monopod is important. You can also bring a few 'fast' 400 ISO films for low-light situations where a tripod or flash is no option.

Dust and heat

Dust and heat are often a problem. Keep your equipment in a sealed bag, stow films in an airtight container (eg: a small cooler bag) and avoid exposing equipment and film to the sun. Digital cameras are prone to collecting dust particles on the sensor which results in spots on the image. The dirt mostly enters the camera when changing lenses, so be careful when doing this. To some extent photos can be 'cleaned' up afterwards in Photoshop, but this is time-consuming. You can have your camera sensor professionally cleaned, or you can do this yourself with special brushes and swabs made for the purpose, but note that touching the sensor might cause damage and should only be done with the greatest care.

Light

The most striking outdoor photographs are often taken during the hour or two of 'golden light' after dawn and before sunset. Shooting in low light may enforce the use of very low shutter speeds, in which case a tripod will be required to avoid camera shake.

With careful handling, side lighting and back lighting can produce stunning effects, especially in soft light and at sunrise or sunset. Generally, however, it is best to shoot with the sun behind you. When photographing animals or people in the harsh midday sun, images taken in light but even shade are likely to be more effective than those taken in direct sunlight or patchy shade, since the latter conditions create too much contrast.

Protocol

In some countries, it is unacceptable to photograph local people without permission, and many people will refuse to pose or will ask for a donation. In such circumstances, don't try to sneak photographs as you might get yourself into trouble. Even the most willing subject will often pose stiffly when a camera is pointed at them; relax them by making a joke, and take a few shots in quick succession to improve the odds of capturing a natural pose.

Ariadne Van Zandbergen is a professional travel and wildlife photographer specialising in Africa. For photo requests, visit www.africaimagelibrary.co.za or contact her on ariadne@hixnet.co.za.

Hassles
Rip-offs

It may be worth giving suspected 'rip-off merchants' the benefit of the doubt in Cape Verde. Often when you think you are being mistreated it is really a problem with the language barrier, or the local custom (as, for example, with a two-hour wait in a restaurant), or the fact that prices are genuinely high for everyone (for example with taxi fares).

Begging

In a small but growing number of places in Cape Verde the children have become beggars, pursuing passers-by with persistent demands for money, sweets, pens or photos. Handing them out gives the donor a brief feeling of beneficence but does nothing to alleviate poverty. Instead it causes rivalry amongst children, upsets the family balance (in the case of cash gifts) and, worse, instils a vigorous sense among the children that tourists owe them gifts.

Think of the next batch of tourists that will pass through; successful hassle breeds more hassle, which can ruin an otherwise peaceful outing.

We suggest you do not hand out money unless it is to people who have earned it – for example through employment as guides. If you would like to help the children, then seek out the local school and give a box of biros or paper to the ill-supplied teachers. Alternatively, consult *Giving something back* on page 59, for bodies looking for donations for Cape Verdean good works.

There are some effective ways of replying to demands for money – smiles and good humour being the best accompaniments to whatever you say: '*Desculpe* (*deshculp*)' – 'sorry'; '*Não tenho (Now tenyu) livro/stilo/caneta/dinheiro*' – 'I don't have book/pen/money'; '*Não trabalho, não dinheiro*' – 'no work, no pay'.

All this advice does not apply to genuine beggars – for example the disabled – who ask for money from locals and tourists alike.

Women travellers

Females can travel a lot on their own in Cape Verde and never feel threatened, although they might regularly feel mildly irritated. Cape Verdean men will flirt outrageously, and hassle levels probably rate somewhere between southern and northern Europe, with a few anomalies thrown in. If a firm 'goodbye' is not appropriate then the casual mention of a husband back in town makes most men lose interest pretty swiftly. However, if you reveal that you are childless – whether married, with a partner or single – you will attract huge sympathy, mystification and interest. You will have plenty of offers from potential fathers. If you go to a man's home, or invite him back to your place, he will expect to have sex even if you tell him it is not on the agenda.

Women who stay for a long time in one place – for example volunteers – can have more serious problems. The concept of an unattached woman is incomprehensible in Cape Verdean society and it seems that some communities just cannot tolerate it, so sexual predation can build up until it is, in some cases, quite frightening. Meanwhile, local women can become angry with visitors who take a boyfriend from their already limited supply of men.

Photography

It is best to ask people before you take their photo; smile and say hello, pause, ask to take a photo, offer to take their address and send them a copy. Then, when they are relaxed, you can take the real atmospheric ones. Do not try to photograph the *rebelados* in Santiago, who have scruples about photography; or the hot-tempered market women in Praia. Some old people may have objections as well.

Although most brands of regular print film can be easily found, those using slide film should bring all their supplies from home.

Hiring guides

We indicate in the text whether a guide is necessary or not. Where a guide is not absolutely essential, you may still prefer to hire one in order to get to know a local person, embellish the walk with more information and help the local economy.

Local resources

Water is scarce and has invariably taken toil and money to reach your basin; big hotels have to fetch lorry-loads of barrels. An example of water costs is given in the *Fogo* chapter, page 172.

There are many endangered plant species on the archipelago (see *Perspective*, page 30). Ultimately, the goats may get them all. Nonetheless, picking flowers is absolutely out of the question.

GIVING SOMETHING BACK

Despite the obvious new climate of foreign investment, and indeed local investment by former emigrants and returning Cape Verde citizens, there remains an alarming amount of poverty. Much of this new money is limited to the tourist sector and will not necessarily filter down to much of the population living outside the influence of tourism. In fact, on the less-developed islands like Maio, a large influx of tourist and foreign buyers may actually put the cost of land and produce up beyond the reach of those left on the sidelines.

That said, visitors travelling independently throughout the islands will, by the very nature of their adventures, be contributing in a useful way to the local town and village economies. By using local tour operators, staying in the many family-run *pensãos* and eating in restaurants, you will help give something back directly.

If you would like to contribute to charitable work in Cape Verde you could contact one of the following:

The Cape Verdian Society 53 Ty Mawr Av, Cardiff, Wales CF3 8AG; ☎ +44 029 2021 2787. This charity (registration number 1018138) seeks to help with education, relieve need and provide facilities for Cape Verdeans, inc expatriates in Cardiff. In the past it has contributed to the upkeep of schools, orphanages, a children's hospital and a malnutrition centre.

Aldeia Infantil SOS Achada Santo António, Praia; ☎ +238 264 7379. It is orientated to helping orphans and deprived children.

Institute Cabo-Verdiano de Menores Edifico CECV, Av Lisboa, Praia; ☎ +238 261 6869. Amongst other activities, this lobbies for legislation protecting minors and shelters street children.

Fundação Criança Cabo-Verdiana This supports impoverished children through day-care centres. It was founded in 1993 by the first lady, Dr Antonina Monteiro. It is not currently listed locally but you can try to get further details from the office in Portugal; Urbanização Vale de Alcantara, Bariro da Liberdade – Lote 4 nivel 2 loja 3 o 4, 1070 Lisbon; ☎ +351 213 861 311. Also for the Cape Verde section contact Sonia Maria Gomes Rocha, ☎ +238 242 1681.

Africare Africare House 440 R St NW, Washington, DC 20001-1935, USA; ☎ +1 202 462 3614; f +1 202 387 1034. Gifts should be marked 'for development projects in Cape Verde'.

Church World Service www.churchworldservice.org

Agricultural Co-operatives Development International 50 F St, Suite 1100, Washington, DC 20001, USA; ☎ +1 202 638 4661. Donations to this organisation, which supports agriculture and rural co-operative development, should be marked 'Cape Verde'.

Red-billed tropicbird (rabo de junco)

Health

Cape Verde does not suffer from many of the diseases that are a menace in mainland Africa. There is a limited incidence of malaria – and polio, diphtheria and measles have successfully been combated. Food-borne diseases, from diarrhoea to cholera, are common though, and for the tourist, accidents are a threat.

PREPARATION
Travel insurance
It is important to ensure that you have comprehensive travel insurance. American travellers should also remember that US medical insurance is not always valid outside their country. The Medicare/Medicaid programme does not provide payment for medical services outside the United States. You may need to take out supplementary medical insurance with specific overseas and medical evacuation coverage (see *Travel clinics* below).

Immunisations
Several weeks – or, to be on the safe side, two months – before you go make sure you are up to date with the following: tetanus (ten-yearly), polio (ten-yearly), diphtheria (ten-yearly), and hepatitis A. One dose of hepatitis A vaccine (eg: Havrix Mondose, Avaxim) gives protection for up to one year and can be given even close to the time of departure. A booster dose given at least six months after the first dose provides protection for up to 20 years, so is well worth having. If you are going to Cape Verde from a country that has reported yellow fever infections over the last six years you must carry a certificate of vaccination unless there are specific contraindications. Consult your doctor before you go, as it may be necessary to have an exemption certificate if the vaccine is deemed unsuitable.

Typhoid vaccine (Typhim Vi) is about 85% effective and needs boosting every three years. It is recommended unless you are travelling at short notice for a week or less, when the vaccine would have insufficient time to be effective.

Hepatitis B vaccination should be considered by anyone working within a medical setting or with children. It is also recommended for stays longer than four-six weeks. A course of three doses of the vaccine is ideal and can be taken over as little as 21 days (Engerix).

Rabies vaccine is also recommended for those working with animals or for longer trips (four weeks or more) when you are likely to be more than 24 hours from medical help. Again, three doses of the vaccine are ideal and like hepatitis B can be taken over 21 days – see below. Immunisation against cholera is not required unless specific outbreaks are reported. There is now an effective oral vaccine (Dukoral) available in the UK. Two doses of vaccine should be taken at least one week apart and at least one week before entry for those over six years of age. At the time of writing, however, there are no specific concerns in Cape Verde. Your family doctor or a commercial travel clinic (see below) can tell you if this list has changed recently.

If you need more than one of these immunisations then the cheapest approach should be through your family doctor, who may make an initial charge plus a small fee for each jab. Remember though that not all GP's offer these services, so you should contact your clinic to check. Travel clinics can also be faster and are used to dealing with the last-minute traveller. The rabies jab can also be about £20 cheaper from a commercial clinic.

Travel clinics and health information

A full list of current travel clinic websites worldwide is available from the International Society of Travel Medicine on www.istm.org. For other journey preparation information, consult www.tripprep.com. Information about various medications may be found on www.emedicine.com.

UK

Berkeley Travel Clinic 32 Berkeley St, London W1J 8EL (near Green Park tube station); ☎ 020 7629 6233

British Airways Travel Clinic and Immunisation Service There are 2 BA clinics in London, both on ☎ 0845 600 2236; www.ba.com/travelclinics. Appointments only Mon–Fri 9.00–16.30 at 101 Cheapside, London EC2V 6DT; or walk-in service Mon–Fri 09.30–17.30, Sat 10.00–16.00 at 213 Piccadilly, London W1J 9HQ. Apart from providing inoculations and malaria prevention, they sell a variety of health-related goods.

Cambridge Travel Clinic 48a Mill Rd, Cambridge CB1 2AS; ☎ 01223 367362; e enquiries@cambridgetravelclinic.co.uk; www.cambridgetravelclinic.co.uk. Open Tue–Fri 12.00–19.00, Sat 10.00–16.00.

Edinburgh Travel Clinic Regional Infectious Diseases Unit, Ward 41 OPD, Western General Hospital, Crewe Rd South, Edinburgh EH4 2UX; ☎ 0131 537 2822;

LONG-HAUL FLIGHTS

Dr Felicity Nicholson

There is growing evidence, albeit circumstantial, that long-haul air travel increases the risk of developing deep vein thrombosis. This condition is potentially life threatening, but it should be stressed that the danger to the average traveller is slight.

Certain risk factors specific to air travel have been identified. These include immobility, compression of the veins at the back of the knee by the edge of the seat, the decreased air pressure and slightly reduced oxygen in the cabin, and dehydration. Consuming alcohol may exacerbate the situation by increasing fluid loss and encouraging immobility.

In theory everyone is at risk, but those at highest risk are shown below:

- Passengers on journeys of longer than eight hours duration
- People over 40
- People with heart disease
- People with cancer
- People with clotting disorders
- People who have had recent surgery, especially on the legs
- Women who are pregnant, or on the pill or other oestrogen therapy
- People who are very tall (over 6ft/1.8m) or short (under 5ft/1.5m)

A deep vein thrombosis (DVT) is a clot of blood that forms in the leg veins. Symptoms include swelling and pain in the calf or thigh. The skin may feel hot

www.link.med.ed.ac.uk/ridu. Travel helpline (↘ 0906 589 0380) open weekdays 09.00–12.00. Provides inoculations and anti-malarial prophylaxis and advises on travel-related health risks.

Fleet Street Travel Clinic 29 Fleet St, London EC4Y 1AA; ↘ 020 7353 5678; www.fleetstreetclinic.com. Vaccinations, travel products and latest advice.

Hospital for Tropical Diseases Travel Clinic Mortimer Market Building, Capper St (off Tottenham Ct Rd), London WC1E 6AU; ↘ 020 7388 9600; www.thehtd.org. Offers consultations and advice, and is able to provide all necessary drugs and vaccines for travellers. Runs a healthline (↘ 0906 133 7733) for country-specific information and health hazards. Also stocks nets, water purification equipment and personal protection measures.

Interhealth Worldwide Partnership House, 157 Waterloo Rd, London SE1 8US; ↘ 020 7902 9000; www.interhealth.org.uk. Competitively priced, one-stop travel health service. All profits go to their affiliated company, InterHealth, which provides health care for overseas workers on Christian projects.

MASTA (Medical Advisory Service for Travellers Abroad) London School of Hygiene and Tropical Medicine, Keppel St, London WC1 7HT; ↘ 09065 501402; www.masta.org. Individually tailored health briefs available for a fee, with up-to-date information on how to stay healthy, inoculations and what to bring. There are currently 30 MASTA pre-travel clinics in Britain. Call ↘ 0870 241 6843 or check online for the nearest. Clinics also sell malaria prophylaxis memory cards, treatment kits, bednets, net treatment kits.

NHS travel website www.fitfortravel.scot.nhs.uk provides country-by-country advice on immunisation and malaria, plus details of recent developments, and a list of relevant health organisations.

Nomad Travel Store/Clinic 3–4 Wellington Terrace, Turnpike Lane, London N8 0PX; ↘ 020 8889 7014, travel-health line (office hours only) 0906 863 3414; e sales@nomadtravel.co.uk; www.nomadtravel.co.uk. Also at 40 Bernard St, London

to touch and becomes discoloured (light blue-red). A DVT is not dangerous in itself, but if a clot breaks down then it may travel to the lungs (pulmonary embolus). Symptoms of a pulmonary embolus (PE) include chest pain, shortness of breath and coughing up small amounts of blood.

Symptoms of a DVT rarely occur during the flight, and typically occur within three days of arrival, although symptoms of a DVT or PE have been reported up to two weeks later.

Anyone who suspects that they have these symptoms should see a doctor immediately as anticoagulation (blood thinning) treatment can be given.

Prevention of DVT
General measures to reduce the risk of thrombosis are shown below. This advice also applies to long train or bus journeys.

- Whilst waiting to board the plane, try to walk around rather than sit.
- During the flight drink plenty of water (at least two small glasses every hour).
- Avoid excessive tea, coffee and alcohol.
- Perform leg-stretching exercises, such as pointing the toes up and down.
- Move around the cabin when practicable.

If you fit into the high-risk category (see above) ask your doctor if it is safe to travel. Additional protective measures such as graded compression stockings, aspirin or low molecular weight heparin can be given. No matter how tall you are, where possible request a seat with extra legroom.

WC1N 1LJ; ℡ 020 7833 4114; 52 Grosvenor Gardens, London SW1W 0AG; ℡ 020 7823 5823; and 43 Queens Rd, Bristol BS8 1QH; ℡ 0117 922 6567. For health advice, equipment such as mosquito nets and other anti-bug devices, and an excellent range of adventure travel gear.

Trailfinders Travel Clinic 194 Kensington High St, London W8 7RG; ℡ 020 7938 3999; www.trailfinders.com/clinic.htm

Travelpharm Their website, www.travelpharm.com, offers up-to-date guidance on travel-related health and has a range of medications available through their online mini-pharmacy.

Irish Republic
Tropical Medical Bureau Grafton Street Medical Centre, Grafton Buildings, 34 Grafton St, Dublin 2; ℡ 1 671 9200; www.tmb.ie. A useful website specific to tropical destinations. Also check website for other bureaux locations throughout Ireland.

USA
Centers for Disease Control 1600 Clifton Rd, Atlanta, GA 30333; ℡ 800 311 3435; travellers' health hotline ℡ 888 232 3299; www.cdc.gov/travel. The central source of travel information in the USA. The invaluable *Health Information for International Travel*, published annually, is available from the Division of Quarantine at this address.

Connaught Laboratories PO Box 187, Swiftwater, PA 18370; ℡ 800 822 2463. They will send a free list of specialist tropical-medicine physicians in your state.

IAMAT (International Association for Medical Assistance to Travelers) 1623 Military Rd, 279, Niagara Falls, NY 14304-1745; ℡ 716 754 4883; e info@iamat.org; www.iamat.org. A non-profit organisation that provides lists of English-speaking doctors abroad.

International Medicine Center 920 Frostwood Drive, Suite 670, Houston, TX 77024; ℡ 713 550 2000; www.traveldoc.com

Canada
IAMAT Suite 1, 1287 St Clair Av W, Toronto, Ontario M6E 1B8; ℡ 416 652 0137; www.iamat.org

TMVC (Travel Doctors Group) Sulphur Springs Rd, Ancaster, Ontario; ℡ 905 648 1112; www.tmvc-group.com

Australia, New Zealand, Singapore
TMVC ℡ 1300 65 88 44; www.tmvc.com.au. 23 clinics in Australia, New Zealand and Singapore inc:
Auckland Canterbury Arcade, 170 Queen St, Auckland; ℡ 9 373 3531
Brisbane 6th floor, 247 Adelaide St, Brisbane, QLD 4000; ℡ 7 3221 9066
Melbourne 393 Little Bourke St, 2nd floor, Melbourne, VIC 3000; ℡ 3 9602 5788
Sydney Dymocks Building, 7th Floor, 428 George St, Sydney, NSW 2000; ℡ 2 9221 7133
IAMAT PO Box 5049, Christchurch 5, New Zealand; www.iamat.org

South Africa
SAA-Netcare Travel Clinics Private Bag X34, Benmore 2010; www.travelclinic.co.za. Clinics throughout South Africa.

TMVC 113 D F Malan Drive, Roosevelt Park, Johannesburg; ℡ 011 888 7488; www.tmvc.com.au. Consult the website for details of 8 other clinics in South Africa.

Switzerland
IAMAT 57 Chemin des Voirets, 1212 Grand Lancy, Geneva; www.iamat.org

Malaria prophylaxis
All the islands except Santiago are free from malaria, and Santiago suffers only between September and December. Current advice is not to take any prophylaxis, but if a fever develops (in Cape Verde, or at home) it should be investigated promptly.

Medical kit
Pharmacies are widespread and well-stocked but, just in case, bring a small medical kit containing soluble aspirin or paracetamol (good for gargling when you have a sore throat and for reducing fever and pains), plasters, antiseptic, insect repellent and suncream. Many travellers are reassured by investing in a blood transfusion kit which contains sterile equipment such as needles for use during surgery. Some travel clinics will try to persuade you to take antibiotics but there is no need as doctors' prescriptions and the drugs themselves are readily available. Self-medication should only be a last resort.

COMMON MEDICAL PROBLEMS
Traveller's diarrhoea
This afflicts half of all visitors to the developing world and can ruin a short holiday. The bacteria are borne on traces of faeces which get into food sometime between when it is growing in the soil and when it arrives at the table. If you are scrupulous you should be able to keep the bacteria from reaching your mouth. Only eat freshly cooked food or peeled raw fruit and vegetables. In particular avoid unpeelable raw food such as lettuce or cabbage and avoid raw seafood. Avoid fruit juice, unless it is from a sealed bottle, and ice-cream.

Avoid the local water including ice-cubes. Tea and coffee should be fine, simply because bringing water to the boil kills 99% of bacteria. Wash your hands after going to the toilet.

If you do fall ill then you should rest, stop eating your normal diet, avoid alcohol and take lots of clear fluids. If you are hungry then eat bland food such as biscuits and boiled rice or potatoes. The idea is to avoid stomach cramps caused by the belly trying to expel food. It is dehydration that makes you feel rotten during a bout of diarrhoea and dehydration is also the principal danger, so it is of paramount importance to drink plenty of fluid. Sachets of oral rehydration salts such as Dioralyte, Electrolade or Rehidrat give the perfect biochemical mix – so put some in your medical kit. You can make your own such drink with eight teaspoons of sugar, one teaspoon of salt and one litre of safe water. A squeeze of lemon or orange juice improves the taste and adds another vital ingredient: potassium. You can create an approximation to this wonder-drink with flat Coke-Cola and a pinch of salt. Drink two large glasses after every bowel action and more if you are thirsty. If you are not eating you need to drink three litres every day plus enough fluid to compensate for what you are losing through diarrhoea.

Diarrhoea blockers such as Imodium, Lomotil and codeine phosphate are not a treatment and should be avoided: your body is trying to expel poisons, not lock them in. However, it may be necessary to use them if for example you are facing long bus rides. If the diarrhoea lasts more than 36 hours or you are passing blood or slime or have a fever you will probably need antibiotics. Seek medical advice as soon as you can, but if this is not possible then you may wish to take ciprofloxacin (one 500mg tablet should be taken and repeated 10–12 hours later).

Giardiasis is prevalent on Cape Verde. It can take about ten days to incubate. Stools are loose, greasy and sometimes watery; there can be pains in the upper abdomen, and sulphurous belches from both ends. If you suspect you have it, seek help.

Skin infections

Any insect bite or cut gives bacteria the opportunity to foil the skin's usually strong defences. Skin infections start quickly in warm and humid climates so they are not such a problem in Cape Verde. Creams do not keep the wound dry so they are not as effective as a drying antiseptic such as dilute iodine, potassium permanganate (a few crystals in half a cup of water) or crystal violet applied three times a day. If the wound starts to throb, if it becomes red and the redness begins to spread, or if the wound oozes then you may need antibiotics and should seek a doctor. Fungal infections take hold easily in moist parts of the body so wear cotton socks and underwear and shower frequently, drying thoroughly. An itchy and often flaking rash in the groin or between the toes is likely to be a fungus and will require treatment with a cream such as Canesten (clotrimazole). If this is not available then try Whitfield's ointment (compound benzoic acid ointment) or crystal violet.

Insects and parasites
Insect bites
There is a slight risk of malaria on Santiago Island, so it is worth protecting yourself against mosquito bites between dusk and dawn by covering up with trousers, a long-sleeved shirt and applying insect repellent containing the chemical DEET. Ideally you should sleep under a mosquito net. Cape Verde's waterless climate keeps insects down but they pop up all year round in odd places where there is stagnant water.

Tumbu flies or putsi
The adult fly lays her eggs on soil or drying laundry. When those eggs come into contact with human flesh (when you put on your clothes or lie on a bed) they hatch and bury themselves under the skin. There they form a crop of boils, each of which hatches a grub after about eight days. Once they are hatched the inflammation will die down. Avoid *putsi* by drying clothes and sheets within a screened house or by drying them in direct sunshine until they are crisp or by ironing them.

Jiggers or sandfleas
These bury into bare feet and set up home under the skin of the foot, usually at the side of a toenail where they cause a painful, boil-like swelling. A local expert must pick them out. If the distended flea bursts during eviction the wound should be dowsed in spirit, alcohol or kerosene to avoid more jiggers infesting you.

Ticks
There are several nasty, tick-borne diseases, such as typhus. Avoid ticks by wearing long clothes and repellent, especially if walking takes you into scrubby countryside where you are brushing through vegetation.

Remove any tick as soon as you notice it – it will most likely be firmly attached to somewhere you would rather it was not – grasp the tick as close to your body as possible and pull steadily and firmly away at right angles to your skin. The tick will then come away complete as long as you do not jerk or twist. If possible douse the wound with alcohol (any spirit will do) or iodine. Spreading redness around the bite and/or fever and/or aching joints after a tick bite imply that you have an infection which requires antibiotic treatment, so seek advice.

Heat and sun
Dehydration
It is easy to get dehydrated, especially in the first week. If you wake up in the morning feeling nauseous and tired that may be the reason. Water requirements

depend on temperature, humidity, amount of exercise taken, and the length of time the person has been in the country. Those who get into trouble are people who do not allow themselves to acclimatise, a process that takes up to two weeks. Eager adolescents are particularly vulnerable. In the tropics you need to drink about three litres a day, more if you are exercising. Take it easy for the first week. In Cape Verde it is very likely you could end up on a long, hot and shadeless hike for a day. In those conditions you will need to have drunk five litres by the end of the day to avoid dehydration. If you are going on a day's hike drink plenty before you go, try to carry two litres per person, and fill up again in the evening.

Prickly heat
A fine pimply rash on the trunk of the body is likely to be heat rash. Take cool showers and dab (do not rub) yourself dry, finishing off with a sprinkling of talc. If the rash doesn't improve it may be necessary to check into an air-conditioned room for a while, slow down, wear only loose, cotton clothes and sleep naked under a fan.

Sunburn
Cape Verde is notoriously lacking in shade so you must bring your own in the form of a broad-brimmed hat, umbrella, or even a windbreak for a day on the beach. The best solution is to cover up: a light-coloured, loose cotton shirt and long skirt or trousers is also cooler than shorts and a T-shirt. Try and keep out of the sun between noon and 15.00 and, if you must expose yourself, build up gradually from 20 minutes per day. Be particularly careful of sun reflected from water and wear a T-shirt and plenty of waterproof suncream (SPF 15) when snorkelling or swimming. Tanning ages your skin and can give you skin cancer.

Heat exhaustion and heat stroke
Heat exhaustion develops gradually, caused by loss of salt and water through excessive sweating. It is most common in people new to the heat or new to exercise in the heat and in people who have recently had an illness in which they lost fluids (diarrhoea or vomiting). Sufferers have fast shallow breathing and a rapid weak pulse. They may feel dizzy and sick, be pale and sweating, have a headache and have cramps in the limbs and abdomen. Sit or lie the casualty down in a cool place, raise and support the legs to allow blood to flow to the brain. Give plenty of water.

Heat stroke is less common and is most likely to happen as a result of prolonged exposure to very hot surroundings. Symptoms include confusion, swiftly deteriorating to unconsciousness, a strong pulse and slow, deep breathing. The sufferer's skin will be hot, flushed and their temperature will be over 40?C. The essential thing is to cool the person quickly – do this by moving them to a cool place, removing their outer clothing, wrapping them in a cold, wet sheet and fanning them. Call for a doctor immediately.

SERIOUS ILLNESS
AIDS
With a mobile population and no stable family structure Cape Verde is facing a big problem with AIDS. About 40% of HIV infections in British people are acquired abroad. Bring condoms or femidoms with you. If you notice any genital ulcers or discharge get them treated promptly. The presence of a sexually transmitted disease increases the chance of contracting AIDS.

Cholera

This arises sporadically in Cape Verde and in 1995 killed 240 people and sickened 13,000. Avoid it through the precautions described under *Traveller's diarrhoea*, page 65. However, it is very unlikely to affect visitors. The severe form of cholera, which almost never hits travellers, is sudden and copious diarrhoea without any pain, very watery with white flecks in it. There is vomiting but usually no fever. Rehydration is vital – up to 20 litres a day in serious cases. Seek immediate help.

Typhoid

Symptoms are fever, headache, loss of appetite, abdominal pain and sometimes pink spots on the skin. The heart rate may slow. Seek immediate help.

Elephantiasis

Also known as *filariasis*, it is spread by mosquitoes and causes massive inflammation of the leg in long-standing sufferers: another reason to avoid insect bites between dusk and dawn.

Trachoma

This is a disease of the very poor and not something that travellers get. However, in trachoma-affected countries the risk of travellers contracting ordinary conjunctivitis increases – so a course of antibiotic eye-drops might be useful in the medical kit.

ACCIDENTS

Hospitals on the smaller islands can do little and have to evacuate to São Vicente or Santiago, even for the resetting of a broken leg. The hospital on São Vicente is the best. The inter-island planes always reserve space for medical emergencies.

Vehicles

Vehicle accidents – not exotic diseases – are often the biggest killers of visitors to Africa. Cape Verde vehicles are in better condition than those on mainland Africa and many drivers are careful of their investments. But the roads are vertiginous and a few drivers compete with each other in heart-stopping races along the cork-screw routes – there is plenty of scope for hundred-metre cliff plunges. Make sure your driver has not been drinking alcohol and try not to travel along precarious roads at night.

Swimming

Swimming accidents are the other danger. The blue waters may be seductive but they are also the wild mid ocean, abounding with hidden reefs, strange currents and hungry wildlife. The golden rule is to ask local people whether it is safe to bathe (*Não e perigoso tomar banho?* – 'It's not dangerous to take a dip?') and don't dive from boats that are far from the shore, or you could end up getting nibbled by shark. In the shallows a pair of plimsolls will protect against coral, urchins and venomous fish spines. The trick after being stung by a venomous fish is to denature the poison by heating it – so stick your foot in a bucket of hot water until some time after the pain subsides – perhaps 20–30 minutes overall. If the pain returns, immerse the foot again. Then ask a doctor to check for fish spines in the wound.

Hiking

Much of the classic walking on Cape Verde is through populated areas or at least on paths trodden regularly each day by local people, but some hikes are so abandoned you will meet no-one. On Santo Antão in particular, once off the beaten track it is dangerous, with scree, gullies and landslides and no sign of water or food. It can be easy to leave the path in some of the Santo Antão ribeiras, particularly the many tributaries of Ribeira Grande, in which case you could get stuck on a path that has dwindled to a crevice, unable to descend without sliding along the rubble and unable to ascend because there are no footholds – and with the mist approaching. The really remote region is the west of Santo Antão where only experienced hikers should go.

Walking accidents are not uncommon. Cape Verdean terrain – hard, bone-dry soil sprinkled with tiny, rolling bits of grit – can be slippery even for those in good walking boots and even when it is flat. Sometimes you must watch each step, placing the foot on any available vegetation, stone or clear ground and avoiding the mini landslides waiting in the middle of the path. If you break a bone insist on having it set by a qualified doctor rather than a nurse, or you could end up needing it reset later.

If you go hiking don't forget the basic principles: it is essential to wear walking boots with ankle support; plan your route before you set off so that you know which villages to ask for along the way; tell someone who might care where you are going and when you are expecting to be back; drink plenty of water before you go and take two litres of water for a full day away (this assumes you can stock up beforehand and replenish in the evening); bring food – assume you will not find any on the way; take a whistle and protect yourself from the sun.

For walks in the Fogo crater and on Santo Antão peaks take a jumper, it can get cold. Cuts and grazes can be avoided by wearing long trousers.

Animal bites

The only mammals to watch out for on Cape Verde are village dogs, cats and monkeys. Some people keep monkeys as guards or pets on long stretches of rope. They are accustomed to being fed and may bite. Although the UK lists Cape Verde as a country free from rabies, it is best to assume these animals are rabid. Rabies can be carried by all mammals and is passed on to humans through a bite, or a lick of an open wound. If you are bitten, seek medical help as soon as is practicably possible. In the interim, scrub the wound thoroughly with soap and bottled/boiled water for five minutes, then pour on a strong iodine or alcohol solution. This can help to prevent the rabies virus from entering the body and will guard against wound infections, including tetanus. The decision whether or not to have the highly effective rabies vaccine will depend on the nature of your trip. It is definitely advised if you intend to handle animals, or if you are likely to be more than 24 hours away from medical help.

Ideally three pre-exposure doses should be taken over a three-week period although if time is short even one dose may be considered better than nothing. If you think you have been exposed to rabies by any of the routes described above then you should seek treatment as soon as possible. At least two post-bite rabies injections are needed, even by immunised people. Those who have not been immunised will need a full course of injections together with rabies immunoglobulin (RIG), but this product is expensive (around US$800) and may be hard to come by– another reason why pre-exposure vaccination should be encouraged in travellers who are planning to visit more remote areas. Treatment should be given as soon as possible, but it is never too late to seek help as the incubation period for rabies can be very long. Bites closer to the brain are always more serious. Remember if you contract rabies, mortality is 100% and death from rabies is probably one of the worst ways to go!

The other risk with animal bites is tetanus which is caught through deep, dirty wounds. Make sure your immunisation is up to date and clean wounds thoroughly.

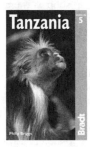 

Living and Working in Cape Verde

This chapter covers business visits to Cape Verde, setting up a business there, gaining residency, considering property investments and working as a volunteer. Regulations are liable to change so you need to contact the relevant agencies to get the latest information.

BECOMING A CAPE VERDE RESIDENT
If you are thinking of settling permanently in Cape Verde, particularly if you are retired, the government claims it can process your application within 30 days. Once you have a residence permit, you qualify for certain privileges, including the import of personal effects such as a car and electrical equipment free from taxes and fees; exemption from property tax when buying your house; and no tax on any financial resource brought in from outside the country. Also, if you decide to invest any of your savings in a Cape Verdean business, you will qualify for foreign investor status (see below).

To qualify, you must have a monthly income of no less than US$1,300 (this figure is sometimes reviewed) and provide your own medical insurance. Contact the Ministério dos Negócios Estrangeiros e das Comunidades, Gabinete de Estudos, Documentação e Assessoria; ☎ 261 5733; f 261 5729. Also you may contact the Camara, Rua Ceasario Lacerda No 6, Tenis, CP 105 Praia, Cabo Verde; ☎ 261 7234/5352; f 261 7235; e cciss@cvtelecom.cv.

BUSINESS VISITS
People who are used to the tribulations of mainland west Africa generally find it quite a relief to make business visits to Cape Verde. There is less endemic corruption, deals tend to be reasonably straightforward and the big towns have a less fraught atmosphere. The administration can be slow and bureaucratic but less than is usual for the region.

Preparations
Much of the chapter on *Practical information*, page 41, applies here, particularly sections on *Getting there*, *Red tape*, *Money*, and *Getting around*.

You obtain a visa with the same form and for the same price as a tourist visa. You must submit, however, a letter of guarantee from your company or a copy of an invitation from a Cape Verdean organisation.

Flights
European travel agents recommend that business travellers use **TAP Air Portugal** or **TACV**. For regular travellers to Cape Verde, TACV offers various discount schemes. Regular travellers can join a frequent-flyer scheme. TACV and TAP Air Portugal signed a flight-share agreement in 1998 which means that you can now travel out on one airline and return on the other without having to buy two single tickets.

THE PACE OF LIFE IN CAPE VERDE
Steven Maddocks and Gabi Woolf

Life in Cape Verde has some of the characteristics traditionally associated with life in Africa. So things that are quick and easy in Europe or the US might be expected to take a long time here and be fraught with difficulties. But anyone who has travelled beyond Europe, especially to countries like Africa, South America, India, or China, will find life in Cape Verde a comparatively smooth ride.

People who consider themselves officials – behind counters, in uniforms, with name badges – refuse to be hurried. The more impatient you look, the more they will seem to enjoy taking their time. Lots of apparently simple procedures are unnecessarily complicated, involving baffling bureaucracy and pointless paper. Be prepared to wait around a lot, maybe even to have to come back tomorrow. People have a lot of time on their hands. If they have to sit in a waiting room for three hours to pay their electricity bill, so be it. What's the rush?

Queuing is a fluid art form. People will go to the bank, stand in the queue for five minutes, go away, do some shopping, have lunch, come back, and expect to reclaim their place. You may have been standing there in the queue for an hour and a half, finally reach the front, only to find two or three women suddenly appear from nowhere and 'reclaim' their places in front of you. Very frustrating. Women (yes, unfortunately it's always women who do this) go into the supermarket and grab three empty baskets. They put those baskets on the floor in the queue. They then walk round the shop, grabbing this and that, bring it back to their baskets, and go back for some more things, ingeniously moving forward in the queue and doing their shopping at the same time.

Cape Verdeans accept situations without feeling the need to enquire into the whys and wherefores. So if you find yourself in a crazy predicament, and want to know why the post office hasn't got any stamps, or why the baker doesn't sell bread, or why you can't buy the cheese even though it's there in the fridge with a price on it, don't expect an explanation. That's just the way it is.

Money

The top hotels generally accept Visa or Mastercard, but it is still advisable to have cash and travellers' cheques. The TACV airline office in Praia will accept payment directly with major credit cards and travellers' cheques.

Where to stay

The details of all hotels mentioned below are in the relevant island chapters.

In Praia the business hotels are all off the Plateau to the south, a taxi ride from the business centres on the Plateau and Achada Santo António. Hotels that cater for business travellers (eg: telephones in rooms, faxing facilities, electricity generator, conference facilities) are principally the Hotel Pestana Trópico and Hotel Praia Mar.

On São Vicente, in Mindelo, the business hotels are the Hotel Porto Grande and the Mindel Hotel. The Foya Branca, near the airport, offers business, conference and secretarial facilities for up to 30 people and corporate rates.

On Sal the business hotel, Atlântico, is in Espargos. In the resort of Santa Maria the big beach hotels have good facilities, including faxes, but are very much geared towards tourists. Oasis Belorizonte and Novorizonte are Portuguese-managed, Djadsal has a fully equipped 250-seat hall for conventions and meetings. Hotel Pousada da Luz and Hotel Central are a grade lower but are spacious and quiet.

On Fogo the Hotel Xaguate and the Pousada Belavista can provide good accommodation for business travellers. A little more downmarket, the Pensão Las Vegas is nevertheless smart and has a generator, fax and the proprietor speaks English. On Boavista prospective businesspeople can find comfort at the Dunas Hotel, the Estoril or the Migrante in Sal Rei. Near the airport is the tranquil Parque das Dunas.

Communications
A large number of businesses now have email. See *Practical information*, page 54.

Help
In Praia contact Promex, also now known as the Centre for Promotion of Tourism, Foreign Investment and Exports, out on the headland near the upmarket hotels in Praia (*CP 89-C, Praia;* ❧ *262 2621/2689;* f *262 2657*). In smaller islands contact the town hall (*câmara*), which is generally the biggest, smartest building in town. Ask to speak to a councillor (*vereador*). The following is a list of telephone numbers to contact:

Boavista Fundo Figueiras; ❧ 252 1255
Brava Nova Sintra; ❧ 285 1314
Fogo São Filipe; ❧ 281 1295; Mosteiros; ❧ 283 1038
Maio Vila do Maio; ❧ 255 1334
Sal Santa Maria; ❧ 242 1136; Espargos; ❧ 241 9000
Santiago Praia – see Promex; ❧ 622736
Santo Antão Porto Novo; ❧ 225 1169; Ribeira Grande; ❧ 222 1223; Ponta do Sol; ❧ 225 1179
São Nicolau Ribeira Brava; ❧ 235 1242
São Vicente Mindelo; ❧ 232 5218

Other suggested contact links:

Banco de Cabo Verde www.bcv.cv
Cabo Verde Telecom www.nave.cv
Governo de Cabo Verde www.governo.cv
Promex www.promex.cv, www.promex.org or www.virtualcapeverde.net
Those looking at the possibilities of investment within the construction industry could approach the local consultants below:
Engeobra Engineering CP 902 Achada Santo Antonia, Praia, Santiago; ❧ 262 6030; f 262 3275; e engeobra-pr@cvtelecom.cv

For commercial, industrial and other services contact:

Camara Sovavento Rua Cesario Lacerda No 6 Tenis, CP 105 Praia; ❧ 261 5352; fax 261 7235; e cciss@cvtelecom.cv

Also try the following in connection with property development:

www.eurolaw.com
www.smartinvestmentproperty.com

INVESTMENT OPPORTUNITIES
In the last few years there have been some big initiatives to promote the sale of apartments to foreign residents. This is particularly expanding on Sal, and also now

on Boavista. Italian investors comprise much of the market. We have no idea at all how secure these arrangements will be in the future. With all such ventures you must do as much research as possible into these deals, and be prepared to take time doing this. Politically the Cape Verde Islands have been among some of the least-disturbed countries, but that is no guarantee for the future. Not all the local population will welcome such intrusions, although that is more likely on the other islands than on Sal.

The following information is given as a guide to prices and expectations as of May 2005:

Apartments of 50m²	39,000
Apartments of 55m² 2nd floor	55,000
Apartments of 120m²	160,000
Apartments of 50–60m² with furniture	85,000
Apartments of 80m² with furniture	125,000
Prices of buildings before completion	1,100 per m²

Deposits of 2,000 are required, plus full details of names, nationality, etc. Taxes are 3% record office, 3% owner's liabilities, annual tax varies with location and could be 3–5% plus 0.075% of property value. Contracts are in English/Portuguese.

Sambala Village Santiago, ☏ +44 (0)1608 813160; e info@sambaladevelopments.com; www.sambaladevelopments.com

Affitti Turistici Santa Maria; ☏f 242 1895, m 993 7663; e info@oceano-azul.com; www.oceano-azul.com

Agencia Imobiliare em Cabo Verde Santa Maria; ☏f 242 1668, m 994 1004; www.gesturim.com

Oceano Azul Rua 15 Agosto, Santa Maria; ☏f 242 1895, m 993 7663; e info@oceano-azul.com; www.oceano-azul.com. In the same building as Affitti Turistici and part of the same group.

SETTING UP A BUSINESS IN CAPE VERDE

A government committed to a free market economy was elected in 1991 and re-elected in 1995. Then, in 2001, the more socialist party, PAICV, regained power. Current investments continue to rely both on overseas aid revenue and tourist development, but the situation may change with the next elections, due in February 2006. For the last decade the country has had legislation designed to encourage foreign investment, particularly in fishing, light industry and tourism. It has promoted Cape Verde's advantages as the following: a strategic position close to Europe, west Africa and the Americas; a large, young and motivated unskilled workforce which is 70% literate; a professional workforce whose members generally have degrees from foreign universities; a stable political system with an unblemished human rights record and low crime rate; and a moderate tropical climate.

The fishing industry needs substantial investment but is said to have huge potential. Cape Verde has an exclusive economic zone of 180 times its land area, or 734,000km² and is therefore one of the last significantly under-used fishing zones in the world. The estimated annual sustainable catch is 45,000 tonnes, of which 6,000 is caught at present, mainly by artisanal fishermen. There is potential for large catches of tuna, lobster, shark and molluscs.

Over the last few years there has been substantial investment in ports, including wharves, warehousing, cold storage and repair facilities. A business park has been built at Praia.

Tourism

Various regions have been earmarked for beach tourism development (zones on Sal, Boavista, Maio, Santiago and São Vicente – the last two in small areas). Other regions have been targeted for adventure tourism (in particular Santo Antão, Fogo and São Nicolau) and there is also believed to be scope for cultural tourism in Santiago, São Vicente and São Nicolau.

Investors must provide their own, desalinated water and meet various architectural standards, amongst other requirements. In return there are tax exemptions mentioned below.

Light industry

Cape Verde has unfulfilled quotas for products sent to the USA through the Most Favoured Nation status and the Generalised System of Preferences. It has preferential access to European markets through the Lomé Convention; and to west African markets through the Economic Community of West African States (ECOWAS).

Infrastructure

The lack of adequate infrastructure, in particular inter-island transport, sanitation and water, has put a significant brake on tourism development. Many ports have been modernised, including Porto Grande at São Vicente and Porto Vale de Cavaleiros on Fogo, and the harbours on Boavista and Maio.

The Amílcar Cabral International Airport on Sal has a main runway 3,270m long and another, 1,500m long. A second international airport for Santiago, funded by the African Development Bank, has been much delayed. It will accommodate Airbus 310 aircraft. All islands except Santo Antão and Brava have frequent air connections, though the planes are small and often over-booked.

Marine connections between the islands are under even more pressure. The problems were alleviated somewhat by new boats introduced in 2000, but in 2005 there are almost no scheduled services in operation.

Cargo transport to the mainland is seen as a problem. A limited number of vessels operate between Mindelo or Praia and the African mainland.

Water is a perpetual problem and more desalination plants are being built. There is plenty of water underground, but its use is limited by the complex geology.

Inducements

A foreigner with a regular monthly income of at least US$1,300 and private health insurance can apply for residency in Cape Verde. Citizenship is available to any foreigners on payment of at least US$35,000, or if they are resident for two years, or if they set up an 'external investment company' and employ a minimum number of Cape Verdeans.

The important step is to achieve status as an 'external investor'. Once registered in this way, a business qualifies for various privileges. It is allowed duty-free import and export of materials, which is essential because tariffs are otherwise extremely high – in the case of a car they can equal its cost, for example. Registered businesses are also supposed to receive streamlined customs procedures.

Foreign businesses also qualify for total tax exemption for the first five years and, after that, pay 10% tax. Exports qualify for tax incentives and there are special tax deals on industrial, tourism and fishery projects. If you train Cape Verdean staff the costs are exempt from tax. There is Free-Zone Enterprise Status for companies producing goods and services exclusively for export.

How to go about it

An application for foreign or external investment must be made to Promex, from whom forms and instructions can be obtained. Once you have obtained a certificate of external investment (in the case of a tourism facility, *autorização turístico*) you have access to the tax incentives. This can be quite a laborious process. It is useful to cultivate a good relationship with the president of the town hall of the relevant island. It is also essential to speak Portuguese or it will be very difficult to oversee the project.

Labour system

Local people can be employed either on 'limited time' or 'unlimited time' contracts. If your staff are on the latter type, and you wish to fire them, you have to compensate them with three months' salary for every year you employed them. This can make an extraordinary total in the case of long-serving employees. There is no minimum wage.

Obstacles

Cape Verdean culture is complex – at once west African, European, American, cosmopolitan and parochial. Politically it is still coming to terms with the liberalisation of its economy, to which it has until recently reacted by electing the old familiar leaders from the time independence was won. For this and many other reasons it will take a while to understand the people around you.

The following are tips from people who have recently set up businesses in Cape Verde:

- Try to learn the language as soon as possible.
- Cultivate a good relationship with the president of the town hall (*câmara*) on your chosen island.
- Even small investors should employ a lawyer for dealing with Promex and other bodies.
- Although imports made by 'external investors' are exempt from tax, they are not free from a variety of fees. For example, one must pay for each day the goods spend at the harbour, and for the compulsory hiring of a lawyer to deal with freight. One small-scale investor has calculated that these charges have cost him 5–10% of the value of each batch of imported goods.
- Customs bureaucracy can delay the release of imported items, sometimes by up to six months.
- Cultivate the virtue of patience.

Further information

Promex, now known as the Agencia de Promoção de Investimentos (*CP 89-C, Praia;* ☎ *262 2621/2689;* f *262 2657*), promotes itself as a one-stop shop for information, contacts, and the processing of applications and permits. It has in-depth brochures on all of the above issues. The amounts needed to obtain citizenship and invest in Cape Verde are constantly under review, so you should always check with Promex for the latest information.

For a good summary of Cape Verde's economy, politics and recent history see the latest edition of *Africa South of the Sahara*, Europa Publications, available in most good libraries.

VOLUNTEER AND DEVELOPMENT WORK

Many volunteers and other development workers in Cape Verde have a superb, and sometimes life-changing, time. They have the opportunity to absorb the people and landscape in a way that tourists can only dream of. They have the chance to understand this singular people, impoverished in some ways yet deeply resilient and formidably artistic. Some who have spent time in Cape Verde say they feel it has qualities that Europe and the USA have lost in the stampede for material success. Returning *emigrantes* from the USA, as well as foreigners, enjoy the peace, the relaxed pace of life, and the high value (and consequently time) invested in friendships, free time, parties and making music.

Trying to work in such a culture can pose problems, however, which are all the more frustrating if your work is designed to help local communities rather than produce a successful business for yourself. Your success is uniquely dependent on the enthusiasm and co-operation of the people with whom you work, and if they are not co-operative, you may end up with nothing to show for your efforts. The ability to motivate and inspire is essential.

'The culture here is a double-edged sword,' says one volunteer. 'They are an island nation, which makes them somewhat isolated and entrenched in their own ways. Yet by African standards they are sophisticated, better educated, and more European.' Some volunteers arrive with an idealistic notion that the people will greet them with 'outstretched arms, waiting for them to teach, train, and show them a better way of life', he says. It can be a shock to discover indifference – or pride in the current way of life – combined with a reluctance to change.

English teachers may find that schoolchildren do not have the docile enthusiasm to learn that is found in mainland Africa. Pupils – adult or children – are also unlikely to have come across educational methods we take for granted in the West. 'A lot of the people trying to learn English have had very little formal education and find learning itself extremely difficult,' says one teacher. Community workers may find their job descriptions have changed by the time they arrive, or the job disappears totally after a few months. Unless you have the type of character that can deal with this type of disruption you may come unstuck.

An invaluable attitude derives from realising that you are in Cape Verde to learn as well as to give. Every new situation, however discomfiting, can provide insights into this foreign culture. Ask why it has happened, search for the answers in the history and culture, find it interesting. In this way you will derive a deeper understanding of another culture – one that only comes when you spend time in a place and which will be invaluable through life.

Another approach to irritation is to do some mental gymnastics and find something to admire in, for example, the failure to turn up to a meeting. 'My ploy is to think not "where the hell are they?" but "Ah yes, these people are great the way they refuse to be intimidated by time",' says another English teacher.

Above all you must be able to switch off. This does not rule out caring deeply about your work, and putting in more than 100%. But it does mean that when things get beyond your control you can shrug, laugh and say: 'I did my best, and the rest is out of my hands.'

Essential characteristics
Consider whether you have the following before you go:
- Linguistic ability, especially the ability to pick up a spoken-only language like Creole, but also the wherewithal to learn a formal written language like Portuguese, used for all official purposes
- Patience
- Sensitivity to other cultures
- People skills

Volunteer programmes

The British honorary consul arranges for volunteers to come on short postings to teach English on the islands. Contact him (see *Practical information*, page 46) or the British embassy in Senegal.

Many volunteers in Cape Verde have been sent there by the US Peace Corps on two-year postings. The volunteers tend to be employed in schools teaching English, training English teachers, working with the town hall, or in rural areas dispensing basic health education.

Peace Corps ⟩ +1 800 424 8580; www.peacecorps.gov

TEFL (TEACHING ENGLISH AS A FOREIGN LANGUAGE)

The English Language Institute (*CP 823, Rua 5 de Julho;* ⟩ *261 2672*) has schools in Praia, Mindelo and Sal. Lessons are generally business or general English, taught to adults, although there are some classes for children. The pay can sustain a good lifestyle in Cape Verde and the institute helps people get started – for example by organising a flat to be ready on your arrival. They are looking for Celta-qualified TEFL teachers. Some would-be teachers have just walked in off the street with their certificates and secured jobs, but it is probably best to arrange it beforehand.

High schools are desperate for English teachers, so it might be quite easy to find such work. The pay would be about 50,000$ a month and you are likely to be left to yourself to sort out issues such as accommodation and medical insurance. The work can be tiring, with classes of 40, and those who do not already speak Portuguese may have problems with class control.

It may be possible to give private classes, charging 1,000–2,000$ per hour. There are plenty of people who want to learn English for work or to visit the USA, but they might be hard to find until you have links with the local community.

Part Two

The Guide

Raso lark (calhandra do Ilhéu Raso)

Sal

You live – sleeping mother
Naked and forgotten
Arid,
Whipped by the winds
Cradled in the music without music
Of the waters that chain us in …

Amílcar Cabral, quoted in Basil Davidson,
The Fortunate Isles (Hutchinson, 1989)

There can be nowhere on earth as elemental as Sal. It lies like an oil slick on the Atlantic – any mountains, streams or vegetation that may have adorned it in the past have been obliterated by the wind over millions of years. Now Sal is just stone, sand and salt, still blasted by the same winds. On Sal the transience of life – animal or vegetable – becomes dismally clear.

The arrival at Sal on an international flight is one of the most deliciously depressing descents. For hours the traveller has scanned the Atlantic from the aeroplane window, searching for the lost islands of Cape Verde with an increasing sense of their isolation. Then Sal appears: relentlessly brown and featureless, etched with dry cracks through which rain occasionally flows. As the descent begins one feels like the Mars Pathfinder as it fell towards the Red Planet – except that Mars is believed by some to be capable of sustaining life.

Disembarking from the aircraft to cross the heat of the runway you will gaze at the rocky plains in puzzlement, trying to remember why you decided to come. There are two possible reasons: either you are going to the white sands and windy waters that lie on the island's south coast – be reassured that they are there and they are beautiful; or you are passing through to other islands of much greater interest.

HIGHLIGHTS

On Sal you can windsurf, surf, sunbathe, swim, enjoy the international hotels with their pools and other facilities, dive and go deep-sea fishing. You can take a day trip by sail or motorboat to Boavista.

You can take lonely walks along its treeless coastline. You can visit the imposing volcano crater and salt lake of Pedra de Lume and you can swim, dive, or do a little underwater caving at the foaming lagoon of Buracona.

Sal abounds in interesting birds and shells. It is not, however the place for mountain walkers or those who love verdant scenery. There is little point allocating days for sightseeing here because the few places of interest can be fitted into transit times at the beginning and end of the holiday.

BACKGROUND INFORMATION
History
On Sal the living has always been marginal, based on whatever need could be found for its four products: rock, salt, sand and wind. Today, for the first time in its history, it is flourishing on three of those commodities. Merely as a rock in the Atlantic it is proving useful as a refuelling stop for international aircraft. White sand is now in demand from beach-loving tourists. And the wind now catches the sails of delighted windsurfers who have discovered one of the best places in the world for their sport.

For the last five centuries Sal's economy has risen (always modestly) and fallen with international demands for its fourth element: salt. It is thought that even before the island was sighted by Gomes and de Noli in 1460 it was known by Moorish sailors for its rich saltpans.

The colonisation of Cape Verde had little consequence for Sal for hundreds of years – salt was procured more easily from the island of Maio, closer to the capital island, Santiago. Nothing much disturbed Sal except perhaps the off-loading of some perplexed goats in the 16th century as part of the archipelago's drive to increase its meat production. For much of the time there were probably also a few slaves on Sal, digging for salt. Early reports from passing sailors also show that people sometimes hunted marine turtles on Sal.

Even by 1683 the passing English sailor William Dampier reported just six men, a governor and an abundance of flamingos. There are no longer any of the last – it is

believed they disappeared with the rise of the salt industry. The men survived by trading salt and goat skins for food and old clothes with the odd passing ship.

It wasn't until 150 years ago, when a Cape Verdean business-man, Manuel António Martins, set up a salt export business, that Sal's population began to grow. A thousand souls came to join the 100 occupants between 1827 and 1882 – 'souls' was the word used by the British businessman from São Vicente, John Rendall, to describe both free men, of whom there were 300, and the 700 slaves.

The salt business was based at two sites: Pedra de Lume in the east and Santa Maria in the south. Its fortunes fluctuated with the trade barriers in Brazil, the African mainland and even Portugal itself. Eventually it was wound up in the first half of the 20th century and the island returned to desolation. Archibald Lyall, an English journalist who visited in 1936, reported:

Not even the most rudimentary garden is possible among the shifting dunes, and all the landward windows of the houses have to be kept perpetually shuttered against the penetrating yellow grit.

Sal's prosperity in the 20th century began when the Italian dictator Benito Mussolini was looking for a site where aircraft could stop to refuel between Europe and South America. Portugal sold him the right to build an airport on Sal, then bought back the resulting facility in 1945. Since then the airport has grown bigger and the town of Espargos has developed with it.

Another nation found Sal a useful refuelling point: South Africa. Throughout the years of apartheid, when all other African countries refused to allow its planes to land on their ground, South African Airways stopped in Sal, which it still uses as a refuelling base.

Responding to the need to house airline crews was Sal's first, tiny step towards tourism. Today Sal's income comes mainly from tourism, the airport and its petrol storage facilities, and there is a fish-processing factory in its harbour, Palmeira.

Geography
Sal is the most barren of the inhabited islands. Its highest peak, Monte Grande, in the northeast, reaches just 406m. The island is 30km long and nowhere more than 12km wide. Ten thousand people occupy its 216km^2 and they live almost exclusively in Espargos, the capital in the centre of the island, and Santa Maria, the village and tourist resort on the south coast. Its landscape is of brown, stony plains and desert sands deposited by the wind from mainland Africa. Many of the inhabitants are immigrants from São Nicolau who have arrived since the airport began to expand in 1939.

Wildlife
Turtles frequent some of the eastern beaches of Sal. Birdwatchers will find interesting waders in the saltpans including, if they are lucky in Pedra de Lume, the black-winged stilt (*Himantopus himantopus*), known locally as *pernalonga*. This extraordinary, elegant creature has long red legs which extend behind it as it flies, as well as a long, thin beak. Pedra de Lume is its last remaining breeding site in Cape Verde.

Festivals
Festivals, when everything may be closed, are as follows:

São Jose	19 March (Palmeira)
Santa Cruz	3 May (Espargos)
Santo Antonia	9 June (Espargos)
São Joao	24 June (Espargos)
São Pedro	29 June (Hortela, Espargos)
Santa Ana	Last week of July (Fontona)
Nossa Sra de Pliedade	15 August (Pedra de Lume)
Municipality Day	15 September

GETTING THERE AND AWAY
By air
International arrivals in Sal
Long-haul flights will deposit you in Sal, although this may change after the construction of a longer runway and opening of the new international airport in Praia, Santiago. Those with visas can obtain an entry stamp at the booths. Those

with pre-arranged visas should go to the office before the immigration booths on the left. Visas are stamped into your passport here – yours for   45. You then collect your bags and go out into the entrance hall. There you can change money at two *cambios*, as well as use an ATM at the Banco Commercial do Atlantico. Changing travellers' cheques at the *cambios* here incurs a 1,000$ commission and even cash exchanges are charged at 600$. There are also offices for TACV Airlines, South African Airways, TAP Air Portugal, Hertz, Avis, Cabetur and an information booth; some of these services may not be open. There is also a restaurant. Most of the big tourist hotels meet international flights with free minibuses.

Airport ❧ 241 1468 or 241 1305

Airline telephone numbers

South African Airways	❧ 241 3786
TACV (Cabo Verde Airlines)	❧ 241 1656
TAP Air Portugal	❧ 241 1195
Air Luxor charters	❧ 241 3494
Cabo Verde Express charters	❧ 241 2600

Neos Air (*www.neosair.it*), an Italian charter airline, has flights to/from Rome, Bologna, Milan and Verona.

International departures from Sal
It is worth getting your hotel to obtain updates from the airline about the time of the plane – better to sit out a delay on the beach than in the airport.

In transit through Sal
If you are in transit to Praia Airport on Santiago then your baggage should have been checked all the way through. You will, however, have to go through immigration and customs yourself, after which you should check in immediately for your onward flight and exchange money in the bank in the arrivals hall (30-minute queues at the bank build up very soon after international arrivals); you can't change money at any other airport in the archipelago. If you are in transit to any island other than Santiago you will have to collect and re-check in your baggage.

Internal flights
There are frequent inter-island flights with TACV between Sal and other islands:

Santiago	Numerous, every day
Boavista	1 a day, with 2 on Mondays
São Vicente	Between 2 and 4 a day
São Nicolau	Several a week
Fogo	2 a week

To reach Maio or to find more frequent flights to and from Fogo, go first to Santiago. To get to and from Santo Antão, you must go via Santiago or São Vicente and travel there by boat from Mindelo.

From the airport
From the airport there are plenty of taxis to Espargos (180$) or Santa Maria (from 700$); after dark prices go up by 30%. You probably won't find a public *aluguer* waiting at the airport. The cheapest thing to do is to start by walking: with your back to the airport building you follow the road to the left and, after a few minutes, you'll reach a turning on your right. Take this for Santa Maria – once you are on

the road you should pick up either a public *aluguer* or a lift. Go straight on for Espargos (25-minute walk).

By ferry

At the time of research no regular ferries were operating from Sal. Most boats geared to tourists will go to Boavista, but it may be hard to negotiate a one-way passage (see *Excursions*, page 86). If any ferries are running they leave and arrive at Palmeira, the island's main harbour. A taxi for the 4km to Espargos costs about 200$. You can walk it in about 40 minutes.

By yacht

Sal is the most upwind of the islands. There is a very good anchorage in the western harbour of Palmeira. It is a good place for making crew changes because of the international airport. Shell will fill you up alongside; water is available in the same way. There is a small shipyard where they can do welding. If this is the first island you visit you will be dispatched in a taxi to the airport for an immigration stamp – an easy process. Other anchorages lie in the broad Baia da Murdeira in the west, just south of the promontory of Pesquerona and in the southern bay of Santa Maria.

GETTING AROUND

A tarmac road runs down the spine of the island between the capital, Espargos, and Santa Maria. The journey takes 25 minutes by car. The other roads run from Espargos to Pedra de Lume, and Espargos to Palmeira.

By public transport

Aluguers run regularly between Espargos and Santa Maria (100$) and between Espargos and the airport; less regularly from Espargos to Palmeira and infrequently to Pedra de Lume. In Espargos they depart from the square beside the town hall and Hotel Atlântico; in Santa Maria from in front of Matheus Restaurant.

By taxi

Taxis (and chartered public *aluguers*) from Espargos to Santa Maria cost 700–1,000$; from Espargos to Pedra de Lume 300$ (600$ return); Espargos to the airport 150$. There is a 30% surcharge in the evenings.

Car hire

Many require a deposit of about 20,000$. Prices are from 3,600–7,000$ per day depending on size and may include 80km mileage. Some of those listed below are also *aluguer* operators:

Alucar Santa Maria; ℳ 242 1187
Avis Santa Maria at Hotel Novorizonte and Belorizonte; ℷ 242 1551
Hertz Santa Maria at Crioula Hotel; ℷ 242 1661
Hifacar Santa Maria; ℷ 241 1054/1934, m 991 2044/6585; f 242 1651; Espargos;
ℷ 241 3015; e anacleto@cvtelecom.cv or hifacar@cvtelecom.cv
Sulcar Santa Maria at Restaurant Atlantic complex; ℷ 242 3718/1940, m 992 7755/995
4472; f 242 1940/241 3583; e sulcar@cvtelecom.cv

Others listed by Unotur are:

Cartur Santa Maria; ℷ 242 1700
Melicar Espargos; ℷ 241 1666

Mendes and Mendes Espargos; ✎ 241 2860
Neves Aluguer Santa Maria; ✎ 242 1039
Porto Novo Car Espargos; ✎ 241 2880
Rentavetra Espargos; ✎ 241 3519

WHERE TO STAY

There are two places to stay: Espargos and Santa Maria. Espargos is cheaper, near the airport and almost entirely unaffected by the tourism in the south. Staying in Espargos and commuting to Santa Maria carries the added cost of the transport.

Often Santa Maria is completely booked up. A trick, if you are planning to stay there at the end of your holiday, is to book a room through Cabetur while passing through at the beginning of your holiday. Cabetur has an office at the airport opposite the airport building.

There is an increasing number of self-catering options, with a huge number of apartments being built: see below.

ACTIVITIES
Excursions

Several agencies offer day trips by air to other islands, day trips by boat to Boavista, and boat excursions and sightseeing around Sal.

Typical prices are:

Half-day island tour	1,900$, minimum 6 persons
Full-day island tour including lunch	4,000$, minimum 6 persons
Day trip to Fogo	20,000$ by plane, minimum 17 persons
Day trip to Santiago	19,000$ by plane, minimum 17 persons
Day trip to Boavista	13,500$ by trimaran, minimum 4 persons
Day trip to Boavista	16,500$ by plane, minimum 17 persons
Day trip to Sao Nicolau	15,500$ by plane, minimum 17 persons

Mini cruises

Usually these trips go to Boavista for the day. A trip with the HD catamaran for four hours, minimum ten persons, costs 3,300$ per person. A sailing boat trip for eight hours, minimum ten persons, costs 6,600$ per person. A special trip aboard the trimaran at the Hotel Morabeza in Santa Maria costs 13,500$ (minimum 4 persons). Contact the hotel, or James Sarkies, who has a hand in its operations. For further details about the boat, see www.nigelirens.demon.co.uk.

Local operators

AVT ✎ 242 1020
Cabetur At Sal Airport; ✎ 241 1545; f 241 1098
Cabo Verde Time Next to Vasco de Gama Restaurant; ✎ 242 1618
Centro Excursions At the Centro Windsurfing Atlantis, Santa Maria; m 996 3427; f 242 1871; e centroexcursoes@cvtelecom.cv
CVTS Rua 1 de Junho 10, Santa Maria; ✎ 242 1260/1220; f 242 1224; e cvtssal@cvtelecom.cv
Jumbo Tours Next to Vasco de Gama Restaurant; ✎ 242 1725
Morabitur At Sal Airport; ✎ 241 2672; f 241 2673; e morabitur@cvtelecom.cv
Odisseia Praia de Santa Maria; m 997 7441/2; www.odisseia.org. Also in Portugal.
Planeta Cabo Verde Turismo Zona Tanquinho Sul, CP 68, Santa Maria; ✎ 242 1575; f 242 1727; e booking@planeta-caboverde.com; www.planeta-caboverde.com. Also close to Hotel Morabeza.

Unotur Rua 15 de Agosto, CP 97, Santa Maria; ℝ 242 1771; f 242 1744;
e unotur@cvtelecom.cv. This organisation is a non-profit agency that seeks to promote the
Cape Verde Islands; it is sponsored by a number of hotels, agencies, car hire, island
promoters and real estate agents. In effect it is the only functioning tourist office and
tourism promotion organisation.

Windsurfing
For a description of windsurfing conditions on Sal, see *Practical information*, page 36.
More and more windsurfing centres are setting up in Santa Maria.

Angulo Watersports Close to Hotel Sab Sab; ℝ 242 1899; www.angulocaboverde.com.
Offers windsurfing, kite rentals, private tuition and island trips.
Bravo Club At Vila do Faral Hotel, e bcfarol.recep@renthotel.org. Offers windsurfing.
Chiensee Surf Club On the beach in front of Hotel Leme Bedje; ℝ 242 1339. Offers
windsurfing, kitesurfing and bodyboarding.
Morabeza Beach Club m 997 8804; e srodi@aol.com; www.cabokite.com. Has a 'surf
station' offering kitesurfing; introduction lessons for 60, day rental 70. Windsurfing
lessons, 3 hours 55; rental 5 hours 55.

Equipment can be bought at the **Ponta Preta surf shop** near Pensão Relax.

Fishing
For a description of Cape Verdean fish, see *Practical information*, page 37. Fishing is
best done between July and October, but wahoo is available almost nine months
of the year. There is a good wahoo fishery about 20 minutes away, by sea, from
Santa Maria. Game fishing, bottom fishing and pier fishing are all available from
the companies below.

Big Game Fishing m 991 5505
Fishing Centre Next to the Barracuda Restaurant.
Morabeza Fishing Club In the Hotel Morabeza. Offers a variety of experiences in
conjunction with Odisseia, inc surf casting, 4 hours 3,200$; shore spinning, 4 hours 5,400$;
offshore trolling, 4 hours 300 per boat; big-game fishing, max 4 people, 4–7 hours
 234–468 per boat.

Diving
Diving in Cape Verde is discussed in *Practical information*, page 36. There are some
exciting dives on Sal, including one to the 1966 freighter *Santo Antão* and the
Danish ship *Demfior*, which foundered on the east coast in the late 1940s and
abounds in colourful fish. There is a cave dive at Buracona where, 20m (60ft)
down, you pass through a tunnel and journey through blackness for about 130ft
until the tunnel turns upwards, revealing a chink of light, and you follow it till you
reach a huge, open-topped cave, 10m in diameter. There are also good dives at the
many other small caves and inlets north of Palmeira (10–15m drops). Salão Azul,
200m (600ft) off Pedra de Lume, is a reef with a wall that stretches to a depth of
45m, peppered with recesses full of marine life. Another highlight is Ponta do
Farol (45m), another dramatic reef wall dive ending at a large cave. Make sure you
feel confident with whoever is in charge at the diving centres below.

Baia Village Dive Centre At the Baia da Mordeira bay north of Santa Maria.
Manta Diving Centre At the Hotel Belorizonte; ℝ 242 1540; f 242 1550;
e manta.diving@cvtelecom.cv; www.mantadivingcentre.com
Odisseia On the beach outside Hotel Morabeza; m 997 7441; www.odisseia.org. Offers
courses such as Discover Diving, 7-dive basic course, and single dives with guide.

Planeta www.planeta-caboverde.com. Also offers diving; see *Locally based operators*, above.
Pro Atlantic Diving Center Hotel Leme Bedge; ↘ 241 2621, m 997 7360; f 241 2622;
e proatlantic@cvtelecom.cv. A NAUI centre offering NAUI scuba diving and single-dive courses.
Stingray Dive Center Hotel Odjo d'Água; ↘ 242 1134; f 242 1381;
e info@stingraydive.de; www.stingraydive.com. Offers courses inc Discover Diving, bronze course inc 6 open-water dives, as well as single dives.
Prices range from 4,000$ for a single dive to around 32,000$ for a 7-dive basic course. Contact the companies concerned for more details.

Surfing
The world-class break is at Ponta Preta. For more information see *Practical information*, page 35.

Hiking
You can go for lonely long walks virtually anywhere on the island. Just take plenty of water and a hat. See page 97.

Cycling and motorbikes
Sal is a pretty good venue for exploration by bike: as with hiking, wear a hat and take plenty of water.

KidBoy Next to Pensão Les Alizés in Santa Maria has bicycles for hire, 1 hour 2, All day 10.
Moped Rental In Santa Maria; enquire at Pastelaria Relax.
Quad Hire Motoquad guided excursions cost 4,400$ for 1 person, 6,600$ for 2 persons. Contact Hotel Morabeza, Santa Maria.

Driving
It is very popular to rent a car and see the island in a day. Such a trip should take in Palmeira and Pedra de Lume and cover much of the coast (so a 4x4 is necessary). For a description of a round-island trip, see page 99.

ESPARGOS
Poor Espargos has an undeserved reputation for desolation. In fact, it is just an ordinary town. There is no reason to visit it but then it hasn't asked you to come: you are meant to be in Santa Maria. Still, it has some good restaurants and at night it is pleasantly lively in the main square.

Espargos draws its unlikely name from the wild, yellow-flowered, red-berried asparagus bushes that are said to grow on sandy parts of the island. It is a young town, expanding with the airport.

There is nothing to do in town except perhaps walk up Morro, the mound covered in satellite dishes, for a view of the island.

Where to stay
Hotel Atlântico CP 74, Rua Amílcar Cabral; ↘ 241 1210; f 241 1522. This 3-star hotel is one of the most comfortable in Espargos, on the airport edge of town. It caters mainly for flight crews, heavily delayed passengers and business people. There is a tennis court and disco. *Sgl 2,900$; dbl 3,600–3,900$; breakfast 465$.*
Residencial Santos ↘ 241 1900, m 992 3850; f 241 2695;
e residencialsantos@hotmail.com. A pleasant place east of town with restaurant and upper terrace. *Sgl 2,800$, dbl 3,800$; inc breakfast.*

Residencial Central CP 27, Rua 5 de Julho; ☏ 241 1366; e central@cvtelecom.cv.
Located on Espargos's main street, the hotel has rooms arranged around a courtyard, some
with balconies. *Sgl 2,120$; dbl 3,180$.*
Pousada Paz e Bem CP 161, Rua Jorge Barbosa; ☏ 241 1782; f 241 1790;
e pensaopazbem@cvtelecom.cv. *Sgl 2,120$; dbl 3,180$; triple 3,710$; all rooms inc breakfast.*
Casa da Angela Rua Abel Djassy 20; ☏ 241 1327. Friendly hotel towards the north of
town. Some rooms have fridge and spare bed. *Sgl 1,900$; dbl with cold shower 2,500$, with hot
shower 3,000$; breakfast 350$.*
Residencial Monte Sentinha Lada Zona Travessa; ☏ 241 1446; ☏/f 241 1720, m 994
3459/991 8671. *Sgl 2,000$; dbl 3,000$.*

Where to eat and drink
Hotel Atlântico Serves breakfast, lunch and dinner. Main dishes start at 800$.
Residencial Santos See above. Restaurant and upper terrace with views; fish 800–1,300$,
meat 850$, pasta 650$.
Churasqueira Dinamica A local café serving hearty plates of fish or stew. Behind the
aluguer park.

Esplanada Bom Dia A café with outside seating. Head east from the Hotel Atlântico and it is on your left.

Restaurante Salinas ⟍ 241 1799. Bright airy restaurant serving grilled lobster and fine steak. Main dishes start at 750$. It is on the main street into town from the *aluguer* park.

Restaurante Sivy Traditional menu, with main dishes starting at 450$. Kiosk serves ice cream. On the main square but often closed.

Tanha Fina Snack bar. A good breakfast place if all others are closed; egg, bread and tea 180$.

Bar Ziquipa On the square for drinks.

Nightlife
The **Millennium nightclub** is situated several minutes' walk east from the Hotel Atlântico.

Practicalities
Airlines There are no travel agents in Espargos. Angola Airlines has an office in town, see map; ⟍ 241 1355. Major airlines have offices at the airport; ⟍ 241 1468.

Bank Caixa Económica; Banco Comercial do Atlântico

Ferries If any are running, they depart from Palmeira.

Hospital ⟍ 241 1130

Internet Cyberspace; open daily 09.30–midnight; third road on the right off the main street; offers other services such as photo scanning. There is also the Suzy internet café in the centre of town and another internet café near the Casa da Angela.

Pharmacy Farmacia Alianca; ⟍ 241 1109

Police ⟍ 241 1132. With your back to the Hotel Atlântico, follow the main road to the right for 10 minutes.

Shopping There are 2 music shops; Tropical Dance (Rua 5 de Julho, the main road through town, on the right) and west off the main road heading towards Casa da Angela. Minimercados are to be found opposite the church, just off the main square, and next to Residencial Central, which faces the square.

SANTA MARIA DAS DORES
This settlement has all the charm of a wild-west town: strangely empty, devoid of vegetation and scourged by wind. Its few, wide streets are lined with pastel single-storey houses and its people potter, as if they are waiting for something big to happen. Santa Maria has three layers: tourism is the topping, lining the beach; affluent locals live along three parallel streets behind, where there are some tourist restaurants, bars and shops; beyond that the poor part of Santa Maria stretches inland where people live in rambling hovels made of rough concrete and boulders – the one commodity that is not in short supply.

Archibald Lyall, the English journalist, reported:

> Never was a place better named than these two or three dozen little
> houses by the sad seashore. There is no vegetation and nothing to do but
> steel oneself against the unceasing wind which blows the sand into food
> and throat and clothes. At night, when the red-eyed people retire to their
> shuttered, oil-lit houses, the great white crabs come out of the sea and
> march through the streets like a regiment of soldiers.

But Santa Maria is more cheerful now. Instead of crabs it is tourists that walk the streets at night.

History
While the bay at the south of the island was probably frequented over the centuries by salt-diggers and sailors, Santa Maria only officially came into existence at the

beginning of the 19th century, when Manuel António Martins of Boavista arrived to exploit the saltpans that lie behind the village.

Martins's workforce scraped away the sand to the rock beneath. They guided seawater inland along little trenches and then pumped it by means of wooden windmills into the rows of broad shallow pans. The water would gradually evaporate leaving white sheets of salt which were dug into pyramids. These were loaded into carts which were pulled by mule, along the first railway tracks to be built in Portuguese Africa, to a newly built harbour. Around 30,000 tonnes of salt were exported each year from the port of Santa Maria and much of it went to Brazil until disaster struck in the late 1880s when that country imposed a high customs tax to protect its own new industry.

In the early 1900s, several new ventures with European companies collapsed, forcing the people of Sal to leave in search of work on other islands. Just a few peasants were left, making a living from salting fish and exporting it to other islands.

Santa Maria's fortunes surged again in the 1920s when a new market for salt opened up in the Belgian Congo and some Portuguese companies revived the business. By the mid 1900s Sal was exporting 13,000 tonnes a year and there was enough money to build the Santa Maria of today but, as always, international events were to snatch away whatever prosperity they had bestowed. Independence for the Belgian Congo, changes in Portugal and then independence in Cape Verde brought an end to the business. By 1984 even the routine maintenance of the saltpans ceased.

Santa Maria had a small but significant role to play in Cape Verde's liberation. In September 1974, hearing that Spínola, the new Portuguese ruler, was secretly to visit Sal, Cape Verdeans immediately hired whatever planes and boats they could find. They arrived at Sal and picketed him, daubing slogans on the road from the airport and braving threats that they would be shot.

In return an embarrassed Spínola sacked the Cape Verdean governor on the spot and ordered a stronger one to the colony immediately.

Where to stay
Many new hotels are being built, including the five-star Club Hotel **Rui Funana**, a vast complex west of the town beyond the Hotel Farol, as well as many new apartment blocks for tourists. Santa Maria can become very full in summer, so it is advisable to book ahead.

Upmarket
Crioula Hotel CP 45 Santa Maria; ☎ 242 1615/1647/1654; f 242 1376; e crioulahotel@cvtelecom.cv. Reservations in Italy; ☎/f +39 030 370 0630; e vilacrio@tin.it. Santa Maria's first 5-star hotel lies to the west of town, constructed of pleasant, muted terracotta and stone architecture with quiet rooms arranged around gardens. Large, freshwater pool, excursions, car rental. *Sgl 9,925$; dbl 18,745$; triple 26,463$; suite 27,566$.*

Djadsal Holiday Club CP 29; ☎ 242 1170; f 242 1070; e djadsal_h_c@libero.it or info@caboverdetime.it; www.caboverdetime.it. A 4-star hotel to the west of town, built within Moorish-style walls and a favourite of Italian package tourists. Swimming pool, sports and activities, Italian restaurant. *Room only: single 6,500–14,000$; double 8,000–22,000$; suite 15,000–24,000$; breakfast 1,000$.*

Hotel Morabeza CP 33; ☎ 242 1020; f 242 1021; e info@hotelmorabeza.com; www.hotelmorabeza.com. Reservations in Belgium; 15–17 Kaarderijstraat, 9000 Ghent, Belgium; ☎ +32 9 226 1947; f +32 9 226 9472; e ciem.nv@skynet.be;

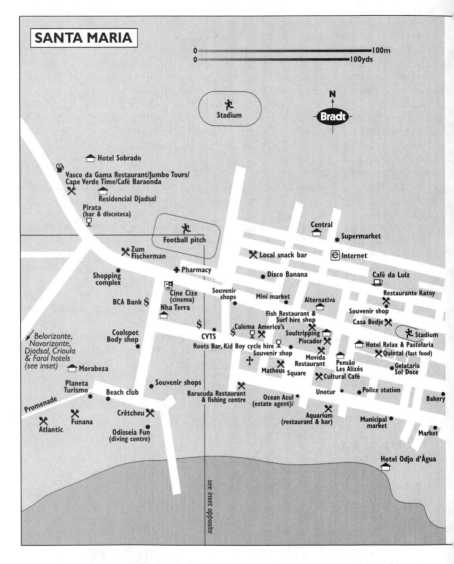

SANTA MARIA

0 — 100m
0 — 100yds

N

Bradt

- Stadium
- Hotel Sobrado
- Vasco da Gama Restaurant/Jumbo Tours/ Cape Verde Time/Café Baraonda
- Residencial Djadsal
- Pirata (bar & discoteca)
- Central
- Supermarket
- Football pitch
- Zum Fischerman
- Local snack bar
- Internet
- Pharmacy
- Disco Banana
- Café da Luiz
- Shopping complex
- Souvenir shops
- Mini market
- Restaurante Katoy
- Cine Cize (cinema)
- Alternativa
- BCA Bank
- Nha Terra
- Souvenir shop
- Casa Bedje
- Fish Restaurant & Surf hire shop
- Coolspot Body shop
- CVTS
- Calema Americo's
- Soultripping
- Stadium
- Belorizonte, Novorizonte, Djadsal, Crioula & Farol hotels (see inset)
- Roots Bar, Kid Boy cycle hire
- Piscador
- Hotel Relax & Pastelaria
- Quintal (fast food)
- Morabeza
- Souvenir shop
- Movida Restaurant
- Pensão Les Alizés
- Gelataria Sol Doce
- Matheus Square
- Cultural Café
- Planeta Turismo
- Souvenir shops
- Beach club
- Baracuda Restaurant & fishing centre
- Unotur
- Police station
- Bakery
- Promenade
- Ocean Azul (estate agent)/
- Aquarium (restaurant & bar)
- Municipal market
- Market
- Atlantic
- Funana
- Crêtcheu
- Odisseia Fun (diving centre)
- Hotel Odjo d'Água

see inset opposite

www.hotelmorabeza.com. The hotel offers B&B only, so that guests can eat in town if they wish and support other establishments as well. Built in the 1960s as a private house for a pioneering Belgian couple long before tourism hit Sal, the Morabeza has expanded over the years and is now a centrally positioned, 4-star hotel run by their granddaughter, Sophie. Attractively laid out, each room has a veranda giving sea or garden views. There is a large open-air swimming pool, and various sports are offered, inc, 4x4 excursions, archery, mini-golf, watersports and trips on the hotel's trimaran. See *Mini cruises* on page 86 for more information. Further extensions are in progress and there is a new rooftop restaurant serving local-style food. There are 2 restaurants and 3 bars. *Sgl 7,710–11,010$; dbl 8,820–15,420$; duplex 13,230–23,130$.*

Hotel Oasis Belorizonte CP 63; ☎ 242 1045; f 242 1210; www.oasisatlantico.com. Just beyond the Morabeza, this 4-star hotel has a mixture of rooms – bungalows or

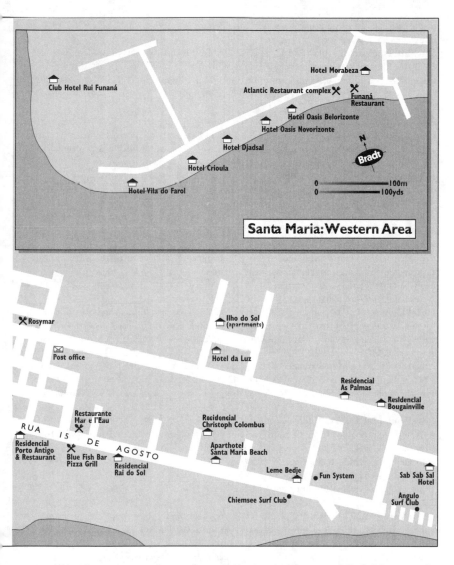

Santa Maria: Western Area

conventional rooms arranged around a pool. Also has the Restaurant Salinas. Now part of the Portuguese Oasis group. *Sgl 78–140; dbl 98–175; suite 125–199.*

Hotel Oasis Novorizonte CP 63; ☎ 242 1551; f 241 2574; www.oasisatlantico.com. Sister hotel to the Belorizonte, with some shared facilities, the hotel consists of individual chalets and facilities include a small pool. Now also part of the Portuguese Oasis group. *Sgl 117–165; dbl 146–206.*

Vila do Farol/Bravo Club CP 59 Praia Santa Maria; ☎ 242 1725; f 242 1730; e bcfarol.recep@renthotel.org; www.bravoclub.it. Located further west of the Hotel Crioula. Facilities include 234 rooms with AC, 2 restaurants, windsurfing club, bars disco, satellite TV, daily entertainment programs. *Prices by email on request.*

Odjo d'Água ☎ 242 1414; f 242 1430; e odjodagua@cvtelecom.cv; www.odjodagua.net. Down on the shore to the east of the pier, this is a quiet and pretty hotel with small, well-

planted gardens and spectacular sea views. Small pool. *Sgl 5,100–9,700$; dbl 8,300–15,500$; suite 9,700–25,000$.*
Sab Sab Sal Hotel CP 49; ❧ 242 1301; f 242 1161; e cabo.campo@cvtelecom.cv. Formerly the 3-star Albatros, this hotel is at the east end of town close to the open beaches. It is spacious and quiet with gardens, swimming pool and the Angulo sports facilities. *Sgl 6,100$ (B&B), 8,900$ (FB); dbl 7,700$ (B&B), 11,600$ (FB); triple 8,800$ (B&B), 11,650$ (FB).*

Mid range
Ilho do Sol ❧ 242 1633, m 991 8724 . Next to Hotel da Luz, these are balconied apts, each with kitchen, double bedroom, living room with 2 sofa beds and 1 further tiny room. Apartments have TV and AC. *Each apt 6,000$; no breakfast.*
Hotel da Luz CP 19; ❧ 242 1138; f 242 1088; e pousadadaluz@cvtelecom.cv; www.pousadadaluz.cv or www.caboverde.com/pages/421138.htm. Inland and to the east of Santa Maria's centre, the da Luz has large rooms, many arranged around a communal atrium. Rooms have TVs and fans. Small pool. *Sgl 3,300$; dbl 4,500$; triple 5,500$; with breakfast.*
Residence Leme Bedje Rua 15 de Agosto; ❧ 242 1146; f 242 1727; e lemebedje.caboverde@tiscalinet.it; www.lemebedje.com. This apartment hotel is at the eastern edge of town. It is bright with most apartments having basic kitchens. Small pool, lively restaurant and bar. Planeta Turismo is close by. *Sgl 3,600–7,100$; dbl 5,000–9,400$; 4-person apt 9,600–14,600$; 6-person apt 11,000–16,100$; breakfast 500$.*
Hotel Central Rua das Salinas; ❧ 242 1503; f 242 1530; e centralhotelcv@hotmail.com. On the inland side of town, the Central is spacious and spotless and has a rooftop terrace with a bar, shade and views over the town and the sea. *Sgl 4,500$; dbl 5,500$; suite 6,500$; all with breakfast.*
Aparthotel Santa Maria Beach CP 58, Zona da Tanquinho; ❧ 242 1450; m 994 3410; f 242 1478. Reservations in France ❧ +33 1 43 00 87 32. Along the coastal road out to the east, the rooms in this hotel are mostly balconied, some with sea views. *Sgl 3,700$; dbl 5,200$.*
Residencial Nha Terra Rua 1 de Junho; ❧ 242 1109; f 242 1534; e nhaterra@hotmail.com; www.caboverde.com. Conveniently positioned at the western edge of town, this airy hotel is great value: bright and cared-for with balconied rooms, all with fans, and spotless bathrooms. *Sgl 3,200–4,000$; dbl 4,200–5,000$; triple 5,200–6,000$.*
Pensão Les Alizés CP 74, Santa Maria; ❧ 242 1446/1008; e lesalizes@cvtelecom.cv. It has 10 rooms with private bath, hot water, TV and veranda sea view. *Sgl 3,700–4,300$; dbl 5,300–6,300$.*
Cabo Verde Palace ❧ 242 1238; f 242 1004; www.caboverdepalace.com. This new place, typical of the latest developments, is located near the Leme Bedje area. It has a charming atmosphere with 4 1-bedroom apts and 2 2-room apts. Breakfast is offered. *VIP studio (2 persons) 73; studio with kitchen (2 persons) 50; dbl room 41; 4-person apt 91.*
Residencial Bougainville e eurim.lda@virgilio.it. On the northeastern side of town but not yet open. Apartments for rent.
Residencial As Palmas e eurim.lda@virgilio.it. Close to the Bougainville and also not yet open.
Residencial Christoph Colombus e nuestisal@virgilio.it. Another new apartment complex.
Residencial Onde Bcu ❧ 242 1895; www.oceano-azul.com. Has apartments for weekly rent, cost 350–390. Contact Oceano-Azul Estate Agents.
Residencial Porto Antigo ❧ 242 1819, m 997 7393. This is a very new place not far from the Odjo d'Água. *Prices not yet available.*
Residencial Rai do Sol ❧ 242 1679. New apartment building east of the centre close to the beach. Virtually completed in mid 2005.

Djadsal Residencial ⟍ 242 1170. Part of the Djadsal Hotel group and with some apts for rent; or at the Djadsal Hotel – see details above.
Pensão Soares ⟍ 242 2020, m 991 2849; f 242 2000; e pensaosoares@cvtelecom.cv. It has 10 rooms, TV and breakfast included. *Prices on application.*

Budget
Residencial Alternativa Rua Amílcar Cabral; ⟍ 242 1216; f 242 1165. Beside the Nazarene church, this is a no-frills place, though it has large rooms, some with shared bathrooms. Nice first-floor terrace. *Sgl 2,420–2,850$; dbl 3,160–3,580$; inc breakfast.*
Hotel Sobrado CP 25 Santa Maria; ⟍ 242 1720; f 242 1715; e hotelsobrado@cvtelecom.cv; www.hotelsobrado.cv. With 25 rooms and a quiet location, this hotel is very good value. Restaurant and swimming pool. Aps Spa is available through the hotel. *Sgl 1,650–4,000$; dbl 2,200–4,900$; triple 3,300–3,800$.*
Pensão Relax Rua Amílcar Cabral, ⟍ 242 1680; f 242 1586; e majoduarte@cvtelecom.cv. Hotel across the road from the restaurant, next to the Vino Shop. *Sgl 2,500–3,500$; dbl 3,500–4,500$; inc breakfast.*
Gestão Turistica e Imobiliaria Rua Amílcar Cabral; ⟍/f 242 1668; e gesturium@cvtelecom.cv. Estate agency that lets apts to tourists.

Where to eat and drink
There are many restaurants in Santa Maria, but most visitors stick to a favourite few around the square in Santa Maria, though it is worth hunting out the little gems on the back streets. Not every restaurant is mentioned in this list. All the upmarket hotels – **Crioula, Djadsal, Belorizonte, Novorizonte, Morabeza, Sab Sab** – also have restaurants that welcome non-residents, generally with live music

Barracuda Restaurant Right on the beachfront next to the fishing centre. It has a good choice.
Café Baraonda next to the Vasco de Gama, but a cheaper option.
Casa Bedje Imaginatively conceived open-air restaurant tucked away behind the sports stadium. Main dishes start at 700$. Was formerly called Sabura.
Crêtcheu Almost on the beach, just before the Hotel Morabeza. Pasta and grilled fish with a view of the sea, the pier and all the boats moored nearby. Open daily 10.00–22.00. Fish starts at 700$.
Cultural Café Hip venue, of mixed Cape Verdean/European design, tumbling out on to the square in the centre of Santa Maria. Promotes a lot of local foods and drinks such as punches, *grogues*, cakes and *cachupa* (order the last in advance).
Fish Restaurant Located nearly opposite the Alternativa Hotel is this well-known speciality restaurant.
Funaná On the beach between the Morabeza and Belorizonte hotels. Attractive, straw-roofed restaurant on the beach, serving Cape Verdean and international evening meals as well as a more limited menu through the afternoon and later at night. Live music every night. Main dishes start at 800$.
Leme Bedje Beside the hotel of the same name. Popular bar and eatery serving grilled fish, pasta, sandwiches and omelettes in a relaxed environment at the quieter end of town.
Matheus Restaurant Ever popular staple of touristic evening life, this open-air restaurant on the square serves fish and meat. Main dishes from 700$. Closed Mon.
Odjo d'Água Beside the hotel of the same name. Attractively designed restaurant open for breakfast, lunch and dinner. Main dishes start at 900$.
Pastelaria Relax Downstairs it serves excellent cakes, coffee and snacks. Upstairs is an evening restaurant with some outdoor seating, and an extensive menu inc fish, meat, pizza and pasta. Fish dishes start at 700$.

Piscador Mainly fish dishes, starting at 800$. Closed Mon.

Restaurante Americo's ↘ 242 1011. A tourist favourite, it serves seafood and grilled fish. It is on the main street beyond Calema Bar.

Restaurante Atlantic On the sea front near the Morabeza Hotel, this large new complex has pizza, gelateria, snack bars and a varied main restaurant. Also in this complex is Sulcar car hire, a cyber café and various shops.

Restaurante Lomba-Branca Above the bakery, Padaria Dâdo. Mainly a local haunt, this place used to serve food from 07.00–01.00. Fish dishes started at 350$. It appeared to be closed in 2005.

Restaurante Movida Serves mainly fish and pasta dishes; fish dishes 650–1,000$. Formerly the Vulcão d'Fogo.

Restaurante Nha Terra 'Chico' Being the first restaurant you meet if you walk to town from the upmarket hotels, this fish restaurant is well frequented, especially in the evenings. Main dish prices start at 650$. Live music sometimes.

Restaurante Praia On the beach in front of the Hotel Belorizonte. Serves sandwiches and grills each day 12.00–15.00. Bar open all day. Grills start at 800$.

Quintal Fast Food Hidden in a side street near the Pastelaria Relax, it serves basic Italian favourites at very good prices. Pizza 300–450$. Tea is also very good value.

Vasco de Gama is a smart new restaurant on the road to Espargos. It has a wide range of dishes starting from 800$.

Zum Fischerman Under German ownership, this restaurant specialises in seafood. You can go out on their boat and catch your own dinner! Cost €35 for a half day (5–6hrs fishing), or €120 for trawling. Dishes from 550–1,000$.

Tam Tam, Katoy and **Café da Luiz** not far from the Hotel Central are local cafés for a different atmosphere.

Fresh bread can be bought from **Padaria Dâdo** (located beneath Restaurante Lomba-Branca); vegetables from the **municipal market**.

Nightlife

The most popular tourist restaurants, such as Matheus and Nha Terra, and the upmarket hotels that line the beach, have live music most nights.

Disco Hotel Morabeza In the hotel (see page 91).

Bar Discoteca Pirata On the airport road, opposite the turning to Djadsal Hotel. Bar open every day 21.00–06.00; disco from midnight–06.00. Pizza served.

Practicalities

Airlines Book through agents such as CVTS (see *Excursions*); Cabo Verde Express (mainly for day charters to Fogo) ↘ 241 2600, m 991 2813 (but people generally book through agents).

Bank Banco Comercial do Atlântico *open Mon–Fri 09.00–15.00*; Caixa Económica *open Mon–Fri 08.00–15.00*.

Ferries Try to ask in Palmeira. Don't expect a clear answer.

Hospital In Espargos

Internet There's one near the supermarket and Central Hotel. Telephone/internet shop, Rua 1 de Junho.

Police ↘ 242 1132. On the way to Sab Sab Sal Hotel.

Post office The large, pink building to the east of town. *Open Mon–Fri 08.00–12.00, 14.00–17.00.*

Pharmacy Rama, near the Cinema Cine Cize; ↘ 242 1340.

Shopping Souvenirs, crafts and Cape Verdean literature in Portuguese can be bought at the cultural centre and also at shops dotted over town, for example on the road down to the Crêtcheu Restaurant and on Rua 1 de Junho. Music can be bought at a number of places (and at the airport shop). The closest to a supermarket is Supermercado Central beside the Hotel Central (see *Where to stay*, above). There is a number of souvenir shops and vendors close to the Hotel Alternativa, which sell artefacts from Senegal, Guinea and parts of west Africa. Look for 'Mama Frica' near Tam Tam café and also 'Akuba' near the Ponta Preta surf shop. Near the beach is Coolspot. The former disco/internet bar – Wind Pub – is now a shop.

Tourist information No official outlet, so talk to the agents (see *Excursions*) or your hotel reception.

What to see and do

Santa Maria is a base for the surfing, windsurfing and fishing that are the chief activities of the island. See page 86 for activities. Beach-basking on its stunning white sands is popular. You can also visit the Santa Maria saltpans – walk through the shantytown inland of Santa Maria, and they are on the other side.

OTHER PLACES TO VISIT
Pedra de Lume

This is a spectacular place, and best appreciated in silence, so the poetic should rise early to reach it before anyone else. Inside a ring of low mountains lies a sweeping geometry of saltpans in blue, pink and green depending on their stage of salt formation, all separated by stone walls. The old rusted cables and a dirty mountain of salt testify to more prosperous days. You can sit on the crater slope in the shade listening to the water lapping in the lakes below and the cry of an occasional bird circling the crater rim.

History

Manuel Martins, who developed Santa Maria, had a business here as well. Bags of salt were strapped to pack animals, which had to climb up the slopes of the volcano and down the other side to reach the port. In 1804, a tunnel was cut through the volcano wall, then in 1919 transport was made easier when a businessman from Santa Maria and a French firm bought the salt company and built the tramway, the remnants of which can be seen today. They could then shift 25 tonnes an hour to the port, from where it was shipped to Africa. But markets shifted and the saltpans fell into disuse by 1985: today they do not even produce enough salt for Sal. Pedra de Lume is still inhabited but it feels like a ghost town.

There is disagreement about how salt water rises into the bottom of this crater – some believe it comes from deep in the earth, but the most orthodox explanation is that it infiltrates through the natural holes in volcanic rock along the kilometre distance from the sea.

Getting there

The village is off the main Santa Maria to Espargos road and you can reach it by taxi from Espargos (300$: if you are being driven into the crater and then back to town, from 600$) or, sometimes, *aluguer* from Espargos. You can try hitching but you might end up walking all the way.

Where to eat and drink

Cadamosto Restaurant 241 2210. This seaside restaurant in the village at Pedra de Lume has an inviting terrace and good seafood.

What to see and do

When you have looked around the village with its important-looking housing blocks and its little white church you can examine the relics of the pulley system for taking salt from the crater and loading ships. Turn inland then, following the old overhead cables uphill and, after ten minutes, through a tunnel into the crater.

It is possible to walk at least halfway round the crater rim by leaving the crater through the tunnel, taking a track to the right and just choosing a shallow part of the slope to ascend.

A longer walk leads north between the third and fourth pylons from the sea. After 15 minutes, through a graveyard of old machinery, you reach a fork. The left road is the coastal track. The right one goes towards the hill of Sol Azul, soon diminishing to a path that leads round the headland. It's a narrow, pebbly path, only for the sure-footed, but you should be able to get all the way round.

Palmeira

Palmeira harbour has a little of interest: a lobster-storage facility which you can visit, and often fine yachts in the harbour. Get there by *aluguer* from Espargos or by walking or hitching

Where to eat and drink

We cannot give any personal opinions about the following, but they have been listed in the sparse tourist information we were able to obtain. Other than in Santa Maria, information is hard to come by.

Da Romano's A nice little Italian spaghetteria on the left as you drive in on the main road (about 350$ for a plate of pasta).

Rosario, Continental Try these two places for sustenance.

What to see and do

Yacht Sailing Piersan Lda, Rua Principal, Palmeira; ⟋ 241 3861, m 993 1474; f 241 3860; e piersan202@hotmail.com. Sail in the *Loverly Bimba*.

Baia da Murdeira

This bay lies about 8km north of Santa Maria and is being developed with well over 100 villas. The coast here is quite rocky, with some smaller sandy areas. The main complex here is called both Baia Village and Murdeira Tourist Resort.

Baia Village/Murdeira Tourist Resort CP 164, Ilha do Sol; ⟋ 241 1604/2550/2308; f 241 1605; e turimsal@cvtelecom.cv. All apts here have TV, hot water and telephone. Facilities also include swimming pool, snack bars, market, diving centre, car rental and leisure boats for up to 12 people. Prices not available.

Buracona

This is an exhilarating natural swimming pool encased in black lava rock over which white foam cascades every few minutes. Nearby is the Blue Eye, an underground pool reached through a large hole in the ground. Divers can swim along an underground tunnel out into the sea.

If you are not in a car you'll have to walk the 6km from Palmeira. Follow the main road into Palmeira until just before the port gates. On the right is the yellow customs building. Turn right before you pass it. Immediately, take the left fork which goes round the front of a desalination plant, and take a turn left towards the sea. The road continues, past a boat yard, and then into a land which is about 25 shades of brown (including chocolate, wine-stain and rusted) covered with a few bent-over trees. Superimposed on this is a wind farm, a few scavenging goats and the odd anti-litter sign with plastic bags caught round it. The coastline itself is wildly beautiful, a jumble of black lava rock and waves. You pass a lesser pool but walk the full 6km to reach Buracona, which is just before **Monte Leste** (263m).

It's a great place for a swim and a picnic but it is notorious for an invisible thief who waits until you are in the pool before snatching belongings.

DRIVES

You can hire a car (make sure it is a 4x4) and do a clockwise tour of the island starting in Santa Maria. Leave the village on the Espargos road and when the main road bends right and goes a little uphill take a track to the left. It's not scenic to begin with – there's a dump on the left. But after ten minutes you are travelling on a rough track parallel to Agadoeiro beach. Keep going past a new house on the shore and on along the wild rocky coast softened by the beauty of the waves.

You rejoin the main road but leave it again 2km later, just as it turns away from the coast, and you drive along a track past the Baia da Murdeira. At the far end of this bay you can take a dead-end track to the west, which leads to the coastal foot of **Monte Leone**, the unmistakable 'lion' gazing out to sea, or you can immediately take the right fork and continue north. The track seems to disappear for a bit but you can see where you are meant to be, up a hill on the right where the route is clearly visible and from where the land stretches away like a vast car park, with the airport on your right. The only movement is the odd plastic bag tossed from a drainage channel by the wind.

Descend to Ribeira da Fontona, filled with palm trees, and on into Palmeira (drive round the front of the Shell and Enacol oil terminals, turn right to meet the main road and turn left on to that same road) where you can stop for lunch. Afterwards follow (in your car) the walking directions (above) to go on up the west coast to Buracona, from where you can continue northeast and round the tip of Sal, Ponta Norte. The track then turns south along a coast of low cliffs and down to Pedra de Lume, where you can drive right into the volcano crater.

Leaving Pedra de Lume, watch out for a track on your left or you will end up following the main road into Espargos. The track will take you down the east coast and back to Santa Maria.

Cape Verde peregrine (soutador)

Boavista

Mornas Dancing
In the sensuous bodies of the sensuous girls
In the dyspnoea of the brave waves
Dying in the sand
In the rolling of the
Languid and gentle waves,
Boa Vista,
The unforeseen
Scenery
Of sands marching on the village

Jorge Barbosa

Boavista is the siren island. For many seafarers down the years, it has been the first sight of land for months. The white dunes, like cusps of icing, must have been an alluring sight but Boavista's beaches have drawn many to a watery grave. It is ringed by reefs and its iron-rich rock formations send ship's compasses spinning. Over 40 ships have foundered here, within sight of land.

Beyond the idyllic beaches another story unfolds. The bleached land has a terrible beauty but it will leave you feeling parched and a little crazed by the sun. The only forests are petrified remnants on the shores: aeons ago, Boavista must have been a fertile place.

In many places the struggle for existence has become too much. Villages are abandoned, and sand drifts across the empty floors of their houses.

HIGHLIGHTS
Go for walks on abandoned beaches, over drifting dunes and in desert oases; go for windsurfing that is claimed by some to be better than on Sal; and for game fishing. There is diving, though currents and wind mitigate against exploring many shipwrecks and impair the clarity of the water. Birds, turtles and shells abound. Don't expect any mountain walking.

BACKGROUND INFORMATION
History
With little to offer but salt, Boavista, like Sal, did not receive much attention after its discovery on 14 May 1460. It was named Saint Cristovão until, it is said, a storm-tossed sailor's triumphant cry: *'Boa vista!'*, the equivalent of 'Land ahoy!', led to its present name.

Island life has been punctuated by shipwrecks – tragedies that were often fortuitous for the starving islanders who would clamber over the rocks after a stormy night to retrieve food and goods from the debris. It is said that in times of starvation the people would tie a lamp to a donkey's tail and send it in the darkness along the coastal reefs in the hope of luring ships to their doom.

Most ships were wrecked by a strange conflation of circumstances. A strong and gusty tradewind combined with a powerful current pulled sailing ships towards the island. Flat, and often shrouded in a dusty haze, Boavista could be invisible until those boats rammed into the hidden rocks of its northern and eastern coasts. Meanwhile, maps and charts have consistently placed Boavista several miles to the west of where it actually is.

Against this background, modern life began very slowly. It was visited early in its history, in 1498, by Christopher Columbus on his third voyage. By then the island already had a few inhabitants and was also used as a leper colony for well-to-do Europeans. After three days Columbus left, made a brief stop at Santiago and went on, reporting that the islands had: 'a false name... since they are so barren that I saw no green thing in them and all the people were infirm, so that I did not dare to remain in them.'

Apart from that, little happened on the island for the first 150 years after its discovery except desecration by goats. In 1580, there were only 50 people living there and in 1619 there was just a group of hunters, there for the goats.

Then English sailors discovered Boavista's high-quality salt and an economy began in about 1620, based at Povoação Velha – its first village. By 1677 Boavista even had a priest, but periodic sackings shook its economy. English sailors attacked the island in 1684, taking chalices from the churches to trade on the African coast. There was another attack in 1697, and by 1702 the population of Povoação Velha was routinely armed.

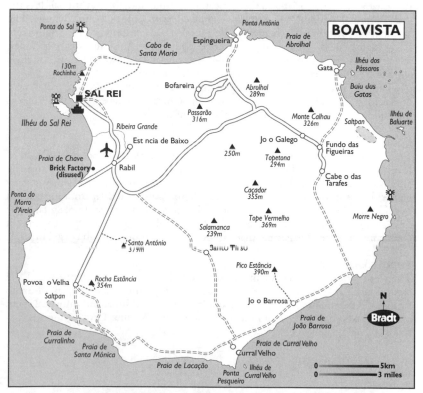

Nearing the 1800s, Porto Inglês (now Sal Rei) became the most important town on the island and salt production was increasing, reaching its zenith in the first half of the 19th century.

But the pillages continued in 1815 and 1817. The final desecration came in 1818 when the town was razed. As a result a fort was built on the Ilhéu do Sal Rei, and with this protection Boavista began an era of relative prosperity, becoming an important cultural centre. In 1834 it was even argued that the town should become the capital of Cape Verde. The Luso-British anti-slavery commission made Boavista its base in 1843.

The fortunes of even the prosperous dwindled, however, when the building of the port at Mindelo made São Vicente the new trading centre. When Charles Thomas, chaplain to the American Africa Squadron (an anti-slavery police) visited in 1855 he found the inhabitants to be starving and the cattle 'with sad faces and tears in their eyes, walking solemnly in cudless rumination over grassless fields'. The chief amusements of the people, he reported, were 'fishing, salt-making and going to funerals'. Fortunes changed again towards the end of the 19th century with increasing business in lime, clay tiles and castor oil. In the last hundred years or so the island has been the victim of drought, famine and grasshopper infestation which has led to emigration.

Perhaps the island's most famous son is Aristides Pereira, the 12th son of the priest of Boavista, who became the first president of Cape Verde in 1975.

Geography

Boavista is the closest island to the African mainland, and 50km from Sal. It is the third largest, at 620km², and sparsely populated, with only 4,000 inhabitants. The island is very flat with the highest peak, Pico Estância, at only 390m. The barren, stony landscape is covered in many areas with white sand and drifting dunes, which pile up on its western coast. The dunes have swallowed various buildings and covered the once-busy saltpans just outside Sal Rei.

There are 55km of white beaches and, in the centre, Sahara-like oases filled with date palms. Since independence, environmental measures have been taken such as the building of catchment dams and planting of trees.

Economy

There is some business exporting dates and fishing (limited because of lack of investment in the large boats needed to withstand the stormy seas). An unusually poor soil thwarts agriculture. Villages across Boavista are supplied with water by tanker from a desalination plant in Sal Rei. Some water is drawn from the ground by windmills (many of which are broken) but this is brackish and not suitable for drinking. It is used for washing, and also for agriculture, although the salt content constrains the type of vegetable that can be grown. Salt production ceased in 1979.

Festivals

There are various festival days, including goat fighting and processions to mark the festival of Cruz nho Lolo on 28 May; processions to the deserted Rock of Santo António in the middle of the island to mark his day on 13 June; and a musical event on an unfixed date in the summer, on the beach of Santa Cruz. Others are as follows:

Twelfth Night	6 January (João Gelego)
Santa Cruz	3 May (Rabil)
Pedrona	4 May (Rabil)

São Roque	8 May (Procãoa Velha)
Santa Isobel	4 July (Sal Rei)
Praia d'Cruz Festival	In August

GETTING THERE AND AWAY
By air
There are regular inter-island flights to Boavista with TACV from:

Sal	1 a day, with 2 on Mondays
Santiago	Daily, mostly via Sal
São Vicente	Daily, mostly via Sal

The airport is 6km south of the capital, Sal Rei, just before the town of Rabil. *Aluguer* buses and trucks wait outside and charge 400$ to transport one person; 200$ each for more than one. To reach the Marine Club (see *Where to stay*, page 107) is more expensive. Transport back to the airport can be found by loitering in the main square, but if your flight is at an odd time (eg: on a Sunday) it's better to ask your hotelier to arrange a vehicle.

In 2005, the airport runway on Boavista was being extended to accommodate international flights direct from Europe and elsewhere. Currently aircraft cannot land at night. Apparently, in the dire event of an evacuation of a seriously-ill person after dark, the town's resident car owners light up the runway with their car headlights.

Airport Rabil; ↘ 251 1313

By ferry
The port is in Sal Rei. Tourist links between Sal and Boavista at present consist of day trips from Sal, but this may improve as Boavista tries to attract more visitors.

By yacht
A very good anchorage is off Sal Rei. Most people anchor between the southern end of the islet and the shore. Harbour officials are generally on the pier. There are few facilities for yachts. Try the shop beside the Oasis Bar.

THE ORIGINS OF THE MORNA
The origins of the morna are obscure but it is said to have emerged on Boavista, named after the English word 'mourn' or perhaps the French word morne, meaning sad. There are a multitude of theories as to how its characteristic melodies arose. According to the Cape Verdean historian António Germano Lima, one theory is that it came from the sound of fishermen's oars hitting the water on their long journeys, and their marking of the rhythm of the rowing with the call 'vo-ga... vo-ga'. Others say it came from a mixture of musical types, such as the medieval Portuguese ballad, the *cancioneiro*, the Portuguese–Brazilian *modinhas* and the priests' liturgical chants. Lima himself favours the idea that the melancholy music must have been born from the hearts of slaves longing for home.

The morna was developed into its modern form by Eugénio Tavares (see *Brava*, page 189). Boavistan mornas are much livelier than Tavares's tearful versions. They can be full of satire, caricature, ridicule and dreams of revenge.

SHIPWRECKS

A few years ago, divers plunged into Cape Verde waters on a hunt for shipwrecks, and surfaced clutching a gold coin bearing a 1760 date. They believed they had discovered the remains of the *Dromadaire*, a French trading ship that sank in 1762, carrying more than £3 million of gold and silver. It is said the crew of the *Dromadaire* only realised their plight when they saw under the prow the surf on the reef.

Some 17 miles south of Boavista lies the notorious reef, Baixo de João Leitão: it has wrecked many a vessel. One man who spent tormented hours battling (successfully) to avoid it was Captain James Cook on his third and last voyage to the South Seas, in 1776.

Old people on Boavista still tell of a legendary cargo of gold brought to their ancestors by shipwreck. This may have been the wreck of the English vessel *Hartwell* on 24 May 1787. The ship suffered a mutiny while on the seas and in the confusion the crew let the boat stray to Boavista's shallows. The reef that sank it is called now the Hartwell Reef and lies at the northeast side of the island – it is partly above water, and extends for about 6km.

Cape Verde's version of the *Titanic* disaster occurred in the 19th century – the tragedy of the *Cicília*. It was the night of 5 November 1863 and the Italian ship was carrying emigrants destined for South America. Their spirits were high and there was a dance going on in the ballroom when the ship foundered near Boavista. When the captain realised what had happened he commanded the door of the ballroom to be locked. He made a great error. According to the poet José Lopes: 'There inside was true horror... a dance of life was transformed into a macabre dance of death...' Passengers were later found dead in the act of struggling to get out of the portholes; in all 72 died.

The *Santa Maria* was wrecked in August 1968 on the northwest coast. It was en route from Spain to Brazil with a cargo of cars, drink, melons, cork and cheese. The year 1968 had until then been a bad one for Boavistans: they spent the next 12 months salvaging booty.

GETTING AROUND
By public transport

Aluguers run frequently between Sal Rei and Rabil (100$); and between Sal Rei and the airport at relevant times. To other destinations they leave Sal Rei in the afternoon, and do not return until the following morning, generally arriving in Sal Rei at about 07.00. Don't get stranded. Buses for the northeast leave from the west side of the main square in Sal Rei at about 13.00. Those heading south depart from beside the makeshift market stalls at the south of the square.

By taxi

In the form of chartered *aluguers*, these can be hired for about ten times the public fare (eg: to Rabil 500$; to Santa Monica 5,000$; to Morre Negro 6,000$; one day around the island 9,000$). To do a thorough tour of Boavista it is essential to have a 4x4.

Car hire

Most of the hotels can put you in touch with a car and driver.

Autobraza ⤷ 251 1519
Cab Auto Rent a Car; ⤷ 251 1166/1540

ACTIVITIES
Excursions
ATC Lda Located on the southeast corner of the main square; ℩ 251 1872, m 992 7306/994 6139; e l_ripa@yahoo.it or fuji_em@tiscali.it; www.quadland-boavista.com. Specialises in quad hire and scooter hire in particular, but has day excursions into the dunes etc.
Dunas Hotel Offers various excursions. Day 4x4 tour 10,000$ per person, Quad tour 4,400$.
Morena Tourist Agency Located in the north of the main square; ℣f 251 1445. It offers day trips from 22 per person to such places as the dunes and further afield to Santa Monica beach.
Olitur Also on the square; ℣f 251 1743. It lists half- and full-day tours into the dunes etc from 15 per person.

Diving
See *Practical information*, page 36 for a discussion of diving in Cape Verde.

Dive School Submarine Center Located along the beach south of the Hotel Estoril near Tortuga beach; m 992 4865; e atilros@hotmail.com. Currently housed in 2 cargo-shipping containers. Small and personal PADI–NAUI centre with 2 qualified instructors (Atila and Rose) offering introductory diving courses, snorkelling day trips, and dives from their zodiac boat. PADI Open Water course 300; Discover Scuba course 80; snorkelling trip with guide 30; 10-hour kite course 250; private lesson 30. Can accommodate small groups.
Sharkys Diving Centre Located next to the Tortuga Beach Restaurant.; ℩ 251 1311; m 992 3050; www.sharkys-divecentre.com. Rates and prices are similar to above.

Windsurfing and other watersports
The excellent windsurfing potential of Boavista is discussed in *Practical information*, page 36. Listed below are the prices specific to the Boavista Wind Club, but these can be taken as a guide to such activities elsewhere in Cape Verde where they exist.
Boavista Wind Club is located at Tortuga beach on the south side. Facilities and prices are as follows:

Windsurf hire	3 hours	35 plus 8 insurance
	Day	50 plus 8 insurance
	Week	220 plus 30 insurance
Windsurf lessons (private)	90 minutes	30 (20 per person for 2–4 persons)
	6 days	150 (100 per person for 2–4 persons)
Kayak	1 hour	4 plus 8 insurance
	3 hours	9 plus 10 insurance
	Day	14 plus 15 insurance
Surfboards	1 hour	5
	3 hours	10
Catamaran Dart	1 hour	30
	3 hours	40
Kite school	1 hour	45 (1 person), 40 (2 persons)
	3 hours	90 (1 person), 75 (2 persons)

Fishing
Ask at the Morena Tourist Agency or Olitur (see above).

Cycling and motoquad
Cycling is an excellent way of seeing parts of Boavista, though the cobbled roads and relentless sun make it a tiring activity (see *Practical information*, page 50). Motoquad, though available, is frowned on by some who wish to preserve the Boavista beaches as quiet havens for visitors. It is, however, increasingly popular.

DRIVING IN BOAVISTA
Colum Wilson

I left Cabeço das Tarafes and the scant vegetation of a *ribeira*, and the road deteriorated to a dusty track. Now I was in open upland dominated by Pico Estância on the right. It is not a large mountain but in this emptiness I had lost all sense of scale and as it shimmered in the heat it seemed massive.

All around was dry rock. Once, I stopped and there was no movement except for the drifting trail of dust thrown out by the jeep. There was silence except for the droning of the hot wind. The land was an endless brown and the skull of a donkey gleamed like a white flower amongst the rocks. At last, after an eternity on the plateau of dry bones, the track swung towards the coast and soon I was driving just above the white sand.

Curral Velho is a crumbling village next to a salt lagoon just behind the shore. It is built in warm honey-coloured stone: a place of stone, built on stone, amongst stone. The wind murmured through the gaping windows. Two of the largest, blackest crows I had ever seen watched me from a broken gable as I picked my way round the ruins. I found a path over the dunes amongst the twisted roots and stumps of a fossilised forest. At the beach I sat for a little and watched the patterns of fine sand stream over the ground. Beyond, the sea crashed on to the steep shore.

From Curral Velho I drove inland. Walls criss-crossed the dry landscape – impressive monuments to generations of Boavistans who have put to good use the two resources that are not in short supply here: rock and time. From time to time I passed the ruins of farmhouses and here and there an abandoned well – there is water, but it is bitter now.

In places the track threatened to disappear altogether beneath thick drifts of dust. Elsewhere, the route was no more than a cleared path across boulder fields.

The sun sank and Santo António became an outlandish silhouette. I passed a tree blasted into a tortured sculpture by the prevailing wind – it was the first living thing since the crows, hours before. There were low scrubby bushes and then, at last, an attempt at cultivation. The field was more like a fortress than a garden: first there were walls to keep the goats out and then there was an embankment around each plant to keep the water in.

ATC Scooter On the southeast corner of the main square; ⟍ 251 1872; m 992 7306/994 6139; e l_ripa@yahoo.it or fuji_em@tiscali.it; www.quadland-boavista.com. Scooter rental 30 per day plus fuel; 2 days 50, 1 week 140. Quad Tours with guide – 4 hours 85.

Hiking
A couple of hikes can be done beginning from Sal Rei (see page 116). Other than that, it is a question of driving to places and making forays from the car.

Driving
The only way to see the island is to hire a 4x4, preferably with a driver. Then you can see many of the places listed later in this chapter. See also box above.

SAL REI
There is a charm about this town that seeps in slowly, as you sit in the main square watching life go by or drink coffee in thankful shade overlooking the beach. The

water is a glorious turquoise and the mounds of sand are a true, desert-island yellow. Men maintain their painted boats and children shout and play around the decrepit ones. From the town, the hillocks of Boavista appear like craggy mountains.

At night, you may become aware of a canine sub-culture, characterised by ferocious barking matches and brawling in the empty streets. Next morning traces of fur in the square are all that remain. You will need dogged determination to sleep through this canine cacophony.

Sal Rei is quietly busy and will hopefully be able to absorb the increasing numbers of tourists for whom hotels and villages are being built. Town planners made the cobbled roads wide and planted acacias, their trunks painted a tidy white. The main square is large with bandstands, children's play areas, benches and even urinals. The square has improved markedly with added shade from developing trees.

Where to stay

For most of the year, it is vital to book accommodation in Boavista well in advance. Prices given below may rise by about 20% during high season, whereas in May it should be quiet.

Upmarket

Marine Club Closed at the time of research but expected to reopen some time. The new prices are unknown, so the rates below are listed only as an indication from past prices. ↘ 251 1285; f 251 1390; e marineclub@cvtelecom.cv. A 30-minute walk from the north of Sal Rei, this is an upmarket concern in a prime position overlooking the water and with a beautiful pool. There are 2- and 3-room villas as well as rooms. *Sgl 7,000–8,500$; dbl 9,200–18,000$; triple 14,800–21,000$; 6-person apt 30,000$.*

Hotel Dunas Av Amílcar Cabral, CP 30 Sal Rei; ↘ 251 1225/1088; f 251 1384; e dunas@bwscv.com. Bright, spacious hotel on the seafront with an open-air restaurant. Guests have free access to Tortuga Beach Resort (basically a beach restaurant and parasol-studded beach area) about 5 minutes' walk away. Massage available 2,500$ per hour; reiki 1½ hours 4,000$. Room rates vary with the season. *Sgl 8,000–11,000$; dbl 12,000–15,500$.*

Estoril Beach Resort Hotel ↘ 251 1078, m 991 8663; f 251 1046; e info@estorilbeachresort.com; www.estorilbeachresort.com. Almost on the beach, down the road opposite the Shell petrol station, the 3-star Estoril is a tasteful, stone-built hotel with gracious rooms built around a courtyard. The new construction to the south is part of the Estoril and should be open very soon. *Sgl 5,100$; dbl 8,100$; 1,200$ HB.*

Aparthotel Ca Nicola Is located close to the Estoril Beach Hotel; ↘ 251 1793/4, m 991 8307; f 251 1549; e francesco@canicola.com; www.canicola.com. A pleasant retreat in a similar mould to the Estoril. Prices vary with season. *Sgl from 5,900–7,500$; dbl 8,600–11,000$.*

Mid range

Migrante Guesthouse Av Amílcar Cabral, CP 80 Sal Rei; ↘ 251 1143, m 995 3655; f 251 1143; e info@migrante-guesthouse.com; www.migrante-guesthouse.com. Contact in Italy: ↘/f +39 04 7126 0813; m +39 0338 866 8345. This superb place is set in a renovated traditional house with courtyard and has great charm. A good place for afternoon tea. *Sgl 5,500$; dbl 6,600–7,700$; rates include breakfast.*

Pousada Boa Vista Rua dos Emigrantes, CP 40 Sal Rei; ↘ 251 1145; f 251 1423. Positioned on the right as you enter Sal Rei from the airport. Large, bright, mostly balconied rooms and with a communal terrace offering views over Sal Rei to the sea. *Sgl 3,800$ B&B, 5,500$ FB; dbl 4,200$ B&B, 8,200$ FB; suites 5,300$ B&B, 8,700$ FB.*

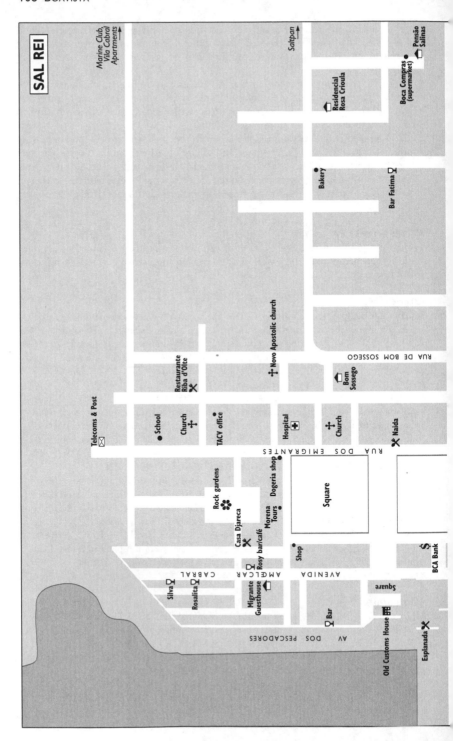

SAL REI

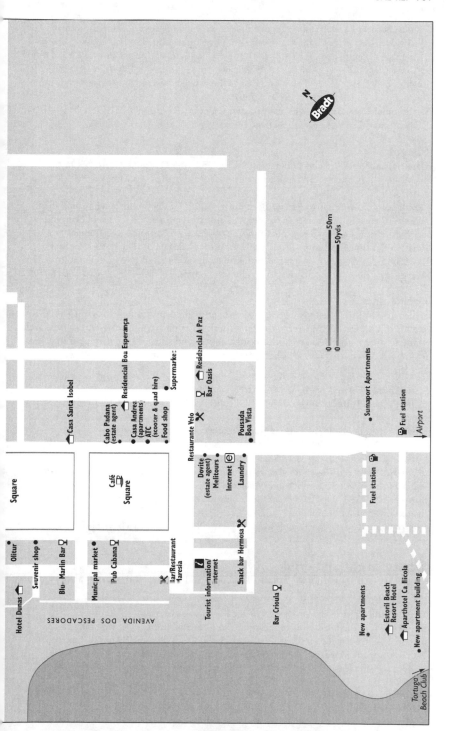

Hotel Dunas

Olitur

Souvenir shop

Square

Casa Santa Isobel

Blu Marlin Bar

Municipal market

Pub Cabana

Café Square

Cabo Padana (estate agent)

Residencial Boa Esperança

Casa Andrea (apartments)

ATC (scooter & quad hire)

Food shop

Supermarket

AVENIDA DOS PESCADORES

Bar/Restaurant Taresia

Tourist Information/Internet

Restaurante Velo

Residencial A Paz

Bar Oasis

Dovite (estate agent)

Melitours

Internet

Laundry

Snack bar Hermosa

Pousada Boa Vista

Bar Crioula

New apartments

Fuel station

Sumaport Apartments

Estoril Beach Resort Hotel

Aparthotel Ca Nicola

New apartment building

Fuel station

Airport

Tortuga Beach Club

50m
50yds

N

Bradt

Pensão Salinas Located east of the main part of town almost overlooking the saltpans; ✓f 251 1563, m 992 4854; e salinabvc@yahoo.it; www.boavista2000.com. The area is likely to develop significantly here. *Sgl 2,400–3,300$; dbl 3,500–6,100$; rates include breakfast and vary with season. The higher rates include HB. Weekly rates are available: sgl 120–172; dbl 172–259.*
Residencial A Paz Located just southeast of the main square and is associated with the Estoril Beach Hotel; ✱ 251 1078. *Dbl 3,500$.*
Residencial Rosa Crioula Located east of town near the bakery; ✱ 251 1786, m 992 7854. *For rates contact the Merceia bar in Rua Bom Sossego.*

Budget
Casa Santa Isobel Rua dos Emigrantes; ✱ 251 1252, m 992 7990; f 251 1625. On the inland side of the square and renovated, this was formerly the Casa Miranda. *Sgl 1,800$; dbl 2,700$.*
Residencial Bom Sossego Rua de Bom Sossego; ✱ 251 1155. In the block behind the church – the lively owner lives at Bar Sossego around the corner. A couple of bedrooms have verandas. *Sgl with bathroom 2,000$; dbl 2,000–2,500$. Higher rates include bathroom.*
Residencial Boa Esperança Rua Tavares Almeida; ✱ 251 1170. The hotel is located in the road east of the main square. It is proud to be the cheapest in town. Some rooms have shared bathrooms. It remains clean, friendly and homely. *Sgl 800–1,150$; dbl 1,000–1,550$.*

Apartments
Following in the footsteps of Sal, Boavista and the outer zones adjacent to Sal Rei are set to change beyond recognition in a short time. At the time of our research many new apartments were under construction and should be completed in a year. Many are for renting, while others will be for sale to foreigners. Below are some agencies to contact:

Casa Andrea For apts on the main square.
Cabo Padana Immobiliare Lda Largo S Isobel, Sal Rei; ✱ 251 1448; f 251 1577; www.cabopadana.com
Dovita Opposite the Pousada Boa Vista; e info@dovita.it; www.dovita.it
Imotur ✱ 251 1574, m 992 2357. They are constructing a vast apartment complex – Vila Cabral – on the road to the Marina Club near the Salinas, which will be offered for sale and to rent to foreigners. You could also try contacting their main office in Praia for details: ✱ 261 7652; f 261 76 53; e imotur@cvtelecom.cv.
Sumaport ✱ 251 1720/1781; www.cfs.cv. This is a new apartment complex for sale and rent on the road south of town.
Bovita Contact: Claudio Morlin; ✱ 251 1873, m 996 7581; e info@bovita.it; www.bovita.it. It also has apts.

Where to eat and drink
Apart from in the bigger hotels, finding food in Sal Rei is not always easy, particularly in the low seasons.

Bar Crioula Close to the beach west of the Hermosa snack bar.
Bar Naida On the inland side of the square. A local establishment serving rather basic food in a whitewashed yard with banana-leaf roof. Closed temporarily but due to reopen.
Bar Restaurant Maresia The only place open all the time during our visit in March. Good food and pleasant service. Starter 350$; egg & chips 300$; spaghetti 450$; fish 600$; dessert 250$.
Casa Djareca Local food at good prices, eaten in the family dining room. Order at least 2 hours beforehand. In Rua de Rego, a small road off the north of the square.
Esplanada Currently closed but may well reincarnate. Used to have live music on Fri and Sat.

Estoril Beach Serving a high standard of mainly local and Italian cuisine, inc pasta that is handmade on site, the restaurant is open all day and can be found in the hotel of the same name.

Hermosa This small snack bar serves all the traditional dishes all day and until midnight. Order 1–2 hours beforehand.

Hotel Dunas Restaurant in the hotel with live music various nights of the week.

Migrante At the hotel, but you may need to order in advance.

Pousada Boa Vista Restaurant may be open for lunch and dinner.

Restaurant Riba d'Olte m 992 4292. It looks like it will be a popular spot when it opens in season.

Restaurant Velo On the south of the square, has a reasonable offering and is open in the evenings.

Rosy bar/café Close to the Migrante Guesthouse. Serves drinks and light sustenance.

Tortuga Beach bar/café Open all day; in season there is more choice and live music most nights. Walk south along the beach south of town.

Other bars
Blue Marlin, Bar Oasis, Bar Sal Rei, Bar Fatima, Saturno

Nightlife
Crystal Disco Transport to this Rabil disco (see *Rabil*, page 113) generally materialises in the main square of Sal Rei at about 23.00–midnight. The *aluguer* drivers will sell you an all-in-one ticket to take you there, get entry, and transport you home afterwards.

Dancing Silva 'Seridja' A ground-floor bar and an upstairs area serving *cachupa*; sometimes empty, sometimes heaving. Doesn't warm up until 01.00; open Fri and Sat.

Practicalities
Airlines TACV; *open Mon–Fri 08.00–12.00, 14.30–17.00; Sat 09.00–11.00.*

Bank Banco Comercial do Atlântico; on the main square. *Open Mon–Fri 08.00–14.00.*

Hospital Beside the church, on the square; ` 251 1167. More a clinic than a hospital really.

Internet At the tourist information centre and opposite the Pousada Boa Vista.

Pharmacy Drogeria Rodrigues on the square

Police Av 5 de Julho; ` 251 1132. On the airport side of town.

Post office Open Mon–Fri 08.00–15.30; up the hill to the north of town, near the TACV office.

Shopping There is a few small craft and souvenir shops in a street west of the tourist information centre. There is a minimercado on the southeast corner of the square. You can (fortunately) buy fresh bread from the *padaria* east of the Bom Sossego bar in the mornings, and generally cheese and vegetables from the women at one corner of the square. A new supermarket close to the Hotel Salinas has tinned hot dogs, water and other basics.

Tourist information Try the information/internet centre listed on the map, or the 2 listed travel agencies, but don't expect maps and handouts.

What to see and do
For sporting activities see page 105.

In Sal Rei itself there is little to do of a non-sporting nature except soak up the atmosphere, or bask on the beach south of town. However, there are quite a few places to visit within walking distance of Sal Rei (or walking plus a short spell on public transport). These are listed below and can be visited individually or put together into hikes.

The chapel and the Ben'Oliel graves

These lie near the Marine Club which you reach by following the signs out of Sal Rei and across a brown wasteland – the sand-covered saltpans – on the hotel's incongruous road of concrete cobbles studded with toy-town street lights.

Before you reach the hotel, on the right, are the graves of the Jewish Ben'Oliel family, whofled here from the Moroccan persecution of the Jews in 1872. There is also the tomb of a young English woman, Julia Maria Pettingall, daughter of Charles Pettingall, who was one of the administrators of the Luso-British Commission. Julia was the 19-year-old victim of a plague of yellow fever that struck Boavista in the 1840s. She left with her family to the safety of another island, but her father later decided the threat had receded and returned to Boavista. He was wrong. Julia died in November 1845. While on board the boat returning to São Nicolau after her death, Pettingall himself died and later his daughter's fiancé died too.

Rejoining the road, go through the Marine Club (or along the cliffs to its left-hand side) and out the other end, by which time you will be able to see the ruins of the chapel and the path to it. Beside it there was once a house with steps leading down to the beach.

Islet of Sal Rei

This was the site of the fort of the Duque de Bragança, but little remains today. You should be able to persuade a fisherman to take you out there for a fee. You can swim there: the water is never deeper than 1.5m.

Chave beach

One of the most exhilarating beaches of Cape Verde, Chave lies to the south of Sal Rei and stretches for ever down the coast. The walk from Sal Rei is wonderful although the return journey can be a bit sand-blown. Two new developments have been initiated on the southern end of this beach. See *Rabil*, opposite.

Brick factory

This eerie building is slowly being submerged by the dunes. It takes just over an hour to walk to it down Estoril beach to the south, crossing Rabil Lagoon after about 35 minutes and continuing towards the chimney, which you will see poking out of the sand. There is a track leading inland from the factory to Rabil from where you can travel back to Sal Rei.

Rabil lagoon

The lagoon stretches between the airport road and the sea. The quickest way to reach it is to take an *aluguer* destined for the airport and ask to be deposited at the bridge (*ponte*), after about 3km. From the road, however, the lagoon looks rather uninviting, so it is better explored from the beautiful beach end. Birdwatchers have recorded sightings of many interesting migrants in the lagoon.

OTHER PLACES TO VISIT

The rest of Boavista is almost impossible to see except from a chartered vehicle or by hiring a quadbike and guide. It is a big place, and touring it all in a day is tiring. A good route is clockwise via Fundo das Figueiras and Curral Velho, north to the main road and then south again to Povoação Velha. Take local advice about the state of the track directly linking Curral Velho to Povoação Velha. Chartering a 4x4 for this trip may not be so easy, as many drivers are loath to take their vehicles along these tracks, some of which are atrocious.

Rabil

This was the capital of Boavista until the early 19th century. It is a bit short on attractions, but has a pottery open to visitors. Look inside the imposing church of Santo Roque, built in 1801. You can visit Rabil by *aluguer* (see *Getting around*, page 104) or as part of the hike on page 106. The canyon east of town is very Saharan in scenery, with palm trees and the dunes to the northeast adding to this feeling.

Where to stay

Parque das Dunas Village ❭ 251 1283/1288/1290; f 251 1339; e info@parquedasdunas.com; www.parquedasdunas.com. Located on the southern end of Chaves beach, south of the brick factory chimney, this is a quiet retreat with 28 villas slowly being improved, with shady trees and a good bar/restaurant area with large pool. Guests are warned to be very, very vigilant in the strong waves of the beach. At times sea bathing is too dangerous, so ask at reception before swimming. Turtles apparently visit the beach at certain times; ask the hotel to be sure when. Rates vary with season as follows: 32–45 (B&B),   43–57 (HB),   55–70 (FB).

A new complex, further south, is as yet incomplete and nameless, but it looks like being a large new tourist complex.

Where to eat and drink

Restaurante Sodade di nha Terra ❭ 251 1048. A large building with flight of steps in front.
Parque de Dunas Tourist complex to the south, about 25 minutes' walk from Rabil.
Bar Estrela When we visited, it appeared to be serving a private group.
Also **Bar Pinto, Bar Carmilo, Bar Lulucha**

Nightlife

Crystal Disco On the left before you reach town. Often popular with the folks from Sal Rei (see above). Open Sun nights.

There's also dancing at the **Belo Horizonte** and the **Tropical Nightclub** in town.

Povoação Velha

In the words of a Povoação Velha landlord: 'It's a slow place, this.' It doesn't look much, but a settlement has endured here for almost 500 years and today it has a sleepy appeal: old folk ruminate on doorsteps, dogs scratch in the sun and donkeys twitch their ears on street corners.

There are two main, parallel streets with a handful of shops. Both the Bar António and the Club di Africa will prepare food on request; they need about two hours' notice so you could place your order before you ascend Rocha Estância, and return to the village as the meal arrives on the table. See *Hikes*, page 116.

You can reach Povoação Velha from Sal Rei by *aluguer* – there's one at 13.00 and one at 16.00 – and hope to hitch back later in the day. Buses go only very early in the morning.

Praia de Santa Mónica

This beach is well worth a visit, but do come prepared, particularly if you are walking. You will need food, suncream and loads of water (see *Health*, page 66). In a 4x4, follow the road through Povoação Velha. After 6km a very rough track deposits you on the beach, named after the famous Californian strand. The Boavistan version is undeniably magnificent but a good deal bleaker.

Praia de Curralinho

This is a beautiful beach and, like Santa Mónica, is reasonably accessible – a two-hour walk from Povoação Velha. Don't expect ice cream kiosks – the most Curralinho beach offers is the possibility of shelter from the wind in the lee of rocky outcrops. Bring your own shade.

As you enter Povoação Velha on the main road, turn right by the bright-green school and head towards the hill that looks like a large slag heap. The track is uncobbled, but the surface stays good for 4–5km until you reach the sand. This is not the beginning of the beach – you are still about 3km away. The dunes can be crossed in a 4x4 but it takes an experienced driver. Beyond the dunes there is a dusty flat land, pock-marked with a reafforestation programme. Then, at last, is the sea. The shore is steep so take care when swimming.

Praia de Lacação

This can be reached by following the track from Santa Monica. It is more of the same, impossibly beautiful beach, but even further from drinking water.

Praia de Curral Velho

This beach is glorious but exposed and remote. Come prepared for a day in the desert. At 15km from the nearest civilisation, it is probably too far to attempt by foot. Curral Velho is, however, accessible by 4x4 from Povoação Velha, from Cabeço das Tarafes, or directly across the heart of the island from Sal Rei. This last route is 43km from town and takes just over an hour by jeep. On the road south from Rabil, bear left at the fork towards Fundo das Figueiras, and after about 1.5km, strike right on a track. For the next hour or so, you will feel as if you are driving across the surface of the moon, and then at last you will reach a T-junction near the coast. Turn right and, after about 300m, take the rough track down to the left through the deserted village of Curral Velho. Then head round to the right of the salt lagoon until the track runs out at the back of the dunes. Beside the date palms and immediately up the dunes in front are the petrified remains of a forest. Beyond is a blindingly white beach, with extensive, Sahara-like dunes to your right, providing the unwary motorist with ample opportunity to get stuck.

There is only one islet in the whole of the eastern Atlantic where the magnificent frigatebird or *rabil* (*Fregata magnificens*) deigns to breed. You can see that islet ahead: Ilhéu de Curral Velho. Watch out for the bird with its long, slim, black wings that have a span of 2.5m. The female has a white breast and the male's is red. There are thought to be about only ten left.

Bofareira and Espingueira

If you have hired a 4x4 for the day, and are looking for a taste of another type of desolation and a visit to a remote but inhabited village, then this long detour is worth making.

After leaving Sal Rei, bear left at the fork south of Rabil and take the road to João Galego. After about 11km turn left at the small, incongruous shrine to the Virgin Mary at the side of the road. Stay on the cobbled track and after 20 minutes you emerge at the tiny village of Bofareira. This place is serviced by a daily *aluguer* but there is not much else happening – there's a shop and a telephone box. The focal point of the village is the standpipe, when there's any water (it all has to be tankered in from Sal Rei).

From the Bofareira road it is possible to get to the shore: about 4km from the village take the rough track which resembles the bed of a river to the coast and the ruined village of Espingueira. There is a small fishing camp out on the point.

TURTLE ISLAND

Turtle-watchers have been astonished to discover in recent years that there are huge numbers of turtles around Boavista. Now they think that Cape Verde may play host to the world's fourth-largest population of turtles (after North Carolina, Libya and Oman).

They are also anxious that development on Boavista should be done sensitively, leaving crucial beaches in their isolated state so that turtles can get on with their lifestyles undisturbed.

Researchers spent a summer on a Boavista beach in 1998 tagging loggerhead turtles (*Caretta caretta*): they counted 92. The following year they changed beaches to what they now think is the island's biggest nesting beach: they tagged 500–600. In 2000, another 1,000 were spotted and tagged.

'We were surprised,' says Pedro Lopez, a biologist working for Dr Luis Felipe López, who runs the turtle project.

The main nesting areas are on the east coast and the mother turtles go there from late May to late October. Once they have laid their eggs they disappear, leaving the hatchlings to fend for themselves. When the baby turtles emerge from their eggs in late August to late December, they make for the sea. It is thought that the glimmering surface of the ocean is what attracts them – hence the fears that lights from houses and hotels could cause them to head inland instead.

'As soon as we see a turtle coming ashore we lie on the ground and crawl. After she is on her way back to the sea, we put a chip in the turtle and ID attached with tags on the flippers,' says Pedro.

The loggerhead is categorised as endangered. The hawksbill (*Eretmochelys imbricata*), which is critically endangered, also feeds at the islands. The green turtle (*Chelonia mydas*), which is endangered, calls at the islands, as do the leatherback (*Dermochhelys coriacea*) and the olive ridley (*Lepidochelys olivacea*).

Looking west along the beach there is a good view of the hulk of the *Santa Maria* – for details of how to visit the wreck, see page 117.

João Galego, Fundo das Figueiras, Cabeço das Tarafes

Rejoining the main road at the Virgin Mary, and continuing southeast, you come to these three villages strung out at the fertile end of a *ribeira*. After the flat, dry plain you have crossed from Rabil, it is refreshing to be near vegetation again. These villages enjoy modest renown as the source of delicious goat's cheese.

João Galego has a smattering of shops, a bar (Moirasa Bar) and a nightclub. In Fundo das Figueiras, a few kilometres further on, there are shops and a snack bar (Bons-Irmãos). If you phone ahead to Gracinda at the Tiéta Restaurant (✆ 252 1111) you can order food in advance.

Baia das Gatas

The bay is a 15-minute drive by 4x4 along a reasonable track 7km from Fundo das Figueiras. The bay is named after the tiger sharks that have been seen from the point. There is a small, semi-permanent fishing camp here, with racks of salted fish hung out to dry. The fishermen will let you have a piece very cheaply – it is probably best to strap it outside the vehicle on the way home. You can see dolphins here.

The largest of the islets in the bay is Ilhéu dos Pássaros, home to the white-faced storm petrel or *pedreiro-azul* (*Pelagodroma marina*). Travel to the islets is prohibited.

Dolphin graveyard

Here lie the bones of nature's equivalent of the Boavista shipwrecks. They litter the sand near Morre Negro which is alleged to have magnetic properties that draw dolphins and whales to their deaths. Ask for directions at Fundo das Figueiras.

HIKES
Sal Rei–Estoril beach–Rabil lagoon–Estância de Baixo–Rabil

Distance: 10km (18km if done as circular walk); time: 3 hours (circular walk: 5 hours); difficulty: 1 (AI)

This walk begins down the beach and over disorientating high dunes with views over the sea, inland up a bird-filled lagoon and up a silent *ribeira* filled with *tamareira* trees and surrounded by sand hills. There's a hill to ascend up to Rabil but in general it is a flat and easy walk. At Rabil it should be possible to organise transport back to Sal Rei – the alternative is to walk.

Go to the beach at Sal Rei and turn left (south), following the coast. After ten minutes you'll pass Tortuga Beach Resort, where you can pick up a drink and watch people skidding across the bay.

Set off again south, walking up the dunes until you reach a disorientating world composed of nothing but expanses of hard-packed white sand. From those high dunes there is a vertical drop to the beach below and superb views of the cobalt sea and the islet of Sal Rei. There are often whales in the bay and you may spot turtles on the beach. Further on you will see the black masts of a shipwreck poking out of the water.

Half an hour from the windsurfers is the lagoon. All you can hear is the waves, the wind on the dunes and, increasingly, the tweets of a multiplicity of birds who thrive on the salty water. The mud is covered in millions of their footprints.

Walk inland up the side of the lagoon. If you choose the left side then ascend a great beer-belly of a dune and after that follow your instinct – there is no path and sometimes you must leave the lagoon edge out of sight in order to find a way between the thick trees. After 20 minutes is a rough track to the main Sal Rei–Rabil road. Follow the road south as far as the bridge and then clamber down into the *ribeira* on the landward side and follow it inland.

It is a broad, dry riverbed full of *tamareira* trees (*Phoenix atlantica*), a speciality of Boavista. After the rain it is lush, full of grass and small plants. The *ribeira* is hauntingly quiet except for the sounds of goats and the occasional child on a donkey collecting water.

The *ribeira* broadens and turns to the right; at times it must be 200m wide. Soon you are between two ridges – inland the hills look as if they are covered in snow with just the tips of plants poking through. Always stay where the trees are thickest. To the left appears a cliff with the village of **Estância de Baixo** on top. Keep well away from that side of the *ribeira* and stick to the right until, eventually, you see Rabil church, on the ridge; tracks lead up to it.

From Rabil you may find transport back to Sal Rei or you can walk down to the airport (look for the windsock), before beginning the 8km trek back to town, hopefully picking up a lift on the way. If you want to walk, it's more scenic to take the old road, which begins after the main road crosses the *ribeira*, and goes straight on where the main road bends to the left.

Sal Rei–Wreck of the *Santa Maria*–Sal Rei

Distance: 14km (alternative route: 16km); time: 4¹/₂ hours (alternative route: 5 hours); difficulty: 1 (CW)

The old hulk of the *Santa Maria* dominates the beach to the north of the island and is within walking distance of Sal Rei. Looking northeast out of town from a high point you will see a ridge – and it lies over that. There are two routes for this walk, which could be mixed to produce a round trip.

There are two ways to get there. The first route is an 18km round trip overland. Head south out of town towards Rabil and just past the small houses at the edge of town you will see the old road to Rabil branching off on your left. It was abandoned because it was considered to be too undulating. Follow the old road for about 2km until a left turning. Take this rough track for about 7km, or until you hit the beach where you cannot miss the wreck.

The second route is from the Marine Club. At Julia Pettingall's grave, turn inland behind the Marine Club and up over the shoulder. The track will eventually lead down the other side of the headland on to the beach at its western end. If you don't want to go by foot (it is not particularly scenic) you will need a 4x4 for this track. About 7km from the Marine Club you will have to get out and walk anyway, as the track peters out just above the beach in a haphazard rock quarry: the calcareous stone here has been used for some years by wealthy Boavistans to face their houses. The wreck is clearly visible – about half an hour's walk along the beach. Just before it, in a low cliff which has been eroded by the sea, are the twisted roots of a petrified forest.

Santo António (379m)

(CW)

From the waterfront at Sal Rei, Santo António can be seen on the left. Take an *aluguer* towards **Povoação Velha** and disembark at the point which seems closest to the mountain. The castellation near the summit means that it cannot be ascended from this side, so cross the rough ground to the mountain (past the men breaking rocks) and skirt round its north side, past some small ruins, before beginning the ascent from the east, which is straightforward.

Rocha Estância (354m)

(CW)

From the waterfront at Sal Rei, Rocha Estância is on the right, with the antennae on top. There are two routes to the summit. The first involves a scramble. Go straight out of the back of the village of **Povoação Velha** near the Bar di Africa, and strike slightly up to the right towards the saddle. Once on the saddle, head left towards the summit. Alternatively, go towards the church on the low ridge to your right as you are looking north at the mountain, and then follow the shoulder up to the left. It is longer this way but more gentle.

For a less arduous walk around the base of the mountain, continue past the church and go round the *rocha's* north side. It is not possible to reach the summit from this side.

Pico Estância (390m)

Time: 2¹/₂ hours (CW)

At 390m this is the highest of Boavista's peaks. From Curral Velho take the track cast towards **Cabeço das Tarafes**. The route, which is very poor, eventually turns inland at a *ribeira* where there are some scrubby bushes and date palms. Some 3.5km from the T-junction at **Curral Velho** there is a regular, well-built lime kiln a few metres in diameter. This is the place to stop the car and start walking.

Santiago

The delirium of the drums of the batuque
   echoing!
Santiago sluggards
Twisting their bodies,
Causing spasms
   In the wombs
At the heat of the rhythm of the
   Do batuque drums
– this ancestral dance!…
memories and screams are still alive in the
   tabancas
And the spirits
Of the invisible grandparents
   From Guinea!
   In the city
The children play
In the cemented pavement of the garden
And men walk around it in
Small groups
Whispering about politics …
…In the air lies this dull
tiredness
of the tropical heat.

Jorge Barbosa, born on Santiago island, 1902

Among the extremes of the Cape Verdean archipelago – the desert islands and the islands so mountainous there is barely a scrap of level ground – Santiago stands out as the normal relation. It is more balanced, more varied and more wholesome. At its heart are craggy mountains cut into exotic outlines and afforested on their lower slopes. Sliced in between are green valleys alive with agriculture. To the south lie irrigated plantations; to the southwest a sterile and gravelly landscape where nothing grows; and in the north and southeast there are some beautiful beaches.

In Santiago the black and the white ingredients of the archipelago's past are at their most vivid. On the southern shore is the old capital of Cape Verde – Ribeira Grande – the first European city in the tropics. But up in the mountains the people are as African as Cape Verdeans can be – their ancestors were escaped slaves from the city below.

HIGHLIGHTS
Go for history in Cidade Velha; music in Praia; a limited number of rewarding hikes; beach-lounging – there are two top-quality beaches, one with facilities, one without.

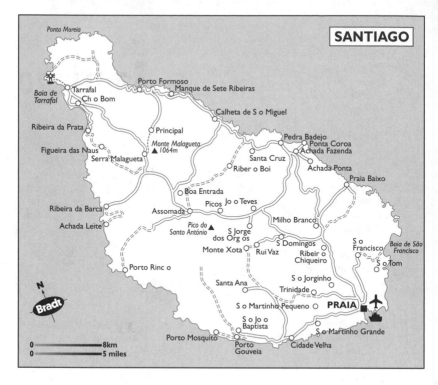

There is some diving and game fishing. Santiago has some surf spots but most surfers choose other islands. Sightseeing can occupy several days – this is the only island with a lively hinterland. For birdwatchers, most of the endemic species are here.

BACKGROUND INFORMATION
History
Santiago *was* Cape Verde for hundreds of years. It was here that the two discoverers of the islands, António de Noli and Diogo Gomes, together with a small group of settlers from the Algarve in Portugal, set up in 1462. Their town grew and the business of resupplying ships and trading in slaves flourished. The other islands, except for Fogo, remained unexplored or were exploited merely for salt or grazing. Even today, inhabitants of Santiago refer to the island as Cabo Verde – as if it was the mainland – and to the other islands as just that: '*as Ilhas*'.

Yet from early on Santiago was also a centre of dissent. Its links to west Africa were strong. The *rebelados* and other African renegades escaped miscegenation and lived isolated lives in the interior where they remembered their ancestral tribes. In the 20th century, rebellion stirred primarily in São Nicolau and São Vicente yet Santiago too had its uprisings – and produced the islands' first great poet and dissenter, Jorge Barbosa.

The Portuguese spelling São Tiago (St James) died out early on in favour of the Spanish spelling used today.

Geography
The largest island in the archipelago, at 990km², Santiago has two mountain ranges: the Serra do Pico do António, which rises to a peak of 1,392m, and the more

JEWS IN CAPE VERDE

Wander round some of the magnificently positioned graveyards in Cape Verde and you will notice that many of the headstones bear distinctly Jewish names: Benros, Lopes, Mendez, Cardoso and Levy for example. Some of the words on older headstones are even in Hebrew. Jews have a long history on Cape Verde and were a major cultural and genetic ingredient in Creole culture. Most of the Jews who washed up on Cape Verde's islands were Portuguese exiles escaping the Inquisition, or forced to work there and in other Portuguese colonies as *degredados*. On the Rivers of Guinea they became trading intermediaries.

Santiago Island was the first to receive Jews though they were banished to a ghetto in Praia. There are Jewish graves there (now engulfed by the expanding cemetery they were originally buried outside) and in Cidade Velha. Jews reached Boavista early on.

In the 1820s some fled from Portugal to the mountains of Santo Antão and became leading traders: there is a village in the northeast named Sinagoga and a Jewish cemetery at Ponta do Sol. Another influx of Jews came from Morocco in the 19th and early 20th centuries. There are also Jewish graves in Brava, at Cova da Judeu. (See *Further reading*, page 268.)

northern Serra da Malagueta. There are lush valleys in the centre and several permanent sources of water. Some 240,000 people live here – about 120,000 in Praia, the capital.

The volcanic rocks on Santiago are 4–5 million years old while the rocks from the sea floor are older, at 8.5–9.5 million years. An important feature of Praia's landscape is the *achadas* (elevated plains) on which the different districts of the city are built. Santiago is the principal agricultural producer of Cape Verde.

Festivals

The most important festivals are the Tabanka processions in June and July (see *Perspective*, page 28). The Festival of Nossa Senhora da Graça, the first patron saint of Praia, is held on 15 August. Others celebrated throughout Santiago are as follows:

Municipality Day	15 January (Tarrafal)
Nho Fenrero Festival	2 February (São Domingos)
Ashes Day	The Wednesday after Carnival
Municipality Day	13 March (São Domingos)
São Salvador do Mundo	15 days after Easter (Picos)
São Jorge	23 April
São Jose	1 May
São Miguel Arcanjo Feast	8 May (Ribeira Calheta de São Miguel)
Nossa Sta De Fatima	13 May (Assomada)
Imaculada Conceiceo	31 May
Nossa Sta Do Socorro	15 August
Municipality Day	25 November (Santa Caterina area)

GETTING THERE AND AWAY

Santiago is a hub of the archipelago and thus easy to get to. The international airport in Praia (✆ *263 3380*) should improve this further when it opens.

By air

Please note that this information will change when the new, international airport opens, not far from the current one. Long-haul flights from Europe will be able to land at Praia.

The airport has a café. Taxi drivers crowd the airport exit but there is little hassle: just go to the head of the line. Even then arguments can develop between the drivers over who 'owns' you. The fare to town is 200–300$, depending on your destination. It is possible to walk the 2km.

International flights

Planes from the African mainland – Senegal, Guinea-Bissau and The Gambia – generally land at Praia. See *Practical information*, page 42. **Air Senegal** has an office in Praia; see below.

Internal flights

Regular inter-island flights with TACV link Santiago with:

Sal	Several every day
São Vicente	2 or 3 a day
Fogo	2 or 3 a day
Maio	4 a week
Boavista	3 a week, and daily via Sal
São Nicolau	A few a week, via São Vicente

By ferry

The port is at the northern end of the harbour. Taxis there or back cost 200$. The *Tarrafal* runs from Santiago to São Vicente and São Nicolau twice a week and the *Barlavento* to Brava and Fogo. For further information try the following:

ANAV Shipping CP 58, Rua Serpa Pinto; ☏ 261 7858/260 3100; f 261 2162; e anavpraia@cvtelecom.cv

Polar Shipping CP 120, Rue Candido dos Reis, Praia Plateau; also try Rua Serpa Pinto 141; ☏ 261 5223/5225/7177/7224; f 261 4132; e polarp@cvtelecom.cv. Contact them for existing options and for further information about new ferries planned in the future,

SAMPLE TIMETABLE PRAIA–FOGO–BRAVA

Day	From–To	Dep	Arr
Monday	Praia–Brava	23.00	07.00
Tuesday	Brava–Fogo	13.00	14.00
Wednesday	Fogo–Brava	08.00	09.00
	Brava–Fogo	15.00	16.00
	Fogo–Praia	19.00	03.00
Thursday	Praia–Fogo	23.30	07.00
Friday	Fogo–Brava	14.00	15.00
	Brava–Fogo	19.00	20.00
Saturday	Fogo–Brava	08.00	09.00
	Brava–Fogo	15.00	16.00
	Fogo–Praia	19.00	03.00
Sunday	No service		

Note that this timetable is given as a sample only and is highly likely to change.

possibly a high-speed catamaran service. They are very helpful. A company called Moura may be the operator of this new catamaran service.

Cabo Verde Shipping Agency ↘ 261 1179; f 261 3913; e csa.rai@cvtelecom.cv

Viagens Cabo Verde Also on Rue Candido dos Reis, for shipping.

Cargo vessels Between Praia and São Vicente.

By yacht

Praia provides a well-sheltered harbour, where yachts are asked to anchor in the west between the two jetties. It is essential to follow all the entry procedures, whether or not this is your first stop in Cape Verde: port captain and immigration office; on departure get clearance again from the port captain. Yacht facilities are poor. There is no boatyard or chandlery. Fuel and water have to be collected by can. The next-best anchorage is Tarrafal, at the north of the island. Visit the harbour office on arrival. Other anchorages are at Ribeira da Barca (but there is swell and northeast winds funnelling off the island).

> The sea
> You enlarge our dreams
> and suffocate our desires
>
> Jorge Barbosa, born on Santiago island, 1902

GETTING AROUND
By public transport

Aluguers travel up and down the spine of the island – the road between Praia and Tarrafal – all day and evening. Villages down the west coast are reached on roads extending from this central spine, so catch one of these *aluguers* and change at the relevant junction. Aluguers are also frequent along the slower, eastern coastal road between Praia and Tarrafal. They all leave from the Sucupira market west of the Plateau. For Cidade Velha there are regular *aluguers* leaving from Terra Branca in Praia, southwest of the Plateau. Sucupira market is a noisy melée of drivers and their assistants trying to get you to choose their *aluguers*. Pick the one with the most people inside, as they don't leave until they are full.

A grey-haired driver may be a safer bet than most.

By taxi

There are many taxis in Praia, marked and unmarked, and a journey within town costs 150–200$, sometimes 300$ (especially after 23.00). Particularly with unmarked taxis, agree the price beforehand. A taxi for the day costs about 7,000$.

Eurotaxi ↘ 262 6000. A 24-hour taxi service which appears to be very reliable.

Taxi Lopez ↘ 262 1043

Car hire

There is quite a choice in Praia. Remember that only a 4x4 can take you on the dirt tracks down to the west coast.

Abreu In Fazenda district; ↘ 261 2757

Alucar At the Hotel America

Atlantico In Prainha; ↘ 261 6424

As the Best In Varzea; ↘ 261 5409

Autobraza In Fazenda ; ↘ 261 6352

Avis At the Hotel Oasis Praia-Mar in Prainha; ↘ 261 8748. Sample prices: 6,900$ per day for a small car or 6,268$ per day for 4 days.

TRACING THE ANCESTORS

Romantic stories abound of brave Cape Verdean men who risked their lives to sail across the Atlantic and find fortune for themselves and their families in the USA. But these days, many Cape Verdeans in the USA have lost track of their personal family histories. They may have a forgotten great, great grandfather who toiled on whaling ships on the wild ocean, risking his life to harpoon whales, earn promotion and set up life on the east coast. They may be descended from a couple of lost generations who worked themselves to the bone in the cranberry bogs of New England, returning home with their earnings at the end of each season. You may be descended from a young man who left his sweetheart on Fogo; you may own a stone cottage or great *sobrado* house, now standing forgotten on Brava.

Of all the Africans who went to the USA in the era of mass migration, Cape Verdean Americans are the only ones who can trace their families back to their original villages, according to James Lopes, author of a genealogy website (*www.umassd.edu/specialprograms/caboverde/jlopes.html*). This is because there are excellent records of Cape Verdean arrivals in the USA. Those who have made the journey of rediscovery often find they have relatives, or ancestors, from all over the world, including Europe, Asia, and South America.

To decipher your family tree, begin by questioning your immediate family,

Classic Auto Rental In Achada Sto António, Praia; ↘ 262 1808; e rentcarclassic@cvtelecom.cv
Ferreira Cars In Plateau; ↘ 261 6949
Gomescar & Filho In Achada Sto António; ↘ 262 2018
HR Rental In Prainha; ↘ 261 8260
Hertz At the Hotel Pestana Tropico in Prainha; ↘ 261 4200
Oasis Motor In Grande Frente; ↘ 263 5143
Pajero Sport In Prainha; has racy vehicles: 9,715$ per day or 8,910$ a day for 3 days
Rentmavetra In Chas d'Areia; ↘ 161 3834
Tecnorent In Fazenda; ↘ 261 9393

In nearby Assomada, try the following:

Garagem Monteiro ↘ 265 1351
Veiga Car ↘ 265 4590

ACTIVITIES
Excursions

Try the following operators for guided tours to highlights of the island:

G and S Schellmann Viagens dos Sonhos, CP 36, Ponto de Calhetona, Calheta do S Miguel; ↘ 273 2240, m 996 7930; www.reisetraeume.de or www.reisetraeume.de/kapverden/viadoso/index.html. They are specialists in hiking tours on Santiago.
Cabetur Rua Serpa Pinto 4, CP 318; ↘ 261 5551/2; f 260 0686; e cabetur@cvtelecom.cv; www.cabetur.com. This is one of the larger agencies, with offices in Tarrafal, Santiago, on São Vicente, and on Sal at the airport and in Santa Maria.
Executive Tour Av Lisboa, Fazenda; ↘ 261 7837; f 261 7839; e executiv@cvtelecom.cv
Hotel Marisol Travel Desk m 991 6719; f 261 3273; e servicos_turismo@hotmail.com. They offer tours to Tarrafal via São Domingos, Picos and Santa Caterina; 8 persons 1,100$ each, 14 persons 700$ each.

advises Mr Lopes. Write down everything you unearth – in particular the dates of birth, marriage and death of each remembered person, and how they made a living. Then, when a particularly dim but fascinating figure emerges from the past, there are several sources to help you investigate. For those whose families went to the USA before 1920 the arrival should have been recorded in the passenger and ships lists of the Port of New Bedford. Most Cape Verdeans passed through there, though Boston and Providence were other ports of entry.

The voyages of all Cape Verdean whaling ships are also listed, and kept in New Bedford Free Public Library (see *Further reading* for contact details).

One mine of fascinating information is the Old Dartmouth Historical Society at the New Bedford Whaling Museum (*New Bedford, MA 02740, USA*). The original logbooks of many of the whaling expeditions that took Cape Verdeans to the USA are stored here. Details of the trip, including how much your ancestor was paid, might be found.

There are several other useful places to begin digging, including the Arquivo Historico Nacional in Santiago (see *Further reading*). Staff there will research birth records on request. For more information on where to search, see James Lopes's website, above.

Finally, Marilyn Halter's book *Race and Ethnicity* gives spellbinding accounts of life in the cranberry bogs and other features of the emigrante life.

Orbitur Av Amílcar Cabral, Praia; ↘ 261 5737
Mundialtur In Achada Santo António; ↘ 261 6339
Novatur Av Lisboa, CP 80; ↘ 261 8424; f 261 8344; e ognovatur@hotmail.com
Praiatur Av Amílcar Cabral 36, CP 470; ↘ 261 5746/7; f 261 4500;
e praiatur.lda@cvtelecom.cv. Open 08.00–12.00, 14.00–16.30; does 1-day tour of Santiago; half-day or full-day tour of Cidade Velha; trip to Praia Baixo for swimming and lunch. Price per person drops considerably for groups of 5 or more.
Tropictours Next to the Hotel Praia Maria; ↘ 261 1240/5012; f 261 1253. Sells air tickets.
Verdeantours Rua Serpa Pinto; ↘ 261 3979

Hiking
The interior of Santiago is filled with spectacular craggy mountains, *ribeiras* and plantations. Though it does not have the breath-catching drama of Santo Antão, or the sheer strangeness of Fogo, it has walks that are beautiful and rewarding, for which it is definitely worth putting aside some time. Many walks consist of finding a point along the spine of the island and walking down a *ribeira* to the coast (or vice versa). The big hike is to the top of Pico do Santo António – a twin peak that protrudes from the landscape like a canine tooth. Unfortunately the path to the Pico is not clear, the final ascent borders on the hazardous and knowledgeable guides are hard to find. See *Health*, page 66, for advice on hiking.

Fishing
You can link up with local fishermen in almost any village – pay them about 1,000$ if they take you out on one of their trips. See *Practical information*, page 37, for a discussion of fishing.

Diving
This is only possible in Tarrafal at present.

Surfing

There are some reasonable surfing spots in Santiago, though it is not worth coming to Cape Verde especially for them. The swell is best between January and March.

In Tarrafal, a short walk southwest from the main bay, there are some reef breaks, in particular at Ponta do Atum and at Chão Bom. The other well-known spots are in the southeast of the island: the coast south of Ponta do Lobo lighthouse which marks the easternmost point of Santiago (accessible only by 4x4) and the local bodyboarding beach at Praia itself, just in front of the Plateau. See *Practical information*, page 35, for general surfing information.

PRAIA

Built on a tableland of rock, with the city overflowing on to the land below its steep cliffs, the centre of Praia is attractive. It has a disorientating feel: it is indisputably African and yet Mediterranean as well. During the day, people of every shade of skin go about their business. At night, though, the plateau is empty – life continues in the scattered regions beyond. To its south rises another level plain, the Achada Santo António, where the more affluent live in apartment blocks and where the huge parliament building is. Between the two lies Chã de Areia, and, behind Achada, Prainha, where there are embassies, expensive hotels and nightclubs. Other districts include Terra Branca to the west and Fazenda district to the north. Palmarejo is a new, upmarket residential area to the southwest. To the northwest is a huge sprawl of half-built houses and burning litter – Cape Verde's version of the urban drift from the countryside.

History

From the early 1600s, Portugal tried both to entice and to force its citizens to make Praia da Santa Maria their capital instead of Ribeira Grande (now Cidade Velha). But the colonisers ignored instructions and stuck to their preferred settlement, 13km away. By ignoring Praia, they left themselves open to attack from behind: Praia, with its poorly fortified beaches, was a place where pirates could land. From there it was an easy overland march to attack the capital.

This happened on two disastrous occasions. Francis Drake (see pages 10–11) used the tactic in 1585 and the Frenchman Jacques Cassart did exactly the same more than a century later in 1712. After the first assault the population built the fort, which survives to this day. The second sacking signalled the demise of Ribeira Grande as investment was made in the fortification of Praia. Its shacks were replaced by permanent buildings and it grew. By 1770 it was the official capital achieving, in 1858, the rank of *cidade*. Today Praia remains the administrative centre while culture seems to gravitate towards Mindelo.

One of Praia's most distinguished visitors was Charles Darwin, who anchored there at the start of his famous voyage on the *Beagle* on 16 January 1832, and spent

THE LINDBERGHS

Charles and Anne Morrow Lindbergh, the famous aviators, arrived in Praia while trying to circumnavigate the North Atlantic. The plane was called the *Tingmissartoq* ('big flying bird' in a Greenland Inuit language). They took six hours to come from Morocco, arriving on 27 November 1933. They were not impressed with the island, which Anne said was 'boring'. In Santiago they recalculated their course and returned to the African mainland, deciding instead to attempt the transatlantic leg to Brazil from The Gambia.

some time examining the flora and fauna, as well as making forays to Cidade Velha and São Domingos. He reported that he 'feasted' upon oranges and 'likewise tasted a Banana: but did not like it, being maukish and sweet with little flavour'. He wandered through a valley near Praia:

> Here I saw the glory of tropical vegetation: Tamarinds, Bananas and Palms were flourishing at my feet. I expected a good deal, for I had read Humboldt's descriptions, and I was afraid of disappointments: how utterly vain such fear is, none can tell but those who have experienced what I today have. It is not only the gracefulness of their forms or the novel richness of their colours. It is the numberless and confused associations that rush together on the mind, and produce the effect. I returned to the shore, treading on Volcanic rocks, hearing the notes of unknown birds, and seeing new insects fluttering about still newer flowers… It has been for me a glorious day, like giving to a blind man eyes, he is overwhelmed with what he sees and cannot justly comprehend it.

He also wrote about the more barren slopes of Cape Verde:

> A single green leaf can scarcely be discovered over wide tracts of the lava plains; yet flocks of goats, together with a few cows, contrive to exist. It rains very seldom, but during a short portion of the year heavy torrents fall, and immediately afterwards a light vegetation springs out of every crevice. This soon withers; and upon such naturally formed hay the animals live. It had not now rained for an entire year. When the island was discovered, the immediate neighbourhood of Porto Praya was clothed with trees, the reckless destruction of which has caused here, as at St Helena and at some of the Canary islands, almost entire sterility.

Where to stay
It is advisable to book ahead if possible, particularly outside of Praia itself.

Upmarket
Hotel Pestana Trópico CP 413; ↘ 261 4200; f 261 5225;
e hotel.tropico@cvtelecom.cv; www.pestana.com. On the coast road in Prainha, the 4-star Trópico is the most luxurious hotel in town. With 47 rooms and 4 suites, it is a good choice for business travellers, with conference room and internet facilities. Spacious, pleasing and well-equipped rooms, all with AC, minibar, cable TV and hair dryer, are arranged around a seawater swimming pool and new bar. The restaurant has an excellent reputation for its food, and expatriates visiting from other islands come especially for its steaks. Restaurant meals: steaks or pork from 12; fish 12–15. An extremely helpful and friendly place with excellent management. Sgl 9,800$; dbl 12,000$; triple 13,650$; suite 18,000$.
Hotel Oasis Atlantico/Praia-Mar CP 75; ↘ 261 4153; f 261 2972;
e reservas@oasisatlantico.com; www.oasisatlantico.com. Attractive, low-rise hotel on the headland of Prainha with plenty of space for terraces and balconies, as well as a swimming pool and tennis court. Sgl 10,800–12,700$; dbl 13,450–15,880$; suite 17,100–28,450$. Half board plus 15, FB plus 27.

There's also talk of one forthcoming venture: **Hotel Santiago Golf Club and Resort** (*Calada São Martinho, CP 157-A;* ↘ *262 8321;* f *262 8356;* e *santiago-golf@cvtelecom.cv*). This complex seeks to transform a vast area of rocky shore and barren land into an upmarket resort with a white sand beach. Despite

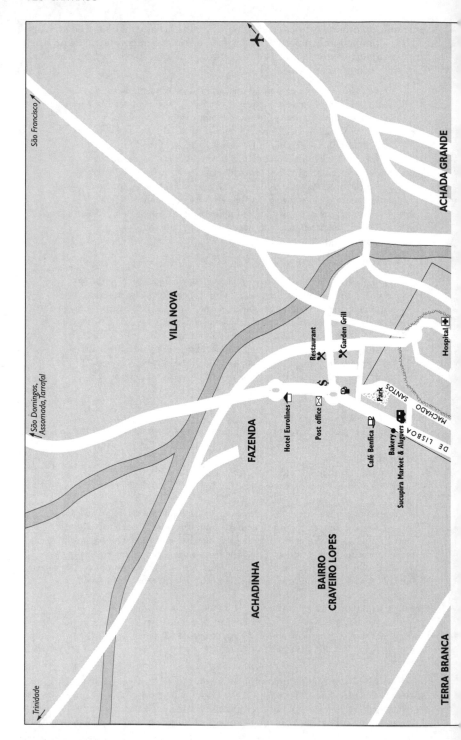

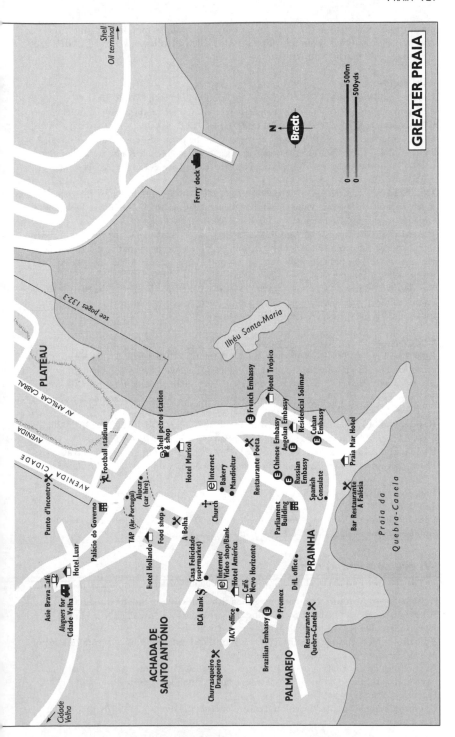

GREATER PRAIA

Shell
Oil terminal

Ferry dock

N

0 ____ 500m
0 ____ 500yds

see Pages 132-3

PLATEAU

AV AMÍLCAR CABRAL

AVENIDA

AVENIDA CIDADE

Punto d'Incontro

Football stadium

Shell petrol station
& shop

Palácio do Governo

TAP (Air Portugal)

Alucar
(car hire)

Hotel Marisol

Internet
Bakery
Mandioltur

Church

Restaurante Poeta

Hotel Luar

Asie Brava Café

Aluguers for
Cidade Velha

ACHADA DE
SANTO ANTÓNIO

Hotel Hollande

Food shop

A Bolha

Casa Felicidade
(supermarket)

BCA Bank

Internet/
Video shop/Bank

Hotel América

Café
Novo Horizonte

TACV office

Promex

D+L office

Brazilian Embassy

Churrasqueiro
Drageiro

Restaurante
Quebra-Canela

PALMAREJO

PRAINHA

Parliament
Building

Russian
Embassy

Spanish
Consulate

Bar Restaurante
A Falésia

French Embassy

Chinese Embassy

Angolan Embassy

Cuban
Embassy

Residencial Solimar

Hotel Trópico

Praia Mar Hotel

Ilhéu Santa-Maria

Praia da
Quebra-Canela

Cidade
Velha

Bradt

continuous advertising for this project, it was still suspended at the time of research. A Portuguese contact address is also listed as follows: f +351 213 019 928; e santiagogolfresort@hotmail.com.

Mid range

Residencial Praia Maria CP 27-A; Rua 5 de Julho; ❧ 261 8580; f 261 8554; e res.praiamaria@cvtelecom.cv; www.praiamaria.com. A bright and fresh 3-star hotel with large rooms. *Sgl 4,200–6,000$; dbl 5,200–7,000$; triple 6,500–8,000$.*

Hotel América CP 55/A; A little out of the way, in the peace of Achada Santo António; ❧ 262 1431/1527; f 262 1527/1432; e hotel_america@cvtelecom.cv. It is a bright and modern hotel, all rooms with fridge, TV and AC. Look for 'Club Love es terra' here. *Sgl 4,500$; dbl 5,500$; suite 7,200$.*

Hotel Luar CP 88; ❧ 261 5947/6019/6024; f 261 6038. In Terra Branca near where public transport leaves for Cidade Velha, this is an acceptable 3-star hotel. Rooms overlooking the entrance are quieter. Restaurant. *Sgl 3,550–4,700$ (AC); dbl 4,650–5,800$ (AC).*

Hotel Felicidade Rua Serpa Pinto/Rua Andrade Corvo; ❧ 261 5585/260 0246; f 261 5584; e felicidade@cvtelecom.cv. Centrally positioned on the Plateau, above the supermarket of the same name, its entrance is in the street east of the supermarket. All rooms have AC and have recently been upgraded. *Sgl 4,800$; dbl 6,000$.*

Residencial Solimar ❧ 261 8549, m 997 5769/991 2939; f 261 9868. On the coast road leading to the headland at Prainha, this is a shiny, new establishment; rooms have AC, fridge and TV. *Sgl 4,230$; dbl 5,300$; inc breakfast.*

Budget

Aparthotel Holanda CP 59-A, Rua C Saúde; ❧ 262 3973; f 262 3839. Up in Achada Santo António, this distinctive and attractive hotel is filled with the owner's sculptures. Its restaurant with big pots of tea has become a lively strumming ground for musicians in the evenings. Library with Dutch, English and German books. A very clean and well-run hotel. *Sgl 1,500–2,500$; dbl 2,500–3,500$; suite 5,000$.*

Residencial Sol Atlantico On the south end of Av Amílcar Cabral; tel 261 2872; f 261 3660. A reasonable choice for a stay on the Plateau. *Sgl 1,725$; dbl 2,875$.*

Residencial Anjos Rua Serpa Pinto; tel 261 4337; f 261 5701. On the northern half of the Plateau; rooms vary from dark and tatty to more upmarket, with balcony and fridge. *Sgl 3,000$; dbl 4,000$.*

Pensão Paraiso Rua Serpa Pinto; ❧ 261 3539. At the far, northern tip of the Plateau. *Sgl 2,645$; dbl 4,000$; inc breakfast.*

Pensão Eurolines CP 115-C, Av Cidade de Lisboa; ❧ 261 6655/260 3010; f 261 6660; e eurolines@cvtelecom.cv. *Sgl 2,700$; dbl 3,500–4,000$.*

Where to eat and drink

There are many eateries in greater Praia; here is a selection:

Achada Santo António. At night, buy grilled fish with salad on the street for 100$.

Alkemist Located at Quebra Canela, along the seafront west of the Praia Mar Hotel; Italian and traditional cuisine with a panoramic view of the sea.

Aparthotel Holanda Meals enlivened by informal gatherings of musicians, on the edge of Achada Santo António. See *Budget* listings above.

Aquarium Popular lunch spot on Rua Serpa Pinto, the central street along the Plateau.

Artica Achada Santo António; for ice creams, burgers and hot dogs. It also has a branch in Fazenda. Open 12.00–19.00 daily.

Cachito On the Plateau at the cultural centre/internet building; ❧ 261 9278. One of the oldest places.

Café Benfica Along Av Cidade de Lisboa, a local retreat.

Café Bordalo On the first floor of the mall. Near the French Cultural Centre on the Plateau. Serving fruit juices, milk shakes and cakes.

Café Lee/Sodadi Opposite Café Bordalo on the Plateau. Charming, poky place serving sandwiches, cakes and excellent coffee plus plate of the day. Excellent value – a real backpackers' delight.

Café Novo Horizonte In Achada Santo António, a pleasant spot for a while if you're in the area.

Café Plateau Just north of the east end of Av Eduardo Mondlane, a bright place for some comfortable dining.

Churrasqueiro Benfica In Achada Santo António; ↘ 262 2195. The place to go for piles of barbecued chicken, pork kebabs and beefsteak.

Churrasqueiro Dragoeiro Av UCLA-Meio, on the west side of Achada Santo António; ↘ 262 3335. The place to go for piles of barbecued meats, popular at weekends.

Fashion Coffee Sophia One of the few places on the Plateau where you can sit outside under a parasol and enjoy watching life go by. Also has limited internet availability inside.

Flor de Lis ↘ 261 2598. Apparently moving to a new location. See map.

French Cultural Centre Used to have a delightful outdoor café, inside the cultural centre; closed in 2005 but may reopen.

Garden Grill This open-air restaurant is currently closed but may be reopening.

Hotels Praia Mar, Pestana Trópico and Marisol All have restaurants open to non-residents. Meals at the Tropico, although relatively expensive, are some of the best in town.

La Cucina Cape Verdean pizzas in an open-air restaurant with garden, in Achada Santo António.

O Poeta ↘ 261 3800. Upmarket restaurant admired for its views over the harbour. At weekends, get there early to secure a seat with a view. Main dishes start at 900$. Go up the hill that leads from Chã de Areia to Achada Santo António and it is on your left.

Punto d'Incontro Av Cidade de Lisboa, opposite the football stadium in Chã d'Areia; ↘ 261 7090. Italian bar and restaurant serving fine pizzas and pasta.

Restaurante Panorama Rooftop restaurant, a lunchtime escape from the noise and heat below. Above Hotel Felicidade on the Plateau.

Sovaco de Cobra The cuisine is as interesting as the name (*sovaco* means 'armpit'), with crêpes, raclette, pancakes and huge sandwiches and a small terrace on which to eat them. Some of the food is a bit greasy. Coming from Chã de Areia, go up to the Terra Branca roundabout and turn right, walk for 5 minutes then ask for directions.

Sucupira market Great platefuls of cheap lunchtime eats can be found in the kiosks of the market, round the back in the covered area.

Vilu Rua 5 de Julho for food, bar, entertainment and handicrafts.Vilu Rua 5 de Julho for food, bar, entertainment and handicrafts.

Nightlife

There are bars at O Poeta, Marisol, Pizza Roma and Flor de Lis. Live music is regularly performed at the Aparthotel Holanda. The following are popular:

A Capital Part of the Hotel Praia Mar complex, in Prainha. No admission charge but some drinks are expensive. There is a small dance floor but plenty of tables and chairs. It appeals to a slightly older, more affluent crowd; busy Fri and Sat nights.

Bomba–H Off the road to Cidade Velha: turn left at the Terra Branca–Hotel Luar roundabout. This open-air place appeals to the younger crowd.

Quintal da Música ↘ 261 7282. On the Plateau, open every night except Sun, but Thu, Fri and Sat evenings are the best. Formed by some members of the Cape Verdean band Simentera to promote traditional music and stimulate local musicians, its courtyard and little

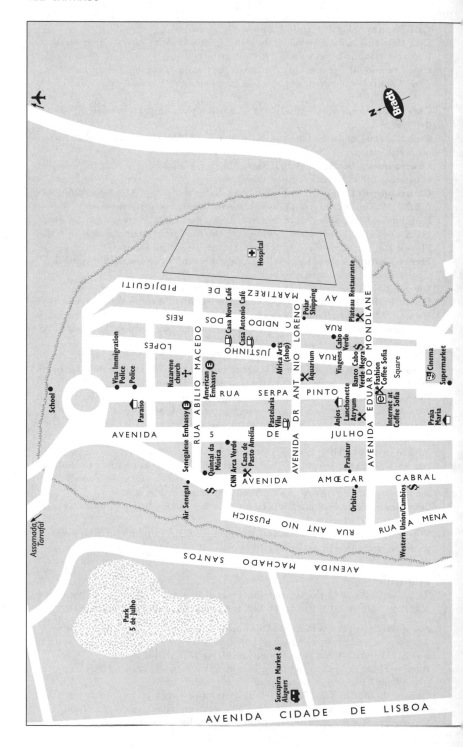

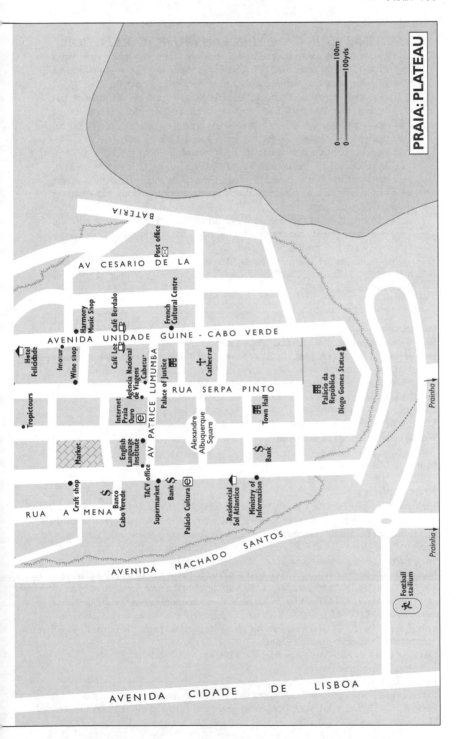

PRAIA: PLATEAU

STARTING YOUR CAPE VERDEAN MUSIC COLLECTION

If you want to buy some recordings of modern Cape Verdean music, here are some ideas to start you off. The list is designed to be small and of course there are many other bands and singers to look out for.

The grande dame is of course Cesária Evora, producer of at least ten albums, including *Miss Perfumado* and her latest, *São Vicente di Longe*. Bau, a musician who plays regularly in Mindelo, has produced *Djailza*, *Tope da Coroa*, *Inspiration* and *Bli Mundo*. Go for the last if you are buying only one.

A popular instrumental collection is *Travadinha*.

Cordas do Sol is a band from Santo Antão whose CD is widely on sale, especially in their home island. In Fogo Agusto da Pina, the blind violinist who inspired the introduction to the first edition of this book, now has his own CD, *Agusto Cego*.

Simentera, a band founded in 1992 and greatly inspired by traditional Cape Verdean music, has three albums, *Raíz*, *Barro e Voz* and *Cabo Verde Serenade*. Perhaps the last is the best.

Finally, for some compilations try *Funana*, an album dedicated to that musical form. Try also *The Soul of Cape Verde*, for a good mix of some of the bands above.

stage make an evocative place to while away warm evenings. Rolling programme of local and invited musicians. Gets chilly later on – take a jumper.

Discoteca Zero Horas Achada Grande. On the road to the airport take the right turn past some warehouses and it is about 400m down on the right, a big purple building inside which is an open-air disco. It opens at midnight and there is a 500$ admission charge. Popular with all ages.

Complexo A Teia In Fazenda

Disco Mar Mar In Tira Chapeu; ☏ 263 2396

Nos Morna In Achada Santo António

Sons d'Africa In Fazenda

Violao In Meio de Achada

Practicalities

Airlines TACV, Av Amílcar Cabral; ☏ 260 8241/8200/261 7529; f 261 5905; *open Mon–Fri 08.00–17.00; Sat 09.00–12.00*. TAP, Chã d'Areia; ☏ 261 5826; overlooking the roundabout beside the vast Palácio do Governo. Air Senegal, Av Amílcar Cabral; ☏ 261 7529/4795/7539; f 261 5483; e praia@airsenegalinternational.sn; www.airsenegalinternational.com; at the northern end of the Plateau.

Banks On the Plateau: Banco Comercial do Atlântico, Praça Alexander Albuquerque; *open Mon–Fri 08.00–14.30*. Caixa Económica, Av Amílcar Cabral, at the northern end; *open Mon–Fri 08.00–13.00, 14.00–15.00*. In Fazenda: Caixa Económica, Av Cidade de Lisboa; *open Mon–Fri 08.00–13.00, 14.00–15.00*. Banco Comercial do Atlântico, Av Cidade de Lisboa; *open Mon–Fri 08.00–14.30*. Banco Cabo-Verdiano de Negro, Av Eduardo Montlane; various *cambios* along Av Amílcar Cabral.

DHL Av OUA, Achada Santo António, CP 303A, Praia; ☏ 262 3124; e dhl_praia@cvtelecom.cv

Embassies See *Practical information*, page 45.

Ferries Polar Shipping, Rua Candido dos Reis (see *Ferries*, pages 39 and 49). *CNN Arca Verde*, Av 5 de Julho; ☏ 261 5497; f 261 5496; at the northern end of the Plateau. Agência Nacional de Viagens, ☏ 261 7858.

Hospital Av Martirez de Pidjiguiti, at the northeastern edge of the Plateau, overlooking the airport road; ➤ 261 2462
Internet Palácio di Cultura, Praça Alexander Albuquerque; this is on the main square on the Plateau; *open Mon–Fri 08.00–12.00, 14.30–18.30*. A good place is Praia Ouro on the northeast side of the same square. Also at Fashion Coffee Sophia. Café Lee/Sodadi advertises it but it was not functioning in May 2005. Try also the French Cultural Centre; it plans to have a service.
Pharmacy Various places throughout the city, inc: Africana, ➤ 261 2776; Central, ➤ 261 1167; Farmacia, 2000; ➤ 261 5655; Moderna, ➤ 261 2719; Santa Isabel, ➤ 261 3747.
Police ➤ 261 1332
Post office On the Plateau, behind the Palace of Justice, and in Fazenda near the big roundabout; *open Mon–Fri 08.00–12.00; 14.00–18.00*.
Shopping Cape Verdean literature in Portuguese and French, music and artefacts are on sale in Palacio di Cultura on the main square on the Plateau. There's a craft shop on Av Amílcar Cabral, nearly opposite the municipal market. Another is Africa Arts. Other music shops include Harmonia Music Shop, Quintal da Música (see *Nightlife* above) on the Plateau, but the best is Tropical Dance in Sucupira. The main supermarket on the Plateau is near the Hotel Felicidade on Rua Serpa Pinto.
Tourist information None on the Plateau. Along Av OAU in Achada Santo António, near the Brazilian embassy, is the Agencia de Promoção de Investimentas de Cabo Verde, formerly known as Promex; ➤ 262 2621/260 4110/260 4111; f 262 2657; e promex@cvtelecom.cv. Taxi drivers and officials still know it as Promex.
French Cultural Centre has some outdated guidebooks. Its hours, however, are a little odd: *open Mon–Fri 09.00–12.00, 14.30–19.00; Sat 10.00–13.00; Sun 14.30–19.00*. On the Plateau, east of the main square.
Visa extensions Go to the police station opposite the Hotel Paraiso in the northern end of Praia; ➤ 261 1845
Business contacts Camara de Comercio; ➤ 261 5352

What to see and do
Museum
Av 5 de Julho
Small but well-laid-out display in a restored 18th-century building on the Plateau. One of the few places you will see the beautifully woven *pano* cloth that was so important in Cape Verde's history. There are also relics from shipwrecks and artefacts from rural life. *Open Mon, Tue, Sat, Sun 10.00–12.00; Wed, Fri 10.00–12.00, 15.00–18.00; Thu closed. Entry fee: 100$.*

Centro de Restauração e Museologia
Rua da Alfândega, 3 Chã de Areia; ➤ 261 1528; e crm@arq.de; www.arq.de
Stunning display of treasure retrieved by the company Arqueonautas from various shipwrecks around Cape Verde. The scientists themselves will show you round, explaining their detective work in piecing together the histories of the various wrecks and their painstaking restorative efforts. See box, page 145. *Open Mon–Fri 09.00–12.00, 15.00–17.00.*

Main square
On the Plateau, this houses the old Catholic cathedral, the old Palace of the Council, the Presidential Palace and the newest building, the Palace of Justice. Behind the square is the statue of Diogo Gomes, one of the two discoverers of the southern islands. Wander a little further and enjoy the views off the Plateau down to the sea.

Beaches

One beach, to the east of Hotel Praia Mar, is very small, and busy at weekends. Ten minutes to the west of the same hotel is Quebra-Canela, which is less busy. The arid cliffs to the east of town are not particularly interesting but have an attractive beach at the end of them. Take a taxi as far as the Shell oil terminal and continue for a few kilometres, at the end of which you will find the beach.

Lighthouse

Wild and windswept with a good view of the town; the caretaker should let you climb to the top.

CIDADE VELHA

This once proud town has had nearly 300 years to decay since the French robbed it of its wealth in 1712. Now there is just an ordinary village population living amongst the ruins of numerous churches, the great and useless fort watching over them from a hill behind. Its inhabitants, whose only wealth is derived from what can be pulled from the sea, spend their time either fishing or bickering, while children and old women harass tourists with demands for money. But it is a beautiful place and it is magical to wander through the vegetation in the *ribeira* and in the surrounding hills to discover the ruins of what was once a pivot of Portuguese empire.

Some tourist developments have started to spring up in the area.

History

Ribeira Grande is where the history of Cape Verde began – where the first Cape Verdeans were born. It was chosen by António de Noli as the centre of his portion of Santiago and it flourished. It had a reasonable and defensible harbour which was the second safest in all of Cape Verde, Madeira and the Azores. It had ample fresh water and a stony landing beach. One of its early illustrious visitors was Vasco da Gama, in July 1497, who discovered India later on the same journey.

Just 70 years after the *ribeira* was settled it was granted the status of *cidade*, and by 1572 some 1,500 people walked its streets (many of them slaves whose job was to till the plantations up the valley). They were watched over by a bishop, dean, archdeacon and 12 canons. Portuguese ships called there on their way to India and Brazil.

The upper valleys were planted with 'vast groves... of oranges, cedars, lemons, pomegranates, figs of every kind, and... palms which produce coconuts,' according to one 16th-century account. Although there are still plantations in the valley it is hard to imagine such foliage there today.

But this was an isolated outpost, helpless under attack and victim of any country that happened to have a grudge against its colonial masters. In 1585, forces supporting the Prior of Crato, fighting for the succession to the throne of Portugal, attacked the town.

When Drake's force landed in mid November 1585 his 1,000 men found the city deserted. Everyone had fled into the mountains, where they remained for two weeks while the Englishmen were below. Drake marched 600 men inland to São Domingos but they too found it deserted. They torched the settlement, went on to Praia and did the same and then left, having acquired food and water but none of the gold they were after. Two weeks later a fever contracted on the island killed hundreds of Drake's crew.

Nevertheless Ribeira Grande continued to grow. By the end of the 1600s it had a population of about 2,000. The grand cathedral was completed in 1693 but little

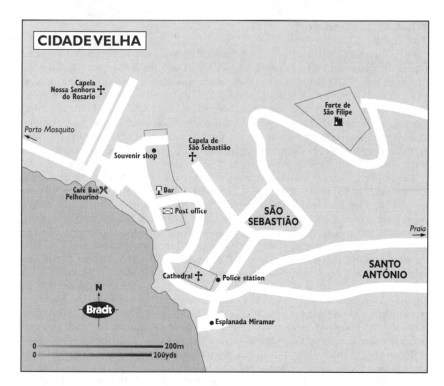

did the people know that the demise of their city was imminent. The French raid of 1712 began the drain to Praia and the city's fate was sealed by the decision of a new bishop in 1754 not to live at Ribeira Grande. Soon it was to be known only as Cidade Velha.

Getting there

Take the approximately hourly *aluguer* (30 minutes, 80$) from Sucupira market or from Terra Branca in Praia. A taxi costs 1,000$ one way. *Aluguers* depart from Cidade Velha from the tree in the centre of the square.

Where to stay and eat

Several new pensions are planned for this town. Until then, there is a limited selection.

Residencial Por do Sol CP 7600, Pedia Flipo is a new project just over 1km west of the town; ☎ 267 1622, m 991 2136/992 8487. Contact Xisto Almeida at Imotur, Rua Andrade Corvo 35, CP 7600 Praia; ☎ 261 7652; f 261 7653; e imotur@cvtelecom.cv or axa@cvtelecom.cv. Take a minibus *aluguer* for 150$ or private taxi 1,000$ to get there from Praia. *Sgl 4,000$; dbl 5,000$*.

Pensão Abel Henry Borges ☎ 267 1374. At the northeast corner of the square, this is a small craft shop with 1 room to rent, so book ahead. *Sgl 2,000$; dbl 3,000$*.

Practicalities

Police ☎ 267 1132
Hospital ☎ 267 1111

What to see and do
The ruins
Fort Real do São Filipe was built after the 1585 sacking and was intended to guard primarily against attack from overland. Walk up there from the town or ask to be dropped, before you descend into town, at the road that leads from the main road to the right. The fort's extraordinarily thick walls were built with brick from Lisbon; its turrets with their little windows give a wide view over the Atlantic and the village. Behind are long views over flat-topped hills and lonely, rocky moors, and also deep into the canyon of Ribeira Grande with its sprinkling of plantations spreading up the valley floor. Inside the fort are some of the old cannons. A museum has been opened there.

Descending into the town you pass the remains of the cathedral on the right, surrounded by high wire netting. Ask around for the key (chave – 'sharve') as the curator lives nearby. Inside are the remains of its 1m-thick walls, begun by the third bishop of Cape Verde, Francisco da Cruz, in 1556. After his initial impetus, the work was half-hearted and construction funds were diverted elsewhere. In 1676, the ambitious original plans were scaled down and it was proposed to build only a sanctuary about 24m long. But the energetic Bishop Vitoriano Portuense, who arrived in 1688, returned to the original design and it was completed in 1693.

Archaeologists have done occasional digs here and revealed the gravestones in the floor; the balustrade between the central nave and the transept; the baptistry, with red-tiled floors and the foundations of the font; and the tomb of António José Xavier, first bishop of Cape Verde. Once the cathedral had a gabled façade, a tower on either side and a flight of steps which led down to the square.

Returning to the road and descending into town you will find at the far left of the square a 16th-century pillory – pelhourinho – used for the punishment of slaves. It is not much more than a century since slavery was abolished in Brazil and the pillory is an arresting symbol of inhumanity – as long as it is there the memory will never slip away.

Leave the square at the pillory end, by the coastal road, and turn right into the wide and dry ribeira. This was once a great stream, which, before it reached the sea, formed a wide pool which was dammed at the mouth by a maze of pebbles through which the water trickled out slowly to the ocean. Fresh water was loaded from it into small boats and brought out to the ships, for which a huge charge was made.

You can walk up the ribeira, turning left on to a track that joins it after about 100m, after the ruins. The track bends round to the right and peters out into the valley above after five minutes. Now, hiding among the trees up to the right are the ruins of the Igreja c Convento de São Francisco, which include a bell tower.

Returning to the track, walk up amongst the trees of the valley to reach, after 15 minutes, a small water tank in which the local people bathe and which used to supply water to Praia. You can return to town along the concrete water channel that leads from the water tank just below you. It follows a contour round the hill and affords good views of the town and the hills behind. When the channel turns to the right at a road, jump off it and follow the track back to the main road.

As you return to town, after 50m, you will see a narrow path between stone walls off to the left. This leads up and then to the right to the church of Santa Luzia. There's little left of it, but there's a good view up to the fort and the cathedral.

Before crossing the ribeira to return to town, take the road on the left which leads to Nossa Senhora do Rosário. This fine church is over five centuries old and Mediterranean in feel with its ochre-tiled roof and patterned blue tiles on the walls. Laid in the floor are 17th-century tombstones. This church served as the

BADIUS AND REBELADOS

The *badius* were at the heart of the Santiago peasant population. Whenever there was a pirate attack, or drought caused some social chaos on the island, some of the slaves would seize the opportunity and flee into the mountainous interior. There, though in exile in a restricted and infertile area, they had freedom. The *badius* form the African core of Cape Verdean society, reflected in their music, which harks back to the African coast for inspiration, and in other aspects of culture. Because of this they have been despised by many. It was from the *badius* that the *rebelados* movement arose as a reaction against the arrival in the 1940s of the Portuguese Catholic priests of the Holy Spirit Congregation. They wished to purify Catholicism, eliminating the many native practices which were based on a clashing personal spiritualism. It is said that those who stuck to the old ways of carrying out baptisms, marriages and other rituals were imprisoned or persecuted.

Ultimately the movement coalesced around practices such as the communal farming of land, the refusal to deal with money and the prohibiting of killing living creatures. As their rebellion centred on treasuring traditions and rejecting change, they also renounced many of today's luxuries such as television and radio. Some still live in the Santiago highlands in distinctive dwellings; their houses can be seen from the main road. They object to being photographed.

When they thwarted an anti-malarial campaign by refusing the fumigation of their homes, their leaders were arrested and dispersed to other islands.

settlement's principal place of worship until the cathedral was built, and is still full on Sundays. Wander through the few little roads here, for example Rua Banana is a pretty one: the houses are like the thatched cottages of rural Ireland – except that cacti grow around them.

If you have time you can also wander further up Ribeira Grande among the plantations. The road continues up the coast for about 20km as far as the small village of Porto Mosquito.

SÃO DOMINGOS

The main reason to stop here is for drives or walks up to the west into the hills. Look out for the *Artesanatos* of São Domingos and their pottery, *pano di terra* (literally 'bread of the earth'), and other local arts and crafts.

Getting there and away

Aluguers leave Sucupira market all day for São Domingos (60$). Any Tarrafal or Assomada *aluguer* will stop there. They run back to Praia well into the evening. By hire car from Praia, take the road north, signposted São Domingos, Assomada and Tarrafal, passing through the urban sprawl and into the countryside. About 12km later there is a sharp bend to the right at which you should take the left turn. After that, just stick on the same road.

Where to stay and eat

There is little accommodation actually in São Domingos, but nearby Rui Vaz offers a pleasant hotel; otherwise it is probably best to stay in Praia.

El Dourado ͱ 265 1865. *Dbl 2,500$.*
Restaurante Morena In Cutelo Branco; ͱ 268 1159
Quinta da Montanha Rui Vaz; ͱ 268 5002/3, m 992 4013; f 268 5004;
e quintamontanha@cvtelecom.cv; www.reisetraeume.de/kapverden/viadoso/c-u2/00.html.
Set in a tranquil place with scenic landscapes. There is a good restaurant at the hotel. Most
of the ingredients come from their own fields. At the weekend they have a self-service
buffet dinner for 10,000$ per person. *Rooms 2,000–4,200$.*

What to see and do
Artisan Centre
At this centre Cape Verdeans are trying to rejuvenate old crafts, in particular the
weaving of *pano* cloth and the production of ceramics. You can watch them
practising their skills around the back. In the front is the craft shop, which sells
foods (jams made from sweet potato, papaya and a green fruit known as *azedinha*;
biscuits) and locally made dolls, as well as trinkets made from coconut and cow
horn. Crafts imported from Senegal are also for sale. Open every day.

Rui Vaz and Monte Xota
The road up into the mountains to this village and up to the peak is magnificent.
To find the turning, take the left turn towards the end of São Domingos, then take
the first right. *Aluguers* go as far as Rui Vaz fairly regularly – the rest of the journey
can be completed by walking. Alternatively, charter an *aluguer* in São Domingos
(630$ one way). At the top it is sometimes possible to enter the antennae complex
and go up to the viewpoint for a panorama of the interior of Santiago. To do Rui
Vaz and Monte Xota as a hike, see page 150.

Botanical gardens and São Jorge dos Orgãos
Cool, verdant and pretty, this village is reached by going up the main road as far as
the village of João Teves (*aluguer* from Praia 150$, one hour) and turning left.
Above you tower the mountains of the Serra do Pico do António.
   Here, houses rise up the crevices between the mountains, all relying on a single
little mountain spring to water their many crops. The agricultural research station
here, Inida, just near the blue church, has a national botanical garden (Jardim
Botanico Nacional), which lies up a turning to the left just beyond its main
buildings. Here they are trying to study endemic species and conserve those
threatened with extinction. Inida, meanwhile, selectively breeds plants in the quest
of ever hardier species and develops more efficient irrigation techniques. If the
researchers are not busy they sometimes show visitors around the garden. Look for
lingua de vaca (*Echium vulcanorum*, if they've managed to get this inhabitant of Fogo
volcano to grow) and the purple flowers of *contra-bruxas-azul* (*Campanula jacobea*).

ASSOMADA
Recently granted the rank of *cidade* (city), Assomada nevertheless still feels like a
country town and does not possess the infrastructure of the two other Cape
Verdean cities, Praia and Mindelo. It is the capital of the region of Santa Catarina,
the grain basket of Santiago. It is an ancient town, as old as Cape Verde's human
history, and was often more highly populated than Cidade Velha.

Getting there and away
By public transport, the journey from Praia takes 1½ hours (200$) and *aluguers*
leave all day. *Aluguers* leave for the return journey to Praia until late at night. Private
taxis cost 3,000–5,000$ for half a day.

The drive to Assomada is spectacular, particularly after João Teves, when jagged clifftops rear into view and there are vistas into valleys on both sides of the road. A rock formation that looks like the profile of a recumbent face has been christened the Marques de Pombal rock, after a statue of that nobleman in Lisbon. Climbing out of the Pico you can see the island of Maio to the east, before the descent into Assomada.

Where to stay and eat
There are now two good new places to stay in Assomada, so it is no longer necessary to stay in Praia and visit this town on a day trip.

Pensão Avenida Av Amílcar Cabral; ℺ 265 3462; www.reisetraeume.de/kapverden/reisebuero/hotels/santiago/avenida.html. A new upmarket 3-star hotel, with AC. *Sgl   30; dbl   40.*
Pensão Monraci Bolanha; ℺f 265 1932; e racine532000@yahoo.fr; www.caboverde.com. Joint Cape Verdean and French management. Follow website links as follows: Ilha de Santiago, accommodations, Cidade de Assomada, Pensão Monraci, to get further information.
Pensão Café Paris 2000 ℺ 265 4767. Currently being renovated. *Rooms from 2,500$.*

Practicalities
Bank Banco Comercial do Atlântico (BCA); ℺ 265 3110
Hospital ℺ 265 1130. Opposite the police station.
Police ℺ 265 1132
Pharmacy Farmacia Santa Catarina; ℺ 265 2121

What to see and do
Museu de Tabanka
This museum is located in a former treasury and mail government building. It covers the history of Assomada and Santa Catarina and gives extensive coverage to the musical form of *tabanka*. There are also interesting displays of pictures, instruments and other objects. Sometimes there are exhibitions by Cape Verdean artists and poets and there is frequent entertainment, usually at night. It has been considerably enhanced with the addition of cultural events and further artistic contributions. There is a gift shop, café and French library.

African market
All the colours, smells and noise of a west African market. Held on Wednesdays and Saturdays.

Porto Rincão
This little fishing village is reached by turning left at Assomada (or catching an *aluguer* from beside the market or from the road junction) and following a fantastic road to the coast. There are deep red canyons and a stunning view of Fogo sitting on a cushion of cloud across the water. Halfway along the cobbled road turns to dirt. It's a 24km round trip, and if you have time for just one foray down to the west coast we recommend the more northerly one, to Ribeira da Barca.

Boa Entrada
North along the main road from Assomada, just slightly out of town lies a turning to this village, which lies in the green valley that meanders down to the right of the road. You can walk down from Assomada. Dominating the valley is a magnificent,

centuries-old kapok tree, in which nests one of the only two known colonies of Cape Verde heron, known locally as *garca-vermelho* (*Ardea purpurea bournei*). The other colony is at Banana de Ribeira Montanha, near Pedra Badejo. This tree is probably the biggest you will ever see and is said to have been there when the island was discovered.

The valley can be reached by several obvious paths. One leads down to a white church with pinnacles and a green door and from there to the tree. There is also a cobbled road that leads down from the main road about 100m further on.

House of Amílcar Cabral

National hero Amílcar Cabral lived as a child in a yellow-walled, red-roofed house set back from the main road that leads north from Boa Entrada, on the left-hand side. He spent most of his short life, though, in São Vicente, Portugal and the African mainland. The house is not open to the public.

Ribeira Barca

To reach this village by *aluguer* should be possible but may involve some long waits at the road junction. It's a 6km walk so it could make a pleasant day trip.

As you leave the vicinity of Boa Entrada start counting churches that possess separate bell towers. After the second one on the left there is a fork in the road – turn left and follow the cobbled track as it swings past a dramatic canyon on the left and continues past deeply carved *ribeiras* all the way to this beautiful beachside village. There are two restaurants. Once you've eaten you can visit one of the most enchanting places on Santiago – Achada Leite and the Grotto d'Águas Bellas. There is an oasis packed with trees and, further on, a grotto with a beach inside it where you can sit and have a picnic, the light glimmering through a gap in the roof of the cave. It's a 6km drive – much longer than it looks because the dirt road bends inland and then out again – but there's a footpath at the bend of the road which reduces the walk to just over 2km. You can hire a local fisherman to take you; it's 2,000$ for a boatload.

TARRAFAL

A cobalt sea, a string of little coves and a flat land under the forbidding mountains are what make Tarrafal. The beach is of lovely soft sand and there's a jumble of life going on there: fishermen, local sports fanatics, sunbathers, and lots of dogs. This place becomes packed at weekends so a midweek visit is ideal. It can be a bit windy and depressing during the harmattan period, December–March.

It is a good base for doing some of the walks the island offers and it is easy to laze away a few days here – the beach is cosier than Santa Maria in Sal. There can be quite a few mosquitoes at night.

Tarrafal's mention in the history books comes from its notorious prison, 3km before town on the main Praia road, on the left (see page 144).

Getting there and away

The 80km trip from Praia along the central road takes two hours and *aluguers* leave all day from Sucupira market (400–500$). To return to Praia on the same, inland road catch an *aluguer* from where the Praia road joins the main square of Tarrafal. They run until early evening. To return along the coastal road find an *aluguer* behind the church in the main square along with women returning from their early forays to Tarrafal beach to buy fish. Ask for Calheta: *aluguers* on this road rarely go all the way to Praia so you will have to change where necessary (150$ to Calheta, 200$ Calheta to Praia).

Where to stay
Upmarket
Hotel Tarrafal Rua Senador Vera Cruz 57, CP 50; ℩ 266 1785/6; f 266 2273;
e htltarrafal@cvtelecom.cv; also cabetur@cvtelecom.cv. The best hotel in Tarrafal in terms
of service, facilities and comfort with 20 rooms. Small pool, terrace, sea views. *Sgl 5,000$;
dbl 6,000$; suite with sofa bed 9,000$.*
Hotel Baía Verde ℩ 266 1128; f 266 1414. Chalets scattered in the shade of coconut palms
on Tarrafal beach. Each has TV, fridge and minibar. Some have hot water. Used to be
good, but has deteriorated in recent times, and may no longer be considered upmarket. *Sgl
2,000–4,000$; dbl 3,000–4,000$; 3-bedroom chalet 6,000$.*

Mid range
Hotel Marazul CP 33; ℩/f 266 1289. Situated where the town starts to peter out towards
the west. *Sgl 2,000$; dbl 2,500$.*
Pensão Mille Nuits ℩ 266 1463; f 266 1878. At the heart of town with acceptable rooms
arranged around a bright atrium. The cheapest have shared bathrooms. All have fans. *Sgl
1,500–2,000$; dbl 1,500–2,500$.*
Pensão Tata ℩ 266 1125. *Rooms 1,500–2,000$.*
Hotel Solmarina ℩ 266 1219; e hotelsolmarina.cv@hotmail.com. Practically on the
beach, Solmarina is endearing in an arty kind of way. The hotel is due to close in Nov
2005, according to the management. It remains to be seen if it will reopen. *Sgl
1,600–2,000$; dbl 2,000–2,500$; no breakfast.*

Where to eat and drink
Crioulo Food is excellent and very cheap.
Hotel Baía Verde Open-air restaurant overlooking the beach, with main dishes starting at
700$. Now rather run-down.
Hotel Tarrafal Has an upmarket restaurant.
Restaurante Bonanza Has only 4 dishes, and is run by a Spanish man who speaks several
languages.

The hotels **Marazul**, **Mille Nuits** and **Tata** also have restaurants attached, and
the Italian restaurant at the Solmarina is recommended.

Practicalities
Bank Banco Commercial do Atlantico BCA; ℩ 266 1170. *Open Mon–Fri 08.00–15.00.*
Hospital ℩ 266 1130
Police ℩ 266 1132
Post office On the Assomada road, on the right as you leave town. *Open Mon–Fri
08.00–15.30.*

What to see and do
Diving
Hotel Solmarina Ask at this hotel for dives from the boat, but the hotel may be closed
from Nov 2005.
Kings Bay m 992 3050. A new diving centre, being set up at the time of research.
Monaya A Cape Verdean diving instructor – ask in town or at the hotels.

Boating
Local fishermen can take you down the coast, for example to Ribeira da Barca and
on to the oasis (see *Ribeira Barca*, page 142). One hour can cost 2,000$.

THE CONCENTRATION CAMP AT TARRAFAL

It was known as the *Campo da morte lenta* (slow death camp) to some; *Aldeia da morte* (death village) to others. The concentration camp just outside Tarrafal had at its centre a cemented building whose temperature would soar during the day. Each cell was a completely enclosed cement box about 3m long by 2½m wide. At one end was the iron door. The only ventilation was a few holes of less than 1cm in diameter in the door, and a small, grilled hole up near the ceiling.

Into this camp, after it was built in 1936, were put 150 Portuguese antifascists. The prison continued to house such political prisoners until 1954, when it closed after international protest. But it opened again in the 1960s, this time to be host to independence fighters from Angola, Cape Verde and Guinea-Bissau.

The camp's gruesome history came to an end on 1 May 1974, a few days after the Carnation Revolution in Lisbon which would usher in democracy. The gates were thrown open and out tottered a bewildered group, many of them crying. Waiting for them was a crowd of thousands who had rushed from Praia in cars, trucks and on bicycles as soon as they heard of the telegram ordering their release.

There are plans to open the camp as a museum.

Surfing
Before midday the break to the west of the bay is good and extends all the way down to Ribeira da Prata.

Hiking
Tarrafal is a good starting point for several hikes, including the short walk to the lighthouse and the walk down Ribeira Principal (see *Hikes*, page 147).

Museum
Close to Tarrafal is the **Museum of Resistance of Tarrafal**. It was effectively a concentration camp that was built in 1936 and used as a prison for political prisoners. It was closed after the 1970s. It has now been restored and opened for visitors.

OTHER PLACES TO VISIT
Calheta de São Miguel
There's no particular reason for stopping the night here, except to use it as a base for hikes up into the interior. It's a pretty enough coastal town with a good hotel. To get there from Praia take an *aluguer* from Sucupira market that is travelling up the coastal road; from Tarrafal catch an *aluguer* from behind the church in the main square. From Assomada you can catch an *aluguer* that takes an interesting route down a cross-country road to Calheta.

Where to stay
Hotel Mira Maio ↘ 273 1121. At the southern end of town, off a road leading down to the shore. Varied rooms, some large, some with balconies, some with TV and fridge. Rooftop terrace with coastal views. Restaurant. *Sgl 1,300–2,800$; dbl 2,500–3,000$.*
Hotel Amazoni m 991 8204. *Dbl around 2,500$.*

Praia Baixo

This developing place is located on the northeast coast of Santiago about 20km from Praia. It is noted for its safe beach. Sir Francis Drake is thought to have made a landfall here.

Where to stay and eat

Aparthotel Praia Baixo ↘ 268 7105; f 261 2629. This is the main option but it is reputedly not that cheap, with prices in the mid-range bracket.
Poseidon Nauticlub ↘ 268 7103

Pedra Badejo

This growing settlement is located a little further north of Praia Baixo along the northeast coast.

Where to stay and eat

Pousada Mariberto 'A La Française' (5 rooms) CP 35; ↘ 2691900; m 9912298; e contact@hotelmariberto.com; www.hotelmariberto.com. Located in Punta Coroa, 5km before Pedra Badejo on the road from Achada Fazenda to Ponta Coro, this quiet 4-star guesthouse is run by a French-Russian couple, Bernard and Marina. Large rooms face the sea across to Maio Island. Sea-water pool and wine bar. Various excursions offered include Cidade Velha, trekking in Santiago, traditional fishing, and visits to banana/mango plantations and Maio Island. *Dbl 9,900$. No children under 13.*
Residencial Tiara ↘ 269 1819. This was until recently the only place to stay in Pedra Badejo. It would be advisable to call ahead.

São Francisco

With superb beaches and deserted coves, this is the best place near Praia for a day in the sun. Unfortunately it's a pain to get to, with little traffic and no public *aluguers*. A taxi will cost about 1,400$ each way. You could try hitching. Follow the road that goes to the airport, cross the bridge and turn left, to the north. At weekends it's far busier as the beach is a popular local destination.

There is nowhere to stay at present, however, as the Kingfisher Lodge, a German investment, is not functioning.

DRIVES
Round-island drive

This is highly recommended as the interior of Santiago is a drama worth making an effort to see. It could be accomplished in one day but this would be pretty exhausting – it is better, if possible, to travel from Praia to Tarrafal on the first day and return down the coast road on the second. If you have time take the left turn after Assomada (just before Fundura) and visit Ribeira da Barca for a vivid glimpse of the terrain leading to the west coast.

The drive begins through the urban sprawl of Praia – ever expanding as people move from the villages to the city. As you reach the countryside you should see the long yellow flowers of aloe vera lining the roadside, along with, at the right time of year, maize and haricot beans. About 12km from the centre of Praia, where you take the left turn, you begin to gaze down into a green valley and soon pass the large, irrigated banana plantations. The road passes through São Domingos and Assomada – springboards for visiting all the places described above. After marvelling at the Pico do Santo António and its surrounding craggy peaks you will later come to the Serra Malagueta – the other high point of Santiago.

Non-stop, the journey from Tarrafal to Praia along the coast is 2½ hours. There is less to stop and see than there is on the inland road but the drive is spectacular, following the coast along hairpin bends that take you into verdant creeks and out again into the dry mountainsides. The houses have hay piled high on their flat roofs and occasionally goats live up there. Wires stick out of the top of every house in anticipation of the building of the next storey. Pigs forage round the houses and the dry landscape.

After Calheta the land becomes almost lush with great banana plantations, coconut trees and always the yellow of aloe vera poking up from cacti-like leaves.

HIKES
Serra Malagueta–Hortelão–Ribeira Principal (longer route)
Alexander Hirtle, author of the Santiago hiking guide 'Bemvindos A Assomada' (see Further reading).
Distance: 13km; time: 4½ hours; difficulty: 3
This is a beautiful walk, and the peak time for it is between mid August and early December (late October is probably the greenest and most picturesque). Beware, though, that during the rainy season that usually starts mid/late July and ends mid October, trails can be slippery and often wiped out with streams rushing through them. Visibility can also be limited due to cloud cover and the rain itself. The walks are mainly downhill, but continual downhill jaunts can be very stressful on knees and ankles. You need to get transport up to the area of Serra, commonly called Serra Malagueta. From Assomada, a *hiace* costs 100$. Tell the driver to drop you off at the secondary road with the gate (*portão*), before the primary school (*escola*).

Follow the secondary road, which is clear and wide with generally good footing, up several hundred feet; it makes winding turns, some so sharp and steep you'll wonder how vehicles get up there. There are some excellent views of the *ribeira* off to the left. As you continue upwards, the flora changes. You'll see groups of pine trees, part of a continual reforestation project in which the locals participate. It is a necessary programme, because local residents are always collecting firewood from the area (you may pass several people coming down the road carrying loads of wood on their heads). Continue up the road and it begins to level off. You are near one of the highest points on the island, **Serra Malagueta**. There are spectacular views to the right; you may even be above the cloud cover, depending on the day. Watch the sides of the cliffs though: a misstep will send you hundreds of feet down. Continue on the road, and after a small clearing where at times vehicles are parked.

Stay to the right, along the drop-off, but not too close to it. The paths to the left lead to somewhat dangerous wooded areas. You will begin to descend, as the path takes a left turn and leads you into very green and beautiful woods: thus begins the decline to Ribeira Principal.

The path switchbacks several times; it is important to stay on the main path that generally goes to the left of the ridge and eventually to the bottom of the *ribeira*. If you find yourself going down to the right of the ridge, you will need to retrace your steps and find the correct path again. You will descend to an area with some enclosed animal pens and houses. Most residents here are very friendly, but respect their privacy and property as on occasion you may meet a local who is not always happy with foreigners passing by. After entering the first area of houses, continue through another area with sets of houses and, as the path veers to the right, walk along an area that is a small ridge where the drop off is steep to the left, shallow on the right. You will reach an area where the path quickly drops down, makes a slight turn to the right, and then a sharp turn to the left. This area can be very dangerous when it is wet, so take it slow and steady. The path then takes you along a lower terrace that brings you to the left side of the *ribeira*. You will descend further to more houses, again staying along the lower ridge that overlooks the *ribeira*. There are very good views here: you can see the terracing of the agricultural areas, and the isolated *vilas* below. Several areas will have diverging paths, so you need constantly

---

Piecing together a ship's history, and matching it with a known vessel, requires all sorts of lateral thinking. The cargo provides clues. Sometimes small collections of coins from a variety of countries – perhaps from the pocket of an individual sailor collecting a souvenir from every port – can help plot the ship's route.

'The quality of the cargoes is amazing,' says Piran Johnson of Arqueonautus Worldwide. A massive batch of ivory tusks – eaten away like long thin pieces of cheese – was brought up from the *Princess Louisa*, a 1743 ship that was on its way between London and Bombay. An intact bottle of wine 200 years old and, more irresistible, several bottles of cognac were retrieved from an unknown wreck in the harbour of Praia. One ship yielded huge copper plates that the Swedes once used as unwieldy currency – the ship went down in 1781 on its way from Denmark to China.

Another ship – the *Hartwell* – contained a collection of watches: 'They were the Ratners of the day,' says Piran. 'Gold filigree on top but cheap tat underneath – they were being shipped out to the colonies to buy off the locals.'

Most of the treasures emerge looking most unpromising, in the form of ugly grey concretions formed by the build up of iron, sand and other substances over the decades. It takes a professional eye to spot the underlying shape; then it takes weeks of painstaking work to remove the concretion without damaging the valuables inside.

To visit the collection, see *What to see and do*, page 135.

to ask the locals the way to Hortelão, the *vila* just past Principal. You will come to a converging area that will bring you across to the right side of the *ribeira*. You may not notice it at first, but once you leave the more dense areas with houses, you will be following the lower ridge on the right side of **Ribeira Principal**.

Continue to descend, past some fantastic rock structures on the right including a keyhole in one part of the ridge. Your final climb down is full of tricky switchbacks, so take it slowly. The path eventually takes you to the bottom of the *ribeira*, to **Hortelão**. Waiting vehicles can take you to Tarrafal, or Calheta, where you can change vehicles to return to Assomada, or Praia. Alternatively, you can walk the extra 30–40 minutes along the road to the main road, but it is not the most scenic part of the trip, and may take longer if you are tired and hungry.

Serra Malagueta–Ribeira Principal (shorter route)
Alexander Hirtle (see above)
Distance: 8km; time: 3¹/₂ hours; difficulty: 2
The second, and shorter, way down the pretty Ribeira Principal starts from the *vila* of Serra, at the small market, or *mercearia*. The owner, Marcilino, can point out the path that starts your descent.

The first part is tricky: steep switchbacks where it is easy to slip. Take it slowly, and when you come to the first major fork (about 0.5km from the road) take a left.

This second path is much simpler than the first: the higher part of the walk stays to the left of the *ribeira* the entire time. The path levels off quickly as it leads you on to a lower ridge, again staying on the left side of the *ribeira*. You can see the beautiful terracing of the lower gorge, the isolated houses, and the forested view of the opposite side of the *ribeira* – the route for the longer hike to **Principal** (see above). The path follows the ridge and then cuts inward (to the right), descending towards the centre of the *ribeira*. It cuts back and forth but leads mainly to the right, ending up at the bottom centre of the *ribeira* in a lush oasis of mango trees and sugar cane.

This is a good area to stop and have lunch. You will probably see locals coming and going, carrying water from the tank, or maybe sugar cane. Please respect their area and stay clear of the paths when they are close by so that they can pass easily. As you follow the path, you will pass several *grogue* distilleries. Many owners enjoy demonstrating how their distillery operates; feel free to inquire, but respect their work if they are in the middle of something.

Follow the path that climbs just a bit to the higher area of the oasis and goes through several small *vilas*. If you are lucky you will hear some woman beating on plastic homemade drums, and singing *batuko*, a traditional form of music popular in this area (see page 28). Joining them is not usually a problem, and sometimes they will bring you right into their houses and make you feel very welcome to sing or beat drums with them.

BIRDS
A bird to watch out for is the grey-headed kingfisher (*Halcyon leucocephala*) which is known locally as *passarinha*. Common on Santiago, Fogo and Brava only, you can spot its distinctive blue, rust, black and white feathers in well-vegetated valleys and cultivated areas.

Also watch for the red-billed tropicbird, known as *rabo-de-junco* (*Phaethon aethereus*). It frequents Santiago, Brava and Raso and is one of the most elegant birds on Cape Verde, with a red bill, streaming white tail and white plumage with a little black.

The path continues a little longer, again descending slightly to the lowest part of the *ribeira* where it ends at a large *grogue* distillery. By showing interest in the facility, and some friendly rapport in Portuguese, Creole, or maybe limited English, you may be invited to sample some of their *grogue*. Nearby vehicles can take you on to the main Tarrafal–Calheta road.

Chão Bom–Ribeira da Prata–Figueira das Naus
Distance: 9km; time: 3¹/₂ hours; difficulty: 2 (AI)
This is an attractive, if lonely, walk that begins on the level, following the coast as far as Ribeira da Prata. It then toils uphill along a remorselessly shadeless track, relieved by the drama of the canyons and the vista back towards the sea. The walk is on road and track and there are no problems with slipperiness or steep slopes; but the 1¹/₂-hour upward slog from Ribeira da Prata requires a certain amount of fitness if it is to be enjoyable. To get to the beginning of the walk at Chã Bom (pronounced 'shambome') travel for about five minutes by *aluguer* from Tarrafal along the Assomada road. The turning to Ribeira da Prata is signposted, on the right, at the beginning of Chã Bom.

From the Tarrafal side of Chã Bom, take the road signposted **Ribeira da Prata**, passing initially through slums. Leaving habitation behind, the lonely road passes in and out of the coastal fractals for about an hour, revealing eventually the black sand beach of the *ribeira* with acacia and coconut palms offering a bit of shade. The bottom of the valley is where people pause in the shade to rest. Follow the road out, up, into the village and out of the other side after which it will do a great loop backwards and upwards to ascend into the hills.

This is an extremely quiet road and, as it ascends, there are views back to Tarrafal, to the harshly bright sea and over the rocky ground that characterises the western side of Santiago. There is a huge amount of reafforestation here. Some 1¹/₂ hours after leaving Ribeira da Prata the track begins to pass through a series of villages, including Figueira Muite and Marmulano, most of which have bars tucked away – all you have to do is ask for them. Some 2¹/₂ hours from Ribeira da Prata you reach **Figueira das Naus** with its pretty church. Here the road divides and you can wait for an *aluguer* (there are three or four a day) to take you along the right fork and back to the main Tarrafal–Assomada road.

Alternatively, if you have a taste for more of this rocky, inland drama, you can walk the 8km to the main road. Just take the right fork and remain on the same track, ignoring a single right turn.

Monte Xota–Pico do António–Monte Xota
Time: 6 hours; difficulty: 3 (AI)
This walk is only for the fit, sure-footed and navigationally competent. Even then, the final ascent is up a dangerously steep and crumbling slope. All the rules of hiking apply (see *Health*, page 66), in particular that you should go in a group of at least three and wear boots with good grip. Take two litres of water for each person. Set off before 11.00. For the middle third of the journey the path is obscure or non-existent and one needs to trust to an understanding of the topography to find the way up the ridge to the top. Sadly, it is hard to find a competent guide. There are many local men who will agree to take you but few know the way or understand that most Westerners are less fleet of foot than they – so they may give you a false sense of security. The soldiers at the telecommunications station at the start of the walk work on rotation and may never have been up the Pico.

The walk begins at the telecommunications installation, on a path opposite its entrance. The path disappears into the vegetation and winds back behind the station. Almost immediately there's a view of the curved pincers of the Pico. Climb down the low wall ahead of you and follow the path that goes round the installation and then branches away to the northwest. You emerge on a little ridge and already the views are spectacular, with Fogo visible to the west and within five minutes, views of São Domingos and Serra Malagueta.

For the next half hour the path is clear, descending through pleasant forest, past a couple of smallholdings and in and out of the valleys until you are in the position from which to begin the ascent up the spur that leads to the top.

The ascent will take 2–3 hours depending on fitness and agility. After the first 1½ –2 hours you reach the lesser peak.

Monte Xota–São Domingos
Distance 5km; time: 2 hours; difficulty: 1 (AI)
Spectacular views accompany this downhill walk from the antennae station at the peak of Monte Xota to the town of São Domingos on the main road. The road is cobbled throughout and navigation is simple: just head downwards. If you become tired at any point, you can just sit and wait for the next *aluguer* – these are fairly frequent from Rui Vaz downwards. To reach Monte Xota for the beginning of the walk either take a public *aluguer* as far as the Rui Vaz turning and walk, or charter an *aluguer* in São Domingos, which should cost around 700$.

Try to kick off the walk by gaining entry to the grounds of the Monte Xota telecommunications station and climbing the knoll to the right. The soldiers there may let you in if you ask nicely and they are not too busy. From the knoll you can see spread before you the heart of Santiago. Retracing your steps, join the road and enjoy the greenery and the sharply scented, cool air before it fades as you descend. The magnificent cobbled road takes you through sheer cliffs and craggy rock formations with occasional glimpses of Pico do António, the canine tooth poking up behind them. Watch out for Pico de João Teves, one of many raw, majestic shapes, which looks like the top of a submarine. You will also pass the president's holiday home, on the left.

Further down the road descends towards the valley and travels parallel with it before a left and a right turn deposit you on the main road just in the north of São Domingos.

Assomada–Poilon–Riberão Boi–Santa Cruz
Distance: 16km; time: 5 hours; difficulty: 1 (CW)
This is a long, gentle walk down a shallow *ribeira*. If you want to see rural corners of Santiago without tackling tougher peaks, this is a good walk to do, though it is not as interesting as many of the others. There are several active *grogue* distilleries along the route, where people will be only too happy to let you try some of the raw spirit, often still warm from the still. Your path is an easy, valley-floor track throughout. But if you want to avoid a one-off scramble down a rock face, you have to take a brief detour up the valley side.

The track out of Assomada is a little tricky to find – the best thing to do is to ask for **Poilon**, where there is a tourist-friendly distillery (or *trapiche*). The track to Poilon threads along the right-hand side of the head of the *ribeira*, and finally brings you down to the valley floor about 1.5km out of Assomada.

You will know you have arrived because you will pass two large concrete tanks on your right. Turn right along the *ribeira* floor – the beginning of the path does not look promising, but does improve.

After about 500m, you will pass the Poilon *trapiche* on your right. There is usually pressing or distillation in progress (except Saturday, when the week's produce is taken to market). Look out for the large wooden barrels nearby. Beneath the covering of leaves, the sinister, yellow bubbling liquid is the fermenting sugar cane. It is a natural fermentation, usually taking about three or four days, depending on the weather.

If the fire is burning, you may see the clear *grogue* being carefully collected after it has distilled in a curly pipe passing through cold water. For more on *grogue* production, see box, page 232.

From the *trapiche*, follow the track along the valley floor. Before the track bears round to the east, you will pass the outskirts of **Boa Entrada** on your left. After about 3km of easy walking from the *trapiche* you will see a line of houses on a high crag which projects into the valley from your left. Just before the track cuts up to the left, stay on the valley floor by taking a small path down to the right at the point where the track crosses a riverbed. There is a small, concrete lined spring directly beside the track.

After approximately 1km from the turning, you will pass another *trapiche* on your left. If you continue on at this point, the path enters a tight gorge, and you will have to scramble down a 2m drop that interrupts the path.

You can avoid this by turning right, out of the valley floor, opposite the *trapiche*. After about 15m, take a steep path leading up a ridge on your left. After about ten minutes, this path passes over the shoulder, and you can take a small steep path on the left which will bring you back down to the valley floor, on the other side of the 2m drop.

Continue along the track in the valley floor for another 6.5km (about 1 hour 40 minutes), and you will reach **Riberão Boi**. Just before you arrive, you will pass beneath a high cliff face on your left, where the rock has formed into dramatic faceted columns.

From Riberão Boi to the Calheta–Pedra Badejo road it is about 3.5km. On the road, you can pick up an *aluguer*.

Tarrafal–lighthouse–Tarrafal

Distance: 6km; time: 2½ hours; difficulty: 2 (AI)

WARNING: This walk is currently unsafe and many people have been attacked. We do not recommend it at present. Ask locally if the situation has improved.

This walk will take you from the Tarrafal cove to the lighthouse at the foot of the big headland to the north of Tarrafal, which you can see from the beach. It involves a steep scramble at the end and there is no shade – take at least 1½ litres of water and a hat.

Go to the north end of the most northerly cove of the beach and follow a little sand path up through the rocks and past the last of the holiday bungalows. You can see the path cut into the cliff side ahead. Keep an eye on it as it often disappears underfoot. After 30 minutes clinging to the headland, the path turns inland to face an inhospitable ravine strewn with huge boulders from a landslide. There is a path, though it turns to a scramble at times. When you have reached the end of it follow a path out along the big bulge of land, past deserted dry stone walls built to keep cattle.

Instead of turning to the lighthouse you can continue up the coast and walk for hours, even as far as a distant cove (about 3 hours). It really is empty and there are exhilarating views down green stone canyons and up the coastline.

Maio

Huge heaps of salt like drifts of snow, and most fine and perfect in nature, the abundance whereof is such, and the daily increase so exceeding great, that they serve all countryes and lands about them, and is impossible to be consumed.

Sir Francis Drake, British sailor,
pirate and slave-trader, 1578

Maio is the forgotten island. More than any other it seems to have missed out on finding a modern role. Other islands have snatched the prizes – the international airport, the beach tourism, the agriculture, the port industries. But Maio just lies in the shadow of Santiago waiting to be lifted by the tide. It's the kind of place where one notices a plastic cup blowing along an empty street.

HIGHLIGHTS

This is the island to which tourists are least likely to go at present, though some development (mainly Italian) is starting. It is one of the three flat islands and lacks the development of Sal and the generous supply of beautiful dunes and oases of Boavista. It has little gripping walking. But it is this quiet that attracts some people – there are some lovely white and lonely beaches. There is the biggest acacia plantation of the archipelago – and the trees are mature and green. For naturalists there are turtles in the summer and some interesting birds, particularly seabirds on Ilhéu Laje Branca off the north of the island. Two Italian-run restaurants offer authentic pizzas and seafood etc, and the hotels also supply acceptable food.

BACKGROUND INFORMATION
History

Maio's one resource is its prolific salt and for this reason it was a bustling island from the late 16th century until the 19th. In a good year it exported 11,000 tonnes. Before this treasure was discovered, Maio was a grazing ground for cattle and goats, producing 4,000 head a year at its peak. But soon the fragile vegetation was eaten and there was little left to sell but salt and lime.

It was the English who commandeered the salt production because the Portuguese never had much interest in Maio. One Englishman even made a profit by loading salt at Maio and bartering it at Santiago. The salt was shovelled into sacks at the salt lake, fastened to donkeys and carried to the beach where it was loaded into boats specially designed to cope with the heavy swells in the bay. They would travel out to the boats belonging to the big ships which would themselves be anchored well away from the shore.

The English ships, laden with about 200 tonnes of salt, would leave for Newfoundland to pick up cod, salt it, and take it back to Europe. Other ships took salt on journeys between Europe and the West Indies and between America and Africa. Maio's fort was built by English sailors left behind by Sir Francis Drake in 1588.

All through the 17th century about 80 English ships a year called at Maio for salt; there was usually a battleship standing by to guard English interests. The Maio people were paid with some money but also with old clothes and food. It is said their houses were full of English ornaments.

By the 19th century the principal market for salt switched to Brazil, where thousands of tonnes were sent annually. That business was killed when Brazil introduced protective tariffs at the end of the 19th century.

Maio did not escape plunder. In 1818, a pirate ship from Baltimore sacked the port. A South American ship sacked it in 1827. In the 20th century there were repeated droughts and emigrations.

Geography
Maio, like the other islands, is an old volcano that has slowly been eroded by the wind. But Maio is unusual because beneath the volcano that welled up out of the ocean floor was ocean sediment that ballooned up behind it. Subsequent erosion of the volcanic rock has exposed vast amounts of marine sediments that are 190 million years old, which is why some texts refer to it as the oldest island.

Maio is small, at 268km^2, with a population of about 4,000. It lies 25km to the east of Santiago. Its terrain is similar to Sal and Boavista with one big difference: it has been heavily reafforested in parts, almost exclusively with acacias. The highest peak, Monte Penoso, is 437m. There are saltpans in the southwest and northwest and there is more fertile, agricultural land in the east.

Economy
Farming occupies about 15% of the population and fishing about 7%. The people use their now plentiful wood to turn to charcoal in underground ovens for export to other islands. There are large lime reserves and there is some gypsum.

Festivals
The festival of Santa Cruz on 3 May, and those in June, are the biggest celebrations. Weddings have big build-ups that can last for days. Others are as follows

Nossra Sra Do Rosario	2 February
São Jose	19 March (Calheta)
Santa Cruz	3 May (Maio)
Santo António	13 June (Santo António)
São João	24 June (Ribeira de João)
São Pedro	29 June (Pedro Vaz)
Santa Ana	26 July (Morrinho)

GETTING THERE AND AWAY
By air
There's a 20-minute TACV flight four times a week to and from Praia. If you've booked into one of the two hotels, a minibus should meet you. If not there are taxis. It is easy to walk the few kilometres into town: facing the sea, the capital, Vila do Maio can be seen to the left. Take the only road, towards the sea, and turn left at the T-junction. Pass the saltpans and in about 40 minutes you are in town. On departure, ask around the hotels for transport back to the airport or allow time to walk.

Airport ͻ 255 1108

MAIO

Ponta Cais
Praia Real
Praia de Galeão
Ilhéu Laje Branca
Pedro Vaz
Praia de Santana
Salt-pans
Monte de Santo António 252m
Santo Antínio
Porto Cais
Cascabulho
Praia Gonçalo
Morrinho
Chão do Campo
Pedro Vaz
Praia de Soca
Calheta
Monte Penoso 437m
Alcatraz
312m
Pilão Cão
Praia de Morro
Monte Batalha 294m
Monte Branco
Morro
João
Figueira da Horta
Ribeira de João
Salt-pans
VILA DO MAIO
Barreiro
Lagoa
Praia Preta
Casas Velhas

0 ———— 5km
0 ———— 3 miles

By ferry

There is currently no regular or reliable connection to and from Praia. Apparently roughly once a fortnight a ferry may run. Cargo boats that can take passengers run more frequently but not to any fixed schedule. Costs are expressed as around 1,000$. When you see a crowd of excited people at the port, it may be the cargo boat unloading. There are still plans for a new fast ferry.

By yacht

An unsatisfactory open anchorage with a lot of swell to deal with. Clear in with the police.

GETTING AROUND
By public transport

It is just about possible to do a circuit of the entire island in a day by picking up *aluguers* and hitching. But there is always the small chance of being left stranded and the desire not to be will prevent you from exploring off the main road.

Several of the good beaches lie within walking distance either of the *vila* or of

Figueira da Horta, which is easy to reach by *aluguer*. For other sights take a chance, hire transport, or ask your hotel owner to come and look for you in his car late in the day if you haven't returned.

Aluguers depart from villages such as Morrinho and Alcatraz very early in the morning to come to the *vila*. They return to Alcatraz at around 11.00 and to Morrinho between 08.00 and 10.00, departing from near the hospital.

By bicycle

A great way to see Maio is by bicycle. There is none officially for hire, although it should be possible to find one by asking one of the hotel proprietors. Take several litres of water and remember that every village has a shop somewhere, often indistinguishable from a private home – so ask.

Car hire

Find a jeep: a minibus or car will substantially restrict where you can go. A car can be rented for about 4,800–5,800$ a day. A car plus driver will cost more – about 6,500$.

MaioCar Vila do Maio. On the street continuing northeast of the post/telecom building; ☎ 255 1700

ACTIVITIES
Excursions

Maio is a place for resting and taking early-morning walks along the beaches and around the saltpans. There are no

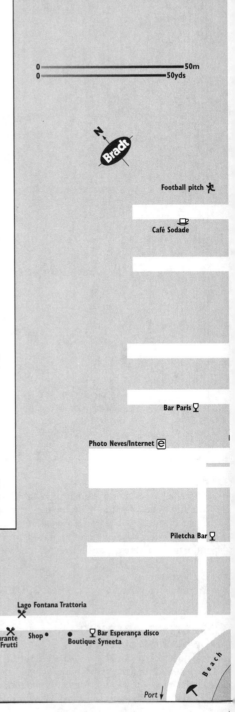

tour companies, but the following agency is planned:

Caboturismo SA Ribinha-Calheta; ☎ 256 1200

VILA DO MAIO

There is a well-kept and gracious town centre with a large square endowed with extra drama because it rises up a small but steep hill to a huge, white Baroque church built in 1872. At the southeast edge of town is an 18th-century fort, now restored and including some cannons.

Where to stay

Hotel Bom Sossego CP 34; ☎ 255 1365; f 255 1327. On the square, this is a bright, modern building run by spirited Senegalese staff. *Sgl 2,120$/2,650$ without/with hot water; dbl 2,968$/3,500$ without/with hot water.*

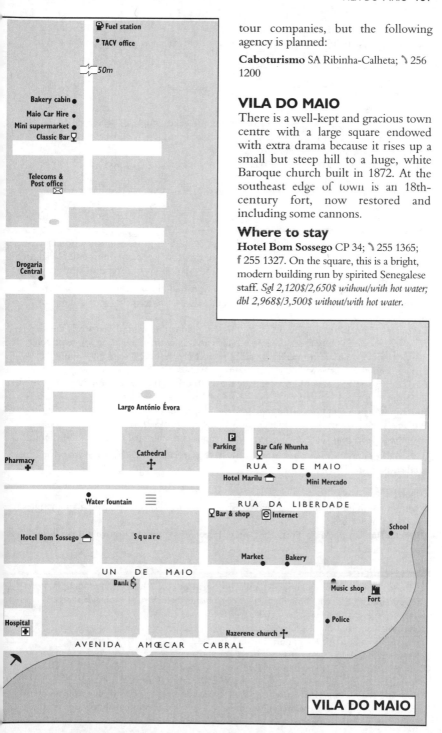

Fuel station
TACV office
50m
Bakery cabin
Maio Car Hire
Mini supermarket
Classic Bar
Telecoms & Post office
Drogaria Central
Largo António Évora
Parking
Bar Café Nhunha
Pharmacy
Cathedral
RUA 3 DE MAIO
Hotel Marilu
Mini Mercado
Water fountain
RUA DA LIBERDADE
Bar & shop
Internet
School
Hotel Bom Sossego
Square
Market
Bakery
UN DE MAIO
Bank
Music shop
Fort
Hospital
Police
Nazerene church
AVENIDA AMÍLCAR CABRAL

VILA DO MAIO

Hotel Marilú CP 48, Rua 24 de Septembre; ↘ 255 1198; f 255 1347. Facing the church, the hotel is to the right. Reasonable quality here with upstairs terrace, games room and fine views. *Sgl 2,500$; dbl 3,180$.*

Marcel Monteiro Quartos ↘ 255 1150

Spencer Quartos m 991 7438

Apartments

Salinas Village These are a series of strange windmill-like complexes developed by Germans on the northern entrance to town from the airport. 2-, 3- or 4-bedroom villas, some with private swimming pools.

Apartments Ilha do Maio ↘ 255 1312; www.ihladomaio.it. On the north side of town close to Salinas Village.

Gianniselva Apartments e gianniselva.bonino@libero.it. On the opposite side of the road to Ilha do Maio.

Where to eat and drink

Although a quick perusal of the list below would indicate a good choice, it is possible that many will be closed for much of the day. Keep an emergency stock of lunch items: bread, water, tinned sausages and mayonnaise instead of butter.

Hotel Bom Sossego The hotel has a reasonable restaurant downstairs.

Hotel Marilú A good standard of fare. Sometimes they have excellent pastries and perfect chocolate cake.

Restaurant Tutti Frutti ↘ 255 1575, m 997 9195. Along the main road towards the airport. Alberto and his wife serve excellent pizza and other fine food using imported food mainly from Portugal. (For interest, he says the electric bill at the restaurant is about 250 a month and duty on the wine is 80%.) Pizzas from 500$.

Lago Fontana Trattoria Almost opposite the Tutti Frutti, they serve meat dishes at similar price levels. Beer 100$.

Bar Esperança Along the seafront north of the hospital, for drinks.

Bar Paris For cold drinks. It is hidden away in the centre of town.

Esplanada Miramar Café has a beach view. Opposite the hospital near the phone booth.

The market may not have any food, but there is a bakery nearby – see map for this vital source of sustenance.

Nightlife

Nhunha Bar in the square (in a converted shipping container) where musicians sometimes play; open all day and in the evenings.

Piletcha Bar Un de Maio Turn right out of Hotel Sossego, right again and it is a little along, on your right.

Practicalities

Airlines TACV; ↘ 255 1256. Friendly but a long way from the centre, almost hiding along the road from the post/telecom building further out towards the town of Figueira da Horta.

Bank On the square. *Open Mon–Fri 08.00–13.00.*

Hospital None, but there is a health centre; ↘ 255 1130.

Internet Try Photo Neves and on Rue da Liberdade.

Pharmacy ↘ 255 1370. Look for Farmacia Forte.

Police ↘ 255 1132. At the far end of Av Amílcar Cabral.

Post office North of the square. *Open Mon–Fri 08.00–12.00, 14.00–18.00.*

Shopping Ramos Supermarket is quite well stocked and hoping to cash in on the awaited expansion of the apartment scene. There are also a couple of boutique-style shops nearby, but they may not be open often.

What to see and do
Beach
After the new pier the beach stretches for miles. See if you can find the pile of dumped boulders that intrigued visitors for years because they cannot be from anywhere in the archipelago. One academic thought they harboured clues to the whereabouts of Atlantis – it was once argued that the islands of Cape Verde might be the tips of a submerged continent. The mystery was solved by a vulcanologist who demonstrated that the boulders were from Brazil and were used as ballast – thrown on to the beach when the boat was loaded with salt.

The saltpans
This extraordinary lake of salt stretches for 5km north of town. At 1.5km wide, it is surrounded by vegetation adapted to the salty conditions. Between the pans and the sea is a raised beach which the sea water rises over at high tide: once it is in the lake the water evaporates in the sun and wind, leaving the crusts of salt. Some salt is still exported to Guinea-Bissau.

Ponta Preta
From the *vila* walk east along the coast, across the refuse tips and past the cemetery on the left – after about 15 minutes there is a small, pretty bay. A further 30 minutes will take you to the beach at Ponta Preta. Ask in town for further directions.

MORRO
The beach at Morro, in common with many in Cape Verde, fluctuates in size with the season's changing currents. In winter about 3m depth of sand vanishes, exposing rocks, and the sea as a result comes many metres further in. It is safe for swimming apart from the odd day when the waves come from the south. Turtles visit in the summer.

From Morro there is a two-hour walk up the nearby hill with good views at the top and a walk along the stunning beach to Calheta where Pedro Tavares Silva (↘ 256 7349) might still be prepared to rustle up some food if you telephone beforehand.

Where to stay
Hotel Belavista ↘ 256 1388, m 995 2087; f 256 1377; e belavista@terra.es. The Belavista, a 3-star hotel, is a series of square stone buildings with shady plants developing. It is on the beach just before Morro. Facilities include tennis, swimming pool, rent a car, excursions and fine restaurant. Sgl 4,650$; dbl 5,800$; triple 7,100$; 4-bedded villas 8,300$; all inc breakfast.

Clube des Tortues This is an astonishing compound whose walls rise from the barren rockscape to encircle a group of chalets built of local stone, and thatched with banana leaves. The hotel has a beach and had a restaurant. At the time of research it was closed, hoping to find new ownership. Reservations were formerly made through Cape Verde Travel in the UK (see page 40).

Where to eat and drink
Bemvindo ↘ 994 2348

Calheta
This settlement to the north of Morro is being expanded to settle more local residents. A considerable amount of building activity was evident in 2005.

WHALES

When Beatrice Jann, a biologist from the University of Basel in Switzerland, can scrape the money together she heads to Cape Verde to indulge her passion – documenting whales. Sometimes she is the guest of the *Sodade*, a schooner that used to take visitors around the islands the old-fashioned way. In 2000 and 2001, she identified 35 humpbacks.

'This is probably only a small proportion of what is around,' she says. Whales are identified from the undersides of their tail flukes. Each underside is unique to that whale. Its shifting patches of black and white look like an ink-blot pattern. Researchers photograph these patterns and send them to a store at Bar Harbour in Maine, USA, where there are now 'fingerprints' of 5,000 whales.

'It's sort of an Interpol of the humpbacks,' says Beatrice. By matching observations, scientists can piece together the whales' migrations. They have found whales photographed in Norway turning up in the Dominican Republic, and whales from western Canada appearing in Japan.

In Cape Verde whales can be seen from December and linger for some time. They are gone by the summer. On her April 2001 trip Beatrice spotted several mothers with calves that were only a few days old – tantalising evidence that Cape Verde is a breeding ground.

'Mothers seek out places where there are not too many waves and it is not too deep, probably because the calf cannot swim very well,' says Beatrice. 'It's important that people don't rush on the whales close to shore.'

Whales are often seen from the beach at Sal Rei in Boavista. Other scientists have recorded them around Sal.

Where to eat and drink
Café Ca Nelhino ⟩ 256 1198

A CLOCKWISE TOUR OF THE ISLAND

The land is flat, desolate brown desert, broken by unexpected patches of acacia forest and, in the east, relief for the eye from the odd fertile valley planted with crops and palm trees. The beaches are hidden from the main roads but many can be reached in a jeep or by walking a few kilometres.

Drive from the *vila* up the west coast. About 3km after Morro is the pretty fishing village of **Calheta**: turn left off the main road to drive through it. At the end of its street, lined with red-tiled pitched roofs and white-painted stones, is the bay. You can swim here, though it is probably cleaner away from the settlement. After Calheta lies the bulk of the forest – low green vegetation in sandy ground. It makes surprisingly little impact, perhaps because the soil itself remains dry and bare.

At **Morrinho** ask for the rough track that leads northwest to **Praia de Santana**, a wild and desolate beach, invisible from the long road you will follow, hidden by a ridge of dunes. About 1km in from the sea, on your right, lies another saltpan. The rough track goes on and on for several kilometres and then peters out: if you want to go further you must walk. Eventually, you reach **Praia Real**: bear in mind that northern beaches are not safe for swimming.

Returning to the main road, between Cascabulho and Pedro Vaz there is more of the green and mature forest followed by a landscape that feels like an abandoned opencast mine. Then **Pedro Vaz** appears. It seems as though it could be the end of the earth but it's not – there's another two rough kilometres to the beach, possible by car. This is perhaps the loneliest and wildest beach, enlivened occasionally by women who come to meet the returning fishermen.

As you leave Pedro Vaz to continue south you'll pass an old village, all that remains is a little white church. They hold a service here on the last Sunday of each month. Just after the church you can walk up the slopes of the hill on your right. Even a short stroll will be rewarded with good views. Continue, and the journey feels increasingly isolated in the abandoned stony plains and lifeless land. **Alcatraz** lies 4km from Pedro Vaz – a single wide and dusty street where you can ask the locals to guide you up to the top of Monte Penoso for the best views of the island.

Continuing, the dry land is broken up a little now by the agricultural areas. Turn left just before **Figueira da Horta** and you will travel past pretty oases to reach Ribeira de João where you can park. Turning right off the main street, down a footpath, it is a ten-minute walk past the football pitch and along an enormously wide *ribeira* to find this magnificent beach with unbearably turquoise water. Look behind you – the village nestles like some Arabian desert town on the top of the bare brown hills. (To reach this beach directly from the vila, take an *aluguer* to Figueira da Horta and ask directions.)

Figueira is a bright village from which you can drive to **Barreiro**, a neat settlement built on two sides of a valley. At the second half of Barreiro take the left fork (the right one goes to Ponta Preta) and continue to Lagoa, a beach to which stalwart locals claim they walk from the *vila* along the coast (about 9km).

Tamarisk palm (tamareira)

Fogo

It is all of it one large mountain of a good height, out of the top whereof issues Flames of Fire, yet only discerned in the Night: and then it may be seen a great way at Sea.

William Dampier, 1683

Fogo rises steeply from the ocean, pokes through the clouds and towers above them. From the coast of Santiago or the peaks of São Nicolau it is as forbidding as a fortress. Fogo is a volcano, still active, and inside the crater the latest eruption still smokes gently.

Fogo is a menacing place: dark lava flows from centuries of eruptions to reach down its eastern side to the ocean. But it has a soft heart. Amongst the clods of cold lava that have covered much of the floor of the crater are fertile fields. Spilling over its northeast side are woods of eucalyptus and cool valleys in which grow coffee and vines. Inside the crater lives a race of people who have defied government orders to evacuate and instead live and farm below the smouldering peak that last erupted in 1995.

HIGHLIGHTS

The crater is a highlight of the archipelago, its drama matched only by the mountains of Santo Antão. Fogo is thus one of the principal hiking islands, but it is also fascinating for its anthropology and its natural history. Much of the island's splendour can be reached by vehicle. There are caves to explore and modest swimming but virtually no white beaches and no watersports. The capital is quiet.

BACKGROUND INFORMATION
History

Geologists have done intricate work to piece together the volcano's history by extrapolating from the directions of lava flows of different ages and combining that information with literary descriptions of the appearance of the volcano at different times.

Fogo erupted from the sea a few hundred thousand years ago, a single volcano reaching a mighty 3.5km high. Its walls were steep and unstable and so, sometime within the last 10,000 years, a great section in the east collapsed towards the sea – reducing the height of its walls by about 300m in one giant avalanche. After the first eruption there were numerous smaller ones, all making craters in the floor of the original large crater, which is now about 10km long and 7km wide.

Volcanoes are fertile places and Fogo's agricultural potential was harnessed from

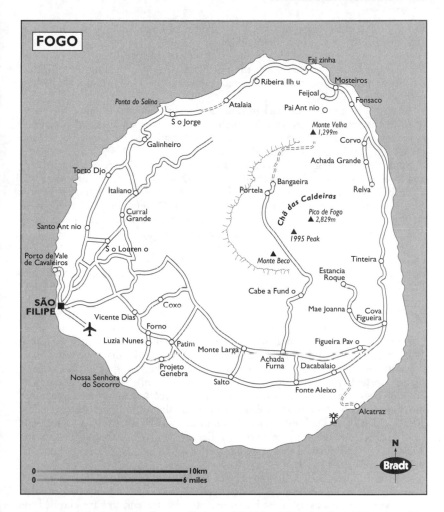

early on – it had acquired a population of 2,000 within the first 120 years of its discovery. It was the second island of the archipelago to be settled and was populated with slaves who grew cotton and developed the skill of weaving – the island was famed for its *pano preta*, or deep indigo cloth (see *Perspective*, page 26). The cloth was shipped to Santiago, and because of this the island remained remote from the trans-oceanic ship trade. But it did not escape attack: the Dutch had a four-day spree there in 1655. Lisbon's response to the ensuing plea for more Portuguese settlers was to dispatch convicts. Fogo was regarded as a hardship posting and, though it is only 50km from Santiago, it was the threatened place of exile for the people of the greater island.

For much of this time the volcano in the background was growing: it appears to have put on several hundred metres between 1450 and 1750, and in the early 1600s black clouds swathed its heights. An eruption in 1680 was savage and gave the island its name, which means 'fire' – before that it had been called, as usual, after the saint's day on which it was discovered. Much fertile land was ruined in that 1680 eruption and many people emigrated permanently to neighbouring Brava.

From the end of the 1600s into the 1700s the fire of Fogo could be seen from afar and was used by ships to aid their navigation.

It was into the open space left by the giant ancient collapse that, in 1785, Pico de Fogo erupted. Lava spewed down the northeastern slopes creating the bulge on which the town of Mosteiros is situated today and the Pico became the highest point of the archipelago.

Against this tempestuous background the people of Fogo welcomed the crews of American whaling ships who came ashore in search of supplies and personnel, as they were doing on Brava. Thus began the emigration to the United States and the creation of the great Cape Verdean diaspora.

Since 1785 all eruptions have been inside the old crater. There was one in 1799 and three in the following century, in 1847, 1852 and 1857, after which there was a century's gap. Each eruption leaves cones in the crater floor which is how it earned its name, Chã das Caldeiras or Plain of Craters. In 1847 there were fatalities, caused not by lava flows but by the associated earthquakes. The eruption of 1852 created the cone known as Monte Preto de Baixo.

In the 20th century there were two eruptions. Lava spewed from one of the two chimneys on the southern side of the volcano in 1951 and also created cones to the north and south of the Pico – such as Monte Orlando, Monte Rendall and Monte Preto de Cima. These eruptions all began along a line of volcanic fissures extending from the flank of the Pico de Fogo summit cone across the floor of Chã das Caldeiras. The lava flows that issued from these vents spread over the northern and southern parts of Chã das Caldeiras and down the eastern flank of the island.

It was just a few years ago that the last eruption occurred, on the night of 2 April 1995. For a week before, the villages had been shaken with small but increasingly powerful earthquakes. Just after midnight the flank of the Pico split apart as a line of fissures opened. It was as if the Pico had been 'cut by a knife', said one villager. The eruption began and a curtain of fire issued from the volcano and poured down into the crater. Thousands of inhabitants fled. By daylight the whole island was covered by a thick cloud of dark ash extending 5km into the sky; lava bombs up to 4m wide landed half a kilometre from the eruption and a day later lava fountains were spurting 400m high: it is estimated that at its height the volcano ejected between 4 and 8.5 million cubic metres per day.

One month later the lava had thickened but was still flowing at 15cm per hour. It was another month before the flow stopped. Miraculously nobody died; perhaps the luckiest escape was made by two guitarists who are said to have climbed the Pico the day before the eruption, to make music and enjoy the view.

The 1995 eruption was different from the others. Unusually, it occurred southwest of the Pico, through a system of fissures that lay in a broadly south-to-west orientation. As a result the lava flows spread west and then north, covering an area of fertile volcanic soils and ultimately much of the small village of Boca Fonte. Today, shells of its houses remain, invaded by monstrous clumps of lava as high as their roofs.

Alternative housing was quickly built on the southern slopes – it can be seen from the road as you ascend to the crater. It was assumed that the people would move there permanently but most of them have returned to their crater homes to cultivate whatever land escaped the lava flow. The road across Chã has been rebuilt.

For most of the duration of the eruption (from 10 April to the end of May) the only active vent was at the northeastern end of the fissure system and it is here that the largest volcanic cone of the eruption grew – the yellow-streaked, smoking black slope that lies at the foot of the Pico de Fogo. You pass it on the right soon after entering the crater by road.

Today Fogo has been boosted by development work, much of it funded by Germany. It has a fine new harbour, and acres of terracing, catchment dams and reafforestation.

Geography

The fourth-largest island, with an area of 480km², Fogo's highest point is the Pico de Fogo which reaches 2,829m. Fogo has a population of 40,000. São Filipe is the third-largest town in Cape Verde.

On the volcano there is little short of an ecological crisis. Locals cut down the wood for fuel and rake in the vegetation for fodder. Goats kill even the trees by chewing away their bark. The entire island could become barren within a few years except for deliberate plantations. There are six plant species endemic only to Fogo. Two to watch out for are *lingua de vaca* (*Echium vulcanorum*), a white flower with a broad leaf, which is confined not just to Fogo volcano but only to the volcano's rim; and *cravo-babo* (*Erysimum caboverdeanum*), a delicate pink flower with long pointed leaves, which is found only inside the crater.

The islanders grow coffee and produce wine. The coffee is grown on the outer northern slopes near Mosteiros. Grapes are grown in the crater by digging pits amongst the little black pieces of basaltic rock known as *lapilli* and planting a vine in each: at night the moisture condenses on the rock and dribbles into the holes. The vivid green of the vines contrasts sharply with the black lava below.

Fogo is thought to have potential for geothermal energy for electricity production. Rainwater filters through the permeable volcanic rock and reaches underground reservoirs. Volcanic activity means that water samples taken during investigations have had temperatures of 200–300°C.

Economy

Agriculture is the main activity, though fishing occupies a small number of people. There's plenty of water underground but hoisting it to the surface is expensive, and directing it higher – to the slopes that carry much of the agriculture – is even more costly.

Festivals

The end of April is the time for Fogo's big party, Bandeira (Flag) de São Filipe. There is horse racing, held on the black sandy terrace outside Le Bistro Restaurant, dancing and processions. Special dishes are made. The island has a distinctive music known as *pilão*, a bit like *batuko*, a chanting and beating of drums that forms the background to the grinding of corn in the run-up to the festival. Others are as follows:

São Sebastião	20 January
São Joao	24 June
São Pedro	29 June
Santa Rainha de Cabo Verde	Second Sunday in July (Chã das Caldeiras)
Nossa Sta do Soccorro	5 August
São Lourenco	10 August
Municipality Day	15 August (Mosteiros)
Santa Caterina	24 November (Cova Figueira)

GETTING THERE AND AWAY
By air

Flying over the flanks of the volcano and landing on a sliver of flat land between the grey slopes and the blue sea is one of the most spectacular experiences you will have on the archipelago. Coming from Praia, sit on the right-hand side. Inter-island flights with TACV are as follows:

Praia	2 or 3 a day
Sal	2 a week, regular day-trip charters
Boavista	Regular day-trip charters

It's 2km into the capital, a 20-minute walk downhill into town. A shared *aluguer* from the airport to São Filipe should not cost more than 100$ (taxi 500$). Some hotels collect their guests if they have booked in advance. There is an *aluguer* for Mosteiros which meets every São Filipe flight.

By ferry
The port lies to the north of São Filipe and a taxi to town costs 150$ (but from town to the port costs 500$). The *Barlavento* runs between Santiago, Brava and Fogo, though services can be erratic. Tickets can be bought, in advance, from the ferry ticket office in the docks.

Another possibility might be to charter a boat from Fogo Adventures.

By yacht
Fogo is bathed in a swell that can only be avoided by anchoring at the harbour to the north of the capital. Unfortunately it is so small that the presence of two ferries or cargo ships may lead to an order for yachts to leave. Mosteiros is not suitable for yachts. Register with the port captain's office in São Filipe.

GETTING AROUND
By public transport
Aluguers leave Mosteiros, the villages in the crater and other outlying villages between 04.00 and 05.30, arriving in São Filipe about an hour and a half later. They depart from São Filipe mid morning and also at midday and at 14.00 for the crater (250$): don't get stranded. There are no *aluguers* to and from the crater on a Sunday. An *aluguer* leaves São Filipe for São Jorge sometime between 09.30 and 11.00 and one returns to São Filipe at 13.00.

Aluguers for the crater and for Mosteiros leave from beside the block that houses the town hall (*câmara municipal*) and the market. Those for São Jorge, Salinas, the airport and the port leave from outside Pousada Belavista. To go to Monte Genebre, take an *aluguer* from outside the post office.

By taxi
Taxis or chartered *aluguers* will go most places (the taxi rank in São Filipe is at the top of town, opposite the post office). Fares are relatively fixed – for example, to the crater 6,000$; around the island 8,000$; to Mosteiros 6,000$; to São Lourenço 1,000$; to Curral Grande 1,300$.

Car hire
Discount Auto Rent and Parts São Filipe; ☏ 281 1480; f 281 1063. 1 day's hire: 7,000–8,000$.

ACTIVITIES
Excursions
Dja'r Fogo CP 101 Alto San Pedro, 8220 São Filipe; ☏ 281 2879, m 991 9713; e agnus@clix.pt; www.djarfogo.net. Specialising in small groups and individuals, this agency can arrange any itineraries to suit. Agnelo also serves great homegrown coffee.

THE SCHOONER 'ERNESTINA'

The schooner *Ernestina*, a beautiful, 112ft sailing vessel over a century old, is one of the most famous of the packet ships that connected Cape Verde with the USA in the early 20th century.

She was still working as a packet ship in the 1960s, making her last Atlantic voyage to Providence in 1965 in an era that had long been dominated by the steamship and which was fast losing trade to the aeroplane.

The *Ernestina* had many lives. After her launch in 1894 she became a Grand Banks fisher and then an Arctic expeditionary vessel. She sank after a galley fire in 1946, and that was when a Cape Verdean, Captain Henrique Mendes, stepped in. The schooner was raised, restored to seaworthiness, bought by Captain Mendes and then began her new life as a trans-Atlantic packet ship. Her work was to carry passengers and goods between Cape Verde and the US. Often she took seasonal workers to New England for the cranberry harvest. Hopeful immigrants would also come. Sometimes she would take successful immigrants on rare trips home; more often it was goods she ferried back to the motherland – bought with hard-won money earned on the bogs or in the textile mills of New Bedford.

For ten years this trade continued between Cape Verde and Providence, Rhode Island. After her last trip in 1965 she continued work between Cape Verde and the African mainland. She also worked the islands. One job was to ferry schoolchildren from Fogo and Brava to boarding school in Praia and Mindelo.

But even this work was being eclipsed by other, more modern ships, and eventually it was decided to return the *Ernestina* to the USA. But the trip home, in 1976, was a disaster – a storm dismasted her and she was forced to return to port. There, the government of the new republic had her rebuilt and, six years later, gave her to the US as a symbol of friendship.

Ernestina is now a sailing school, educational vessel and cultural icon.

For more information on the schooner and a vivid history of the passage of Cape Verdeans to and from the USA, see www.ernestina.org/history/index.html.

Homestays can be arranged on the lower slopes of the crater area at a charming old family home. Contact Agnelo Vieira de Andrade.

Ecotur Rua do Hospital, São Filipe; ☎ 281 2255, m 994 3051/992 6997; f 281 1726; e ecotourfogo@cvtelecom.cv; www.ecotur.cv. Organises mainly group trips to Chã das Caldeiras, and a variety of walks in and out of the crater, with guides. Sample price: day trip to the Pico, 8,700$ per person (minimum 4 people).

Fogo Adventures m 993 2866; f 281 2362. Specialises in sailing yacht trips and fishing. They operate a Bertram 35ft twin-engine boat for fishing for blue marlin, sharks and big tuna. It is also possible to hire the boat for diving, dolphin-watching and trips to Brava. Contact via Ecotur.

Hiking

This is the great activity of Fogo. As well as the big one, up to the Pico in the crater, there are several delightful walks from various points on the crater down its sides. See *Hikes*, page 176.

Fishing

See *Excursions* above.

Cycling

Fogo is steep and cobbled, and cycling anywhere but along contours or downhill can be unbearable. Vulcan Bike, the previous rental concern, is currently closed but ask around anyway.

Swimming

It is often dangerous to swim on Fogo, but when the sea looks really calm it is safe at the beach at the port, and at Praia Nossa Senhora. The best place to swim, however, is Ponte Salina – a stunning cove with black rock formations smothered by white seaspray and riddled with grottos and reefs. It can be reached on the São Jorge *aluguer* – ask to be dropped off there and check what time the *aluguer* is returning. A big disco and bar is planned there.

Caves

There are at least three volcanic tubes to explore on Fogo. The tubes are lava flows that solidify on the outside, after which the inner liquid flows away leaving them hollow inside. Inside they are beautiful, with frozen lava in streams down the inner walls like melted chocolate.

Two of the caves lie on an imaginary line drawn roughly between Pico de Fogo and São Lourenço, on the slopes of Fogo a bit higher than the roads. To reach them ask at Bar Teresa for Robert, who will take you to Ribeira de Aguadinha, to a large concrete water tank and then on to the caves. Access to one involves a 5m crawl before it opens out into a larger area. Bring a good head torch and don't go alone or if you are not an experienced caver. The floors of the caves are uneven.

SÃO FILIPE

This is a large and pretty town full of Portuguese squares, esplanades and *sobrado* houses (see *Architecture* below) – some of them collapsing, a few lovingly restored. The streets are cobbled, the buildings are pastel with terracotta tiles, and vegetation springs from pots on every fragile wooden balcony. Bougainvillea abounds and trees are a healthy size. The town could do with some more outdoor cafés from which its architecture and the views of Brava could be enjoyed. Until then, there is a promenade, adorned with busts of Portuguese heroes, which lines the cliff tops and from which you can gaze down the harsh drop to the black sands and the violent sea below. There's also a large terrace on which to sit, halfway up the hill at the top of a flight of steps (marked on the map).

Where to stay
Upmarket

Hotel Xaguate CP 47; ✆ 281 1222; f 281 1203; e xaguate@cvtelecom.cv; www.caboverde.com. The hotel has been virtually completely renovated. It is set in a spectacular position on the headland, which can be enjoyed from the balconies of some of the rooms, or from the swimming pool terrace. Non-residents may swim there for a reasonable fee. *Sgl 7,170$; dbl 8,600$; extra bed plus 3,640$; inc breakfast. Half board plus 1,655$; FB plus 2,650$. Mastercard and Visa accepted.*

Mid range

Pousada Belavista CP 50; ✆ 281 1734/1220; f 281 1879; e p_belavista@yahoo.com; www.pbelavista.com. It is around the corner of the same block as the TACV office. This

friendly, excellent-value hotel is immaculate, with 11 spotless and very comfortable rooms, all with private bathroom and TV. Rooms vary; some have AC, some have fans; some have fridge and TV; some have hot water. *Sgl 2,000–2,500$; dbl 3,000–3,500$; triple 4,000–5,000$; inc a good breakfast.*
Casa Renate CP 78; ╲ 281 2518, m 994 5939; f 281 1641; e RenateFogo@hotmail.com. This is the building opposite the cathedral. The lady of the house can also be contacted at the Bistro Café – see map. *Sgl 2,700–3,700$; dbl 3,500–4,500$; use of kitchen 200$ extra; inc breakfast.*
Pensão Las Vegas ╲ 281 2223, m 995 6873; f 281 1281; www.caboverde.com. Las Vegas has friendly management, and a variety of rooms, some with balconies giving sea views. *Sgl 2,000–2,500$; dbl 3,000–3,500$; inc breakfast.*
Pensão Open Skies ╲ 281 2726/2012, m 991 4595; e majortelo@yahoo.com. At the top of town east of the main square. Rooms with AC, hot and cold water, TV and minibar. It's the purple building, with a pleasant rooftop terrace. *Sgl 2,000–2,500$; dbl 3,000–3,500$.*
Ecotour CP 93, Rua do Hospital; ╲ 281 2255, m 994 3051; f 281 1726; e ecotourfogo@cvtelecom.cv; www.ecotur.cv. It is nearly opposite the hospital, with equipped kitchen, living room and verandas. *Sgl 2,120$; dbl 3,180$; inc breakfast.*
Pensão Fátima ╲/f 281 1359; www.caboverde.com. Near the cathedral, this is an attractive place with a rooftop terrace which is a good place to meet other travellers. Some rooms have balconies. *Sgl 1,800$; dbl 2,800$.*
Pensão Verdiana ╲/f 281 2678. Just above the central market. This hotel building has been completely renovated and has various bars and restaurants within. It is sometimes closed when the owners are away. *Sgl 1,500$; dbl 2,800$; inc breakfast.*
Pensão Christina On the east side of town. It is linked with the hotel in Mosteiros so contact the Mosteiros number ╲ 281 2623. *Sgl 1,800$; dbl 2,500$.*
Pensão Seafood CP 63; ╲ 281 2623/2624, m 992 2981; f 281 3188. In the southern area of town. A few rooms in a quiet area, no seafood though. *Sgl 1,700$; dbl 2,400$.*
Pensão Inacio A new pension in the orange building just off the airport road, east of the open area, was set to open when we visited and looks very clean and airy. *Prices were not available at the time of research.*
Casa Amelia Restaurant/bar/music has 2 rooms for rent and a hairdresser.

Homestay
Quinta das Saudades ╲ 281 2879. A homestay about 8km from São Filipe (see Dja'r Fogo under *Excursions* above). A quiet retreat on the lower slopes of the crater with walks to the nearby extinct volcanic cones. By taxi it costs 600$, *aluguer* about 70$. Price inc breakfast and afternoon tea with homemade biscuits. *Dinner 1,200$. Sgl 1,800$; dbl 2,200$.*

Where to eat and drink
Bar Restaurante Leila ╲ 281 1214. Consistently good reports about the food in this basement restaurant, opposite the noisy generator in the east of town. Main dishes start at 500$.
Casa Amelia Restaurant/bar/music.
Cape Cod Restaurant is close to the Pensão Las Vegas and has fish from 600–1,200$.
Café Magma Located above/behind the Pousada Belavista, with a good selection and a bright atmosphere.
Hotel Xaguate Has a restaurant with good reports about the food.
Le Bistro Popular with tourists because of its terrace with superb views and its Mediterranean cuisine.
Open Skies Rooftop restaurant at the top of town, in the hotel of the same name. Can be crowded. Food served after 17.00. Right in the centre of São Filipe, halfway up the hill.
Pensão Las Vegas Has a restaurant and bar on an open-air terrace. Good food, available all day, a definite plus in Cape Verde.

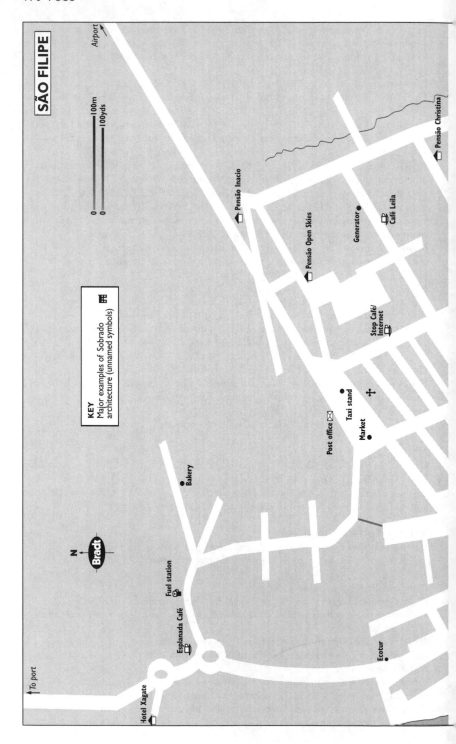

SÃO FILIPE

To port

Airport

Bradt

N

KEY
Major examples of Sobrado
architecture (unnamed symbols)

0 ——— 100m
0 ——— 100yds

Hotel Xagate

Esplanada Café

Fuel station

Bakery

Pensão Inacio

Pensão Open Skies

Post office

Taxi stand

Market

Stop Café/
Internet

Generator

Café Leila

Ecotur

Pensão Christina

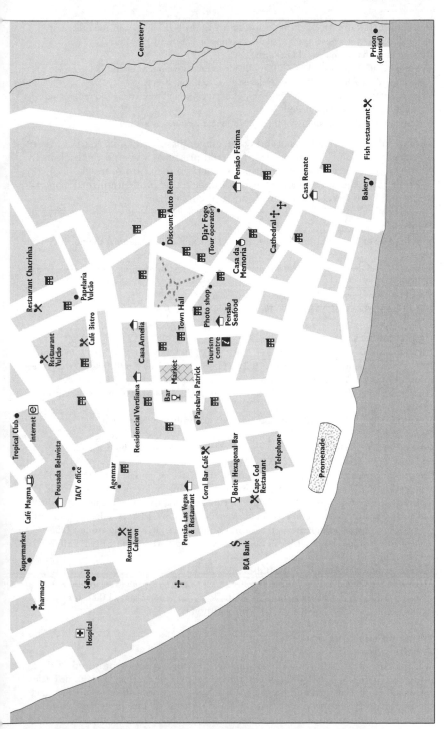

Restaurant Caleron An excellent open-air place for barbecued chicken and other tasty delights. Follow your nose; the barbeques cooking are a sensory overload.
Restaurant Chacrinha An old favourite.
Tropical Club Snacks at a bar with an outside terrace. Live music occasionally. Follow your nose; it's south of the Pousada Belavista between two streets.
Restaurante Seafood ☎ 283 1045. Overlooking the sea, and receiving good reports, this restaurant is down near the prison.
Restaurante Vulcão Copious local fare. No longer operates as a hotel.

Find freshly made bread, cakes and warm ginger biscuits at Dona Maria's bakery on the edge of the cliff, just up from the old prison. It's around the back in an alley next to the sea wall. There is also a bakery in the north of town.

Fresh goat's cheese, fruit and tomatoes can be found in the municipal market in the middle of town, in the same block as the town hall.

Nightlife

Esplanada Tex Traditional music most Fri nights. On the roundabout at the northwest of town.
Tropical Traditional music every Fri night. Discos the rest of the time (see *Where to eat and drink* above).
Coral bar A 'watering hole' in the centre of town.
Bar Boite Hexagonal ☎ 281 2175. Next to the Cape Cod Restaurant.

Practicalities

Airlines TACV; ☎ 281 1340/1701; f 281 1340; *open Mon–Fri 08.00–13.00, 15.00–18.00.*
Banks Banco Comercial do Atlântico, Rua do Hospital; *open Mon–Fri 08.00–15.00.* On the road that runs up the cliff edge of town, away from the esplanades.
Ferries Agenmar; ☎ 281 1012; *open Mon–Fri 08.00–12.00, 15.00–18.00.* Across the square from Pousada Belavista.
Hospital ☎ 281 1130. On the same road as the bank, further up on the left.
Police ☎ 281 1132
Post office Large pink building at the top of town on the big square with a candle sculpture. *Open Mon–Fri 08.00–12.00, 14.00–16.00.*
Shopping Souvenirs, inc Fogo wine and coffee, and crafts, are on sale at Ecotur (see *Where to stay*, page 167). Food supplies can be found at various small mini supermarkets beside.
Tourist information None. Ask the travel agents. Papelaria Patrick sells a map of Fogo and also postcards. There is avery useful information kiosk in Chã das Caldeiras. Look out for a book written by John Rendall, the former British consul in Mindelo around 1856, *Guide des Iles du Cap Verte*, available in English, French and Portuguese (ISBN 2 9510592 5 6; cost 28).
Maps *Fogo* 1:60,000, Attila Bertolan (ISBN 3 934262 03 1; cost 8).
Miscellaneous Water is a very scarce resource on Fogo, so be sparing. Apparently water costs approximately 8,000$ for 6 tonnes – a lorry load – in general, and 11,000$ for 6 tonnes in the crater. In 1856 it cost 10 shillings per tonne.

What to see and do

Architecture

Wander the streets admiring the *sobrado* architecture. About a hundred of these houses remain – built by the rich and decorated with fine woods and tiles imported from Portugal and west Africa. If you can peek into one of them take the opportunity: a central courtyard planted with trees and vines gave coolness and shade and around it, on the ground floor, were the working rooms. The next floor was more beautiful, lined with an inside balcony that overlooked the courtyard on three sides – this was the floor for the master and his family. On the street side there was a balcony of carved wood. Slaves were not permitted to ascend to the first floor except once a year, on the festival of Santa Cruz. During the summer the town house was closed and the family went inland to oversee the farming.

See map (page 170) for the location of some more prominent examples.

Casa da Memória
A private museum (✆ 281 2765; www.chez.com/casadamemoria) in a beautifully restored family house, depicting the history of Fogo from the early to mid 1800s. Full of photos, domestic objects and a patio in which there was Fogo's first cinema, now restored. Cultural events are held there, as well as some conferences.

The beach and swimming
A walk down the grotty ribeira road to the black beach is worthwhile for several reasons. This is a poor part of town, with people scavenging among the rubbish on the hillsides and pigs tethered in makeshift shelters. Below lies a strip of black sand under the ominous Fogo cliffs, lashed by Atlantic breakers. As you begin your descent you will see the prison. Perched on the cliff, its prisoners must have had a vista of the ocean and the cemetery must have afforded many prisoner an inspirational setting for reflecting on his misdemeanours, but it is now closed.

Take a swim at the Hotel Xaguate, which has an enjoyable poolside terrace.

CHÃ DAS CALDEIRAS
The road to the volcano passes first through pleasant countryside dotted with abandoned Portuguese farms and old volcano cones. Later the road becomes a series of terrifyingly steep hairpin bends with views down massive ancient lava spills to the coast and then enters the echoing silence of the crater. Its sinister dark walls, and the vast clods of lava scattered over it, make one feel very small.

The people are as of a different race – light skinned, straight haired, some of them even blond and blue eyed. These are the descendants of the fecund Duc de Montrond (see box, page 174), a French nobleman who came here in the 19th century and brought the vines that began Fogo's wine production.

The people who live in the volcano are trying to improve its fragile ecology and develop an economy. One step has been to define the crater as a nature reserve; another has been to set up small-scale tourism. Around 1,600 people live in this unusual region. Of the five endemic species found almost exclusively in the Parque Natural do Fogo, the lingua de vaca is the most common and spectacular species of scrub vegetation.

Getting there and away
A good plan is to take a midday aluguer for the three-hour journey from São Filipe (500$) and ask to be deposited at the Cooperativa in the crater. There, over a glass of Fogo wine and to the lusty music of the small band that seems to play there permanently, you can ask around for a room. Spend the rest of the day exploring the volcano: some ideas are given below. The next day you can climb the Pico, then stay another night and pick up the very early aluguer the next morning back to town (listen for the horn which sounds loudly in the village at about 05.00). For a small supplement, you can ask to be dropped at the airport first.

If you prefer to walk some of the way to the volcano, then catch an aluguer from town to Achada Furna; it takes three hours to cover the steep road from there.

THE DUKE OF MONTROND

Most of the inhabitants of the volcano crater can trace their ancestry back to an eccentric French duke who made Fogo his home in the 1870s.

The scattering of blue eyes, light skin and yellowy hair among the people of the crater can be traced back to the prolific duke. He had at least 11 children – and now has 300 descendants in the USA alone.

François Louis Armand Montrond was on his way to Brazil when he arrived in Cape Verde in 1872 – and stayed. After testing most of the islands he found Fogo was the one he preferred and he spent the rest of his life there, returning to France several times for visits.

The duke has left more behind him than the intriguing people of the crater: he put to use his background in engineering and medicine. He oversaw the construction of a road from São Filipe to Mosteiros, and he sank wells, some of which are still in use today.

A wealthy man, he supported at least three wives and adopted two children as well. He also imported medicinal herbs and, it is said, the vines that kicked off wine production on the volcano slopes.

At 60, he fell off his horse, broke his leg, and died of an infection.

At first he was not credited for his achievements because the Portuguese felt he showed them up, claims Alberto Montrond, a great-great-grandson who lives in the USA and regularly visits Fogo.

'He did great things for the people on the island,' he says. Alberto's work tracing the Montrond ancestry and investigating the duke's story has been the subject of a French documentary film.

An alternative to the above plan is to set off on the second day on foot, out of the north of the crater and down to Mosteiros, where there is an excellent *pensão*, taking the pre-dawn *aluguer* back to São Filipe the next morning. A walk up the Pico followed by the descent to Mosteiros in one day is too much for most people.

A day trip to the volcano is tricky by public transport, though there are cars in the crater which can be chartered as taxis for the trip back to São Filipe for several thousand escudos.

Where to stay

Pousada Pedra Brabo ❱ 261 8940; f 281 2904; e pedrabrabo@cvtelecom.cv Tasteful, single-storey lava-brick guesthouse with 12 rooms. Has hot water, electricity, excellent food and a stunning view. Patrick, the congenial French proprietor, has a wealth of stories about crater life. *Sgl 1,900$; dbl 2,800$ (add 6% tax to room rates); breakfast 700$.*

Homestays Accommodation is either in the houses of local people or in dormitories they have built alongside. Accommodation is pretty basic (see *Living with the people*, page 51); sometimes just a windowless room made of lava blocks. But the best are clean and careful preparations are made for visitors, who are received with great delight and good spirits. To sample and buy local wine and cheese, ask for the house of Señor Socorro. For booking contact a travel agent in São Filipe or, after you have arrived in the crater, at the tourist office/*Cooperativa* beyond Portela. *Price per person 1,000–1,500$ inc evening meal; breakfast an extra 300$ each.*

Where to eat and drink

Pousada Pedra Brabo A 3-course evening meal from 1,000$. The chocolate mousse is unforgettable.

Nightlife
Head for the *Cooperativa* (see *Homestays*), where there is often wine, music and dancing into the small hours.

What to see and do
Hiking
There are several guides conversant with the natural history of the volcano, having worked with botanists and geologists: ask for them at the *Cooperativa* (see *Homestays*) or at Pousada Pedra Brabo. For some walks it is essential to have a guide. An example is climbing the Pico de Fogo, because the path shifts with the movements of the ash – a guide will cost around 3,000$. For other walks a guide is not essential, but embellishes the experience and takes you to places you would not otherwise find.

The main walks are up the Pico (which can take anything between three and six hours depending on your fitness and your proficiency at running back down through the lava powder – see box, page 176) and the walk down to Mosteiros. You can also ascend to the crater rim and even walk along it, or wander around the crater floor. It's possible to scramble to the top of the 1995 eruption. Some of these walks are described in *Hiking*, page 176.

MOSTEIROS
The town, also known as Igreja, is a useful stopping point during trips around the island but otherwise is not worth a visit. It has a pretty centre, squashed between the mountain and the sea, and a depressing suburbia of black, lava-block houses built on black lava rock.

Getting there and away
The *aluguer* run to and from São Filipe is a fantastic journey along the precipitous eastern slope of the island. You can do the journey in the dark on one of the pre-dawn runs to the capital. In the case of a fast *aluguer* driver this can be quite a relief. The proprietor of Pensão Christine will arrange for one of the drivers to call at the hotel for you at about 04.45. *Aluguers* leave São Filipe for Mosteiros at about midday.

Where to stay
Pensão Restaurante Christine e Irmãos ❜ 283 1045. In a green building on the main road through town; it has 7 lovely, airy rooms. They also have a guesthouse in São Filipe. *Sgl 1,800$; dbl 2,500$.*

Practicalities
Airlines TACV; ❜ 283 1033. In one of Mosteiros's two squares. *Open Mon–Fri 08.00–12.00, 14.00–16.00.*
Bank *Open Mon–Fri 08.00–14.00.*
Hospital ❜ 283 1034. In the same square as the TACV office.
Post office In the other square. *Open Mon–Fri 08.00–12.00, 14.00–16.00.*

OTHER PLACES TO VISIT
Nothing else on Fogo matches a crater visit, but all of the visits below are pleasant ways of filling spare days on the island.

São Lourenço
A large church and a peaceful graveyard – clusters of white crosses all with stunning views of Brava. Visiting it is a pleasant way of enjoying the green Fogo lowlands. It is a 12km round trip but you will probably find lifts for parts of the way. Leave São

Filipe from the roundabout opposite the Xaguate, and, with your back to the hotel, take the second turning on the left (the first leads down to the port).

Monte Genebra and Nossa Senhora do Socorro
Find an *aluguer* to Forno and from there walk to the village of Luzia Nunes, then take the left fork to Monte Genebra. German development workers helped to build these gardens in 1976. Pumping stations take hundreds of cubic metres of water from a natural spring near the sea, to water tomatoes, potatoes, cabbages and fruits. You can go to the top of Monte Genebra, while down towards the sea is the little chapel of Nossa Senhora do Socorro.

Ponto das Salinas
This is one of the few possible swimming creeks on Fogo where the lava here has formed a natural pool. It is located close to São Jorge north of São Filipe. Take an *aluguer* to São Jorge and walk down to the sea, about two hours return for the walk.

HIKES
Cooperativa–Portela–1995 lava flow–Boca Fonte–Cooperativa
Hannah Cruttenden
Distance: 6km; time: 2 hours; difficulty: 1
This two-hour walk starts at the *Cooperativa*. Head back towards the village of **Portela**, but as you leave the village, turn off to the right following the car tracks

---

CLIMBING THE PICO
Simon Day

The Pico de Fogo is one of the steepest and most spectacular volcanic cones in the world. I climbed it one January with a group of geophysicists from Lisbon. The 1,200m ascent and descent took seven hours. Although it was the coolest time of the year, we planned the climb to start at dawn. This meant leaving our hotel in Mosteiros at 05.00, driving up the steep mountain road in the pre-dawn twilight and reaching Portela before 07.00.

In Portela we met up with António and Jose António, two local men who work as guides and have also been field assistants for my Portuguese colleagues. They are good friends but António, who has lived all his life in Chã das Caldeiras, has a hard time adjusting to the idea that not everyone can run (literally) up mountains.

The usual route up the Pico starts from a track on its northern side, and begins with a long march up a gullied slope that is hampered by thick deposits of volcanic *lapilli*. These are fine fragments of lava, a bit like sand or gravel, which were ejected explosively from the vent during the volcanic eruption. It is like walking through deep sandbanks. By the time that we reached a group of small volcanic spatter cones marking the foot of the main ascent – a continuous slope inclined at 30–40° and over 1,000m high – we were already tired. One of the advantages of being with geologists, though, is that whenever you need to rest you stop walking and start discussing the rocks.

Higher up the slope the *lapilli* beds thinned out, leaving a treacherous veneer of loose ash and gravel underfoot: it was like walking on marbles. However, as the going became harder the views grew better: the northern half of the great crater was spread like a map below us: a vast field of lava flows dotted with small volcanic craters now clogged with bits of lava and known as *scoria*. It is truly a 'plain of craters'.

in the grey soil. The track leads you towards the west walls of the crater and continues round the edge of the 1995 lava to the former village of Boca Fonte – now destroyed except for the colonnaded façade of a *Cooperativa* which still stands at the edge of the flow. About 100m further on, climb up on to the lava and clamber across it to get a view of a house marooned in the flow. A short walk later you arrive at the vineyards – the vines look almost pitiful, straggling along the ground like weeds. Next, after curving round to the left and on to the southern side, you'll see several small agricultural and fruit farms. Their produce goes to the market in São Filipe. Shortly afterwards there's a chance to turn back towards the Pico and the main road back to Portela.

Portela–1995 peak–Portela

Distance: 7km; time: 2 hours 10 minutes; difficulty: 2 (CW)
You will never have done a walk like this. Walking through this lava field is like walking through a nightmarish black sea that has frozen in mid storm. Slabs of dark rock rest at jagged angles like buckled plates of ice; elsewhere, rivulets of molten rock have hardened in place. Beyond the lava field, you crunch across a glittering black landscape of *lapilli* that seems to muffle sound and life. The tricky bit is to find the rough path that takes you across the lava field up towards the peak.

From Portela, take the cobbled road that leads to São Filipe. After about 40 minutes you will pass just beyond the 9km² lava field that flows down in an ever-

Beyond that, in the haze that had already begun to form, were the immense cliffs of the original volcano crater. Known as the *Bordeira*, it once rose another few hundred metres before it was destroyed in a great rockslide towards the ocean floor to the east.

The collapse left a scar which has been as much as half filled by the lavas which today form Chã das Caldeiras. The Pico rises out of the centre of the scar. But the old walls still ascend around the Pico as sheer rock faces, a kilometre high in places. Of all the volcanoes in the world, I know of no other where the evidence of a giant lateral collapse, involving hundreds of cubic kilometres of rock, is so spectacularly preserved. Even for professional vulcanologists, this is an awesome place.

We reached the summit after five hours of climbing (and a couple more hours of geological arguments en route). The lavas of the crater walls were coloured every shade from red through oranges and yellows to bleached whites – the result of corrosive attack by the acid gases that still fume from vents on its floor and walls although there has been no eruption in the Pico since 1785.

We did not have long to study them though: the day was hot and humid, and the Pico is not a place to be in a thunderstorm. Fortunately, the thick beds of *lapilli* that had hampered our ascent made the descent quick if not easy: we ran down the scree slopes, braking by ploughing into the *lapilli* up to our knees whenever the pace became too alarming. This is the only way to descend: if you try to go down the bare rock slopes you are liable to have an accident.

António was rather disgusted when we stopped to talk about another outcrop that caught my eye; but even so we reached the track where we had parked the jeep within 40 minutes of leaving the summit. We were just in time: a few minutes later the heavens opened and claps of thunder rattled around the cliffs of the *Bordeira*.

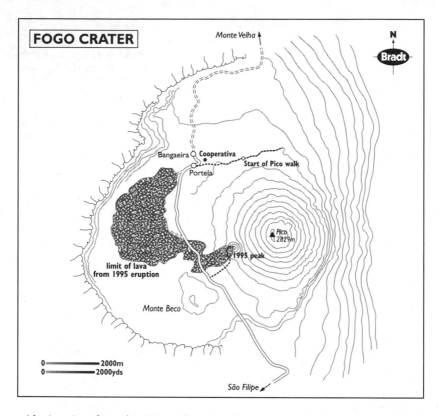

widening river from the 1995 peak and reach a point that is directly between Pico Beco on your right, and the 1995 peak on your left. Looking up at the cone you will see it is made of black, chilled fragments of lava, known as *scoria*. These have been turned a rusty red by exposure to the hot sulphur dioxide that poured out in the first few years after the eruption. The yellow patches are sulphur, precipitated from the gas as it cooled.

A few hundred metres before the road does an obvious turn to the left followed directly by an obvious turn to the right, strike out from the road to the left across the black sand (there is no path) towards the 1995 peak. About 600m from the road, you should join the edge of the lava field, and immediately start ascending on a rough path. This path takes you in a northerly direction across the side of the Pico for a few hundred metres before starting to bear northeast.

The crater of the 1995 peak is a gash a few hundred metres long running in a northeast direction. You are approaching the crater at the point where the lava spilled out and down the side from the southwest end. Twenty minutes after leaving the road, you will be at a low rim within the open southwest end of the crater. If you are prepared to scramble over loose rock and lava for another 50m, you will be able to look into the very eye of the crater, a jumble of massive yellow streaked boulders and lumps of lava.

You must return the same way you arrived, which should take about 40 minutes.

As an alternative, you can approach the northern rim of the 1995 crater from the northeast, where there is no path.

Bangaeira–crater rim–Bangaeira
Distance: approximately 14km; time: 5 hours; difficulty: 2 (AI)
This trip takes you up to the rim of the volcano for a stunning, bird's-eye view of the crater. Parts of the path are steep and slippery.

From the *Cooperativa* walk the 5km north along the road to the barrier that marks the protected forest. Continue down the road for 15 minutes to a fork. The road to the right leads to Mosteiros. Follow the left-hand road which becomes a dirt track, quite precarious in places. It winds its way up the side of the volcano. Soon you find yourself above the low cloud, gazing at a superb view of Santiago. The road eventually climbs steeply upwards to a large white building used to store rice and grain: this is where cars must stop. Walk past the front of the storehouse and on to a path running along the left-hand side of the building and up towards the volcano rim. It's a steep climb and the path is slippery in places but it shouldn't take longer than half an hour to get to the top.

This part of the crater is very green and you will see women from the villages gathering firewood. Recent eruptions are 'mapped out' in the vast area below, covered by lava, which pushes right up to the edge of the villages of **Bangaeira**

SEARCHING FOR THE NGON-NGON BIRD
Hannah Cruttenden
The *ngon-ngon* bird has almost lived up to its name and vanished from the islands. They rate as 'vulnerable' on the international Red List of endangered species because only a few hundred of them remain. Also known as the Cape Verde petrel or *Pterodroma feae*, the birds owe their plight to several factors. In the past the local people have hunted them because traditionally their fat is used in medicines. Also, they lay their eggs in places where cats can get them. Already, local people have agreed not to hunt for them, but without urgent conservation work the black-winged, white-bellied *ngon-ngon* could disappear.

I joined one scientist on a night trek to the edge of the crater to find the birds, which are nocturnal creatures. They are marine birds but they nest mainly in the mountains of Fogo, Santo Antão and São Nicolau. Stumbling around the sides of the crater in the dark clutching my tape recorder I followed him until we reached an area close to the rim at about 20.30. Norman, from Britain's Royal Society for the Protection of Birds, had gone to great lengths to imitate its long low cry for me so I knew what I was listening for. We crouched quietly in the cold darkness and waited. At first all we could hear was the monotonous trilling of cicadas.

'This waiting through the night,' said Norman, 'is the easy bit. Next, ornithologists must try to establish the number of birds living in the colony. This involves some dangerous work, including rock climbing and abseiling down the sheer crater walls to reach the burrows and put rings on the birds.'

Eventually, after about an hour, Norman said he could just hear the *ngon-ngon* up on the rim. He was disappointed – we had been hoping they might come further down into the crater. It took me a minute to tune into a very faint wailing noise, like an extended 'coo' that dropped in pitch as it went on. I had by this time given up on the tape recorder and instead, using Norman's night-vision image-intensifying equipment, tried to spot them. I succeeded: through the machine it was just possible to see two or three of them dancing about through the air carrying out courtship rituals.

and **Portela** to the right. The darkest lava is from the most recent 1995 eruption. Closer to you, the slightly lighter coloured lava is from 1951; the lightest coloured lava, directly in front of you, is oldest of all. It is possible to continue walking round the rim – take a guide.

Crater–Montebarro–Pai António–Mosteiros
Distance: approximately 10km; time: 4¹/₂ hours; difficulty: 2 (AI)
This delightful walk takes you out of the crater and down the volcano's steep, northeastern side, with views across the sea to Santiago, and a host of pretty plantations, in particular oranges and coffee. The hike involves some steep descents likely to produce aching, shaking knees, and those who find such descents difficult could find the walk takes fives hours. Navigationally it is pretty easy.

Begin with a 5km walk north along the road through the crater which takes you out, past a road barrier that marks the protected forest and on past a road to the left that goes to **Montinho**. Two minutes after this turning there is a steep little path down to the right. You can stick with the road or follow this short-cut in which case you will rejoin the road after ten minutes, turning right. Some 15 minutes past this point you arrive in Monte Velho. The road bends to the right over the bridge where there are a few small houses. After crossing the bridge leave the road and turn right, down the right-hand side of the first house. The path takes you down the side of a ravine, across which can be seen the president's house. Giant *carapate* plants stack the sides of the path. Descend through **Pede Pranta**, after which the ban on farming expires. You enter little valleys planted with coffee, mango and orange plants.

Mist drifts upwards and the view of the ocean through the vegetation is beautiful. After a while, descending past little dwellings built on terraces of lava rock you reach the first region of Mosteiros – **Montebarro** – and the air is filled with the scents of oranges and fires and the noise of children and cockerels. Three hours into the walk you reach **Pai António**, with a steeply cobbled street, from where it is a 40-minute walk down the cobbled road (ignoring the left turning to Feijoal) to the centre of Mosteiros. Alternatively, it should be possible to pick up a lift in Pai António to save your knees that last steep descent.

Mosteiros–Feijoal–Mosteiros
Distance: approximately 5km; time: 2 hours; difficulty: 2 (AI)
There are various strolls up into the lower slopes of the volcano. To walk up to **Feijoal** for a drink, leave Mosteiros on the south road and, a little after the big Delegação de Fogo, take the cobbled road on the right (ignore a turning up to the left just before Feijoal). After a drink at the *mercado*, find a little footpath (*caminho para Igreja*) back into the centre of Mosteiros: with your back to the *mercado* turn right and the path is a few metres along on the left, running between two buildings. It's a bit slippery and the less sure of foot may prefer to return by the road.

Walking round the north
At present it is not possible to drive right round the island, because the road is interrupted to the north. But you can walk the missing section if you set off early. From the Mosteiros end, the first 2km north along the coast are dismal – save your legs and hitch if you can. Just before the airport, there is a left turning uphill. This is the beginning of a spectacular road, which goes up to Ribeira Ilhéu and then continues as a 9km track to São Jorge. From there you have to try and hitch back to São Filipe – there is supposed to be an *aluguer* at 13.00.

The better alternative is to take a mid-morning *aluguer* to São Jorge from São Filipe and walk in the other direction, staying in Mosteiros at the end of the walk.

Brava

Special thanks to Gerhard Schellmann (see page 124)

Swallows of the wide seas
What wind of loyalty
Brings you on this bitter journey
To our land of *Sodade*
Eugénio Tavares, quoted in Archibald Lyall,

Black and White Make Brown
Archibald Lyall (Heinemann, 1938)

Brava is the most secret of the islands – a volcano crater hides its town, rough seas encircle it and the winds that buffet it are so strong that its airport has now been closed. Brava lies only 20km from Fogo, but many visitors will merely glimpse it from the greater island's western slopes.

Brava – or 'wild' island – appears at first to live up to the meaning of its name. But its unpromising slopes hide a fertile and moist hinterland filled with hibiscus flowers and cultivation. At least that is how it was: today, after years of drought, it is a parched place, its flowers less visible and its food more likely to be imported than grown.

This tiny, westerly island, dropping off the end of the archipelago into the Atlantic, seems to hide from its companions and look instead towards where the sun sets – it is dreaming of the wealth of the USA. For Brava is the island where the great 19th-century American whaling ships called to pick up crews and spirit hopeful young men away to new lives in another continent (see box, page 197). The legacy is an island full of empty houses waiting for the return of the *Americanos* who have built them for their retirement. Meanwhile, a big container ship from Boston visits twice a year and American goods appear in the streets. Brava Creole is peppered with American expressions.

Approaching by boat, the dark mass resolves itself into sheer cliffs with painted houses dotting the heights above. Just a few fishing hamlets huddle at sea level.

HIGHLIGHTS
Go for the walking, for the peace and for the sheer intrigue of a place that is so out of the way. Don't go for beaches or watersports and don't go if you are pushed for time.

BACKGROUND INFORMATION
History
Brava is, geologically speaking, part of Fogo. The channel between them is just a few hundred metres deep – shallow compared with the ocean floor that surrounds the rest of Brava, whose cliffs plunge 4km down beyond sea level. The oldest rocks of Fogo lie on the side that faces Brava and are very similar to Bravan rock, which is how their relationship has been deduced.

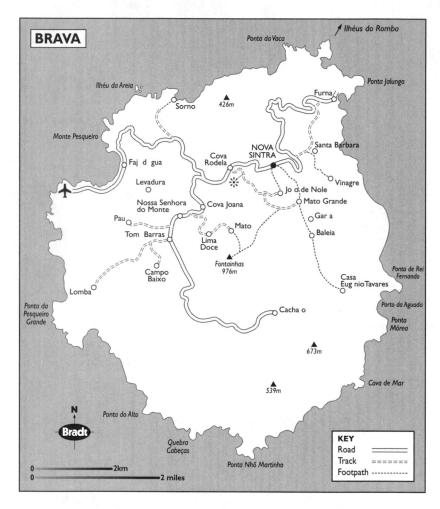

There are no volcanic eruptions now, but the land is not completely calm – clusters of earthquakes shake it, although most are too gentle to be noticed. Yet its active history was recent and its volcano cones are all less than 10,000 years old.

There is a legend about the first settlers of Brava. A young Portuguese aristocrat fell in love with a girl well below him in social class. To prevent their marriage, his parents banished the girl and her family to Fogo, but he pursued her on another ship and escaped with her to the haven of Brava. There they settled in the valley of Fajã d'Água, living with some of the loyal sailors who accompanied them.

Brava was discovered on 24 June 1462 on the saint's day of São João Baptista, after whom it was originally named. Settlers arrived in 1573 and included many fishermen from Madeira and the Azores. This, and the fact that Brava never really took part in the slave trade, are held to be responsible for there being a greater proportion of white skins on Brava than anywhere else.

When Sir Francis Drake's mariners passed by in 1578 they found only one of its hundred inhabitants – a hermit who looked after a small chapel. They probably never discovered the villages hidden in the volcano's crater. By the 1620s there was a proper community there, which swelled 60 years later with desperate boatloads of refugees from Fogo fleeing volcanic eruptions on their own island. Many of them never returned.

By this time the island was owned by Luis de Castro Pereira, who also owned Santa Luzia near São Vicente. In 1686, the population was sufficiently large to merit a pirate attack in which its governor was killed.

Yet Brava remained a relative secret and took almost no part in Cape Verde's thriving 17th-century businesses. Its first major dabble with trade was in 1730 when the Englishman, Captain George Roberts, bought the rights to the *urzella* lichen that covered its slopes (see box, below).

The population was to double in the following 50 years to 3,200.

It was not until the end of the 18th century that Brava became of much interest to the outside world. It became the springboard for the great emigration of Cape Verdeans to the USA: an exile that was to be an important shaper of the whole economy of the archipelago.

That was when the whalers of New Bedford and Rhode Island, venturing further south and east, discovered in Brava a place where they could replenish their ships and recruit eager new crews. English whaling boats recruited there as well – it was easy for the ships to land in Brava's small but secluded harbours. Many of the young men disembarked at New England and set up new lives there (see box *Whalers and the packet trade*, page 197).

Withstanding an attack in 1798 by the French, who were trying to oust the Portuguese from the islands, Brava continued to prosper into the first decades of the 19th century. Intellectually, Brava became the place to be. The parish of Our Lady of the Mountain was created; an American consul arrived in 1843 and a secondary school opened in the 1850s to which students came from throughout the archipelago and from Guinea-Bissau. It was into this environment that the poet Eugénio Tavares was born in 1867 (see box, page 189).

By the late 19th century, Brava was considered one of the most pleasant islands in which to live and its population peaked at 9,200. Income surged into the 20th century, as American *emigrantes* sent their money home. But the prosperity was not to last. The depression came; remittances from abroad dwindled and, confident that the rainy years of the 1930s would continue, many *Americanos* returned home.

ORCHIL DYE

The mountains of Cape Verde yielded one important product – a lichen known as *urzella*, or orchil (*Litmus roccella*), which could be turned into a blue dye. Together with indigo it was used to colour cloth (see page 26). To make orchil dye, lichen was ground to a powder and mixed with stale urine to form a paste. Quicklime was added to make blues, violets and purples, and tin solution for scarlet.

Portugal made a healthy profit from the orchil business, which began as early as 1469. Rights to take the orchil were sold as a Crown Monopoly which was controlled first by a Brazilian group and then by the English because of the country's burgeoning textile trade in the 18th century. An English firm paid over £6,000 for six years' access to the orchil of Cape Verde, The Azores and Madeira and it was in demand into the 1830s but withered when huge growths of the lichen were found in Angola and Mozambique, which sent prices plummeting.

It was a mistake. A drought was looming that was to prove the worst catastrophe in Brava's history. It squeezed the island just as World War II caused foreign remittances to dry up completely. Hundreds died in the ensuing famine. Brava's ageing population rose to 10,000 in the 1960s and then fell back to 7,000. A recent disaster was Hurricane Beryl, which destroyed much of the infrastructure in 1982.

Geography
The archipelago's smallest inhabited island, Brava is 64km² and just 10km across at its widest point. Much of the coastline is steep cliffs, which rise to a dry central tableland with some mountains rising out of it. In the west there is a lush valley – Fajã d'Água – with a small, semi-permanent stream. Offshore there are several rocks and stacks. The highest point is Monte Fontainhas, at 976m often swathed in mist. Even a little lower down, within the crater, there is generally moisture and coolness. Flowering garden plants found on Brava include plumeira, bougainvillea and jasmine. Vila Nova Sintra abounds with planted dragon trees (see *São Nicolau*, page 247).

It is cold between December and April in the *vila* and in higher zones.

Economy
Many people depend on government aid and the island relies heavily on fruit and vegetables imported from Fogo, Praia and Portugal. Maize is planted every year but often turns brown and dies. In better times the islanders grow coffee, bananas, sugar cane, cassava, maize and potatoes. Fishing is the base of the economy.

Festivals
The Festival of São João is held on 24 June and many emigrants return for it. Several days before the festival the women begin a ritual pounding of the corn, joined by others who sing with a high-pitched chanting and clap to a complex beat until the preparation is finished. Another preparation for the festival is the dressing of the mast of *Cutelo Grande* – decorating it with intricately woven breads and also cakes, fruit and drinks and guarding it against pilfering by children. On the day, the mast – all greenery and red flowers and edible ornaments – is raised with a pulley. At the right moment the pulleys are cut, the mast comes plummeting to the ground and the children run to grab what plunder they can. Others are as follows:

Twelfth Night	5 January
São Sebastiao	20 January
São Paulo	First Sunday in July
São Paulinho	Second Sunday in July
Santaninha	Last Sunday in July
Santa Ana	Last Sunday in July
Nossa Senhora do Monte	First fortnight in August (Fuma)
Nossa Senhora da Graca	15 August

GETTING THERE AND AWAY
Brava is very hard to get to. In fact it was so hard in May 2005 that we were unable to visit and so were many others, including a Portuguese TV crew with money to spend. But luckily Gerhard Schellmann made it to the island in August 2005, despite some ferry delays, and provided us with up-to-date details. Other information obtained through Unotur, the 2005 *Cape Verde Tourist Guide*, and travel agents in Fogo has also been incorporated.

There is no air service to Brava now, as the airstrip is disused. Strong crosswinds and the consequent dangers were cited as the main reason for the termination of flights.

Tourists could easily be delayed for days or weeks, because there are currently no reliable ferry services, though this should improve soon according to Gerhard's research. See sample timetable on page 122. If you are keen to visit, make sure you have a lot of time and then make getting there the chief and immediate purpose of your holiday. Santiago or Fogo can at least be visited on the days when you have to wait for a boat. Trying to leave Brava with an international flight looming in Sal or Santiago is not only stressful but also fairly certain to end in trouble. If you get to Brava on a cargo boat, the best advice is to start trying to leave Brava as soon as you arrive – it is such a small and friendly place that someone will give you a daily update on the likelihood of a boat arriving.

Remember too that, because you will not know the date of leaving Brava for certain, booking a plane seat out of Fogo back to Santiago will not be possible for a fixed date. This could also lead to delays in waiting for an available seat. Some years ago one American tourist was forced to charter a passing yacht to make his escape.

In Fogo contact Fogo Adventures in case you can charter their boat; it may be the best option if there is a small group of you (see page 167).

By ferry
The *Barlavento* runs between Santiago, Brava and Fogo, albeit the sailing times are not set in stone. Ask around at the port. A new service launched by Polar is due to run the same route and will hopefully prove more reliable.

Polar PO Box 120, Rua Serpa Pinto 141, Praia; ↘ 261 5225/7177/7224; f 261 4132; e polarp@cvtelecom.cv
Agenmar In São Filipe; may also have some ferry information.

On arrival at Furna get to Vila Nova Sintra either by chartered *aluguer* or shared *aluguer* (100–150$). Alternatively you could walk the steep 3km up the old road, the reverse of the hike described on page 198.

By yacht
Some of the best anchorages in the archipelago are here. Fajã d'Água is secure and beautiful and Furna is secure, except during southeasterly winds.

GETTING AROUND
Aluguers, in the form of trucks or *carrinhos*, travel between Furna and Vila Nova Sintra for 150$ (600–800$ when chartered as taxis); from Vila Nova Sintra to Nossa Senhora do Monte a charter was 500$ and from Vila Nova Sintra to Fajã d'Agua a charter was 1,000$. Up-to-date prices were not available, but are likely to have increased.

ACTIVITIES
Excursions
Try **Ecotur, Dja'r Fogo** or **Fogo Adventures** on Fogo (see page 166).

Hiking
Brava is a superb hiking destination, with numerous circular walks, most of which can start and finish at the *vila*. See page 190.

Swimming
Brava is not really a place for swimming, but there are a few safe lagoons, including one in between Fajã d'Agua and the airport.

FURNA
Furna is the main port and lies in an extinct volcano crater, encircled with rocks on three sides. The bay is just a few hundred metres in diameter – sailing ships used to find it easy to get in but trickier to escape. It is more bustling than the *vila* but not as attractive. Meals are available in a big house on the seafront.

From Furna the road winds up the slopes of the mountain. The sea and the harbour sink far below until, about half a kilometre above and after endless hairpins, it drops suddenly over the rim of a small depression and into Vila Nova Sintra.

VILA NOVA SINTRA
> …an enchanted garden hanging by invisible cords from the clouds
>
> Archibald Lyall

Named after the Portuguese town of Sintra, the *vila* is 520m above sea level. For weeks it can labour under a brigadoon-like fog, inspiring melancholy in the visitor. On a clear day, though, there is a view across the ocean to Fogo: it is said that if you have good eyes you can see the women in São Filipe cleaning rice.

Nova Sintra is a quaint town nestled among the volcanic rocks. Hibiscus trees line many of the streets, scarlet against the ancient cobblestones. In wet years its gardens are full of jumbles of blue plumbago and bougainvillea, almond trees and jacaranda. The houses of the town – all Portuguese whitewash with red tiles – are covered in flowering vegetation, and fruit trees intersperse with fields of corn and cabbage.

The *vila* is very quiet and sometimes you can be the only person in the square. But before meal times the fish vendors are there, crying 'Nhos cumpra peixe' – 'you all buy fish'. Each of the three fishing communities has its own signature cry so that potential customers will know where their dinner is from before they buy it.

Where to stay
Residencial Nazareno ⟩ 285 1375, m 993 1162. In the same building as the TACV office, the Nazareno has around 5 rooms with TV and minibar. There is at least one family apt with two bedrooms, kitchenette and separate bathroom/shower. *Sgl 2,300$; dbl 3,000$. If you stay a few days, you may get a reduction.*

Pensão Restaurante Paúlo ⟩ 285 1312. On the east–west road south of the square, this is an attractive place and some rooms have balconies. Downstairs is a restaurant and sitting room. It has hot water, but some of the rooms are a bit musty. *Sgl 1,500$; dbl 2,500$; breakfast included.*

Pousada Municipal ⟩ 285 1295/1313; f 285 1314. Off the road with the town hall on it, this is an acceptable place with a communal veranda and living room with TV. Out of hours (07.00–15.30) send for Anna Maria or Marie Fernandez to open up. *Sgl 1,000$; dbl 2,000$; no breakfast.*

Where to eat and drink
The following places are listed by Unotur. Others existed at the time of the last research.

Bar Mansa ⟩ 285 1125
Brancaga ⟩ 285 1305

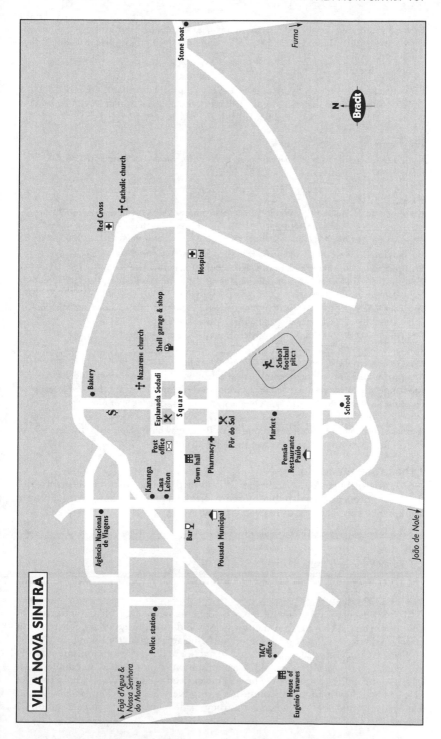

VILA NOVA SINTRA

Stone boat

Furna

N
Bradt

Catholic church

Red Cross

Hospital

Nazarene church

Shell garage & shop

Bakery

School
football pitch

Esplanada Sodadi

Square

$

Pór do Sol

Post office

Kananga
Casa
Leiton

Town hall

Pharmacy

Market

School

Pensão
Restaurante
Paulo

Bar

Pousada Municipal

Agência Nacional
de Viagens

Police station

TACV
office

House of
Eugénio Tavares

Fajã d'Agua &
Nossa Senhora
do Monte

João de Nole

Restaurante Paúlo The best restaurant in town, go and discuss your order several hours beforehand. Main dishes begain at 500$ and previously served prodigious breakfasts. In the *pensão* of the same name.
Ponto de Encronto ❧ 285 1623

Fresh bread can be bought from the bakery opposite the bank and fresh goat's cheese from Paúlo at his restaurant. Fruit and vegetables, if available, can be bought at the market. Shoe repairs are available at the old bakery.

Nightlife
Kananga Open some Fri and Sat nights and every Sun afternoon. Admission: 300$ for men; free for women.

Practicalities
Airlines TACV; ❧ 285 1192. Was in an unmarked house on the road to Eugénio Tavares's house, one up from Casa Silva Bibica. No flights operate into Brava. *Open Mon–Fri 09.30–14.00, 15.00–18.00.*
Bank Banco Comercial do Atlântico; ❧ 285 1254. *Open Mon–Fri 08.00–14.30.*
Shipping Try Agenmar if it still exists. Ask around the port area.
Hospital ❧ 285 1130. Brava's small hospital is on the Furna road out of the square, on the right. No capacity for surgery.
Internet The post office provides an internet service, Should this be down, try the Shell shop which also provides a faxing and photocopying service.
Pharmacy ❧ 285 1223. Look for Farmácia Irene.
Police ❧ 285 1132
Post office On the square. *Open Mon–Fri 08.00–16.00.*
Shopping Postcards are on sale in the post office. For Fogo wine, *grogue* and certain food and drink products unavailable elsewhere try the Shell shop, on the road leading from the square to the Furna road. *Open daily 07.00–21.00; office open Mon–Sat 07.00–15.30.*
Tourist information None, but road maps of Brava may be available from the Shell shop. Staff at the town hall may be able to help; ❧f 285 1314.

What to see and do
The house of Eugénio Tavares is at the top of the town just off the main road. There are plans to turn it into a museum. In the square is a kiosk with a plaque commemorating Tavares. In English it reads:

> There above in planetary spheres
> Shine brilliant and amazing stars:
> But here on earth, one shines
> For ever: Eugénio Tavares

FAJÃ D'ÁGUA
This is probably the most beautiful bay in Cape Verde – a little village at the foot of the mountains, sheltered from the northeast winds and always green. There is not much to do in the village but all the surrounding area is great for hiking.

Fajã is where the whaling boats used to anchor and here lies a monument to the passengers of the *Mathilde*. In 1943, a group of men – some American emigrants on a visit home, others young men who had never been out of Brava – bought the 55ft sloop. They all wanted to flee famine and go to New England. The *Mathilde* was in bad shape but this did not deter them; they made a few repairs and set sail on 21 August 1943.

EUGENIO TAVARES

Eugénio Tavares was born in 1867 and spent his life writing music and in particular developing the art of the *morna*. He wrote in Creole rather than Portuguese which was one reason for his immense popularity. Tavares lived on Brava where the sense of parting was particularly strong. Perhaps his most famous work is *Hora di Bai* (Hour of Leaving), which was traditionally sung at Furna dock as relatives boarded the ships bound for the USA. The first verse is as follows:

Hora di bai	Hour of going
Hora de dor	Hour of pain
Dja'n q'ré	I wish
Pa el ca mantché	That it would not dawn!
De cada bêz	Each time
Que'n ta lembrâ	That I remember thee,
Ma'n q'ré	I would choose
Fica 'n morrê	To stay and die!

Translated in *Atlantic Islands* by Bentley Duncan (Chicago, 1972)

Hora di Bai is traditionally the last song, played at the end of the evening. You need the music and the dancing to appreciate the *morna*. As Archibald Lyall wrote:

Properly to appreciate the work of Eugénio Tavares, it is necessary to see the humble people for whom he wrote gliding close-locked round the whitewashed, oil-lit room and to hear them, drugged for a few hours by his genius into forgetting their sorrows, singing softly to the strains of fiddle and guitar.

Tavares was primarily a composer – the words, it is said, took a couple of hours to invent after he had finished the music. But his lyrics struck deep in the hearts of his countrymen. Famous *mornas* of his include *O Mar Eterno* (inspired by his love for an American woman who visited Brava on a yacht; her horrified father whisked her away one night and he never saw her again), and his lullaby, *Ná ó menino ná*. When Tavares died in 1930, the whole of the island went to the funeral.

Their voyage was a clandestine one because there were wartime restrictions on maritime travel. To make matters worse, they had chosen the beginning of the hurricane season.

Just after the boat left the harbour, a 12-year-old boy on board noticed that it was leaking. He took fright, jumped overboard and swam for the shore, half an hour away. 'There,' says Ray Almeida, an American Cape Verdean, 'he wept as he watched the sloop disappear over the horizon, carrying his compatriots to what he knew was certain death'. It is believed that the *Mathilde* went down in rough weather near Bermuda.

Getting there and away

Look out for the one *aluguer*, which leaves Fajã for the *vila* at 07.00, returning at 12.00 (200$). It is supposed to do an afternoon journey as well, leaving Fajã in the early afternoon and arriving back at 18.00. To charter an *aluguer* there or back costs around 2,000$. Fajã to Furna costs 2,000$.

Where to stay

Pensão Sol na Baia ❱ 285 2070; e pensao_sol_na_baia@hotmail.com. Built and run by Jose and Brigitte Andrade, who speak French, Italian, Spanish and Portuguese, it has 4 rooms. *Dbl 4,500–5,000$ with sea view, inc good breakfast.*
Motel Fajã d'Agua Ocean Front Motel and Sunset Bar Restaurant ❱ 285 1321. About midway along Fajã's only road, the hotel consists of 3 rooms, simple, clean and bright, with a communal balcony gazing directly over the ocean.

Where to eat and drink

Pensão Sol na Baia Try the Jantar Restaurant, where Cape Verdean products are served in a French style. 1,500$ for guests and 2,000$ for other visitors.
Por do Sol ❱ 285 1576
Motel Fajã d'Agua May serve snacks (cake, bananas and coffee) plus meals of fish or meat.

OTHER PLACES TO VISIT
Cova Joana

Cova Joana is a small settlement west of Vila Nova Sintra, just south of the road to Fajã.

Where to stay

Jose Pensão ❱ 285 1081. Run by Jose Teixeira, who lived in the USA for 5 years. It has 4 rooms with hot water, and a bar. *Sgl 1,000$; dbl 2,000$; without breakfast.*

Vinagre

The village derives its name from the mineral water, which still bubbles up here from deep below the mountains. There is not much going on here now – a few broken-down donkeys and some ancient farmers, and an air of faded glory. The elaborate stone irrigation system and the extensive terracing are crumbling and largely overgrown. At the heart of the village is a bridge and a huge bougainvillea – a welcome splash of vermilion against the greys and browns.

On the left before the bridge is a majestic old water tank, fully equipped with gargoyle water spouts and large oval windows. Take a look inside to see how the water used to course through a carefully made tunnel under the road. To sample the water yourself, turn left just before the bridge, and follow the cobbled path down to where the piped spring water issues from a wall.

Further round on the left is the shell of a magnificent old house, inhabited within living memory. There are as many as four lime kilns around the settlement, once used to make whitewash for the houses – look out for their tall brick chimneys.

You can reach Vinagre by following a hike, or part of a hike (see below).

Nossa Senhora do Monte

This village was founded as a place of pilgrimage in 1826 and, within a decade, had become a bishop's palace. Earlier in the last century travellers said that the road from Nova Sintra to Nossa Senhora do Monte was as thickly populated as the Thames Valley. Now emigration has left just a couple of tiny villages.

HIKES

Several of the hikes below pass through Mato Grande, and hikers can therefore mix and match parts of routes.

Vila Nova Sintra–Mato Grande–miradouro–Cova Rodela–Vila Nova Sintra

Distance: 5km; time: 1¹/₂ hours; difficulty: 1 (CW)
This walk takes you up a steep path and then around the ring of hills to the south and west of Vila Nova Sintra on a well-surfaced road. You are always in sight of the *vila*, but you pass through the picturesque village of Mato Grande, clinging to the hillside, and you get some excellent views of Fogo. The *miradouro* (viewing point) is the highlight of this walk, giving an amazing view of the *vila*, spread out beneath you like a map.

From the southeast corner of the main square, take the road out past the building labelled **Casa Teixeira**. After about 100m you will come to a crossroads, where you go straight on. Bear right at a fork after a further 20m. After another 20m, the cobbled road turns sharp left. Go right on an unmade path that heads down to the bottom of the valley. After about 100m you will reach the valley floor.

Almost directly, go past a turning on your right leading up to a white house. After another 30m, turn right up a steep cobbled path between stone walls. This is a steep climb between houses that seem to be built on platforms carved out of the hillside. After about five minutes, the path bears left and you go round a rocky outcrop with a ruin below you on your left. From this point, and if the mist is not swirling around you, you get your first uninterrupted view of Fogo.

The path winds on around the hillside, passing houses in various states of repair. After another five minutes, it crosses a small valley and, directly, you reach a T-junction in front of a two-storey house. Turn right, following the path uphill. As you get higher, you will get glimpses down into the neat courtyards of some of the houses, where bougainvillea spills across ancient walls.

Five minutes later, you cross a second small valley, and then bear left at a fork. Several minutes after that there is a white cross standing on a wall on your right beside a white house. Pass in front of the house on your right, and immediately turn right up beside the house, following the path uphill. Within a couple of minutes you will reach a telephone box, and a larger cobbled path through **Mato Grande**, which is spread out below you on your right as a maze of little paths between crumbling houses. Turn left at the phone box, and after five minutes of ascending, you will reach the Centro Social de Mato Grande (the social centre) on your left. Opposite, there is a table-football table, and a small bar selling fizzy drinks and *grogue*. Inside the shop, the youth of Mato Grande gather to while away the time with a pack of cards.

Looking south (with your back to the social centre), you will see the village of **Garça** down in the valley (look for the bright-green house) and, close by, the white outline of one of a series of stone ships dotted around the mountainside. On the far ridge is the village of **Baleia**, and at the east end of the ridge you will see a further ship.

A few hundred metres down the slope to the left of where you are standing, there is a third ship. If you would like a close look at one, ask at the bar for directions to the *barco*. On 24 June, it is these boats that are decorated with leaves and fruit to celebrate the festival of Sao João (see *Festivals*, page 184).

From the Mato Grande social centre, take the road that leads up to the left of the tapstand, with the *vila* visible on your right. Follow the road around the ridge, past old houses and small areas of cultivation squeezed in amongst the folds of land. After 1km (about 20 minutes), you will reach a T-junction in the road, where the right turning leads down to **João de Nole**. Turn left to continue to the *miradouro*.

Just 100m beyond the T-junction is a small, rough and steep path down on the right. (If you trust your knees, this is a quick way to descend to the *vila*.) The *miradouro* is another 200m beyond this, and gives a breathtaking view over the *vila*.

Continuing beyond the viewpoint, another 600m will bring you to a second T-junction, in the pretty village of **Cova Rodela**. Turn right here, and follow the winding road back down to the *vila*. You will reach the western end of the main street after about ten minutes.

Vila Nova Sintra–Mato Grande–Baleia–Casa Eugénio Tavares–Baleia–Mato Grande–Vila Nova Sintra

Distance: 10km; time: 4 hours; difficulty: 3 (CW)

This walk south of the *vila* is a demanding sequence of ascents and descents, with spectacular views of Fogo out to the east. For much of this walk, the path is unmade and rough, and, particularly on the final steep zig-zag descent to the *casa*, care needs to be taken. Baleia is an attractive, if remote, spot to pause and gaze down vertiginous *ribeiras*. If you want to experience the unspeakable desolation of Brava's dryness, look no further than the *ribeira* where Tavares built his house.

Walk from the *vila* to Mato Grande (35 minutes) using the directions in the first five paragraphs of the previous walk.

In Mato Grande, looking south (with your back to the social centre), take the small path directly in front of you, which leads down in the direction of **Garça**.

At Garça, you can take a detour along the ridge to visit the stone boat (*barco*), which looks like it has been stranded at the end of the ridge in some cataclysmic flood. The path continues up to **Baleia** on the next ridge, about 1km from Mato Grande. Immediately on entering the village, you will see a house on your left that sells biscuits and *grogue*.

Baleia has the feel of a bird's nest perched high on a windswept ridge. The village comprises a single cobbled street and a few houses huddled together against the mist and the ceaseless purring of the wind.

It takes two hours to get from here to Casa Eugénio Tavares and return. People in Baleia will readily point you towards the path to the *casa*. Follow the cobbled path along the ridge through Baleia. Just before you reach the last two houses, turn right and immediately start to descend on an unmade path.

After about five minutes, the path branches. Going left will bring you in a few minutes to Baleia's stone boat. Bear right for the *casa*, down the side of the ridge. After about 20 minutes, you will reach a few scattered houses, mostly ruined. At a fork in the path bear left. You will see some rudimentary crosses on a cairn some tens of metres up the right turning. This is a homemade chapel, and means that the locals do not have to hike over to Mato Grande every Sunday.

You are heading towards what looks like a ruin (but is actually inhabited). Watch out for the dog, which may make you feel less than welcome. Cut close past the right side of this building (where the locals will point you in the right direction for Tavares's house), and descend a few hundred metres along the next ridge. If it is the dry season, you will enter a lunar landscape at this point, where there is nothing but rock and sand. The ruined huts look as if they have grown out of the landscape, rather than been built by human hand.

After less than ten minutes from the inhabited building, the path passes to the right through a small notch in a rocky ridge a few metres high. From here you will see the *casa* a long way below you on the other side of the valley. After a further five minutes, you will pass a ruin on your left. About 50m beyond this, there is a small (and easy to miss) turning on your right down the side of the *ribeira*.

It is a very rough zigzagging path, so watch your step. It will take you about ten or 15 minutes.

The ruin of Eugénio Tavares's house is reached by a five-minute scramble up from the floor of the *ribeira*. His house is surprisingly big – there are two storeys and outhouses. There is also a patio, and what looks like a small swimming pool, but was probably a water tank. In the dry season, you look out across a mind-numbing grey and brown panorama of splintered rock. But it clearly inspired Tavares and, apparently, a host of latter-day scribblers, who have left their poetic offerings all over the walls of the ruin.

Retrace your steps. For the return from Mato Grande to the *vila*, you can either go back the way you came (35 minutes) or go via the *miradouro* as described in the last part of the previous walk. The latter route takes about one hour.

Vila Nova Sintra–Mato Grande–Monte Fontainhas–Mato–Nossa Senhora do Monte–Cova Joana–Vila Nova Sintra
Distance: 9km; time: 3 hours 10 minutes; difficulty: 2 (CW)

This walk takes you to the heart of Brava, to its highest peak, from where you will get superb all-round views if you are not shrouded in mist. It is a steep ascent to Mato Grande, followed by a further steep ascent (on a cobbled path) from near Mato Grande up to the Fontainhas plateau, where it is cool and green, and the air is heavy with sharp pine scents. Note: Mato Grande and Mato are different places.

Walk from the *vila* to Mato Grande (35 minutes) using the directions in the first five paragraphs of the Vila Nova Sintra–Mato Grande–*miradouro*–Cova Rodela walk.

For the 50-minute walk to **Fontainhas**, begin from the social centre in Mato Grande and take the road that leads up to the left of the tapstand. You will see Vila Nova Sintra below you on your right. After about 400m, you will pass a green church on your right, and, cresting a rise, you will see the path you are to take leading up from the left of the road about 200m in front of you. This is the beginning of a steep ascent on to the Fontainhas plateau.

The path ascends the right side of a small valley. After about 200m, a path joins from the right. Your path bends round to the left at the top of the valley, and zig-zags upwards. Some 15 minutes after leaving the main road, the path flattens out and you pass to the right of a small peak with a large antenna on top. Directly after that, a small path joins on the left.

Five minutes after passing the antenna peak, take a right fork, and pass along the right edge of an undulating plateau, where the mist trails through spiky aloe vera and among the red flowers of the cardeal bushes. There are some farming huts, and occasional cattle grazing on the coarse grass. The air is sharp with the smell of pine.

After another ten minutes, you reach a T-junction. The right turning heads down to **Mato**. Turn left, and very shortly you will pass a whitewashed house on your right. Bear right at a fork shortly after this. Follow the path upwards, and after less than ten minutes, you will reach the peak.

To get to Mato, which takes about 45 minutes, go back to the T-Junction before the whitewashed house, but instead of turning right to retrace your steps, head straight on. After about seven minutes of descending from the T-junction along a winding path, you will emerge on a low saddle, and will see the upper end of Mato down on your left.

Continue along the saddle for another five minutes, and then take a deeply worn path leading down on your left. After five minutes, this path will lead you past a concrete water tank on your left.

After another few minutes, the path becomes cobbled, and you are descending through the first of the houses in Mato. Five minutes later, you reach a T-junction with a telephone box on the right. From here, your aim is to reach the main road through Mato. Mato is criss-crossed by any number of small paths, and the best way to the main road is simply by asking.

Once on the road, follow it to the right, descending past a school on your left, and joining at last the main road to Nossa Senhora do Monte at a sharp hairpin.

Turn right on to the main road and walk for an hour, passing through **Cova Joana**, **Cova Rodela** and eventually reaching Vila Nova Sintra.

Vila Nova Sintra–Santa Barbara–Vinagre–Mato Grande–João de Nole–Vila Nova Sintra

Distance: 5km; time: 2 hours 20 minutes; difficulty: 3 (CW)
In this walk, you descend almost to sea level by a zig-zagging cobbled path, and then climb back up again by a very rough (and in places precipitous) ridge path. It is not a walk to undertake if you have dodgy knees or don't like getting out of breath. Vinagre – a village nestling in the mouth of a *ribeira* – is the highlight of the walk, with its old lime kilns and air of decayed grandeur. The mineral waters that flow from a natural spring taste like a mild mixture of lemon juice and soapsuds, and have given the village its name. It is said that those who drink of the waters will never leave.

For the 40-minute walk to Vinagre, set out on the road east from the main square of the *vila*. After five minutes, you will reach the stone boat looking out towards Fogo.

Take the little cobbled path down to the left of the boat, and after just a short distance, you will join the main road snaking its way down to Furna. Cross the road, and double back a few metres to pick up the cobbled path continuing its descent on the other side. Your path is actually the old road to Furna – watch out for the stray vehicles that still use this road. After five minutes descending, take a cobbled turning on your right towards **Santa Barbara**, which you will reach after another few minutes. About ten minutes from the turning, staying on the same path, you will round an outcrop, and catch a glimpse of Mato Grande above you on the hill.

At this point, you will begin a series of sharp zig-zags down towards **Vinagre**, which you will reach after about 25 minutes.

The one-hour hike from Vinagre to Mato Grande is a scramble, and some may prefer to turn round and retrace their steps up to Santa Barbara. The undaunted should cross over the bridge in Vinagre and follow the main path past a white house on the left with a brick kiln behind it. Immediately bear right up a rough path that looks as if it ends in a small rock quarry a few tens of metres from the main path. Pass through this area of broken rock, and, after a few minutes pass a ruin and follow the path as it doubles back up a ridge.

About five minutes after leaving the main path, you will pass an inhabited house on your left, and directly ascend past a ruin. The path is indistinct at this point, and does not look promising, but turn directly left behind the ruin, and you should be able to follow it.

This is the beginning of a very steep ascent on a rough path, where you will sometimes be looking for handholds. After about 20 minutes of arduous zig-zagging, you will emerge at a T-junction on a more major path, where you turn right along a contour. Following this path around the side of the hill will bring you to a small settlement after about ten minutes. From here, you can see Mato Grande on the hill on your left.

Follow the path as it doubles back on itself through the settlement, and then follow the path up the hill under the phone line. After about seven minutes, you cross over a small ridge, and your path improves. Three minutes later, you pass a water point with taps, where you turn left uphill.

After another two or three minutes, a path joins you from your right in front of a white, two-storeyed house. Go straight on, following the path uphill. Five minutes later, you cross a small valley, and then bear left at a fork. Two or three minutes later there is a white cross standing on a wall on your right beside a white house. Pass in front of the house on your right, and immediately turn right beside the house, following the path uphill. Within a couple of minutes you will reach a telephone box, and a larger cobbled path through Mato Grande. Turn left at the phone box, and after five minutes of ascending, you will reach the Centro Social de Mato Grande (social centre) on your left.

To get back to the *vila*, via **João de Nole**, takes about 40 minutes (there are alternative routes, both described in the walk from Vila Nova Sintra on page 194). From the social centre in Mato Grande, take the road up to the left of the tapstand. After about 1km, turn right at a T-junction.

After a further 400m, turn left down into João de Nole. After 100m, go straight across a small T-junction. After this, the cobbled path gets smaller as it starts to zig-zag sharply down towards the *vila*. About ten minutes after the small crossroads, the path emerges on a cobbled street at the edge of town.

Turning left on to the street, you will come to a crossroads after about 50m. Turn right for Pensão Paúlo; go straight on for the Pousada Municipal.

Vila Nova Sintra–Levadura–Fajã d'Agua

Distance: 6km; time: 2 hours; difficulty: 2 (AI)

This is a classic, downhill Cape Verde *ribeira* walk, with your destination sparkling beside the sea during the brief glimpses you snatch as you descend. Before you reach it you have to negotiate a lot of superbly crafted cobbled paths, ghostly villages and the echoey sides of the harsh valley walls. There is a short patch towards the end where there is no clear path and the going is slippery.

The first 25 minutes of the walk is on the road. From the town square head west on the town hall road. At the end of the street turn right up the Nossa Senhora do Monte road. Follow this for just over 20 minutes, passing through the village of **Cova Rodela**, with its superb dragon tree, on the way. Stop at a fork in the road: the high road continues to Nossa Senhora do Monte; to the right is the road to Fajã d'Agua.

Walk for two minutes along the high road, then take a track to the right beside a sizeable tree. Follow this for about five minutes, ignoring another track up to the left, until you reach a crossroads of paths. To the right a track leads to a few houses on a nearby peak. Take the middle path, downhill, which leads you swiftly into a hidden valley of stark cliffs and, beyond them, the sea. Some 25 minutes from the crossroads you reach a water tank around which the path forks. The left path goes to the village of Tomba Has: take the right one instead. You are in a deep valley world of steep, stone wall terracing and startling echoes.

Within a couple of minutes of leaving the water tank you will have your first proper view of Fajã d'Agua, the archetypal nestling village, snug and green between the hostile brown Bravan mountains. Keep going, past two water tanks, through a settlement and, 15–20 minutes after the first water tank, past the quiet village of **Levadura** (to see it take a small detour on a path to the left). Now you are deep in the valley and the path is steep and winding.

Some 15 minutes from Levadura, when you are about level with a wood and a few houses on the other side of the valley, the path crosses a watercourse (generally dry) and a small dam, often full of water. Don't take the little path down to the left but go straight on, crossing, after a few minutes, a concrete barrier and following a path up through the houses ahead. In this jumbled settlement you will find someone who can lead you through to the other side where there is a well-trodden path the villagers all take down to Fajã d'Agua. Beware: it is gravelly and slippery. For half an hour you descend on a path that is a mixture of rock, landslide and gravel, criss-crossing water channels, dams and stream beds and passing a big water tank, until you arrive at the road through Fajã d'Agua.

Vila Nova Sintra–Sorno–São Pedro–Vila Nova Sintra
Distance: 9km; time: 4¹/₂ hours; difficulty: 2–3 (AI)
This spectacular walk encapsulates the essence of Brava: the remote valley hamlet of Sorno making miraculous use of its little stream to farm extensive green terraces up the mountainsides; the vivid, slightly menacing sea; the barren mountains; the ghost villages that are testament to livelier times; and, periodically, big brother Fogo looming from across the sea. The walk is suitable for any walker of average fitness, with just a very small slippery stretch to be negotiated. There is a two-hour walk downhill, mainly along a road, and two and a half hours on a remote path that is steep but not difficult. There are no facilities in Sorno.

From Vila Nova Sintra walk for 25 minutes to the fork, as described in the first two paragraphs of the walk from Vila Nova Sintra to Fajã d'Agua.

Take the right fork (the Fajã d'Agua road), passing a big white water tank on the right after 20 minutes and, after a further 15 minutes, reaching a turning to the right. This road on the right is of much poorer quality and takes you past a small quarry and various houses. You may pass the odd person harvesting grass or loading it on to a donkey but soon you will leave even these few behind, and there is just you, the sea and the odd hawk. The dull brown of the mountains makes a huge contrast with the rich blue and harsh white of the sea.

Eventually one of the road's twists will reveal **Sorno** below, improbably tame below the ominous Brava slopes. The Sorno road takes 1¹/₂ hours to cover, dwindling to a path – slippery in places – some 20 minutes from the village and, all the while, the ingenious village reveals itself in the form of irrigation channels, neat water tanks and endless squares of tended terraces. Follow the path round to the front of a square white building and then follow your nose, and a set of stepped irrigation channels and water tanks, to the sea.

After a break on the beach, it is time for the ascent out of Sorno. Finding the path, which winds out of the other side of the valley from the side you entered, takes a little care. Use as your guide Sorno's first (more southerly) bay. With your back to the water and its twin-peak stacks behind you, gaze up the valley and look for the little path that mounts its left side. For the first five minutes it is a small dirty track, but it then becomes paved and walled, if old and crumbly, soon crossing a concrete water channel and tank.

As you leave Sorno its colours dull and, after a good 20-minute walk, you turn to see its vivid greens already merging with the dull surrounding browns, its charm retreating. Half an hour of climbing out of Sorno brings you round into the next bay, a new set of jagged peaks ahead of you and, after entering a little wood, a turning to the right past a stack of dry stones. Take this and, in less than five minutes, you pass another prehistoric old home on the left – the path goes up and round behind it.

You are now entering the loneliest part of the walk, its stark remoteness made more poignant by the carefully crafted path, with its implication that someone once thought it would be useful. Some 50 minutes from the right turning at the stack of stones below, you reach the ghost village of **Tez Cova** – decaying old piles of stone houses from which folk used to try to farm the now-abandoned terraces. One half expects the ghost of an old Bravan crone to emerge from one of these hovels and share a thought on the fate of the island.

At Tez Cova you should walk through the village, broadly following the contour, rather than heading upwards and inland. The path dips shallowly and then climbs gently, passing on the left No 26, a building with a pale pink door. At the edge of Tez Cova, the final house is inhabited and you pass it on the left and go over a saddle, which reveals the vista of **São Pedro**, the busy overflow from Vila Nova Sintra. From here, it is half an hour to the *vila*, initially through a maze of paths (keep asking for the *praça*).

WHALERS AND THE PACKET TRADE

For a young man with nothing but a peasant's struggle against hunger ahead of him, the prospect of a job on one of the New England whaling ships that pulled into Brava provided excitement and escape.

The first such boats arrived towards the end of the 18th century. Throughout most of the 19th century a new vessel would arrive perhaps every three days so that the crew could resupply, drink and deposit their genes in the ever-absorptive pool. Crucially, the whalers would also be searching for crew – as replacements for obstreperous crewmen who would be abandoned on Brava. The Cape Verdeans were disciplined and took lower wages than their American counterparts, and developed great skill in the arts of whaling.

Stories of life aboard the whalers are full of excitement, courage and horror. The shot of the harpoon sinking into a 30m-long beast; the cries as the men rowed frantically to escape the thrashing of the whale's tail; the speed with which their little boats were towed through the ocean by the fleeing animal until they won control and sank a killer harpoon home. Men frequently died during these battles.

Some used the whaling ships as brief stepping stones to jobs in the USA – manual labour in the ports, in the cranberry bogs of southern New England and in the textile mills of New Bedford.

As steam replaced sail, the schooners and whalers could be bought or even 'inherited' for nothing. Cape Verdeans in the USA took them over, did them up and began the era of the Brava Packet Trade – a regular link between the USA and the islands. The boats would take Bravans to work in the cranberry bogs and return loaded with goods and with *emigrantes* visiting their families. The Packet Trade became an independent link by which Cape Verdeans could keep in contact with their families without depending on the transport system of another country.

There are plenty of dramatic tales about these ships – of charismatic captains, of tussles with disaster and of tragedy. The *Nellie May* was the first to begin a regular journey between the continents, in 1892. One of the longest recorded journeys of such a schooner was 90 days; the record for the shortest crossing was claimed to be 12 but was probably longer. World War II halted the trade, but afterwards one of the most legendary of the packet trade captains, Henrique Mendes, resurrected a sunken schooner and named her *Ernestina* (see box on page 167).

Vila Nova Sintra–Furna

Distance: 3km; time: 50 minutes; difficulty: 1 (AI)
This walk follows the old, little-used cobbled road from Vila Nova Sintra to Furna. It is an easy descent, steep in places, and is a good alternative to being rattled around in the back of an *aluguer* when you are descending to the port for home.

Set out on the road east from the main square. After five minutes, you will reach the stone boat looking out towards Fogo. Take the little cobbled path down to the left of the boat, and after just a short distance, you will join the main road snaking its way down to Furna. Cross the road, and double back a few metres to pick up the cobbled path continuing its descent on the other side.

After five minutes descending, you pass a cobbled turning on your right towards Santa Barbara. Some 25 minutes later, the old road briefly joins the new road, but leaves it again after a short distance.

Just before entering Furna, you rejoin the new road for the last time.

Other walks

There is also an easy path from Fontainhas to Cachaço; and there is said to be a path from Cachaço to Casa Eugénio Tavares: enquire locally.

DRIVES

Brava is very small, so small that in just half a day you can cover all the driveable roads by car. This is well worth doing if you are pressed for time, but also to get a feel for the island – from its plunging mountains scored with deep *ribeiras* above Fajã d'Agua, to the lively fishing village at Lomba, and the dusty poverty at the end of the road in Cachaço.

Take the road west out of the *vila*. A sharp hairpin in the first kilometre takes you out of the *caldeira* and through the pretty village of **Cova Rodela**. Just past the telephone box in the heart of Cova, the road forks – the left-hand fork takes you round the rim of the crater, past **João de Nole**, to where the road ends at **Mato Grande**. It is worth a brief detour along this road: after about 700m, there is a viewing point (*miradouro*) looking out over Vila Nova Sintra towards Fogo.

Continuing from Cova, bear left at a second fork (the right fork will take you to Fajã d'Agua) and descend beneath a hill where there is a large water tank – this is one of a series that serves all of Brava. If you look down the *ribeira* to your right at this point, you will see Fajã d'Agua nestling in a bay far, far below. Below the water tank, you pass through the attractive village of **Cova Joana**, where one aspect of Brava's economy becomes apparent: while emigré money has allowed many of the houses to be restored, the others are just left to crumble away.

A hairpin bend brings you up out of the valley into **Nossa Senhora do Monte**. A turning to the left on the hairpin below the school will take you into the labyrinthine tracks and pathways that make up the villages of **Lima Doce** and **Mato**, further south. Standing over Mato is **Fontainhas** peak, which you will see if the mist is not down. At 976m, this is the highest peak on Brava. Nossa Senhora do Monte is a winding cobbled street between whitewashed houses, where the red flowers of the cardeal bushes spill down the walls. The village commands spectacular views down the *ribeiras* to the north, with the sea beyond. The village is more or less continuous with Tomé Barras, where the road divides. Take the left fork to continue on to Cachaço. At this point, the countryside seems to change, and it starts to feel wilder, emptier and drier. As the road weaves in and out amongst the ridges, note the rows of acacia trees – planted to maintain a semblance of green during the dry season.

Cachação is where the road stops – less than 10km from Vila Nova Sintra. It is a poor place, and epitomises the economic problems besetting rural communities in many parts of Cape Verde. Dependent exclusively on farming, it has been reduced almost to a ghost village. Although the volcanic soil is very fertile, increases in the price of seed and labour, and the unpredictability of the rains over a number of years are factors that have been felt keenly in Cachação. Look about you and you will see traces of old field markings and terracing high up the slopes – all abandoned now – and shattered farmhouses left to the elements.

Returning from Cachação, take the left turning at Tomé Barras. After about 900m, a small turning on the left goes to the small settlement of **Campo Baixo**. Carrying straight on, you will arrive at the fishing settlement of **Lomba**, after about 3km. Although the cobbled road surface stops after about 1km, this journey is worth making just to marvel at the road engineering – in places the track has been cut through ridges of solid rock.

The village of Lomba is strung out along a thin, exposed ridge. Bravans have remarkably limited access to the sea because of the steepness of their volcano. If you have a good head for heights, and are prepared to crane your neck, you will see the fishing boats drawn up hundreds of metres below. The women carry the fish in basins on their heads up an interminable zig-zagging path back up to the village. Depending on the season, they may be carrying bright orange groupers, or swordfish and tuna which, from far off, look like slabs of silver. There is a single shop in the village, selling cold beers. Lomba is a great place to watch the mist rolling down the *ribeiras*, or just to sit on the crumbling white rock of the ridge and try to see where the sea meets the horizon.

Returning along the road, pass the turning to Cachação on your right, go through Tomé Barras, into Nossa Senhora do Monte and on towards the *vila*. Winding up out of Cova Joana, you will come to the turning to Fajã d'Agua on your left. This is another spectacular road – completed only in 1989 – cut through living rock. You will reach Fajã after about 4km. It is a wild and beautiful place, a well-protected harbour where yachts frequently drop anchor beneath mountains which seem to stretch upwards forever.

A few houses line the waterfront, where, on windy days, you will be wet by the spray. A kilometre beyond the village, there is the ill-fated Bravan airport, wedged in between the mountains and the sea. Fickle crosswinds and a runway that is not quite long enough conspire to make the airstrip unsafe – one of the last planes to land here almost ended up in the sea.

On the road back out of Fajã look out for a turning on your left after about 3km. This road is not for the faint hearted. After just over 2km, you will have to abandon your car, and continue to Sorno by foot, but it is well worth it (see *Hikes*, page 196, for a description of Sorno).

THE ILHÉUS DO ROMBO

These islands have been nature reserves since 1990 and are protected by law. The smaller ones are Ilhéu Luiz Carneiro, Ilhéu Sapado and Ilhéu do Rei.

You are only likely to visit the islands if you are a birdwatcher. It should be possible to find a fishing boat in Fajã or Furna to take you there and back for about 2,200$. Most people choose to camp overnight, eating fish that they catch and grill there. There is no campsite; you will need to take all equipment and water with you.

Ilhéu Grande

Some 2km², Ilhéu Grande's highest point is Monte Grande, at 96m. It has a rounded shape. Seabirds used to breed here – the island is covered in thick layers of guano.

BIRDS ON THE ILHÉUS DO ROMBO

Bulwer's petrel (*Bulweria bulwerii*) is known locally as *João-petro*. The birds are only known to breed on Raso Island, which is near São Nicolau, and on Ilhéu de Cima. They are almost totally black with a strip of dark grey stretching along the middle of their wings.

The Madeiran storm petrel (*Oceanodroma castro*) is known locally as the *jaba-jaba* or the *pedreirinho*, and breeds only on these islands and on Branco, Raso and islets off Boavista. It is black apart from a white bit just before the tail.

Ilhéu de Cima

This long and narrow rock is 1.5km² and famous for its seabird colonies. It has a big lump sticking out of its southern end, 77m high, and some smaller rocky outcrops.

São Vicente

Four o'clock in the dawning
São Vicente folk are there
To cry their sorrow
For sons who are sent away
To São Tomé

Mindelo lament

For many people Mindelo, the island's capital, *is* São Vicente. It's a fine city, full of life and a certain grace. In some ways it is one of the most pleasant cities in west Africa. Mindelo's buzz contrasts with a dead hinterland – as dry as Sal but more extraordinary, as it has died at a younger age, while still covered in sweeping hills and mountain ranges. The British called São Vicente the 'cinder heap'.

São Vicente only found a purpose in the very late 18th century, and since then its people have been through great trauma. The promise of trade and riches drew them from other islands to the business of Mindelo harbour. But São Vicente is not a land that can support a peasantry and so its poorest classes have been parasites – extracting what living they could from the insalubrious spin-offs of the shipping trade. Wander outside the capital and that haunting question evoked by the flatter islands returns once again: 'How did people end up here? How have they survived?'

HIGHLIGHTS

Many Cape Verdean writers and thinkers were educated at the São Vicente *lycée* and Mindelo is proud of its intellectual and artistic tradition. It has a liveliness – visit for the music, for the occasional performance, for hanging around in the bars. Cape Verde's two most exuberant annual festivals are here: the exotic Carnival, a miniature Rio, in mid-February, and the beach music festival in August.

Also go for watersports, in particular windsurfing and also surfing. But do not go for an aesthetic experience or for hiking. There is one reasonable beach and a few depressing ones.

Cruises

Cruises that pause at Cape Verde generally stop at Mindelo because of its deep harbour. If there is time to visit the island across the channel, Santo Antão, and enjoy its glorious scenery by taking a trip to Ribeira Grande and back, then that should be the priority. It should be possible to do such a trip in a day (see *By ferry between São Vicente and Santo Antão* page 205).

If there is no time for such an expedition, and it is a clear day, then a walk or drive up to the top of Monte Verde is the most scenic activity; failing that go for a

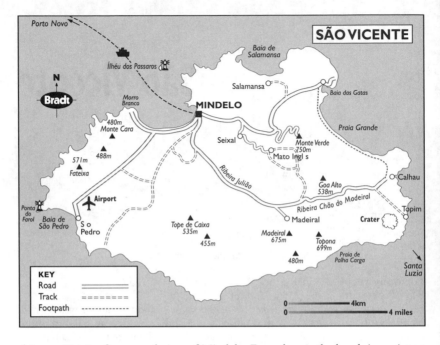

drive up Fortim for a grand view of Mindelo. For a day on the beach jump into a taxi and go to São Pedro (for details, see page 217).

BACKGROUND INFORMATION
History

This rock in the ocean was of little use to anyone before the end of the 18th century. After its discovery on 22 January 1462, and the traditional release of goats to prey on its delicate vegetation, humans forgot about it, except to land there occasionally with dogs and spend a night goat hunting. An attempt to populate the island was made in 1795, but it failed and just a few people remained, at the top of Monte Verde.

But São Vicente has one superlative natural resource. The island's harbour is a sweeping curve formed by a crater rim over whose northern side the sea has breached. A headland to the northeast of the harbour completes the protection while the ring of hills blocks wind from almost any direction. Thus Mindelo is a fine stopping point for ships crossing the Atlantic. When coal replaced wind as the main propellant, Mindelo became the ideal place for refuelling mid journey.

It was the British, by then the lords of the Atlantic and creators of the steam engine, who began to realise Mindelo's potential. By the early 1800s they had established a consulate and depot there. One John Lewis, a lieutenant, brought coal and set up a refuelling station for ships crossing from Europe to South America or to southern Africa. His arrival was followed by the Royal Mail in 1850. Soon Mindelo was busy, and in its heyday thousands of ships a year would pause in its harbour to load with coal brought from Cardiff to São Vicente. At any time 5,000 tonnes were waiting in lighters ready to load on to ships – part of the constant reserve of 34,000 tonnes. A 100,000-gallon tank was kept in the harbour, filled with water ferried over from Santo Antão.

John Rendall, one of the British involved in the coal business, reported of São Vicente in the 1850s:

There is space sufficient to anchor 300 vessels. Two steam packets run to and from England with the Post Office Mails, calling here every month for a replenishment of coals. The place is improving daily, and will no doubt, in a short time, become the wealthiest of all the islands.

São Vicente was also chosen, in 1875, as the site for the submarine cable that allowed telecommunications across the Atlantic, and it filled with British employees of the Western Telegraph.

Yet the trade did not bring much prosperity to ordinary people. Cape Verde earned some money by charging for water and anchorage and exacting coal taxes. But the refuelling was in the hands of foreign companies and many locals scratched a pittance from the sale of rum and from prostitution and dingy guesthouses, though some earned livings heaving coal. For their part the authorities made little attempt to develop São Vicente: there was no investment in a proper pier to ward off competition from Dakar, and little thought was given to the possibility of taking advantage of world events rather than being their victim.

When Alfred Burdon Ellis visited in 1855, he wrote at length about the antics of the characters in his bawdy and squalid lodgings. On leaving, he concluded:

> Taken as a whole it is, perhaps, the most wretched and immoral town that
> I have ever seen; but what can be expected of a colony which is rated at
> such a low value that the salary of the governor is only four shillings and
> sixpence a day?

Thus, at the same time that it was the fourth-greatest coaling station in the world after Egypt's Port Said, Malta and Singapore, the city became a place of beggars, prostitutes, starving invalids and smugglers.

Unfolding world events dealt São Vicente a series of blows. The opening of the Suez Canal between the Mediterranean and the Red Sea in 1869 diminished the port's activity, though it bounced back after a while. Technology advanced and the cable connection became mechanised so the employees of the Western Telegraph returned home. Ships' bunkers were built larger so they could carry enough coal for their entire journeys. Finally, oil replaced coal, drastically cutting the amount of labour required for refuelling. Drought and famine bit viciously and in 1941, the British consul at Mindelo, Captain J L Sands, reported:

> A large number are emaciated, worn out and have lost both heart and
> hope ... the starving seem to accept the situation with an oriental fatalism.
> They do not press their claims to live, they scarcely beg, may ask you for
> alms once or twice, and then simply stare at you as if resigned to what is
> to happen.

It was from Mindelo that the *contratados* were recruited in their thousands to go and labour on the plantations of São Tomé and Príncipe, islands to the south.

Mindelo was the intellectual capital of the archipelago, so it was here that despair and education came together to create the idea of revolution (see *History*, pages 13–14).

Since independence, São Vicente has received some investment. It has developed its pier and several quays as well as ship repair yards.

Geography

The island is 227km² and lies about 14km east of Santo Antão. It is extremely dry. Its highest peak, Monte Verde, is 750m. There is irrigation in some of the principal valleys – Ribeira de Calhau and Ribeira da Vinha. Earlier this century there were irrigated plantations in Ribeira Julião. The population is 55,000, overwhelmingly in Mindelo. There have been many attempts at reafforestation, particularly along the road to the airport.

Wildlife

São Vicente is the most popular nesting site for turtles. The island does not harbour any bird specialities but there are plenty of interesting waders and migrant birds on the wet sand towards São Pedro, 1km from the airport, and on the sewage ponds 2km from the centre of town (reached by going south along the coastal road until just after the Shell oil storage terminals and following a track inland on the left).

Festivals

Municipality Day	22 January
Santa Cruz	3 May
São João (St John)	24 June
São Pedro	29 June
Nossa Senhora da Luiz	8 August
Baía des Gatas Music Festival	August full moon
Mindelact Theatre Festival	September

Music

This is the reason for lingering in São Vicente. There is live music in many of the restaurants, and events going on at the various cultural centres in town. See below for venues.

GETTING THERE AND AWAY
By air

There are regular inter-island flights to São Vicente with TACV from:

Sal	2–4 flights per day
Santiago	2 or 3 flights a day
São Nicolau	A few flights, schedule not available at time of printing
Fogo	Via Praia
Santo Antão	None: flights discontinued indefinitely

The airport has a bar and restaurant and there is a queue of taxis (600–700$ and 1,000$ at night to town). It is 10km to Mindelo and 1km to São Pedro.

Airport ℩ 232 3715

By ferry
International journeys

If you are arriving from abroad in Cape Verde, you will most likely dock at Mindelo. Ships come from Dakar, Conakry and Bissau and cruise ships pause here as well (see *Practical information*, page 43).

To find a shipping passage away from Cape Verde, try Arca Verde, first on Rua Senador Vera Cruz. The company's four biggest ships sometimes abandon their internal timetables to make trips to the mainland. You can also try the cargo-ship agencies, several of which are on Rua Cristiano de Sena Barcelos. Communications with the mainland might improve one day. Arca Verde had originally planned to operate new connections.

Between São Vicente and Santo Antão

Almost everyone travelling to Santo Antão takes the ferry from Mindelo to Porto Novo. The hour-long crossing is beautiful when calm, but it can become very rough.

A large ferry runs between Mindelo and Porto Novo, operated by Naviera Armas, whose ship *Mar d'Canal* is a super car ferry and is much more stable than the older local ferry. Cars cost 2,500$ one way, and foot passengers 600$. Luggage and 'large' hand luggage (more than 5kg and 25cm³) will be taken away from you and stored in a van during the crossing, for reasons best known to the crew. It departs from Mindelo sharply at 08.00 and 15.00, returning from Porto Novo at 09.30 and 16.30. On Sundays there is only one crossing each way.

Seriously big waves may be observed during a rough crossing. Sick bags are provided. Buy tickets at the port and check in at least 30 minutes before departure.

The smaller local ferry *Ribeira de Paúl* costs 600$, but is liable to suffer in rough weather, with waves crashing unexpectedly over the open deck, so waterproof your camera, wear a jumper, and keep your possessions out of the way of the extraordinary number of vomiting passengers. It can be extremely crowded. It departs around half an hour earlier from Mindelo at 07.30, but not always on time.

Buy your tickets at a low building in front of the port gates, available one hour before departure. The timetable is posted outside the office.

Ferry times change every few months, so check the timetable locally. See www.paulbelezanatural.com and *Santo Antão*, page 222.

Between other islands

Cargo ships regularly go to Praia from São Vicente and, less regularly, to other islands. Try the agents up towards the port and on Rua Cristiano de Sena Barcelos.

The ferries *Barlavento* and *Sotavento* have their base in Mindelo but only the *Barlavento* was operating scheduled sailings to Santiago, Brava and Fogo at the time of research and unfortunately the catamaran service did not seem to be running. The *Tarrafal* runs from São Vicente to São Nicolau and Santiago twice a week.

Shipping

Arca Verde Shipping Rua Senador Vera Cruz – no schedules available here but worth asking about ferries and ships to Africa.

AAB Shipping Agencia Viking Rua Libertadores de Africa 37, CP (PO Box) 448, Mindelo; ⟍ 231 7118/9 and 232 1718/9, m 991 2053; f 231 6464; e viking@cvtelecom.cv or vikingcv@hotmail.com

Albino dos Santos Rua do Santo António, CP 27, Mindelo; ⟍ 232 1895; f 232 1898; e albitos@cvtelecom.cv

Madeira Shipping At the Agencia Tropictur, Rua Camões, Mindelo; ⟍ 232 4265; e manoelgmadeira@cvtelecom.cv

Belltrans Shipping Rua Baltazar Lopes da Silva, Mindelo

By yacht

The harbour and anchorage at Mindelo are excellent, offering protection from the northwest winds through to eastern and southern winds. At Mindelo, Shell will deliver alongside and water is available in this way as well. Ship repair is the best in the archipelago – they should be able to repair new instruments here. Whether or not this is your first port of call in Cape Verde, you may have to call not just at the *capitania* in the port radio building but also with the maritime police and the immigration police. The other possible anchorage is at Baia de São Pedro where it is best to anchor off the eastern end of the beach. There are no facilities.

Watch the channel between São Vicente and Santo Antão, where winds can gust up to 40 knots, particularly between December and May.

GETTING AROUND
By public transport
Transcor buses journey around Mindelo and its outskirts (25–30$), visiting Baia das Gatas during July and August. There are no *aluguer* routes to the rest of the island except to and from São Pedro. Buses and taxis gather at the square to the west of the Presidential Palace.

By taxi
Plenty about town (120$). Taxis charge upwards of 1,500$ to go up Monte Verde; 1,200$ return to go to Baia das Gatas and 1,500$ to Calhau.

Taxi 2000 ⟍ 231 4564

Car hire
Alucar In Monte Sossego, southwest of town; ⟍ 232 1295/5194; f 231 5461;
e alucarsv@cvtelecom.cv or alucarstrc@cvtelecom.cv
Atlantic Car 27 Rua Baltazar Lopes da Silva, Mindelo; ⟍ 231 7032, m 991 6229; f 232 7032
Auto Crioula ⟍ 232 8255
Avis Next to Hotel Porto Grande
Belcar Largo 6, Chã de Monte Sossego; ⟍ 232 7330, m 995 7101; f 232 7366;
e belcarlda@cvtelecom.cv
Cabauto ⟍ 991 2629
Castro & Filhos ⟍ 231 6673
Joel Evora ⟍ 230 0303/4
Mindelauto In Monte Sossego; ⟍ 231 7393
Occidental Car Hire In the southern districts
Porto Novo Car In Rua do Coio; ⟍ 232 1978
Rentmavetra ⟍ 230 0253

ACTIVITIES
Excursions
Agencia National de Viagens South of the French Cultural centre
Albino dos Santos Rua de Santo António 49; ⟍ 232 1895/6; f 232 1898;
e albitos@cvtelecom.cv
Cabetur Rua Senador Vera Cruz; ⟍ 232 3847/3859/5860; f 231 3842. Half- and full-day tours. Also on Sal and Santiago.
FLY Viagens e Turismo ⟍ 232 2844; f 232 2846. At the Hotel Porto Grande, does a guided tour of the island inc Mindelo.
Terraventura-cabo verde ⟍ 998 7463; email: contact@terraventura-caboverde.com; www.terraventura-caboverde.com. Specialises in adventure tourism and ecotourism, with a variety of trips including desert exploration, and horseriding in São Vicente.
Tropictur CP 2, Mindelo; ⟍ 232 4188/1560/1785; f 232 2617;
e tropictur.sv@cvtelecom.cv. Is also the Danish consulate. Also has an office in Praia.
Verdemindo On Rua Baltazar Lopes da Silva, Mindelo

Windsurfing
São Vicente is one of the world's greatest windsurfing and body-boarding destinations but, frustratingly, the market for renting equipment has not yet developed. However, there is the possibility of hiring (or buying cheaply) from a surf shop called Maripesca in Mindelo.

WINDSURFING AND SURFING

Surfers love some of the São Vicente beaches and, in 1997, Sandy Beach at Calhau was included in the European professional circuit. But it is among windsurfers, who have reached bullet-like speeds here, that it has become famous.

For one young windsurfer, it was the channel between São Vicente and Santo Antão that posed the greatest challenge. He gazed longingly across the 14km stretch and promised himself that one day, when the winds were right, he would attempt the crossing. He waited a long time for the perfect day and then set out, just as the ferry pulled away from the pier for the same destination.

He raced across and arrived at Porto Novo before the ferry, much to the admiration of the rest of the windsurfing fraternity back in Mindelo. One man left unimpressed, however, was the local policeman, who promptly arrested him.

For advice, sympathetic company and the possibility of a lift out to a beach where the surf's up, get in touch with Joaquim Brito (↘ *231 5184, daytime; 232 3087, evening*) who is president of the Skibosurf Club of São Vicente.

At the time of going to press there were plans to improve access to windsurfing on São Vicente, so it is worth making inquiries. For more on the potential of windsurfing on this island, see *Practical information*, page 36.

Sailing
Contact the Cape Verde Sailing Club.

Swimming and surfing
You can swim at São Pedro, but beware of very strong currents, the semi-artificial lagoon at Baia das Gatas and Baia de Salamansa. Don't forget Praia da Laginha, just north of Mindelo. Hotel Porto Grande and Mindel Hotel have swimming pools, the latter a little small but with great views from its rooftop position.

There are some reasonable waves near São Pedro.

MINDELO
The wide streets, cobbled squares and 19th-century European architecture all contribute to the sense of colonial history in Mindelo.

Most facilities lie not on the coastal road but on the next road back, which at the market end is called Rua de Santo António and, after being bisected by the Rua Libertadores d'Africa, becomes Avenida 5 de Julho. Most road names in the centre of town have changed, but many of the old signs linger and firms vary as to which street name they use. Visitors to Mindelo should be careful walking about with valuables on show, as robberies do occur. One or two people may well be hostile to foreigners and there are some beggars, genuine and otherwise.

Where to stay
Upmarket
Hotel Porto Grande CP 103, Praça Amílcar Cabral; ↘ 232 3190; f 232 3193; e pgrande@cvtelecom.cv; www.oasisatlantico.com. The large pink building on one side of the square, this is a pleasant hotel of international standard with terraces and a swimming pool. It is part of the Oasis Atlantico group. *Sgl 8,490$; dbl 10,585$; suite 17,860$.*

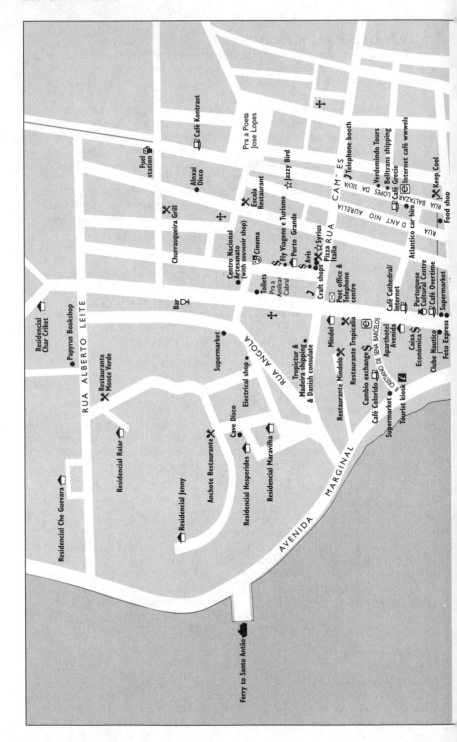

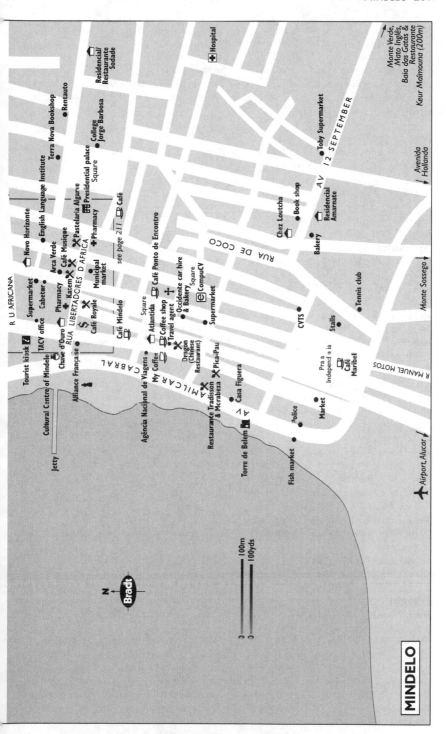

MINDELO

Mindel Hotel CP 844, Av 5 de Julho; ↘ 232 8881/2; f 232 8887; e mihotel@cvtelecom.cv or mindelhotel@hotmail.com. Just off the main square (Praça Amílcar Cabral) this is a smart, 4-star international hotel with all the trimmings, inc satellite TV, hairdryers and AC in good-sized comfortably furnished rooms. Also there is a rooftop swimming pool, but it may not always be open. It is excellent value and the included breakfast must be the best in Cape Verde. Free transport to airport. Visa and MasterCard accepted. *Sgl 5,000–6,500$; dbl 6,500–7,500$; suite 10,500–12,500$.*

Mid range
Residencial Sodade CP 403, 38 Rua Franz Fanon; ↘ 230 3200/7556; f 231 4019; e residencialsodade@hotmail.com. Up the hill behind the Presidential Palace, Sodade commands an excellent view over the town and the bay from its rooftop terrace and restaurant. The architecture is pleasant. Rooms are highly variable, from depressing basement hideaways to good mid-range rooms and slightly rickety suites. More expensive rooms have fridge, TV and AC. *Sgl 2,454–5,287$; dbl 3,030–5,966$; suite 6,111–7,420$.*
Aparthotel Avenida CP 120, Av 5 de Julho; ↘ 232 1178/3435/1176; f 232 2333; e aparthtlavenida@cvtelecom.cv. On the road that heads south from the main square (Av Amílcar Cabral) into the centre of town. Has been renovated and now has TV, AC and hot water. Good views of the harbour from one side. *Sgl 3,000–4,000$; dbl 4,000–5,000$; suite 7,200$. Add 6% tax to room rates.*
Residencial Maravilha CP 533; ↘ 232 2203/2216; f 232 2217; e gabs@cvtelecom.cv. Near the port, off Rua Angola, this is a hidden gem – friendly, helpful management and beautiful rooms with dark, Mediterranean furniture. Some have AC and fridge. *Sgl 2,650–2,900$; dbl 3,700–3,950$.*
Chez Loutcha CP 303, Rua do Côco; ↘ 232 1636/1689, m 999 0339; f 232 1635. Just off the vast Estrela Square, Chez Loutcha has varied rooms. Many rooms have AC, fridge bar and TV. *Sgl 2,050–2,790$; dbl 3,160–4,030$; suite 3,790–5,170$.*
Residencial Hesperides Near the Maravilha; ↘ 231 9019/8688. *Sgl 2,000$; dbl 4,500$.*
Residencial Jenny ↘ 232 8969; f 232 3939; e hstaubyn@cvtelecom.cv. Overlooking the harbour on Rua des Immas od Amar de Deus. *Sgl 2,900–3,900$; dbl 3,500–4,600$.*
Residencial Che Guevara ↘ 232 2449; fax 232 4265; e cheguevara@cvtelecom.cv. A pleasant spot, located in the north of town along Rua Alberto Leite. *Sgl 2,900$; dbl 3,700$; triple 5,500$; inc breakfast and offers a discount for more than 3 days' stay.*
Residencial Amarante In the south of the city, a new place; ↘ 231 3219; f 232 6995. *Sgl 1,783$; dbl 2,300$; triple 3,105$.*
Residencial Raiar/Aluguel da Apartments CP 626; ↘ 231 4740, m 995 1712; f 232 6718; e crair@hotmail.com. In Alto de Sao Nicolau district of Mindelo. *Sgl 1,500$; dbl 2,000$; room only.*
Residencial Alto Fortim CP 701, Mindelo; ↘ 232 6938; f 232 6936. It has 6 rooms, AC, TV and restaurant. It is in the Alto Fortim area. *Prices on request.*

Budget
Residencial Novo Horizonte Rua Senador Vera Cruz; ↘ 232 3915. *Sgl or dbl 1,500$; with a small but pretty balcony. No breakfast.*
Pensão Chave d'Ouro CP 93, Av 5 de Julho; ↘ 232 7050. Centrally positioned on the corner of Rua Libertadores d'Africa and Av 5 de Julho, it claims to be the oldest hotel in Mindelo and the principal bedrooms still have huge shuttered windows and are equipped with ewers and pitchers. It has great character. Rooms vary dramatically in quality; top-floor singles are little more than cupboards with chipboard partitions while it is the first-floor rooms that retain a degree of old colonial charm. No en-suite bathrooms. *Sgl 1,500$; dbl 1,800$; breakfast extra 180–300$ each.*

Residencial Char Criket ❭ 231 0437. North of Rua Alberto Leite. No meals, this is more of a homestay. *Sgl 1,000$; dbl 2,000$.*

Residencial Atlantide ❭ 231 3918. For short stays – even less than 1 night. *Sgl 1,000$; dbl 1,600$.*

Where to eat and drink

There are many places to eat in Mindelo; below is only a selection.

Achote Good-quality food and live music on a Saturday night. Main dishes from 700$. Go up the road that has the Maravilha on its left, and it is at the top.

Café Cathedral Has an internet area and is another popular watering hole along Av 5 de Julho.

Café Colorido Near the Mindel Hotel for snacks.

Café Grecie On Rua Baltazar Lopes da Silva, a quiet snack bar.

Café Kontrast In the northern area.

Café Lisboa A more youthful, hipper version of Café Royale, on Rua Libertadores d'Africa.

Café Maribel In the big square in the south; for snacks and drinks.

Café Mindelo Is close to the French Cultural Centre; for drinks.

Café Musique Remains a popular spot.

Café Overtime A popular spot along Av 5 de Julho.

Café Portugal Across the road from Café Lisboa.

Café Royale Rua Libertadores d'Africa. This was an atmospheric local favourite where little seems to have changed since the 1920s. Closed now but may reopen, and the building is still worth a look.

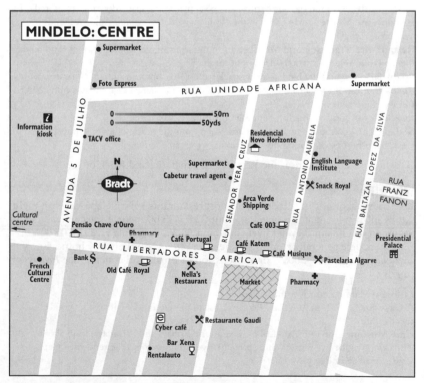

Chave d'Ouro A beautifully designed cake and coffee shop upstairs in the hotel of the same name. Also, a restaurant that is open for lunch (12.00–13.00) and dinner (19.00–23.00).

Chez Loutcha Much-praised restaurant on the ground floor of the hotel of the same name.

Dragon A Chinese restaurant in the south central district.

Keur Maimouna Serves traditional Senegalese lunches and dinners, inc the Senegalese version of *cachupa*. There is usually just one dish on the menu, costing about 300$. To get there, go along the Monte Verde road from Chez Loutcha.

Mindel Hotel Restaurant Outside on the west side of the hotel. Open air and a popular place.

My Coffee A cosy place in the southern district near the Dragon Restaurant.

Nella's Set in one of the beautiful old buildings in the centre of Mindelo, Nella's is primarily a seafood restaurant and dishes are simple and fresh with a Mediterranean twist to the cooking. Food and service are good. Main dishes start at 700$. Above Café Lisboa – access is by stairs on a side street to the left.

Pastelaria Algarve Has a small outside terrace for watching the world go by. On Rua Libertadores d'Africa, up towards the Presidential Palace.

Pica Pau Rua Santo António 42, one road in from the coastal road, to the south of the city; ❧ 232 8207. A bit of a Mindelo institution, this restaurant is as eccentric as it is minuscule, its walls plastered with notes of praise from previous customers. Specialising in seafood, it is most proud of its *arroz de marisco* (seafood risotto).

Pizza Italia Below the Hotel Porto Grande; has a good selection.

Ponto de Encontro ❧ 232 8207. Smart little cake and coffee shop down the southern half of Av 5 de Julho. Open until 20.00.

Restaurante Escale In the northern area; a posh place for expats. Bookings preferred.

Restaurante Monte Verde Close to the Residencial Raiar, evenings and weekends in general.

Restaurante Tradisson and Morabeza On the seafront, Av Amílcar Cabral south end, in an old building, has a good selection of meals.

Snack 003 Pleasant little hidden-away snack bar on Rua António Aurelio Gonçalves.

Snack Bar Katem Very cheap eats in a busy local atmosphere; *cachupa* for around 200$. On Rua Libertadores d'Africa.

Snack Royal Near the English Language Institute.

Sodade This rooftop restaurant offers an escape from the bustle of town, with a panoramic view that is best before dark. Above the hotel of the same name.

Bakeries can be found near the Residencial Amarante and My Coffee.

Nightlife

Live music abounds in Mindelo and most restaurants have a Cape Verdean night. Clubs in Mindelo tend to open at about 22.30–23.00; people start arriving about midnight–00.30 and they get lively by about 02.30, emptying at about 05.00. On a Sunday people generally stop somewhere for *cachupa* on their way home. Entry to most clubs costs 200–300$. For a discussion of music and dancing, see *Perspective*, page 27.

Le Bienvenue Popular live-music venue.

A Cave ❧ 232 7802. In Alto São Nicolau, close to the Hotel Maravilha, it's a good choice for nightlife.

Café Musique Opposite Café Lisboa. Live music Fridays and Saturdays, from about 23.00. The most popular live music venue, particularly among visitors. The renowned Cape Verdean musician Bau played here.

CESÁRIA EVORA

Cesária Evora, the 'barefoot diva', has a dedicated international following, particularly in Paris. Her appeal lies in the quality of her voice which, in addition to its mellow qualities, is untrained, simple and unaffected – the perfect vehicle for expressing the poetry of the *morna*. It has earned her the names Aguadente and Red Wine. Evora is also loved because she sings as if she has just stepped into one of the Mindelo bars – lack of pretension, even bluntness, are her hallmarks. She sings the *morna* accompanied mainly by violin, acoustic guitar, accordion, piano, clarinet and the mandolin-like *cavaquinho*.

Evora was born in 1941. It was a friend of Evora's who remarked on her voice when she was a teenager. She joined a band at the age of 16 and sang in the bars of Mindelo. She made no money from it, apart from a little when she performed at Portuguese official functions – but even that source disappeared with independence in 1975. Her humble career seemed to have evaporated and for a decade she refused to sing.

In 1985, at the age of 45, Evora was invited to Portugal by the Organisation of Cape Verdean Women to contribute to a record. She went, but the record was not a hit. However, while she was there she met a businessman, José da Silva, who offered to work with her. Three years later she cut a record, *La Diva aux Pieds Nus* (The Barefoot Diva), in Paris. She has made several more albums, including *Destino di Belita*, *Cesária*, *Miss Perfumado*, *Mar Azul* (Blue Sea) and *Cabo Verde*. She lives in Paris and has houses in São Vicente.

Alnxai 'the real thing' ͻ 231 5979. Was formerly Pimms.
Fantastique ͻ 232 2572. In Monte Sossego.
Praça Amílcar Cabral On Sundays at 19.00 the municipal band plays here.
Syrius ͻ 232 3190. Under Hotel Porto Grande, very pleasant inside.

A little outside the very centre of the city are some other popular nightspots: **Le Bateau** in Fonte Frances; **Je T'aime** in Belavista; **Astro** in Chã Cemeterio and **Hi Step** in Fonte Ines.

Practicalities

Airlines TACV, Av 5 de Julho; ͻ 232 1524; f 232 3719; open Mon–Fri 08.00–12.00, 14.30–17.30; Sat 09.00–11.30. Agência Nacional de Viagens, Av da Republica; ͻ 231 1115; f 232 3083, for most internal and international flights. *Open Mon–Fri 08.00–12.30, 14.30–18.00.*
Banks Caixa Económica, Av 5 de Julho, near Aparthotel Av; open Mon–Fri 08.00–15.00. Banco Comercial do Atlântico, Praça Amílcar Cabral. *Open Mon–Fri 08.00–14.30.* Also on Rua Libertadores d'Africa. ATMs at the banks near the Porto Grande Hotel.
Ferries Try at any listed above and at Arca Verde, Rua Senador Vera Cruz; ͻ 232 4979; f 232 4973. *Open Mon–Fri 08.00–12.00, 14.00–18.00.*
Hospital Southeast corner of town; ͻ 232 7355 and 231 1879.
Internet Along Rua Baltazar Lopes da Silva is www.els internet café, which charges 50$ for 10 minutes, 100$ for 30 minutes and 150$ per hour. Try also Alliance Française de Mindelo (which also offers scanning, photocopying and print-out services).
Pharmacies Includes a large one at the top of Rua Libertadores d'Africa.
Police ͻ 231 4631. At the market end of the coast road.
Post office Posto Telefonico, Praça Amílcar Cabral. *Open Mon–Fri 08.00–22.00; Sat 08.00–11.30, 15.00–17.00; Sun/holidays 08.00–11.30.*

Shopping The best array of Cape Verdean products is at the Centro Culturel do Mindelo (see *What to see and do* below). Crafts, mainly from mainland Africa, can be bought in many shops around town; music from a shop on Rua d'António Aurelia. Supermarkets are common; try Fragata Overtime, Av 5 de Julho, which is one of the few open over lunch and late at night. For books try Terra Nova on Rua Franz Fanon.

Tourist information None really. There are 2 small kiosks, which basically sell maps (17) and postcards. Centro Culturel do Mindelo on Av Amílcar Cabral has a bookshop. Open Mon–Sat 08.30–18.00 (but in reality opening is unpredictable).

French Cultural Centre (Alliance Française de Mindelo) *Open Mon–Fri 10.00–12.30, 15.00–19.00; Sat 10.00–12.30.*

Maps Of Mindelo and São Vicente, sold at the kiosks. Produced in Germany; e info@goldstadtverlag.de; www.bela-vista.net or www.reisetraeume.de.

What to see and do

Sturdy English architecture, with sloping roofs and the odd bow window, is pervasive in Mindelo. There is the old **Miller and Cory's** building, now the ferry ticket agency; the old residence of the employees of Shell, now the **Portuguese consulate**; and the **Western Telegraph building**, beside TACV.

A wander through the city should begin with a stroll up to the fort, **Fortim d'El Rei**, on the headland to the east of town. From there you can understand the layout of the city. This hilltop fortress housed the local militia as well as many of São Vicente's notable rebels, including resistance fighters imprisoned there in the 1960s before being deported to Angola. Some 30 years before that, in 1934, the militia descended from Fortim on to a food riot incited by a famous carpenter, Ambrósio, who led the looting of the food stores in the Customs House. His story is the subject of plays today.

Now the headland affords a more peaceful scene: the busy port and Mindelo beyond it, the hills curling round the magnificent harbour; the strange stump of **'Bird Island'** poking out of the harbour; and Santo Antão. **Monte Cara**, or Face Mountain, on the other side of the harbour, is one of several places in the archipelago where the sharp erosion has sculpted a remarkable human profile out of the mountains.

On your return along the coast road, just after the port, is a **monument** surmounted by an eagle, commemorating the first air crossing of the southern Atlantic in 1922 by Cabral and Coutinho. They stopped here after their leg from the Canaries.

Other places to visit in Mindelo include **Centro Nacional Artesanato** where the rebirth of Cape Verdean craft is underway and it's possible to watch people weaving traditional cloth and making ceramics.

In the middle of town is the spotless, pink **Presidential Palace**, which is not open to the public. Stroll down the main street from the palace to the harbour. If you turn left you will see on your right the **Torre de Belem**, built in imitation of the monument of the same name in Lisbon and which housed the Portuguese governor from the 1920s. There has been a restoration plan for many years. Ahead and in to the left lies the market and the vast **Estrela square**. One half of the square has been filled with permanent market stalls, and on the wall at the end of each row an artist has depicted a scene from the history of Mindelo, painted on to ceramic tiles. The pictures are lifted straight from photographs taken in the early 1900s. They allow us to imagine Mindelo at its economic height: great wooden piers, cranes and rail tracks forever hauling coal onshore to the storage bunkers; the grand and busy customs house; the ships' chandlers lining the front street. Old men wandering Mindelo today will reminisce about the golden time in their youth when there was plenty of work, abundant food, ships jostling for space in the harbour, coal piled up high – and it always rained. From there, head back towards the Presidential Palace, passing through the **Pracinha de Igreja**, the oldest part of town where the first houses were built and where there is a pretty church, constructed in 1862.

If when you reach the coast road from the Presidential Palace you turn right instead of left you can walk up the *avenida*, with its shady trees down the centre of the road, and past some fine old storehouses. These date from the height of the shipping days: many of them have been transformed for new uses. The **Centro Culturel do Mindelo** occupies one of them. It houses the Instituto Caboverdiano do Livro, which sells a wide variety of publications in Portuguese and Creole, and the French Cultural Centre, which organises films and has its own bookshop. There is also a café, Radio Cabo Verde station and exhibitions. It is open Monday–Friday 08.00–12.00 and 15.00–19.00; Saturday 08.00–12.00.

A little further up the road, opposite the pier, is the **old customs house**, now the nautical club. The harbour is always busy with cargo ships, ferries and yachts. Near the shore, rusting hulks turn to silhouettes as the sun dips towards the horizon. Take a right turn before the road bends left to the port and head up to **Praça Amílcar Cabral**, a huge square dominated by the Hotel Porto Grande and with elegant houses lining its other sides. This is where people gather in the evenings.

Just out of town you can walk to **Morro Branco**, 10km there and back along the shore road to the west. This is not scenic – probably only worth it if you have exhausted everything else on the island. First you pass the Shell oil terminal, and then rusting shipwrecks close to shore. Do not attempt to take photographs as you approach Morro Branco, as the soldiers in the barracks at the end of the road get jumpy.

OTHER PLACES TO VISIT

Baia das Gatas and Calhau are the settings for weekend parties and therefore best visited on Saturdays and Sundays. Monte Verde is stunning on a clear day but rather unexciting otherwise. A trip round the island is not a conventional aesthetic experience but it is a profound one.

Monte Verde

It's best to visit nearing sunset on a clear day. This is easier in July, August, December and January when Casa Branca, a hotel, bar and restaurant at the foot of the mountain, is open.

Leave town along the Avenida 12 de Setembro and travel on the Baia das Gatas road for 8km as far as the right turn to Monte Verde's summit. If travelling by *aluguer* or taxi, ask to be left at the large, white Casa Branca Hotel. You can instead be driven to the top, of course.

From the hotel a good cobbled road zig-zags up the north and east sides of the mountain to the top. At the summit the mist may be down, in which case there is little to see but the radio antennae, guarded by three soldiers and a cat.

On a clear day, however, the view is of a forest of black, misshapen crags, and the harbour beyond. Sunset beyond the forbidding peaks of Santo Antão is fabulous.

Salamansa

In São Vicente terms, this is a thriving place – people actually live here, drawing their livelihood from the sea, and there is a shop. But there is really no reason for the visitor to come here except to muse on why this fishing village exists at all: it's too exposed for launching boats and the fishing fleet is drawn up some 5km away on the other side of the peninsula.

Baia das Gatas

This resort is 12km from town. During the week it has the feel of an English seaside resort out of season. In front of rows of boarded-up bungalows, a pack of smooth-haired dogs trots along the wind-whipped sand. There's a children's play area with gaunt metal swings and slides reminiscent of gallows, and at the extreme end of the bay, a low pier. However, it's a brilliant place to fish where you can easily pull in two-pounders from the shore and then light a fire and grill your own supper. It's also great for swimming because of a natural barrier that creates a huge lagoon. At weekends the place is much more colourful. Unfortunately tourists have been robbed here.

As you drive back out of the village there is a ruin on the shore on your left. This is the old fish-processing factory – it is here that the Salamansa fishermen draw their boats up. If the wind is in the right quarter you may be lucky enough to see them running home under full sail. They venture as far afield as the uninhabited island of Santa Luzia, staying overnight there and returning with cold boxes full of snake-like moray eels, squid and grouper (like giant, bloated goldfish but more tasty).

Music festival

During the full moon of August people descend on Baia das Gatas for a weekend of music, dancing, eating and general revelry. The festival began as the best of them do – just a few musicians gathering for all-night jamming sessions. Now bands come from all over the archipelago and from abroad and there is horse racing and watersports.

Calhau

A drive along the 18km road to Calhau is like a guided tour through all the ecological problems facing both the island and Cape Verde as a whole. The road follows Ribeira Calhau, and takes just 25 minutes.

First the road passes through an area where there is a reafforestation programme – a huge proportion of the scant trees planted here are destined to die. Then, as you continue southeast, you will see Monte Verde on your left. The little village on its western slopes is **Mato Inglês**. Lack of water has driven away all but one or two old people.

A few kilometres further on is a right turn for **Madeiral**, a small village in the shadow of Topona Mountain. Old folk claim that the village was once supplied by water running down from the green slopes of the mountain above. Now the mountain has the same scorched, dusty aspect as the rest of São Vicente and its dryness cannot support even the toughest vegetation. Madeiral, like the island's two or three other inhabited villages, is dependent on desalinated water tankered in from Mindelo.

Past Madeiral the *ribeira* opens out and the valley floor is scattered with small squares of green. This is agriculture under siege – strong stone walls keep marauding goats out and despairing farmers are finding that the water that their windmills draw from the ground is becoming progressively saltier. In the search for sweet water, wells are pushed deeper, and windmills require stronger winds to keep the water flowing. In such precarious conditions, water storage tanks are indispensable. Meanwhile the search for water goes on: the piles of earth across the valley floor mark the places where boreholes have been sunk but have struck only dry earth and rock.

THE BRITISH IN CAPE VERDE

Golf, cricket and a smattering of English vocabulary were some of the lighter legacies left by the British in Cape Verde. Their involvement with the archipelago was sporadic but widespread. It included the dominance of Maio in the heyday of its salt-collecting years; the brief 'ownership' of Santo Antão (see page 221); the drastic sacking of Santiago by Francis Drake and the monopolising of the orchil trade in several islands including Brava.

The British have also contributed much to understanding the natural history of the islands. Charles Darwin spent three weeks recording fauna and flora here (see *Santiago*, page 126–7) – his first initiation to the tropics on the famous voyage of the *Beagle*. Since Darwin, there have been others. T Vernon Wollaston visited in the 1870s and 1880s and collected numerous beetles, moths and butterflies which are stored at the Natural History Museum in London.

But it is in Mindelo that the British are now most remembered. They left a golf club that claims to be one of the largest non-grass courses in the world. They also left a feisty cricket team, whose members are now in their seventies and have received a grant via the British consul to teach their skills to a younger generation.

English-derived words that have entered the Creole language were gathered by Frank Xavier da Cruz in 1950. They include: *ariope* (hurry up), *blaquéfela* (black fellow), *bossomane* (boss man), *cachupa* (believed to have been derived from ketchup), *chatope* (shut up), *salongue* (so long!), *ovataime* (overtime), *tunquiu* (thank you), *fulope* (full up) and *ovacote* (overcoat).

Just before entering Calhau there is a small white church and a school on the left of the road. Almost immediately, a rough track leads off to the right towards a volcano crater, clearly visible about 3km away.

At the end of the road is the village. People live here still, and fish, but as with every other village, water is the problem. Calhau is alive and bustling at weekends, however, with city folk coming to their seaside retreats.

The proprietor of Chez Loutcha, the *pensão* in Mindelo, runs a popular bar and restaurant here that is open only on Sundays except over Christmas, when it is open every day. It is clearly signposted down a rough track on the right as you enter Calhau (after the turning to the volcanoes). There is live music and a self-service buffet.

The Hamburg bar and restaurant is also closed during the week but lively at weekends.

São Pedro

An *aluguer* from Mindelo will cost 100–200$ to São Pedro, which is just 1km past the airport. It is a little fishing village with a shop and a bar, colourful fishing boats drawn up on the beach and an air of tatty quaintness.

Where to stay

Foya Branca Resort CP 781; ℡ 230 7400; f 230 7444; e foyabranca@cvtelecom.cv; www.foyabranca.com. This is on the other side of the bay and has nothing tatty or quaint about it. It is dedicated to seclusion with white walls, a pool and discreet and tasteful apartments. Activities and excursions are numerous as detailed below. *Sgl 6,900–7,300$; dbl/twin 10,200–11,400$; 4-bed villa 19,000–20,200$; 8-bed villa 33,000–35,000$.*

Activities

The waves crashing on to the beach at São Pedro are an impressive size, and it may often be unsafe for swimming, so ask before you venture into the water.

Facilities and activities available through the hotel are windsurfing, bicycle hire, horseriding, fishing and boat hire. Gym 350$ for non-guests; tennis 250$ per hour (double for non-guests). Use of the pool is 600$ for non-guests. Micão organises watersports at the Foya Branca Hotel and is to be found at the Casa Café in Mindelo or ask the hotel to contact him direct. Prices are as follows:

Windsurfing	1 hour 1,600$; half day 3,300$; full day 4,900$
Fishing	Half day 29,700$; full day 55,000$ for 10 persons, inc drinks and snacks
Boat hire	Per day 5,500$
Aluguer hire	Per day 1,500$; 300$ per hour
Horseriding	2 hours 3,000$ inc guide
Excursions	Half day 2 persons 8,950$; full day 3–4 persons 7,900$

Santa Luzia

The smallest of the archipelago members that qualify as islands, Santa Luzia is 35km² and uninhabited. Its highest peak, Topona, is 395m. It is extremely dry and barren. It has a rugged north coast and a south coast of scenic beaches and dunes. No seabirds are known to breed there any more.

Santa Luzia lay uninhabited until the 17th century, when it was granted to Luis de Castro Pireira. It has mainly been used for livestock raising when there has been rain. In the 19th century about 20 people continued these activities. A family of goatherds lived there till the 1960s. In 1990, devoid of inhabitants, the island in effect became a nature reserve.

To reach the island, go to Calhau and enquire amongst the fishermen about the possibility of accompanying a journey. To charter a fisherman for the day will probably cost about 12,000$ and the journey takes about two hours.

Black-winged stilt (pernalonga)

Santo Antão

The rugged peaks and canyons of northeast Santo Antão are one of the world's great landscape dramas. Precarious roads trace the tops of its ridges giving sheer views on both sides down thousand-metre cliffs into the tiny settlements below. The people live in a series of deep valleys, their world enclosed by colossal volcanic walls. As you ascend the valleys on foot you discover in astonishment that the settlements reach high into the cliffsides, clinging to ledges and surrounded by banana trees and cassava. In the west of the island is an apocalyptic and inaccessible landscape of steep walls, jagged edges and harsh ravines.

There is a legend that Santo Antão's precipices defeated a bishop who, while visiting the more distant of his Cape Verde flock, tried to reach Ribeira Grande from Paúl across the mountains. It is said that halfway through the journey, having scaled a terrifying cliff, he lost his nerve and could move neither forwards nor backwards. And so the bishop remained, supplied regularly by the more sure-footed of the island who would arrive with tents, food and clothing for him. He waited in a crevice until a road was built to conduct him away in safety.

HIGHLIGHTS

There is one overwhelming attraction: hiking the *ribeiras*. Non-hikers can also appreciate the landscape from the spectacular drives over the ridges and along the *ribeira* floors. The road from Porto Novo to Ribeira Grande is one of the highlights of a visit to Cape Verde and is worth travelling along even if you must return immediately to São Vicente.

However, there are virtually no sandy beaches and there are no watersports. The hotels, while perfectly adequate, clean and friendly, are not luxurious. There are several rare birds to watch out for and fishing is possible with the locals.

BACKGROUND INFORMATION
History

Fertile and green but mountainous and inaccessible, Santo Antão remained without much of a population for the first 90 years after its discovery on 17 January 1462. If people knew it in the 15th century it was because of its use in the mapping of an imaginary line down the Atlantic that divided Spanish and Portuguese colonial rights. The Treaty of Tordesillas in 1494 agreed that this north–south line would pass 370 leagues west of Santo Antao. Land to the west of that line was to belong to Spain. Land to the east – including the islands themselves and Brazil, which protrudes quite far into the southern Atlantic – was to belong to Portugal.

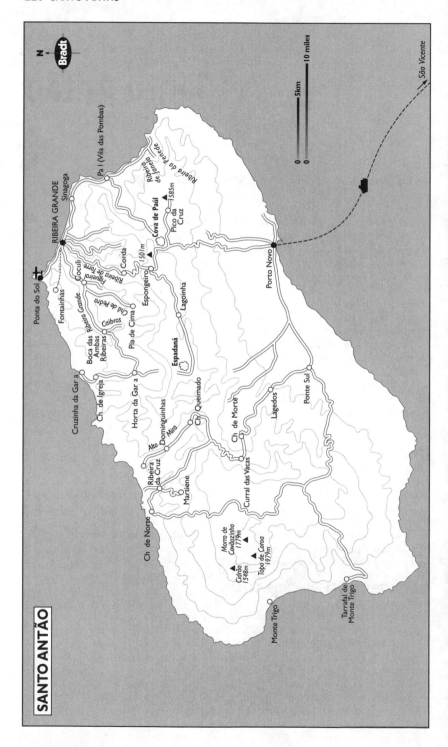

A series of people leased Santo Antão from the Portuguese Crown, the first in 1548. In the 1600s its administration and ownership were granted to the Count of Santa Cruz. It was the son of the fourth Count of Santa Cruz, the Marquess of Gouveia, who was to add brief drama to Santo Antão from as far away as Europe. In Portugal he kidnapped Mariana de Penha de França, the wife of a Portuguese nobleman, and escaped with her from Portugal to England where, having run out of money, he mortgaged Santo Antão to the English in 1732. This went down very badly back in Cape Verde and the Portuguese soon drove the English away.

After that excitement the 18th century granted Santo Antão a little more recognition. Ribeira Grande achieved the status of *vila* in 1732 and, two decades later, Bishop Jacinto Valente chose to settle there, having rejected the crumbling and unhealthy capital of Santiago. It was to be another 120 years before Santo Antão was made capital of the Barlaventos – she was the richest, most populated and least malarial of the northern islands at this time.

Perhaps it was the effect of living between the high and menacing walls of the *ribeiras* but the people of Ribeira Paúl and the people of Ribeira Grande had a major argument in 1894 about their representation in Portugal. The people of Ribeira Grande decided to make war on their cousins down the road, armed themselves with guns, clubs and sticks and roared down the coast.

The people of Paúl were ready, though, and destroyed the road so that no-one could cross it. None, that was, but an athletic horse which leapt across the opening, whisking to safety a lucky inhabitant of Ribeira Grande who had been on the wrong side of the road. The people of Paúl fared the worst in the conflict – many of their men were later imprisoned and spent a lot of money regaining their freedom.

The island lost its position as Barlavento capital in 1934 when the seat of government was transferred to São Vicente. It also recently lost its important role as supplier of water to its barren cousin across the channel, when a desalination plant was constructed on São Vicente. Santo Antão was plagued with an impenetrable interior and also the problem that its only good port – Tarrafal – was a long way from its agricultural area. In recent decades the port of Porto Novo and the road between it and Ribeira Grande have improved the situation slightly.

Geography
Santo Antão is second only to Santiago in size, at 779km², and second only to Fogo in the height of its greatest mountain – Topo da Coroa at 1,979m. It is the most northern and the most westerly of the islands. It has a mountain range stretching from the northeast to the southwest.

The population is about 50,000 and the biggest town is Porto Novo, in the southeast where the port is. Up in the northeast are Ponta do Sol and Ribeira Grande, also known as Povoação. The fertile areas are in the northeast, where there is often moisture on the peaks and intense agriculture, making use of permanent streams in two of the *ribeiras* – Paúl and Janela.

The rest of the island is barren apart from around Tarrafal to the southwest where there is some water, which is used for irrigation.

Santo Antão's annual rainfall has plunged over the last century by about 45%. Engineers have been considering making better use of the island's one abundant source of water: the annual floods during storms between August and November, which can run off the mountains and into the sea in volumes of millions of cubic metres. Conservation dams in the upper mountains could store the run-off and be used for irrigation lower down the valleys.

Economy

Fishing, agriculture and the extraction of *pozzolana* (a volcanic dust used in cement making) are the economy's mainstays. Tourism, bottling of natural mineral water and the marketing of *grogue* are all being developed.

Festivals

The big festival of the year is the festival of São João Baptista on 24 June. It begins with a 20km procession of the cross from the mountains down into Porto Novo – done to the accompaniment of banging drums. On arrival in Porto Novo, the people begin a party which lasts all week. Others are as follows:

Municipality Day	17 January (Ribeira Grande)
Santa Cruz	3 May (Coculi)
Santa António das Pombas	13 June (Paúl)
São Pedro	29 June (Chã de Igreja)
Nossa Sra Da Piedade	15 August (Janela)
Nossa Sra Do Livramento	24 September (Ponta do Sol)
Nossa Sta Rosario	7 October (Ribeira Grande)
Santo Andre	29 November (Ribeira de Cruz)

GETTING THERE AND AWAY

By air

There are currently no scheduled flights to Santo Antão. The runway at Ponta do Sol suffers from frequent and dangerous crosswinds. Flights with different aircraft may resume if demand improves. It is a 20-minute taxi ride (was 500$) to Ribeira Grande from the airfield.

By ferry

Almost everyone travelling to Santo Antão takes the ferry from Mindelo to Porto Novo. The hour-long crossing is beautiful when calm: the view of São Vicente, with the forbidding mountains behind Mindelo, and its guardian rock erupting from the harbour, is stunning.

A large ferry runs between Mindelo and Porto Novo, operated by Naviera Armas, whose ship *Mar d'Canal* takes cars as well. Luggage and large hand luggage (more than 5kg and 25cm³) will be taken away from you and stored in a van during the crossing. The cost is 600$ one way. It departs from Mindelo sharply at 08.00 and 15.00, returning from Porto Novo at 09.30 and 16.30. On Sundays there is only one crossing each way.

The smaller local ferry *Ribeira de Paúl* costs 300$, but is liable to suffer in rough weather, with waves crashing unexpectedly over the open deck, so waterproof your camera, wear a jumper, and keep your possessions out of the way of the considerable number of vomiting passengers.

In Porto Novo, the two ferries, which are run by different companies, have separate offices on the road out of the port. There are stories of tourists being unable to board because the ferries are full. On your return from Santo Antão, take this into account, particularly if it is the first leg of a journey to meet an international flight.

Ferry times change every few months, so check the timetable locally. See also *São Vicente*, page 205.

By yacht

The trip across from São Vicente can be hairy, with winds gusting up to 40 knots from December to May – they are channelled by the two islands, creating a Venturi effect. To anchor at Porto Novo, the only harbour suitable for yachts, requires permission from Mindelo beforehand. It may be preferable to visit Santo Antão by ferry, though leave a watchman back in Mindelo. Tarrafal is a possible anchorage, offering total shelter from the trade winds but constant swell, making it hard to land with a dinghy. Supplies on offer would only be basic (a few food items and water). Ponta do Sol is completely unsuitable for yachts.

GETTING AROUND
By public transport
Aluguers ply the main road between Porto Novo and Ribeira Grande all day (200$), although most of them arrange their journeys to coincide with the ferry arrivals and departures. They are also regular between Ponta do Sol and Ribeira Grande. Elsewhere they follow the usual principle, leaving villages for the town early in the morning and returning at midday or early afternoon. To access the west of the island it is best to stay in Porto Novo to save precious daylight hours driving down from Ribeira Grande. *Aluguer* drivers in Santo Antão are unlikely to overcharge you but they are likely to insist you have missed all public *aluguers* and should therefore hire them as taxis. Be sceptical and hang around for a bit.

By taxi
Taxis are in the form of chartered *aluguers*.

Car hire
Motacar ⟍ 222 1021
Porto Novo Car ⟍ 222 1490

ACTIVITIES
Excursions
Alsatour In Ponta do Sol, Santo Antão; ⟍ 225 1213. Alsatour runs a variety of programmes, mainly hiking. See *Practical information*, page 34.
Dany Careca ('the bald') At the Residencial Ponta do Sol; ⟍ 225 1238/293 2296, m 993 2296; f 225 1249. Organises individually tailored hikes, guides, places to stay, vehicle transport all over the island and fishing trips, for a range of prices.
Santur Travel Close to the Hotel Antilhas in Porto Novo; ⟍ 222 1660, for ferry information about the sailings of the Tarrafal ferry, which may be in operation.
Viagitur In Ribeira Grande; ⟍ 221 2794; f 221 9795. Mainly for air tickets: TACV, TAP and South African Airways.

Hiking
The obvious walks are the grand *ribeiras*. You can either take transport up the main road and disembark for a steep descent or you can walk or take transport along the coastal roads for a steep ascent. After torrential rains these *ribeiras* fill – take local advice about how to ascend them because there is usually an alternative path.

These walks are almost entirely on cobbled footpaths, which can lull your mind should you decide to explore elsewhere on your own. These are high mountains, remote at the top, with racing mists. Paths that are 'off the beaten track' can turn to slippery gullies, and require a guide – even a boy from the nearest village. Between December and February temperatures above 1,000m drop to 10°C.

The west of the island is unfrequented, a hidden world of ravines and cliffs cut into bizarre shapes by erosive winds. There are craters filled with lava flows and looming boulders of white pumice. Interspersed is the odd pool of greenery where irrigation has allowed cultivation. The west is difficult to get to and requires more organisation and expense than the equally fabulous and more verdant northeast – so most people will prefer to ignore it unless staying for some time.

Now that there is a good map of Santo Antão (see *Maps*, page 47) and locals are opening their houses to guests, the west is easier to explore. However, the area is lonely, the roads are sparse and the traffic is scarce. The landscape is full of hidden dangers – landslides, sudden cliffs and lack of water. For this reason we recommend taking a local person with you for any walk there. Official guides are required to complete a two-month course in subjects such as health and safety, history, fauna and flora etc.

Mist can cascade down on to Santo Antão, spoiling the spectacular views from high up in the mountains, and sometimes making it hard to find paths (where they are not obvious cobbled ones).

PORTO NOVO

In September 2005, this busy and windswept town, was inaugurated as a city. It is full of smart new buildings paid for by Luxembourg as well as tended gardens and promenades overlooking the channel. An enjoyable evening can be spent here watching evening fall on the distant, black mountains of São Vicente and the glowing harbour of Mindelo. You can even see São Nicolau, no more than a timid relative beyond. There are one or two excellent restaurants.

Getting there and away

To get to Porto Novo from Ribeira Grande find an *aluguer* in the main street. They run all day (contrary to what the drivers will tell you) but the vast majority time their trips with the ferries. If you have a ferry to meet in Porto Novo allow plenty of time, as the last *aluguers* to leave Ribeira Grande sometimes miss the ferry, or arrive to find all the tickets have been sold.

To get from Porto Novo to Ribeira Grande, choose from the many *aluguers* that queue up to meet the ferry from Mindelo – you may even be recruited as a passenger by a zealous tout on the boat. Outside ferry times, hang around outside the ferry offices near the port, or in the *aluguer* park – keep your eyes open as they are generally driving around town trying to find passengers.

Sometimes, during the rainy season, Ribeira Grande can become a lake, roads can be washed out and visitors can become stuck on the other side of the island for several days.

There are several cars for hire, unofficially, in town.

Where to stay

Por do Sol Fundo Lomba Branca CP 19; ✆ 222 2179; f 222 1166; e pordosolpn@cvtelecom.cv. Dbl 3,255$.

Residencial Antilhas ✆ 222 1193. Just outside the harbour, to the right, the best rooms have balconies with panoramas of São Vicente. Some rooms have shared bathrooms. Sgl 1,000$; dbl 1,500–2,500$ (with TV).

Residencial Girasol ✆ 222 1383. Upstairs rooms with good inland views. Sgl 1,750$; dbl 2,500$.

Where to eat and drink

Restaurante Antilhas In the hotel of the same name with breezy veranda.

Flôr do Dia ✆ 222 1147. Excellent food inc lobster, and great cakes. Main dishes start at 500$. Dishes take about half an hour to prepare but some take over an hour and may be best ordered in advance. To get there take the Ribeira Grande road.

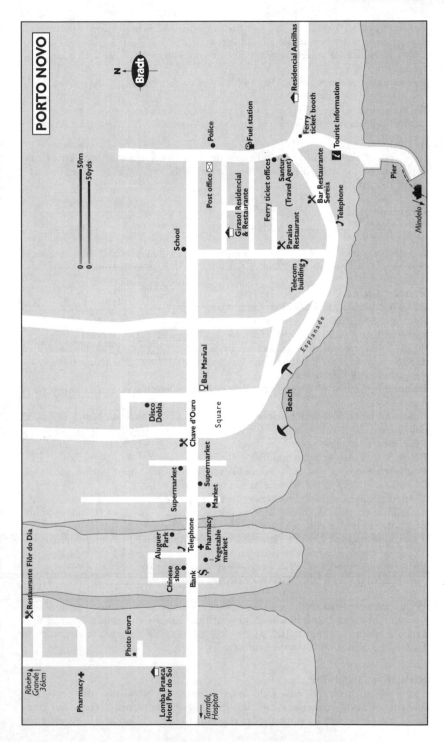

PORTO NOVO

N

Bradt

50m
50yds
0
0

Police

Post office

Fuel station

Girasol Residencial
& Restaurante

School

Ferry ticket offices

Santur
(Travel Agent)

Paraíso
Restaurant

Residencial Antilhas

Ferry
ticket booth

Tourist information

Bar Restaurante
Sereia

Telephone

Telecom
building

Esplanade

Bar Marival

Disco
Dobla

Chave d'Ouro

Square

Beach

Pier

Mindelo

Supermarket

Supermarket

Market

Aluguer
Park

Telephone

Pharmacy

Vegetable
market

Chinese
shop

Bank

Photo Evora

Restaurante Flôr do Dia

Pharmacy

Ribeira
Grande
36km

Tarrafal,
Hospital

Lomba Branca/
Hotel Por do Sol

Bar Restaurante Girasol Popular place that can serve *cachupa rica* if ordered in advance. Also serves pizza. Underneath Residencial Girasol.
Chave d'Ouro Snack bar serving pizza, cakes and drinks. On the corner of the main square.
Restaurante Paraiso A grey building with no sign, on the first road on the right on the coastal road from the port into town.
Bar Restaurante Sereia A superb place to while away an hour or two, perhaps while waiting for the ferry, gazing across the water at São Vicente. On the coast road from the port into town.

Fresh goat's cheese can be bought on the road to the quay at boat arrival and departure times; vegetables from the market at the west end of the main road, beside the bank.

Nightlife
Disco Dobla When open, this is said to get going about 00.30 and to run till about 04.00.
Bar Restaurante Girasol Cape Verdean nights, generally on Fridays and Saturdays, or can be organised for larger groups of tourists (see *Where to eat and drink* above).

Practicalities
Airlines TACV; in Mindelo or Ribeira Grande.
Bank At the west end of the main road through town. *Open Mon–Fri 08.00–14.00.*
Ferries *Ribeira de Paúl* and *Mar Azul* ferries to São Vicente have separate ticket offices on the main road just above the pier. Tickets can also be bought at a kiosk near the Residencial Antilhas in Porto Novo. See also Santur Travel above (⟍ 222 1660) for information about the long-distance Tarrafal ferry.
Hospital ⟍ 222 1130. Huge grey and yellow building with orange roof on the main road as it goes west out of town.
Internet A new place is set to open opposite the market, at the Papelaria Natuds (200$ per hour).
Pharmacy ⟍ 222 1130
Police ⟍ 222 1132. Near the post office.
Post office From the port follow the road north past the petrol station and it is on the left. *Open Mon–Fri 08.00–12.00, 14.00–18.00.*
Shopping Souvenirs (*grogue*, punch and pottery), maps and guidebooks, and postcards can be bought at the quayside shop. The best-stocked supermarkets are Casa Delgado's just off the square and further along the main road, opposite the bank.
Tourist information Not a lot. There is a part-time kiosk uphill from the port exit, but it's mainly a shop selling postcards and maps.
Business opportunities Contact the following: City Hall of Porto Novo, CP 47; ⟍ +238 222 1223; f +238 222 1160; e cmpc.sec@cvtelecom.cv

What to see and do
Visit the little grey beach in town and watch the fishermen hauling up great tuna and the women selling it just a few feet away. Walk east for 25 minutes to Escurralete, the other beach on Santo Antão.

RIBEIRA GRANDE
The road to Ribeira Grande pulls away from Porto Novo past the depressing outskirts of town where the inhabitants live amongst permanent, savage and sand-laden winds. It mounts through the cusps of the brown landscape. Already the

achievement of the road builders seems extraordinary. As it climbs higher and higher forest plantations begin to fill the higher valleys and a chill tinges the air. But you are still in the foothills – on and on you go until you reach the clouds and the eucalyptus and pine trees which thrive in the cold air. The road skates the ridges of the top of the island and sometimes there are breathless sheer drops on either side as you gaze down into the plunging *ribeiras*. Pinnacles, cliffs, and double bends around spires of rock, mark the descent into the verdant side of the island and you will see the puddle of Ribeira Grande long before you drop past the thatched stone houses to reach it.

The town, known to most as Povoação, is a muddle of cobbled streets crammed into the space between the cliffs and the sea, and overflowing up the mouths of the two *ribeiras*, Ribeira Grande and Ribeira de Torre. For a place of such beauty it is strangely lacking in places to while away an hour looking at the view, and the idea of ending a hard day's hike sipping a quiet beer while gazing at some Atlantic panorama never quite materialises. Many tourists still stay here, but it is more refreshing up the coast at Ponta do Sol or tucked away in the few other villages where there are places to stay. A church was first built in the town in 1595. Bishop Valente, who arrived in the mid 18th century having abandoned Santiago, consecrated the large church of Nossa Senhora do Rosário in 1755. However, the transfer of the See to Santo Antão was never officially approved and it went instead, a while later, to São Nicolau.

Getting there and away

To get to Ribeira Grande from Porto Novo get an *aluguer* from the port. From Ponta do Sol, *aluguers* leave from the main square most of the day.

From Ribeira Grande to Porto Novo, *aluguers* leave from the main street (allow plenty of time to get to your ferry). For destinations up the *ribeira* (Ribeira Grande) such as Coculi, Boca das Ambas Ribeiras and Chã de Igreja, wait outside Caixa Económica (walk up the road that goes parallel to the *ribeira* and you will see it on your left). To the more distant of these destinations the *aluguers* follow the usual pattern (into town early morning, out of town midday). For Ponta do Sol, *aluguers* wait for passengers at the junction of the Ponta do Sol road with town (50$). For destinations along the coast road towards Janela, they wait across from town, on the other side of Ribeira de Torre. On Sundays these *aluguers* will not move until after 09.00 and will not go to more distant destinations.

Where to stay

Residencial Trópical ❯ 221 1129. The most comfortable place in town, with a restaurant. *Sgl 2,700–2,900$; dbl 3,500–3,900$; inc breakfast.*
Residencial Cantinho da Varzea ❯ 221 2606. At the south end of town in a quiet spot. *Sgl 2,000$; dbl 2,500$.*
Residencial Marcos Anafortes ❯ 221 1216. On the little road leading up from the petrol station. Good rooms. It can be hard to rouse the owner and there is no sign, so ask around. *Dbl 1,500–2,000$; no breakfast.*
Residencial 5 de Julho ❯ 221 1345; at the end of the main square. It has a maze of rooms and a popular café. Roof terrace. *Sgl 800–1,500$; dbl 1,200–2,000$; breakfast extra 250$ each.*
Residencial Bibi ❯ 221 1149. Down the narrow road opposite the 5 de Julho. Basic clean rooms, some with balconies. Hot water available. Find Dona Bibi in the adjacent food shop, Mercearia Nascimento. *Sgl 1,500$; Dbl 2,000$; breakfast 250$ extra.*
Residencial Aliança Tel 221 1246. Residencial Lagoa Verde and Pensão Conceiçao are also listed under the same telephone number. *Sgl 1,200$; dbl 1,500$.*
Residencial Fami Lar ❯ 221 1533. Down a side street, near the Marcos Anafortes.

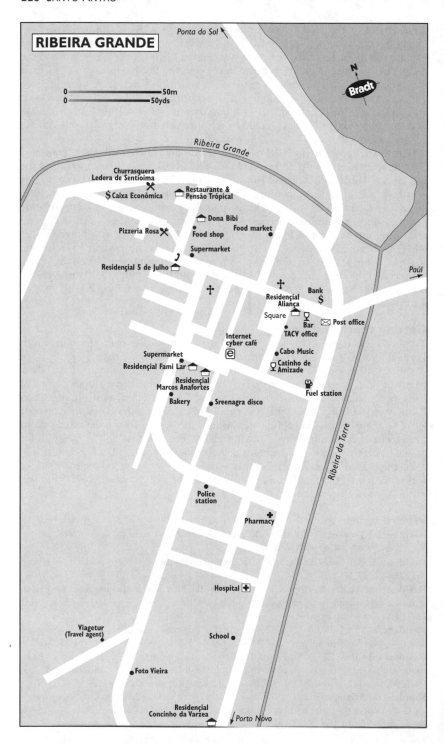

RIBEIRA GRANDE

Ponta do Sol

0 ————— 50m
0 ————— 50yds

Ribeira Grande

Churrasquera
Ledera de Sentioima
$ Caixa Económica

Restaurante &
Pensão Trópical

Dona Bibi
Pizzeria Rosa
Food shop   Food market
Supermarket

Residençial 5 de Julho

Paúl

Bank
$
Residençial
Aliança
Square
Bar   Post office
TACV office

Internet
cyber café

Cabo Music

Supermarket
Residençial Fami Lar
Catinho de
Amizade
Residençial
Marcos Anafortes
Fuel station
Bakery   Sreenagra disco

Ribeira da Torre

Police
station

Pharmacy

Hospital

Viagetur
(Travel agent)
School

Foto Vieira

Residençial
Concinho da Varzea
Porto Novo

Out of town
Pedracin Village ⟩ 224 2020; e pedracin@cvtelecom.cv. A new tourist complex a few kilometres southwest of town. *Sgl 3,800$; dbl 6,000$.*

Where to eat and drink
Aliança Drinks and snacks only.
Café 5 de Julho Basic, but very good value, filling meals. This is definitely one place to find *cachupa* (500$). Also serves egg and chips for 350$ and meat from 600$. At the residencial of the same name.
Cantinho de Amizade Near the petrol station, a pleasant patio bar for an afternoon drink.
Churrasqueira Ledera de Sentissima Is on the road of the Ribeira Grande, with a reasonable choice.
Pizzeria Rosa Near the bank; a good option for hungry hikers. Pizza 550–600$.
Restaurante Trópical (see *Where to stay*) The most expensive restaurant in town, with terrace.

Fresh bread is available from the bakery, **Padaria Sopasa.** Vegetables can be bought at the food market; there is a reasonably well-stocked supermarket opposite Residencial 5 de Julho, and some supplies at Dona Bibi's shop.

Nightlife
Disco Sreenegra In a small alleyway; see map.

Practicalities
Airlines TACV; ⟩f 221 1184.
Bank Opposite the post office at the crossroads on the edge of town. *Open Mon–Fri 08.00–14.00.* Also there is a Caixa Económica on Rua Ponte Lavad: follow the road up the side of the *ribeira* (Ribeira Grande) for a minute or so and it is on your left.
Hospital ⟩ 221 1130. On the main Porto Novo road.
Internet At the Residencial Tropical, Natud's and also the Cyber Café – see map.
Police ⟩ 221 1132. Go along the Porto Novo road and turn right before the hospital.
Pharmacy Near the hospital.
Post office At the end of the main street through town. *Open Mon–Fri 08.00–12.00, 14.00–18.00.*
Shopping Traditional and modern Cape Verdean music can be bought from Cabo Music, on the road that passes down the left side of the square. Food is available in several small food shops, inc a mini market on the same street as Cabo Music.
Tourist information None but try at Viagitur, who mainly sell flights (see page 223).

PONTA DO SOL
A gracious town, built on a breezy peninsula and without the cramped feel of Ribeira Grande, this is one of the oldest *Barlavento* settlements. It is becoming increasingly popular with tourists.

Getting there and away
Ponta do Sol is at the end of the road. It is a 20-minute *aluguer* trip to Ribeira Grande (50–100$), using transport that waits where the main road passes through the square. Transport leaves at times all through the day, but is most common in the early morning. Taxi from Ribeira Grande costs 500$. Taxi to Fontainhas 500$; to Paúl 1,000$; to Porto Novo 3,500$; to Pico da Cruz 2,500$; to Corda 1,500$. Change at Ribeira Grande for transport anywhere else.

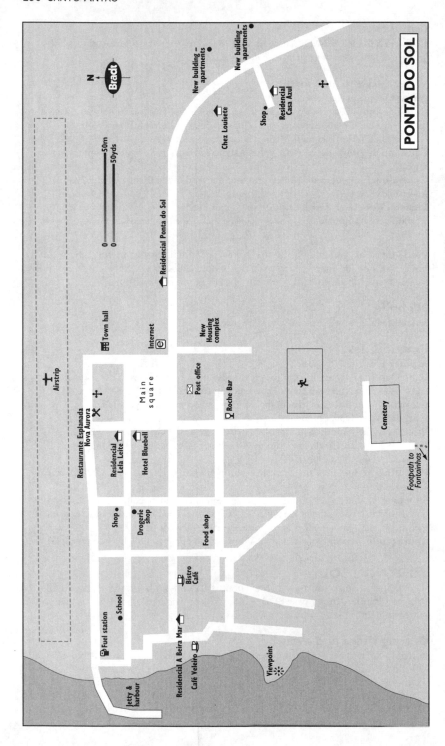

PONTA DO SOL

N

Bradt

0   50m
0   50yds

Airstrip

Jetty & harbour

Fuel station

School

Shop

Drogerie shop

Restaurante Esplanada Nova Aurora

Residencial Lela Leite

Hotel Bluebell

Main square

Town hall

Residencial Ponta do Sol

Internet

New Housing complex

Post office

Roche Bar

Food shop

Bistro Café

Residencial A Beira Mar

Café Veleiro

Viewpoint

Cemetery

Footpath to Fontainhas

Chez Louisete

New building – apartments

New building – apartments

Shop

Residencial Casa Azul

Where to stay

Many new places are opening up, turning Ponta do Sol into an attractive alternative to Ribeira Grande.

Hotel Bluebell ⟍ 225 1215, m 994 1153; f 225 1308; e bluebell@cvtelecom.cv; www.hotelbluebell.info. Located near the square, this is a pleasant new place with an airy restaurant. *Sgl 3,340$; dbl 4,452$; twin 4,876$; suite 7,791$; inc taxes and breakfast.*
Chez Louisete ⟍ 225 1048, m 991 8568; f 225 1115; e chezlouisete@cvtelecom.cv. On the road into town from Ribeira Grande and close to the turning to Fontainhas. Simple but tasteful rooms, with a rooftop conservatory where guests can have their breakfast and evening meals. *Sgl 2,200$; dbl 3,400$; with breakfast.*
Residencial Ponta do Sol ⟍ 225 1238/9, m 993 2296; f 225 1249; e residencialpontadosol@hotmail.com. On the road towards Ribeira Grande, it's a pale blue and white building. *Sgl 2,100$; dbl 3,200$; triple 4,200$.*
Pensão Casa Azul ⟍ 225 1295, m 994 9886; e casaazul-2@hotmail.com. A bright white and blue building, just below the turning to Fontainhas. Clean and modern rooms, some with balconies. Private bathrooms. Proprietor has minibus and driver. *Sgl 1,500$; dbl 3,000$; with breakfast.*
Residencial A Beira Mar ⟍ 225 1018; f 225 1255; e chezfatimaps@hotmail.com. Not far from the harbour. *Sgl 2,000$; dbl 2,600$; with breakfast.*
Leila Leite ⟍ 225 1056. Opposite the Hotel Bluebell; some rooms have shared bathrooms. *Sgl 1,200$; dbl 1,800$.*

Private houses
A number of private houses are listed by the tourist board but are not easy to find – certainly we didn't manage it.
Senhor Rodrigues ⟍ 225 1091. *Sgl/dbl 1,800$.*
Pensão Dona Dedei ⟍ 225 1037. *Sgl/dbl 1,400$; breakfast extra 300$ each.*
Dona Bibi ⟍ 225 1016. *Sgl/dbl 1,000$; breakfast extra 100$ each.*

Where to eat and drink
Bistro Close to the Residencial A Beira Mar and a popular place when open.
Café Veleiro e emanuelrachidsp@hotmail.com. Overlooks the sea and harbour.
Hotel Bluebell (see *Where to stay*) Has a nice restaurant with reasonable prices.
Restaurante Casa Azul At the pensão of the same name.
Leila Leite (see above) Rooftop restaurant; requires half a day's notice.
Restaurante Nova Aurora ⟍ 225 1360. Beside the church on the square. The most expensive restaurant in town, and the only one that requires no notice before eating.
Roche Bar Uphill, on the way to the cemetery, the Roche Bar is a lively place.

Nightlife
Not a lot – look out for **Disco Oceano**.

Practicalities
Airlines TACV in Ribeira Grande; ⟍/f 221 1184
Bank None.
Hospital ⟍ 225 1130
Internet Near the main square – see map.
Police ⟍ 225 1132
Post office Above the main square. *Open Mon–Fri 08.00–12.00, 14.00–18.00.*
Pharmacy Try at the Drogerie shop.
Shopping Very limited so far.
Tourist information Very little. ⟍ 221 2029 or try at the hotels.

TARRAFAL

This isolated spot on the west coast is frequented more by yachties than any other visitors because access is so hard. There are some walks from the village, and the black-sand beach is supposed to have medicinal properties. You can also visit Monte Trigo, which most people do by paying for a lift in a fishing boat.

Getting there and away

Two *aluguer* trucks leave Tarrafal at about 06.00 for Porto Novo, departing on the return journey at about midday. The journey takes several hours and is very uncomfortable, particularly the half nearer Tarrafal, and the trucks are invariably packed. You could charter transport in Porto Novo for ten times the price.

Where to stay and eat

Residencial Mar Tranquilidade ☎ 227 6012; e info@martranquilidade.com; www.martranquilidade.com. Run by Frank and Susi, a German couple. 1 single and 6 double cottages; most with toilet and shower inside, the others very close outside. Reservations are highly recommended, even on the day of arrival, as they are often full. (Although some other local people take in guests from time to time, finding other accommodation in Tarrafal is not always possible, and getting back out of Tarrafal on the same day is practically impossible.) Also, they buy fresh ingredients every day to cook for their guests, so can offer the best choice when they know accurate numbers. *1,500$ pp sgl/dbl, inc breakfast.*

OTHER PLACES TO VISIT
Paúl and Ribeira do Paúl
with thanks to Kayo Shiraishi

A 15-minute drive along the coast from Ribeira Grande town is Paúl, surrounded by valleys of sugarcane, breadfruit and bananas, and with some great hiking. It is also renowned for its *grogue*, with a *trapiche* (sugarcane-juicing apparatus) still operated with oxen.

GROGUE

Sugarcane, the sole ingredient of *grogue*, arrived in Cape Verde with the slaves from mainland Africa. The word *grogue* is derived from 'grog' – used by English seafarers. At first, the production of spirit from sugar cane was forbidden on the grounds that it presented a risk to public health. However, restrictive laws just drove the distillers underground and by 1866 the authorities relented and introduced a brandy tax instead. By 1900, there was even legislation dictating the safe design of sugar cane presses, or *trapiches*.

The *trapiche* is a large machine traditionally made of wood and driven by oxen or mules, plodding round in a never-ending circle. Men feed cut sugar cane through heavy metal rollers and sugar syrup runs out and is collected in barrels where it is allowed to ferment for five to ten days. No water is added, and neither is yeast – there is enough naturally occurring on the cane.

The still is partly buried in a loose stone oven, and the fermented syrup is brought to the boil, producing an aroma that wafts up the valley. After an hour, the steam is run through a pipe cooled by water, and the distilled spirit starts to flow. A skilled eye can tell from the froth in the distillate the point at which a palatable fraction is being produced. That's the theory, at least.

In practice, the *grogue* drunk in villages will not have been produced under controlled conditions. Distillation is likely to have been carried out in an old oil

Getting there and away

The centre of Paúl, Vila das Pombas, is a 15-minute *aluguer* trip from Ribeira Grande (50$), available regularly when events are going on. *Aluguers* can be found by the playground (to Ribeira Grande), or along the *avenida* in front of the carpentry workshop if going up the valley to Cabo de Ribeira (100$). Transport to Pontinha de Janela (50$) can be found in front of the church.

Where to stay

Residencial Marisol Estância; ↘ 223 1294; e helderlima@hotmail.com. On the road next to the sea. The owner, Noémia Melo, offers home cooking, and 5 bright new rooms, some with private bathroom (hot water available), others with a balcony and uninterrupted sea views. French and English spoken. *1,200–1,700$*
Residencial Vale do Paúl Vila das Pombas; ↘/f 221 1319. Claúdia Costa offers 5 simple but clean rooms, with shared bathrooms. The restaurant overlooks the sea (reservations essential). Bar and adjacent well-stocked store. *800–1,300$*.
Casa Familiar (Sabine Jähnel) Eito; ↘ 223 1544. A rare opportunity to stay within one of Santo Antão's great *ribeiras*, this *pensão* can be found by walking up Ribeira do Paúl, beyond Eito, and turning left at the sign for Mercearia Brito. Sabine, who is German, offers 2 rooms (shared bathroom) that open on to a shaded roof terrace. Excellent Cape Verdean meals *en famille*, and friendly hiking advice. German and English spoken. *1,000–1,500$*

Where to eat and drink

Morabeza Vila das Pombas; ↘/f 223 1790. This friendly restaurant offers dazzling views of the ocean and fields. Meals are made to order using locally grown vegetables and freshly caught fish. Open daily 08.00–23.00.
O Curral Chã João Vaz; ↘ 223 1213. This café is perfect for taking a break from the long hike of Vale do Paúl. Try various kinds of grogue made by the owner, Alfred.

Several *mercearias* (small food shops) around the town act as bars, where you can get a cold beer or shots of *grogue*. Try **Docel** (↘ *223 14 28*) for locally made drinks and

drum, and the spirit collected in a rusty tin. It will not kill you unless you binge on a particularly dodgy brew, but it may upset your stomach. After 20 years of sustained drinking, the accumulated methanol may make you blind.

For those who are not put off, *grogue* is an exciting and throaty drink. There are, of course, as many subtleties to *grogue* as there are distilleries in Cape Verde. To fully appreciate the eye-watering gaspiness of it, it is quite acceptable to sip it, although you may be left with the strange feeling that much of what you were going to swallow has already evaporated in your mouth.

If you find yourself recoiling at *grogue*'s rawness, ask for *ponche* (punch). In this amber-coloured liquid the spirit's kick is muffled by honey. For those who dislike the cough-mixture sweetness of this, *coupada* ('cut') is the halfway house – a mixture of *grogue* and punch.

Grogue is something close to the hearts of many Cape Verdeans – an invitation to share a glass in a remote village is not something to be turned down lightly. The drink is an important part of Cape Verdean culture to the extent that the pressing of the cane, with its steady repetitive rhythm, has proved to be a fertile source of inspiration for music. The most famous ballads sung while at work on the *trapiches* are the *abois* or *kola boi*. They dwell at some length on the socio-economic ills which beset the Cape Verdeans. It is said the melodies often reduce the oxen to tears.

sweets or **Senhor Ildo's Trapiche**, to the right of the gas station, for bottled *grogue, pontche* and *mel*.

Nightlife
Disco Discoteca Beira Mar. To the left of the police station. *Open only some Saturdays.*

Practicalities
Municipality office ❭ 223 11 97. Temporarily located at the entrance to Paúl, in Paço.
Health centre ❭ 223 11 30. In the central plaza.
Post office ❭ 223 13 97. Beyond the central plaza on the right. *Open Mon–Fri 8.00–15.30.*
Police ❭ 223 12 92. On the main road before Infantile Park.
Pharmacy ❭ 223 19 72. On the main road, to the right of the police station.
Tourist information Try www.paulbelezanatural.com, a website for tourists created by the municipality office.

What to see and do
The statue of St António is a 15-minute hike that will give you 180° views of the ocean and surrounding valleys. Going up the valley through Eito and Rocha Grande (see hike description pages, 242–3), you will be surrounded by green walls of vegetation or flowering sugarcane, depending on the time of the year. Above that is Passagem, with its charming municipal park nestled among impressive almond trees and bougainvilleas. Beyond the villages of Lombinho and Cabo de Ribeira, up a steep incline, a panoramic view of the valley and ocean opens out. The road ends in Cabo de Ribeira, but a steep cobbled footpath continues to Cova, an ancient crater now filled with verdant cultivation.

East of Vila das Pombas are several options. From Ribeira das Pombas, the flat valley of Neve culminates in a waterfall. From the small fishing town of Pontinha de Janela you can hike up to the lighthouse, from which, on a clear day, you can see the entire northeastern coast of the island, over to São Vicente, Santa Luzia and São Nicolau.

The inscribed rock
From Ribeira de Janela, a path to the small but thriving community of Fajã de Janela leads up to the inscribed rock in Ribeira do Penedo. This large, free-standing rock bears some mysterious inscriptions and a cross. Researchers have thought it to be Aramaic, Phoenician or archaic Portuguese – it bears little resemblance to modern Portuguese or to Arabic, Hebrew, Berber or Tifnaq. Richard Lobban writes in the *Historical Dictionary of the Republic of Cape Verde*:

> The most fruitful investigation rests upon a comparison with the Portuguese inscription of a similar appearance, on a stone at Yellala Falls about 150km above the mouth of the River Congo. This was almost certainly inscribed by Diogo Cão in 1485 [and] appears to have two types of writing systems which range from archaic Portuguese, as well as letters which are in a distinctly different style which is the only form of writing in the case of Janela.

It was also common for the 15th-century Portuguese explorers to mark their landings and passages with stone inscriptions, especially with crosses… In short, the Janela inscription was probably placed there by a 15th-century Portuguese. It is tempting to conclude that it was written by Diogo Gomes or by Diogo Afonso in the 1460s, or by Diogo Cão or his pilots in the 1480s.

Chã de Igreja

This pretty village, with its white church and brightly painted houses, is built on a small promontory of land projecting from the west side of the *ribeira*. A good place to chill for a while. To get there, take an *aluguer* up Ribeira Grande, through Coculi, Boca das Ambas Ribeiras, Horta de Garça and onwards. The best time to try for such transport is about 11.00–14.00. You are unlikely to find public transport back on the same day, as it generally leaves early in the morning.

Where to stay

Senhor Rodrigo (✆ 231 6360) runs his beautiful, recently built home with splendid views as an informal *pensão*. Dbl *4,000$; inc breakfast and dinner*.

Pensão So Nafish ✆ 226 1027. Close to Chã de Igreja on the northern coast, at Cruzinha da Garça, this small establishment is listed as taking guests.

Sinagoga

This lies on the point between Mão para Traz and Paúl. It is where exiled Portuguese Jews settled in the early 19th century. There are Jewish graves here as well as in Ponta do Sol. Later it was turned into a leper colony. For more on Jewish history in Cape Verde, see *Santiago*, page 121.

OTHER PLACES TO STAY

Gradually, a network of remote villages supplying basic accommodation for travellers is emerging. Some people are even building extensions on to their houses to develop such businesses. These are rural homestays, discussed in *Practical information*, page 51.

The great advantage of this change is that it opens up some of the longer walking routes in Santo Antão. Expect to pay 1,000–1,500$ per person, which will probably include evening meal and breakfast. You may want to check whether there is a bed or just floor space. Blankets should be provided. You also need to check the latest on public transport to remoter regions. It varies, but there should be *aluguers* linking Alto Mira and Ribeira de Cruz with Porto Novo.

The remoter of these hosts may have to take a full day to travel to town to buy food for their infrequent guests, so book ahead and, should your plans change, make sure to phone and cancel.

Although there is no-one to coordinate a list of homestay contacts, the following may be worth a call:

Alto Mira Dona Elvira; ✆ 222 3110
Caibros Senhor Zeca; ✆ 224 1174
Catano Senhor Daniel Morais; ✆ 222 3114. Floor space in a room set aside for tourists.
Chã de Pedra Dona Nezinha Oliveira; ✆ 224 1133
Monte Trigo The local teacher may arrange some floor space in the school. *Expect to pay 200–400$ per person.*

HIKES

For the manic, the fourth and fifth hikes can be combined so that the walker goes up one *ribeira* and comes down the next one.

Vila de Ribeira Grande–Coculi–Boca das Ambas Ribeiras–Chã de Igreja

Distance: 12.5km; time: 5¹/₂ hours; difficulty: 2 (CW)

This is a spectacular walk, though not as green and cultivated as the other *ribeiras*. You can halve its length by taking transport from Ribeira Grande (outside Caixa

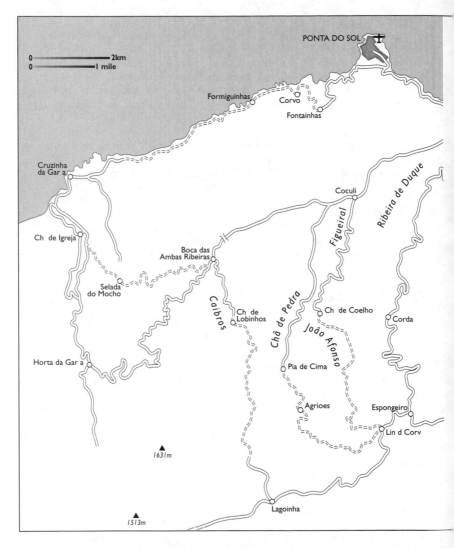

Económica) as far as Boca das Ambas Ribeiras. At the end of the walk you could turn round and walk back, or walk to Ponta do Sol (ie: the reverse of the next walk). Alternatively, you may be able to find an *aluguer* near the church that will take you to Ribeira Grande. If not, you may have to charter one.

Ribeira Grande is at the mouth of two *ribeiras*. The one that gives the town its name is the more northerly one. There's a wide, dusty track that leads up the *ribeira* from where the road to Ponta do Sol leaves town. The riverbed passes through scattered housing and cultivation and on the right, after about 20 minutes, an agronomy station. This was built by the Dutch under an aid scheme but is now run by the Cape Verdeans. A tennis court was included in the package.

Some 45 minutes after setting out there is a large windmill on the left and a small shop which sells drinks. After another ten minutes you reach the little village

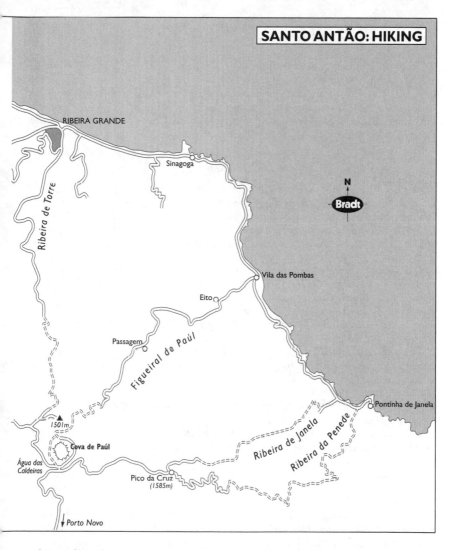

SANTO ANTÃO: HIKING

RIBEIRA GRANDE

Sinagoga

Ribeira de Torre

N
Bradt

Vila das Pombas

Eito

Passagem

Figueiral de Paúl

Pontinha de Janela

1501m

Cova de Paúl

Água das
Caldeiras

Pico da Cruz
(1585m)

Ribeira de Janela

Ribeira da Penede

↓ Porto Novo

of **Coculi** with its prominent white church. This village marks the point where Ribeira Figueiral joins Ribeira Grande on the left. Bearing right at the fork just before the village, you will see that Ribeira Grande is joined almost immediately by another Ribeira on the left, which leads up to **Chã de Pedra**.

The gentle ascent up Ribeira Grande continues and the land empties and becomes less lush, although a lot of sugar cane grows here. Two hours in, there's a slender aqueduct over the increasingly narrow ribeira. It was built by the Portuguese in 1956, and is still carrying water today.

Half an hour later is the small village of **Boca das Ambas Ribeiras**, or 'Mouth of Both Valleys' – the small valley of Ribeira dos Caibros leads up to the left. There is a couple of houses here and two prominent breadfruit trees. Breadfruit, which is in season in March, is considered a great delicacy. It has white flesh that is best cut into slices and boiled in salt water.

A cobbled road leads up the left side of Ribeira Grande. But the more interesting (and direct) route to **Chã de Igreja** is along a small path up the right (north) side of the valley.

You start climbing almost immediately, the path ahead repeatedly seeming to vanish as it curves steeply around the wrinkles of the sheer mountain face. Before long, the view of the valley floor far below is vertiginous, with farms and the occasional vehicle spread out like toys on a carpet. In places, there is nothing but a knee-high dry-stone wall separating you from a sheer drop of 500m. It was the same in the 19th century, when Alfred Burdon Ellis was prompted to write:

> Casualties ... are not by any means uncommon, as the numerous wooden crosses that we passed on our way testified.

Watch out for Egyptian vultures (*Neophron percnopterus*) soaring on the thermals towards the head of the valley. They are unmistakable, a black wing with a white leading edge, and a wingspan of up to 2m.

Finally, 1½ hours after leaving Boca, the path finds a nick in the mountain rim at a height of 830m. Over the saddle, look down on the tiny settlement of Selado do Mocho.

It is a hard descent (40 minutes) on a zig-zagging cobbled path to reach the edge of this remote village. Not long after passing around the head of a small valley into the village, the path cuts up to the top of a low ridge, where you find the village standpipe. Straight away, the path begins the descent into Ribeira Garça. Before long, you will catch your first glimpse of Chã de Igreja, on a small promontory of land projecting from the west side of the *ribeira*.

Unfortunately, to reach it you have to descend into the deep cleft of the *ribeira*, confront the village rubbish dump and find a steep path up the seaward side of the village's promontory.

Ponta do Sol–Fontainhas–Formiguinhas–Chã de Igreja
Distance: 12km; time: 4½ hours; difficulty: 2 (CW)
This coastal walk makes an interesting change from the *ribeiras*, passing through the village of Fontainhas, perched on a knife edge of rock, and with plenty of exposure to the sound and aroma of crashing waves. A lot of the walk is on the level but there are undulations. At the end of the walk you can either stay the night in Chã de Igreja, or catch the *aluguer* that runs from near the church to Ribeira Grande. If you are forced to charter an *aluguer*, it should be about 2,200$.

At the edge of Ponta do Sol on the road to Ribeira Grande, take the very clear turning to **Fontainhas**. The cobbled road winds in and out amongst the folds of the steep mountains and finally affords you a fantastic view of Fontainhas, perched like a fairytale village on a high and precipitous spit of land above a deep *ribeira*. Some 40 minutes after setting out you will be on its extraordinary main street, built on the spine of the narrow promontory. The houses lining this higgledy-piggledy street have a sheer drop of several hundred metres behind them.

As you leave Fontainhas, and as the path climbs back towards the coast, there is a good view of the *ribeira* with its intricate terracing and ingeniously engineered irrigation channels running across the slopes. On the valley floor the wooden structure is a traditional *trapiche* – a mule-driven contraption used for pressing sugar cane in the all-important manufacture of *grogue*.

In the next *ribeira* the path weaves back inland towards the well watered but somewhat gloomy village of **Corvo**, 40 minutes from Fontainhas. Another 20 minutes brings you to the prettier village of **Formiguinhas**, where you descend to the shore.

The next stretch of the walk is the most impressive because much of the path has been hacked out of the massive, ancient rock formations. It is a spectacular but desolate walk, with the air full of the sound of the waves and the taste and smell of salt. At one point you emerge in a small, nameless settlement, where there are four houses and fields of rock. Here, there is no evidence of the passage of the centuries. An hour and a half from Formiguinhas the land opens out again and a broad *ribeira* leads up to the left. The small village of **Felsenquelle** (out of sight of the path) shelters in the mouth of this *ribeira*. After 15 minutes, cross a football pitch with metal goalposts and, 20 minutes later, you descend into the small fishing village of **Cruzinha da Garça**.

Pick up the cobbled road here and follow it for ten minutes out of the village, seeing a cemetery high up on a hillside opposite. There's a track leading into the *ribeira* on the left. Although this does not look very promising follow it inland. The *ribeira* is dry, desolate and dramatic. There is nothing but the rustle of parched leaves and the rattle of pebbles falling from the sheer valley sides. Some 40 minutes after leaving Cruzinha, you arrive at a promontory projecting into the *ribeira* with a steep path up its side leading to **Chã de Igreja**.

Boca das Ambas Ribeiras–Caibros–Chã de Lobinhos–Real–Lagoinha–Espongeiro

Distance: 14km; time: 5 hours; difficulty: 2 (AI)

This walk is a feast of ever more dramatic panoramas and, like the others leading from parallel *ribeiras*, takes you to an eerie, higher world away from the drama of canyons and terraces. No part of the path is tricky, but the unremitting ascent requires a certain degree of fitness. To get to the starting point, take an *aluguer* from Ribeira Grande (outside Caixa Económica) all the way to **Boca das Ambas Ribeiras**, a 20-minute trip. The last part of the hike is a 1½-hour walk along the road to Espongeiro – you may wish to arrange beforehand for transport to collect you from Lagoinha.

Entering Boca das Ambas Ribeiras from Ribeira Grande, you will find a turning to **Caibros** on the left, just before the cobbled main road ascends and bends to the right. Follow this dirt track and, after about 15 minutes, you will begin to ascend the right-hand side of the valley. Five minutes later you pass a small, brick aqueduct on the left and the *ribeira* becomes more interesting, filled with palm trees and plantations. The track ends 30 minutes from the main road, after passing between two high buildings and reaching a little turning area. Continue in the same direction, on the footpath ahead, passing up a valley heavily planted with sugar cane, bananas and vegetables. After five minutes, at **Chã de Lobinhos**, there is a path up the hillside to the left which ascends in a hairpin for 20m. Less than ten minutes after beginning this path, you cross an irrigation channel and a public tap. The path ascends steeply and, after passing the last house for some time, you will see your route ahead, darting back and forth, its cobbled walls camouflaged by the rock.

Reaching a ridge, half an hour from Chã de Lobinhos, you can see into the next *ribeira* and you are already eye to eye with the first of the craggy peaks. The path dips slightly and there's a little path to the left: stay on the main path, the ever more spectacular views of the two *ribeiras*, and of valleys beyond, ample compensation for this breathless climb.

Some 1½ hours from Chã de Lobinhos, the path reaches a T-junction with a path of red earth. Here is the best panorama so far – you can see both the Chã de Pedra and the Figueiral roads. Turn right and arrive ten minutes later at the upper world, whose beginning is marked by a stone house and extensive terracing. The path is varied, sometimes through open agricultural land, sometimes along narrow ridges with cliffs plunging to either side.

Some 50 minutes from the last T-junction you reach another: turn right and go up the hill towards a green concrete water tank and tap. From here, the path becomes a road which, after 35 minutes meets a fork at which you turn right. Five minutes later you pass a graveyard, and five minutes after that the weather station at **Lagoinha**. Turn left after the weather station and begin the 1½-hour trudge to **Espongeiro**.

Coculi–Chã de Pedra–Lin d'Corv–Espongeiro

Distance: 10.5km; time: 4 hours 20 minutes; difficulty: 2 (CW)
Parts of this walk are quite tough – particularly the long, steep and dramatic ascent at the head of Chã de Pedra on an uncobbled path. The approach to Lin d'Corv is across gently undulating agricultural land. To shorten the walk a little, you can try to catch a lift to Coculi and onwards, as far up Chã de Pedra as possible (it is possible to get a lift as far as Pia de Cima, if you are lucky).

From Coculi to Chã de Pedra takes 1½ hours. At **Coculi**, take the right fork, passing Coculi's church on your left, and after about 700m, take a turning on the left. The first part of this road up to **Chã de Pedra** is flat and not particularly interesting. It becomes livelier when it leaves the valley floor as it approaches **Pia de Cima**.

Through Pia de Cima, the road twists itself into mind-boggling contortions as it tackles unnerving inclines; it then deposits you in a rare flat area at the top of the village. Your path leads up to the left by the low wall beside the shop.

Ascending from Pia, you pass houses and the school. Even at the peak of the dry season, water may be rushing down the sides of the path from the pine-clad slopes above. Some 25 minutes after leaving Pia, you will crest a rise and find yourself looking down on the small settlement of **Agriões**. From where you are standing, you can see the path you will take weaving to and fro across the ridge that rises up behind the village.

Ten minutes will bring you down amongst the houses of Agriões. Carry on around a sharp hairpin between two houses and continue down to a *grogue* still. Turn left at the T-junction here, even though it does not look very promising.

Your path crosses the valley floor, and after another few minutes leads you up the ridge. Ten minutes from the valley floor, the cobbled surface stops, and you will find yourself battling up a tough incline. To survive the next half hour, up a steep and winding path, you need to be quite fit. It is all worth it when you finally emerge on a breathtaking ridge, with a deep valley on either side, and Agriões behind and below you. There is a small farmer's hut nearby, with arguably the best view in Cape Verde.

Ten minutes from the ridge, turn left at a T-junction. From here, the path zig-zags up and up, affording great views to the north if you are lucky enough not to be caught in mist. After 20 minutes, the path flattens out and, within a few minutes, goes up a shallow ridge towards a low thatched cottage. Bear right past the cottage and, after a few minutes, you will find yourself walking along the right side of a wide, low valley. Some 20 minutes beyond the thatched cottage you will emerge on a further, smaller ridge. Follow the path down towards the valley floor on your left.

After ten minutes bear left at a fork and, five minutes later, bear right at a second fork and start ascending towards the road at **Lin d'Corv**, which you will reach after just over ten minutes. There is not much at Lin d'Corv except a single house and a large area of the hillside concreted over and walled in to collect rainwater.

Turning left on to the road, it will take about 20 minutes to walk the 1.5km to **Espongeiro**. Wait here for a lift back down to Ribeira Grande. They run all day, though sometimes it can be an hour's wait.

LAST CHANCE TO SEE ... THE CAPE VERDE RED KITE

When researchers travelled round the archipelago searching for the black kite (*Milvus m. migrans*) and the Cape Verde red kite (*Milvus m. fasciicauda*) in 1996–97 they were startled to find fewer than ten of each across the whole of Cape Verde.

The black kite can be found elsewhere – it is a very successful African and European species, and Cape Verde is its westernmost outpost. But the Cape Verde red kite can be found only on Cape Verde (it may be a subspecies of the red kite or an endemic species in its own right).

Scientists returned in 2000 to search again for kites. As birds go, they are quite easy to spot because they soar away from the ground. After two months roaming the cobbled paths and waiting around potential feeding grounds, they produced their verdict: on Cape Verde there remain just one black kite and two Cape Verde red kites.

The red kites were seen on Santo Antão and the black kite was spotted on Boavista. The researchers, Sabine Hille and Jean-Marc Thiollay, say that this means they are 'technically extinct'.

No-one is sure why the raptors have disappeared. It may partly be persecution – they are known to be chicken thieves and so humans pelt them with stones. They eat rats and mice that, these days, have probably been poisoned as part of pest control. Finally, the days are over when goats roamed freely through the plains, leaving the odd goat carcass for raptors to feed on. Now, livestock, and vegetation, are so precious that goats are kept penned up.

The researchers want to round up the two remaining Cape Verde red kites, plus any they have missed, and do a captive breeding programme to enhance their numbers. They would then release them and keep them alive through feeding stations and through a campaign to persuade the local people that raptors do a good job clearing fields of pests.

Espongeiro–Lin d'Corv–João Afonso–Chã de Coelho–Figueiral–Coculi

Distance: 10.5km; time: 3¹/₂ hours; difficulty: 2 (CW)

This hike involves a steep and spectacular descent into the head of João Afonso on a good, cobbled path. It can be shortened by getting transport to Coculi at Chã de Coelho. Get to the starting point by taking an *aluguer* along the Ribeira Grande–Porto Novo road as far as Espongeiro.

Standing on the main road from Ribeira Grande, take the turning at **Espongeiro**, known as the Lagoinha road. Walk for 1.5km until you reach **Lin d'Corv**, where there is a large area of hillside concreted over to collect rainwater. The path down João Afonso begins here. Be careful not to confuse it with the path to Chã de Pedra – the two paths meet at Lin d'Corv. It is important to pick up the right path, otherwise you will end up descending the wrong valley. Stand with your back to the tap at the bottom of the water catchment area, and then follow the path off to your right. The path will lead you down along the side of a low hill through a pine forest, and after about ten minutes, you will see a cottage at the top of a small rise. Take a small turning down to the right about 15m before reaching the cottage.

After less than ten minutes you will reach a few houses at **Lombo de Pedra**. Pass through the settlement and, five minutes later, follow the white arrow painted on a rock to begin a series of zig-zags down the side of the mountain. From here, the path becomes dramatic, sometimes darting backwards and forwards, sometimes tracing down the knife edge of precipitous ridges, and sometimes carving across near-vertical slopes. After a vertiginous 35 minutes, you will pass a tapstand where clear water runs from the mountains above, and will be looking out over the village of **Fajã dos Cumes**.

Continuing the descent, another 30 minutes will bring you to the small village of **Caibros** (not to be confused with the *ribeira* of Caibros) and another 35 minutes beyond that, to **Chã de Coelho**. Passing through here and descending steeply for ten minutes will bring you to the valley floor in João Afonso.

From the point where you hit the valley floor, it will take about an hour to reach **Coculi**.

Agua das Caldeiras–Ribeira de Torre–Ribeira Grande

Distance: 10km; time: 4 hours; difficulty: 2 (AI)

Torre is the most beautiful *ribeira* of them all: a descent from empty, misty pine forest through the clouds, down a steep rocky path with just the jagged peaks and the more adventurous birds for company, and finally through greenery and cultivation to sea level. Navigation is easy but the path is steep. To get to the start of the walk take an *aluguer* along the Ribeira Grande–Porto Novo road to **Agua das Caldeiras**. From Ribeira Grande this takes 40 minutes, and you should disembark at the first sign for the village on the right-hand side of the road. (To do this walk the other way round, leave Ribeira Grande on the Porto Novo road, passing the petrol station, and then the hospital, on the right. Torre is the great *ribeira* on the left.)

Take the cobbled road to the left, fenced off with a chain, and follow it uphill for ten minutes enjoying the sharp coolness. Then take a wide stone track to the left and descend, always through forest. Pine trees were chosen for reafforestation because their needles comb water from the clouds which drips down and moistens the soil.

After another ten minutes there's a clearing. A footpath leads out of the far end. Take it and emerge at a vista of high craggy mountains dropping way below to patches of vivid green, tiny houses and, even this high, the sounds of barking dogs and voices echoing towards you. Two *ribeiras* lie before you – Torre is to the left and after 15 minutes of steep descent you realise you are firmly destined for it as you see the teeth-like crags that now separate you from next-door Paúl. The view is infinitely interesting: crazy terraces inserted into crevices; intriguing local paths disappearing into rock faces.

After 1½ hours you reach the first cultivation. After this, just continue downwards, through coffee and banana crops and past shallow shelving built to capture water. Sometimes the path follows a terrace – there are lots of people around by now so just ask for the footpath (*caminho*).

Ahead is the strange pinnacle of Torre, a rock that has defied the forces of wind and water to rise out of the middle of the *ribeira*. As you descend you pass the extraordinary hamlet of **Raso Curto**, built on a ridge just wide enough for a row of one-room-thick houses and a footpath. Two and a half hours from the beginning, the path meets **Chu Chu** village, green and damp, with dark cliffs on either side. It's another 90 minutes, or 6km, to **Ribeira Grande** along the road track down the *ribeira*. If you are lucky the *grogue* distillery 20 minutes down the road on the left will be in operation. Ten minutes before the end of the walk there is a glimpse of the sea through the crack in the mountains.

Vila das Pombas–Ribeira do Paúl–Eito–Passagem–Cova do Paúl

Distance: 9km; time: 4½ hours; difficulty: 2 (AI)

This is many people's favourite, in a huge, abundantly green valley cloistered among vast, cathedral-like cliff walls. It is so large that there are many villages on the way up, crammed on to every available ledge. Arguments, car horns, barks, drunkenness and radios resound through the valley so that even when you have left them below, and the clouds have intervened, their sounds pursue you into the peaks. You can cut over 90 minutes from this walk by taking transport up the *ribeira* – the road persists a long way. To get to the starting point, take an *aluguer* down the coastal road from Ribeira Grande and alight just before **Vila das Pombas**.

(To go down the *ribeira* instead of up, take a lift along the main island road as far as **Cova**, which lies on the eastern side of the road and has two entrances – you want the one nearer to Ribeira Grande. As you enter Cova you will see the path you want leading up and out of the crater on the other side. Once you are on it, it's the same path down to the coast road.)

Having taken transport as far as the village at the mouth of Paúl, turn right – inland – at the stadium. Reaching an aqueduct after ten minutes, take the road up to the right, and leave the valley below, filled with cornfields and deep green trees. The road ascends through various villages including **Eito**, where you can buy drinks, and **Passagem**, where there is a swimming pool newly filled with water every day during July and August (otherwise, with a day's notice, they'll refill it for you).

Keep going, through **Chã João Vaz** and **Chã Manuel do Santos**. A couple of hours later you will finally leave the most vertiginous local house behind and follow the finely crafted cobbled path with its dry stone walling, gazing upwards to wonder how it can possibly take you through the mountains above. Four hours from the start (assuming no stops) your lonely world of cold and cloud will push you over the top of the ridge and you will be gazing down into a fertile volcano crater filled with crops, orange trees, tomatoes and a few houses. Your exit from the crater is on the opposite side; reach it by following a stumbling path down to the right and into the crater, and then a track across it and out on to the road where, if you walk for a few seconds to the left, you find the final spectacle of the walk – the southern slopes of Santo Antão, Porto Novo and São Vicente beyond. Wait here for a lift back to town.

Penedo–Ribeira do Penedo–Estância de Pedra–Pico da Cruz–Cova

Distance: 14km; time: 5 hours 40 minutes; difficulty: 3 (CW)
Not for the unfit or faint hearted, this hike takes you from sea level up to 1,600m within little more than 7km. After that, it is a less demanding one-hour walk to the main road.

Reach the starting point by taking an *aluguer* along the coast road as far as the little village of **Penedo**, which lies at the mouth of the *ribeira* of the same name.

You strike up the *ribeira* on foot and the climb begins almost immediately, weaving amongst sugar cane plantations and the scattered houses. Follow the path up to the head of the valley and round to where it begins a tortuous zig-zagging ascent up an impossibly steep mountain face. If, as you pause for breath, you look back towards the coast, you will see the smaller Ribeira da Janela running parallel to Ribeira do Penedo, and slightly to the north.

There are small paths that lead off to the right and left but, sticking to the main path, you emerge on a narrow shoulder about two hours after setting out from Penedo. As you continue to ascend, it turns into a narrow ridge with staggering views first down one side, then the other, and a fantastic panorama to the south, east and north. If it is a clear day, **Pico da Cruz** can be seen ahead.

Even at this height (800m), the vegetation has changed – it is much greener here than on the ridges that lead, like dry ribs, to either side. Higher up it becomes cold and alpine with a sharp, resinous smell among the trees.

Along the ridge there are several houses. People have erected frames stretched across with gauze to allow the mist that boils over from the *ribeira* below to condense. After 1½ hours of walking along the ridge, you pass one of these frames and, at the same point, see the cobbled main road that snakes up from the valley towards the Pico. The road is slightly down to your left. Keep to the path, and, after 15 minutes, you join the road, and emerge, after another 40 minutes of steep hairpins, at a small group of houses in the shadow of the summit. Turn right on the road to Paúl past the old, white painted house. Directly behind the house follow the very rough path which cuts up to the right. It's a 15-minute walk to the summit.

Retracing your steps from the summit to the small settlement, rejoin the road you arrived on and follow it straight on towards **Cova** (crater) and **Água das Caldeiras**. Following this road as it gently descends you will get your first glimpse of the crater about 45 minutes after leaving the summit. Ten minutes later you arrive at a crossroads. This is a good place to wait for a lift, or an *aluguer* back to either Porto Novo or Ribeira Grande.

Less demanding walks

The bases of many of the *ribeiras* provide flat walks with mighty views up the canyons. The best such walk is up Ribeira da Torre as far as Chu Chu (see page 242). Ribeira Grande provides a less interesting flat walk. All the *ribeiras* can be ascended quite far by vehicle, at which point you can walk back downhill. Ribeira do Paúl would be a particularly dramatic venue for this option. Finally, it is worth travelling to Cova do Paúl and wandering around the crater.

São Nicolau

Mother dear
I wanted to say my prayer
but I cannot:
my prayer sleeps
in my eyes, which cry for your grief
of wanting to nourish us
but being unable to do so.

Baltasar Lopes, born in São Nicolau, quoted in
*Fire: Six Writers from Azores, Madeira and Cape
Verde* edited by Donald Burness (Three
Continents Press, 1977)

It was in the shady valley of Ribeira Brava in São Nicolau and along the civilised cobbled streets of its town that the seeds of Cape Verdean awareness were planted towards the end of the last century. São Nicolau was for over 50 years the intellectual centre of the archipelago. Yet by 1931 its educational buildings had closed and the scholars had vanished to neighbouring São Vicente.

Now São Nicolau has an air of quiet dignity like a university town in the holidays. It is a victim, like Maio, of being the neighbour of a busy centre of commerce. But this makes São Nicolau a joy to visit. The town is pretty and quiet and there are several outstanding walks in the mountains.

HIGHLIGHTS

Go for beautiful walks almost undisturbed by other tourists (though the mountains' appeal will diminish if you have already visited Santo Antão). Go to fish with the locals: there is a profusion of blue marlin. Go if you are trying to reach Raso Island, but not for white beaches or for windsurfing. There may soon be a museum at the old seminary but at present the details of the island's history are rather inaccessible to the tourist.

BACKGROUND INFORMATION
History

With a fertile hinterland and several almost permanent streams, São Nicolau has been able to produce more agriculturally than the impoverished flat islands. It also has the widest bay of the archipelago, formed by the island's strange long finger that stretches to the east and affording a safe anchorage. Yet São Nicolau has always been overshadowed by Santiago and São Vicente and so, apart from the brief flourishing of its seminary a century ago, it was never an island of importance.

It was discovered, along with the other windward islands, in 1461 – the date was probably St Nicholas's day, 6 December. Families from Madeira and their Guinea

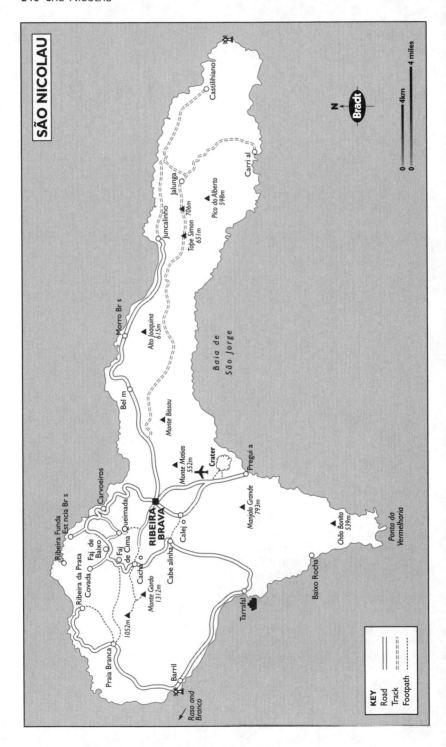

SÃO NICOLAU

Castilihiano

Carri al

Pico do Alberto
598m

Jalunga

Tope Simon
651m

706m

Juncalinho

Baia de
São Jorge

Morro Br s

Alto Joaquina
615m

Bel m

Monte Bissau

Monte Matias
552m

Crater

Pregui a

Manjolo Grande
793m

Carvoeiros

Ribeira Funda

Est ncia Br s

Queimada

Chão Bonito
539m

Faj de
Baixo

Faj
de Cima

Cacha

RIBEIRA
BRAVA

Calej o

Cabe alinha

Baixo Rocha

Ponta da
Vermelharia

Ribeira da Prata

Covada

Monte Gordo
1312m

1052m

Tarrafal

Praia Branca

Barril

Raso and
Branco

N

Brādt

0   4km
0   4 miles

KEY
Road
Track
Footpath

slaves came to settle in the early 1500s. But the island was mountainous and inaccessible – indeed its lush interior is completely hidden from the outside – and so its productive agriculture and livestock potential did not attract more settlers until the 1600s.

Even then, when the English sailor Dampier visited in 1683 he reported only 100 families on the island. He described the green interior, the vineyards producing good-quality wine, the abundance of wood and the great number of donkeys and goats. By 1731 there were only 260 inhabitants.

One great disadvantage of São Nicolau was the ease with which marauders could attack. Dutch, English and French pirates plagued the people, even after they retreated from their coastal settlement to Ribeira Brava, inland. It was not until a fortress was built in 1818 that security and a soaring population came to the island.

In 1805, the wealthy landowner who governed the island, José António Dias, had a son, Júlio José. He was a brilliant student but returned from his medical studies abroad to spend his life as a philanthropist on São Nicolau. Perhaps his greatest legacy came from his decision to move out of his large house in Ribeira Brava in 1866 and offer it to the three canons, three priests and three students who had arrived from Portugal to found a seminary on Cape Verde. This prevented them leaving for Santo Antão, having despaired of finding a building on São Nicolau.

The school attached to the seminary flourished, offering the same subjects as high schools in Portugal. Suddenly the brightest Cape Verdean children were able to learn subjects as varied as the classics, chemistry and political economy. This education groomed them for careers in either the Church or the Portuguese civil service. In this way Cape Verde became the centre for evangelisation of Portuguese west Africa.

The impact created by the generations that passed through this seminary should not be underestimated, for they spread abroad, used by the Portuguese as an interface between themselves and their west African territories. They were articulate and intelligent, wedded to the idea of Cape Verde being part of Portugal, but deeply concerned with the lot of their people. As teachers and administrators they had influence over the next generation, which took their ideas and moulded them into more radical form. The prime example of such a two-generation process was Juvenal Cabral, the seminary-educated teacher who fought for better conditions for Cape Verde and whose son was Amílcar Cabral, the leader of the revolution.

But the life of the seminary was all too brief. It was a victim of the difficult relationship that emerged between the Catholic Church and the government in the democratic republic of Portugal after the Church was separated from the state in 1911. This separation led to the splitting of the seminary – its secondary school function was relocated in Mindelo.

The seminary closed in 1917, reopened in 1923 and shut forever in 1931. Later, it was used to accommodate 200 political deportees from Portugal. The Bishop of Cape Verde, rumoured to be terrified by 'hordes of deported revolutionaries and anti-clericals', fled to São Vicente. All that remained was a highly educated peasant population. One visitor in the 1930s was astonished when a local boy, prompted by a reference in Creole to a rose, quoted: 'Rosa, vita tua diuturna non est'.

The 20th century brought desperate droughts to São Nicolau, in 1921, 1940 and the 1950s.

Geography

The island, 343km², is mainly barren rock with a large semi-humid valley in its centre, cultivated with sugar cane and banana below and maize and beans on the

COAXING LIFE FROM THE SOIL

There are many devices in the Cape Verdean hills and valleys designed to keep precious water and topsoil from being flushed away.

Arretos are lines of small stone walls around the hillsides, designed for erosion control. Although they are not supposed to be used for planting, crops grown behind them are producing double the yield of crops grown before the *arretos* were built.

Terraces are much bigger walls, properly designed for the ubiquitous shelved farming seen all over Cape Verde.

Check dams of concrete or stone are built in the *ribeiras* to try and slow the rainwater's progress to the sea. At the moment, when it rains, about 85% of the water is lost to the sea.

Concreted slopes on the hillside, and sometimes natural rock formations, catch water which then flows into a tank or reservoir at the bottom.

Barrels placed under trees in the highest parts of Cape Verde, such as Serra Malagueta or Estancia de Pedra in Santiago, or the mountains of Santo Antão, can catch the mist that has condensed on the trees, yielding five litres a night.

Nets are being tested around Monte Xota and Serra Malagueta in Santiago. They are supposed to provide a huge surface area on which mist can condense.

Drip irrigation, in which water is directed with minute precision at each individual plant, has increased yields massively while reducing water consumption, in experimental areas such as the valley below the fort of Cidade Velha. However, the initial outlay is expensive, requiring reservoir tanks, filters and a lot of tubing.

higher slopes. In the west is a range of mountains with the highest, Monte Gordo, reaching 1,312m. This peak is the meeting point of two ranges – one runs north–south and the other out to the northwest. The eastern finger of land is a long ridge of barren mountains. Between the central mountains and the western coast are stony plains. Desertification seems to have hit São Nicolau particularly hard – its orange groves and coffee plantations have gone and the old folk reminisce about verdant mountainsides that are now bare – in fact the lines of stone walls that used to divide fields can be traced impossibly high up the mountainsides. There is evidence of much reafforestation. The population is about 20,000.

Economy

Agriculture, and the port at Tarrafal, are the economic mainstays. Catching and canning tuna keeps the occupants of Tarrafal and the remote village of Carriçal busy – and is a great spectator sport.

Wildlife

The fairytale dragon tree (*Dracaena draco*), locally known as *dragoeiro*, is almost abundant on this island – this is about the only place in the archipelago where the endangered species grows naturally. It can reach about 10m high and its flattened top and grey gnarled branches give the landscape the feel of an ancient world – it is said the trees can live for 1,000 years. The 'blood' of the dragon tree has been used in traditional medicines to relieve pain and is also used to colour *grogue*. The tree grows mainly on northeast-facing slopes at altitudes of between 500m and 900m. Conservationists are trying to use it more in reafforestation programmes. The dragon tree also grows in the Canary Islands and in Madeira, where it is also endangered. There are many helmeted guineafowl.

Festivals

Festivals reflect the strong Cape Verdean tradition of music and dancing. The February Carnival, held at the same time as the famous São Vicente Carnival, is the second-most lively on the archipelago. The dress of the young woman chosen to be queen costs over 30,000$. New Year is also big, with a festival on 6 January. In April there is Pascoela, celebrated in Fajã – mass followed by games, horse races and processions. There are lots of festivals through the summer, including one of two days in Juncalinho. Other festival dates as follows:

Santo António	13 April (Preguiça)
São Joao	24 June (Praia Branca)
São Pedro	29 June
São Pedrinho	Sunday following 29 June
Music Festival	August (Praia da Telha)
Potable Water Festival	September (Ribeira Prata)
Nossa Sra do Rosario	First Sunday in October
São Francisco	First Sunday in December (Tarrafal)
Municipality Day	6 December

GETTING THERE AND AWAY
By air

São Nicolau is served by TACV inter-island flights from São Vicente and Sal, but the flights are not frequent. Schedules were not available at the time of publication, but they are likely to be only a few per week.

From the airport to Ribeira Brava costs 400–600$ in a taxi, or 100$ in a shared *aluguer*, but these are hard to find.

Airport ⟩ 235 1313

By ferry

The *Tarrafal* runs from São Nicolau to Santiago and São Vicente twice a week.

By yacht

The best anchorage is at the harbour of Tarrafal, the main problem there being that, should there be northeast winds rushing down the ravines towards you, it can be impossible to shuttle to land. Preguiça – for a long time São Nicolau's main harbour – is more exposed. Carriçal is a tiny, remote village with a pretty bay and shelter from the northeast winds. Anchor outside the cove.

GETTING AROUND
By public transport

Aluguers ply the road between the main square in Ribeira Brava and Tarrafal (50 minutes; 170$). They travel intermittently all day, but are more frequent leaving Tarrafal before 08.30 and leaving Ribeira Brava at 11.00–12.00. Near the check-in time for plane arrivals you'll find *aluguers* for the airport waiting in the Ribeira Brava square.

Aluguers also travel along the eastern ridge as far as Juncalinho but no further, and from Tarrafal north up the coast. These follow the principle: into town in the early morning, out of town around lunchtime. Drivers are very keen for tourists to hire them as taxis. To avoid this, hang around nonchalantly till you are part of a group rather than approaching an empty minibus or truck.

By taxi
Taxis and chartered *aluguers*: Ribeira Brava to Fajã 1,000$; to Tarrafal 2,000$; to Preguiça 600$.

Car hire
Agência Santos e Santos Ribeira Brava; ☎ 235 1830, m 994 5969; e fsantos@hotmail.com or fsantos@cvtelecom.cv. To reach outlying places accessed by dirt tracks, it is best to enquire about a jeep and driver from the *aluguer* drivers or at the town hall.
Monte Gordo Rent a Car ☎ 235 1280

By boat
A fishing boat can take you from Preguiça to Carriçal and from Carriçal to visit caves down the coast.

ACTIVITIES
Excursions
Agência e Transporte Santos & Santos Ribeira Brava; ☎ 235 1830. Organises trips and offers car hire with or without driver.

Hiking
This is the big attraction of São Nicolau and some walks are described below (see page 254). By far the most beautiful walks are in the mountainous interior, though we include one or two others as well. Since a horseshoe road runs through the centre of the walking area, you can alter the walks to suit, using local transport to shorten them or to enable you to walk only downhill or only uphill – or sandwiching several together. Local guides can be found at the town hall.

Do not try to walk around the north coast and make the tempting link between Estância Brás and Ribeira Funda – people have died in the attempt. Bear in mind the timings given may be a little fast for some in the hotter periods. Take water, as supplies are limited outside the towns.

Driving
One of the most spectacular roads in Cape Verde is the road from Ribeira Brava to Tarrafal. This 26km route pulls out of Ribeira Brava and negotiates a series of deep creeks cut into the mountainside of the northern coast before turning inland to the lush Fajã valley. Mountain ranges spike the right-hand side and you ascend gently through Fajã de Baixo (Lower Fajã) and Fajã de Cima (Upper Fajã), almost completely encircled by a ring of mountains.

For a short walk along the most spectacular stretch you can ask an *aluguer* from either direction to deposit you at Cabeçalinha and walk for 30 minutes as far as Cachaço, where you can marvel at the dragon trees and the plantations over a cold drink and wait for the next *aluguer* to take you on in either direction.

RIBEIRA BRAVA
This is a pretty town with houses painted every colour and neat gardens blooming with plants and flowers. It is wedged into the steep sides of a *ribeira* and narrow cobbled streets lead away from the large square decorated with the bust of the town's philanthropist and an imposing cathedral visited by the old ladies of the

town every day. They have first claim to the wooden benches in the square, by the way. Lining the narrow streets are surprisingly well-stocked shops in dim, shuttered interiors. The *ribeira* – green even in the dry season – towers above and cuts the town deeply in two, its narrow floor functioning as an extra road for most of the year.

Where to stay

Accommodation sometimes gets booked up in high season, so book ahead if you can.

Pensão Santo António 235 2200, m 993 4284; f 235 2199. Just east of the main square gardens, this is a new hotel. *Sgl 2,990$; dbl 3,600$; inc breakfast.*

Pensão Residencial Jardim CP 59; 235 1117/1950; f 235 1949. This sparkling white *pensão* on the hillside at the southern end of town is everyone's first choice. In fact prices have fallen as the number of visitors has declined. However this could quickly change, so expect higher prices. Terraces offer shady retreats from which to gaze down on to the *vila*. Rooms have fans. Meals available. *Sgl 2,000$; dbl 2,800$; suite with kitchen 3,000$.*

Pousada Mana Guimara 235 1830, m 994 5969; f 235 1831; e fsantos57@hotmail.com. Down near the Shell petrol station above the agency Santos & Santos, this is a comfortable place. *Sgl 1,500$; dbl 2,000$.*

Jumbo Residencial 235 1315. A good alternative should the Jardim be full. Facing the old town hall from across the *ribeira*, Jumbo has smartened up in recent years and is now great value with spacious rooms. Some rooms have balconies; some shared bathrooms. *Sgl 1,000–1,200$; dbl 1,400–1,600$ with bathroom; breakfast extra 200$ each.*

Pensão da Cruz 235 1282. Just beside the old town hall, its door marked '14', this is a friendly place but basic and dingy. Shared bathrooms. *Sgl 1,000$; dbl 1,200$.*

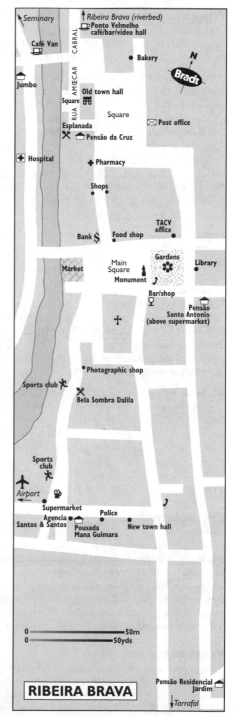

RIBEIRA BRAVA

Where to eat and drink

Order several hours beforehand if you want something other than the dish of the day. In the off season you might almost starve. The São Nicolau speciality is *molho* or *modje* – meat, potatoes and onions with cornmeal and rice.

Restaurante Bar Bela Sombra Dalila One of the best in town, it is down the narrow street that leaves the main square to the right of the cathedral. Closed in low season.
Esplanada This bar is a good place for recovering from the heat of the day. It is beside the gardens of the *praça* opposite the old town hall.
Bar Restaurante Gelataria Jumbo Sells ice cream as well as the usual fare. Underneath Residencial Jumbo.
Jardim Rooftop restaurant serving lunch and dinner, with a varied menu. Above the hotel of the same name. A lifesaver for breakfast and dinner, at the least in low season.
Ponte Vermelho Churrasqueira is also a bar and video hall that serves meat dishes.
Raconte Tasty chicken and french fries.
Van Popular for evening snacks, the van can be found near the Jumbo Residencial.

Fresh bread can be bought from the bakery on a little road off the post office square; vegetables from the municipal market on the street running down from the bank to the *ribeira*.

Nightlife

Locals nicknamed the 'jet set' regularly hold private parties to which it should not be too difficult to obtain an invitation. You pay an entry fee and can expect plenty of food. The population of Ribeira Brava is not generally sufficient to sustain the two Saturday nightclubs, so one is likely to swing while the other fades. Even the owners of the loser venue have been known to give up on a quiet night and go and party at the other one.

Clube de Ribeira Brava and Atletico These two football clubs regularly hold parties. The first is almost opposite Restaurante Bar Bela Sombra Dalila, the other is further down the same road, opposite the Shell petrol station.
Good Look Open Saturdays; looks abandoned on the outside but is fully equipped inside. Follow the Tarrafal road off the map and it is about 50m up, on the left.
Praça On Sunday night everyone goes to the *praça* (the gardens in front of the old town hall) to hang out and listen to a DJ, between 19.00 and 21.00.
Tropicalente Open Saturdays; in Chãzinha, out beyond Residencial Jardim.

Practicalities

Airlines TACV; ⟩ 235 1161. At the top of the central square. *Open Mon–Fri 08.00–12.30, 14.30–18.00.* Agência Santos & Santos, for internal and international airlines.
Bank On the main square. *Open Mon–Fri 08.00–13.30.*
Hospital ⟩ 235 1130. A vast building on the hill across the *ribeira*.
Pharmacy ⟩ 235 1227. Beside Pensão da Cruz.
Police ⟩ 235 1152. On the airport side of town, beside Agência Santos & Santos.
Post office Opposite the back of the old town hall. *Open Mon–Fri 08.00–16.00.*
Tourist information None. Try Agência Santos & Santos.

What to see and do

Igreja Matriz de Nossa Senhora do Rosário, on the main square, is worth a visit. Built in the 1700s, it was then rebuilt between 1891 and 1898 to become the cathedral: the bishopric was in São Nicolau between 1866 and 1940. In the main square is a bust of Dr Júlio José Dias and also the library, in the building that was originally the birthplace of José Lopes de Silva, one of Cape Verde's major poets.

The seminary, the Liceu de São Nicolau, is a little way up the road away from Jumbo Residencial, on the right. You may manage to inveigle your way in and explore its rambling buildings and courtyards.

TARRAFAL

This impoverished port town lies at the base of stony, barren hills that give away little about the lush interior. It can reach 40°C in the summer. The town is strung out along a very long coastal road. At the southern end is the port. A block inland from the port is the long, main square with a Shell petrol station at the centre and the Nazarene church at the top.

Medicinal sand

Some of the black sand beaches around Tarrafal are reputed to have healing powers, particularly in the alleviation of the symptoms of arthritis. Sufferers tend to bury themselves in the sand and lie there; some claim they have subsequently achieved relief for many months. Ask around for the best beach.

Where to stay

Residencial Tocely CP 7; ☎ 236 1220; f 236 1313. To the south of town where the coast road ends, its proprietor is well known. *Sgl 2,000–3,000$; dbl 3,000–4,000$.*

Pensão Tonecas ☎ 236 1220. A similar comfortable option close by, run by the same owners.

Residencial Natui ☎ 236 1178. Going north along the coast road, turn right just before the sports ground and left just after it – the hotel is on your right. Spacious, bright and simple with tiled floors and a roof terrace. Great views both inland and seaward. *Sgl 1,700$; dbl 2,000$.*

Residencial Casa de Pastor Alice ☎ 236 1187. On the coast road; some people develop an affection for this friendly, slightly eccentric place. *Sgl 1,000$; dbl 1,300$; breakfast extra 300$ each.*

Where to eat and drink

Casa de Pastor Alice Thought by many to be the best eatery in Tarrafal, it is a large living room in which guests feel like members of the extended family whose photos cover the walls. Under Residencial Alice.

Esplanada Sandy ☎ 236 1282

Golfinho ☎ 236 1046

Patche ☎ 236 1401.

Tocely Good food, which should be ordered beforehand, in the *residencial* of the same name.

Nightlife

Tarrafal has a livelier nightlife than Ribeira Brava, with the **Disco Paradise** and **Bar-Restaurante Esplanada** (low blue building facing the water), the main disco in town, popular on Saturday nights.

Practicalities

Airlines Proprietor of Tocely Hotel (see *Where to stay*) is a TACV agent.

Bank At the coastal end of the main square. *Open Mon–Fri 08.00–12.00.*

Ferries Try at Avimar; ☎ 236 1170.

Hospital ☎ 236 1130

Police ☎ 236 1132
Post office At the top of the main square. *Open Mon–Fri 08.00–16.00.*

What to see and do
Praia de Baixo Rocha
Praia de Baixo Rocha is a 1½-hour walk south of Tarrafal. Some people rave about the cove, but others consider it a miserable scrap of grey sand and a long walk back. It's a lonely walk over a landscape like burnt fudge with dramatic views of the mountains beyond. Cross the town's southern cove and find the track leading south from it. You pass a new yellow building on the left and a series of dumps as well as the occasional woman breaking stones for a living. You are making for a cove that lies between the furthest headland you can see and the second-furthest – a much lower, smaller headland. The trick is to avoid all the bulges of tiny headlands in between you and the cove and stick to the main track – the route is probably just about possible in a jeep.

OTHER PLACES TO VISIT
Juncalinho
Juncalinho lies along the eastern ridge which is almost entirely devoid of vegetation.

You can go as far as Juncalinho by *aluguer* from Ribeira Brava on a cobbled road. It takes 25 minutes to get there, and it is a desolate village on a plain littered with boulders some of which seem to have randomly assembled themselves into houses. Only the cemetery and the football pitch have been cleared of stones. There's a bar on the road and a dingy sign indicating the *lagoa* – the only sight to see. You can drive the five minutes to the coast and gaze down at the crater – black rock lashed with white foam. On a calm day the *lagoa* lies just beyond the reach of the swell, full of beautiful blue-green water and a pleasant place to bathe.

Carriçal
Check that the road to Carriçal is open – it is sometimes impassable because of landslides. Because of this, there are regular boat connections between Preguiça and Carriçal.

If the road is open then, in a 4x4, it will take another 35 minutes to get to Carriçal from Juncalinho. The road turns right after Juncalinho and climbs in a frightening series·of bends high into the mountains inland, over the ridge and down to the sea again. The terrain is dark brown, with heaps of earth and rock, and a frothy coastline.

Carriçal is a poor but pretty village, probably one of the most isolated in the archipelago. Most families are crammed into two-roomed, concrete houses with hens, pigs, dogs and cats prowling outside. Below the houses lies a tree-filled *ribeira*, a pretty beach and a cluster of boats. You can pay a fisherman to take you out to net a pile of moray eels and bright orange grouper, or to go up the coast to explore the coves and caves.

By the steps down to the shore is a factory. Ask to see inside, where huge pans of tuna are boiled on wood fires and are then canned in tins pressed on the premises.

Preguiça
From the road Preguiça does not look much – a few half-built houses, a football pitch, a signpost. The bulk of the village is out of sight, clinging to the steep slope above the shoreline. A precipitous cobbled street winds down amongst colourful houses past an old church, to a crumbling pier where sizeable boats berth with

cargo from Mindelo. To the right of the pier you can swim from the shingly bay where bright fishing boats are drawn up on the beach.

Fishermen dive from boats to catch the lobsters by hand at a depth of 10–15m. They wear goggles and breathe compressed air piped from the surface, allowing them to stay down for up to an hour at a time.

On the other side of the village is a Portuguese fort with several cannons. The two memorials (one erected by the Portuguese, the other by the Cape Verdeans) commemorate the voyage of Pedro Alvarez Cabral, who in 1500 passed this point on his way to discovering the coast of Mexico.

There are several shops which, as usual, double as bars. You can eat at Preguiça but you must give notice. Try ringing Madame Maria (☎ 235 1584) in the large pink house near the top of the village, before you set out from Ribeira Grande.

Aluguers leave intermittently from the main square (200$) or you can just walk and hitchhike the 8km. Before dark you will find transport back quite easily.

Ribeira da Prata
An attractive place with several shops selling water, biscuits, bread and *grogue*. People visit in order to see Rocha Scribida, the 'writing on the rock'. Ask for directions at the top of the village: it is a two-minute scramble up the other side of the *ribeira*.

There you will see a stratum of rock where localised erosion has revealed some intricate darker lines – or, if you must, rock that bears words written by an ancient people who knew the island long before the Portuguese. Historians have plumped for the former explanation.

There is infrequent public transport between Tarrafal and Ribeira da Prata.

HIKES
Ribeira Brava–Preguiça via crater
Distance: approximately 8km; time: 2¹/₂ hours; difficulty: 1 (CW)
This walk is pleasant but unexciting compared with those in the mountains behind you. There are no steep slopes.

Leave Ribeira Brava on the airport road, ascending past the needles on your left. Bear right at the first junction (the left turn goes to Morro Brás and Juncalinho). After a short distance, bear right again on the road towards the cemetery, which you pass 25 minutes after setting out. The road winds for a short distance in the plantations in the bottom of the *ribeira* before leading you up the other side to rejoin the new road. Follow it away from the edge of the *ribeira* to the airport, which you will reach 35 minutes after the cemetery.

Some 400m past the airport, where the road bends right near the turning to Calejão, a dirt track goes straight on. Follow it past the end of the runway and towards an ordinary-looking brown hill. Twenty-five minutes from the airport you will be staring over the rim of the old volcano into a crater that is surprisingly deep and steep-sided: look out for the yellow sulphur deposits at its base.

Looking to the south you will see a few buildings that mark the beginning of **Preguiça**. To avoid retracing your steps to the airport you can cut down from the volcano rim to the main road. It is quite rough with rocky outcrops.

Ribeira Brava–Calejão–Ribeira Brava
Distance: approximately 4km; time: 2¹/₂ hours; difficulty: 1 (CW)
Take the airport road as described in the Preguiça walk. **Calejão** is the village on your right on the lower slopes of the mountain range and there's a signposted road

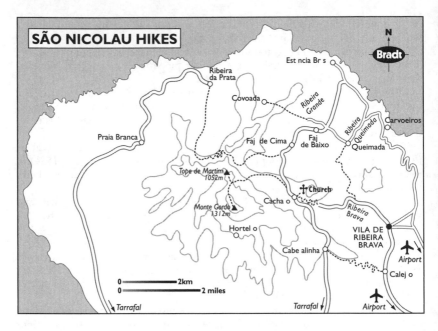

SÃO NICOLAU HIKES

N

Bradt

Est ncia Br s

Ribeira
da Prata

Covoada

Ribeira
Grande

Carvoeiros

Praia Branca

Faj de Cima

Faj
de Baixo

Ribeira
Queimada

Queimada

Tope de Martim
1052m

Monte Gordo
1312m

Cacha o

Church

Ribeira
Brava

Hortel o

VILA DE
RIBEIRA
BRAVA

Cabe alinha

Airport

0 ——— 2km
0 ——— 2 miles

Calej o

Tarrafal

Tarrafal

Airport

to it past the airport. It is a quiet village, strung out along the old road. You will pass a path on your left – the descent from Cabeçalinha described below, which joins your path opposite a graffitied stone on the right. In the building on the corner, just after the path joins you, a craftsman manufactures ornaments from banana leaves. There's a shop selling water, biscuits and soft drinks. The impressive, ochre-coloured building on the left is the old orphanage and bishop's residence.

The road continues, straight at first, and then begins a superb descent into Ribeira Brava along a series of S-bends. There is an excellent view up the valley. The last section of the road is past impoverished suburbia and litter-strewn hillsides followed by some of the biggest houses in town. The track emerges in town beside the old seminary and Jumbo Residencial.

Ribeira Brava–Cachaço–Cabeçalinha–Calejão

Distance: approximately 10km; time: at least 4 hours allowing for stops en route; difficulty: 2–3 (AI)

This is one of the best walks, at least four hours with a steep ascent and descent. Follow the cobbled road up the *ribeira* – a fascinating walk through the villages. After an hour and 20 minutes of puffing you pass between some crags on to a small road leading to **Cachaço**. To the right the road winds up to a wonderfully positioned white church. Turn left to reach the busy main road of the island where there is a couple of shops selling biscuits and drinks. Here the landscape is green, with plenty of perfectly shaped dragon trees. Turn left on the main road for a fantastic view of Ribeira Brava. Peer down the gullies where vehicles regularly tumble – and look up at the mountain on your right down which rocks often fall on to the road. There's a great view of the path you took up the *ribeira* and of the spine of mountains out to the east. Eventually the road turns to the right and you begin to see the gentler slopes that lead down to Tarrafal.

Some 35 minutes after leaving Cachaço the road takes a sharp right turn, just before a blue house. The track to the left returns you to Ribeira Brava but continue on the main road for another five minutes until you reach a white concrete water tank on the right – this is **Cabeçalinha**. Take the left track opposite this. For a good ten minutes the track ascends until you reach the third panorama of this walk – the southern mountains and sea. Now there's half an hour of steep, zig-zagging descent – not for bad knees – until you begin to sink into civilisation again, eventually reaching the dirt road. Turn left at the T-junction, opposite the graffitied stone. From here it is about 40 minutes back to town along the road described in the previous walk.

Cachaçao–Monte Gordo
Distance: approximately 5km (return); time: 1¹/₂ hours; difficulty: 3 (CW)
This steep walk to the highest peak is also one of the most spectacular. You can lengthen it by walking from Ribeira Brava up to Cachaçao first.

Take an *aluguer* to Cachaçao (30 minutes; 200$). There is an obvious turning on your right, to the southwest, near the village standpipe (clearly marked *Água*). You ascend on a well-made path zig-zagging amongst lush plantations. It is attractive and shady, but this ascent is not for the unfit. After 40 minutes, the path flattens and skirts the right-hand side of a hill with radio antennae on top. After gently ascending amongst scattered houses and fields for 20 minutes, you reach a great view over Fajã on your right. Another 15 minutes takes you to a clearly defined saddle. On your right is the **Tope de Martim** (1,052m) and to the left is **Monte Gordo** (1,312m). It may seem close, but don't be fooled – you are still at least 300m below the summit – which translates into a rough scramble of about 40 minutes. The ascent to Tope de Martim is about 30 minutes.

The view of the archipelago from the summits is the best you will find, including the uninhabited western islands – from left to right, Ilhéu Raso, Ilhéu Branco, and Santa Luzia – as well as São Vicente and Santo Antão beyond. It is said that in exceptionally clear weather every Cape Verde island can be seen.

Floating around the peaks and saddle is the neglected kestrel (*Falco tinnunculus neglectus*), a small, brown bird common in the northerly islands. On the lower slopes you may disturb a flock of helmeted guinea fowl. These birds, rather like grey, over-sized hens, were introduced in the 1600s and are found on Santiago, Fogo, Maio and São Nicolau. They are very tasty.

Fajã de Baixo–Fragata–Ribeira da Prata
Distance: approximately 6km; time: 3 hours; difficulty: 3 (CW)
This is a magnificent walk with some steep ascents. The only problem is finding transport from Ribeira da Prata back to Tarrafal at the end of the walk as there are only two *aluguer* drivers resident in Ribeira da Prata and you may find yourself in a one-sided negotiation in which you end up chartering a vehicle for an exorbitant sum. Minimise hassle by beginning this walk early in the morning so you can try hitching back from Prata or picking up the mid afternoon school run. Alternatively, take the midday *aluguer* from Tarrafal to Ribeira da Prata and do the walk in reverse.

Take an *aluguer* to Cachaçao. After Fajã and before Cachaçao, there's a large sign on the right for Pico Agudo Canto Fajã. Take this and, after about 50m, bear left. You will see a prominent finger of rock in the saddle ahead. After about 15 minutes, you reach a T-junction with a small grave marked by a white cross on a mound nearby. Turn left and follow the track as it winds towards the saddle and then becomes a path which ascends steeply. You will reach the saddle about 50 minutes after setting out.

From the saddle, descend on a beautifully cobbled hairpin track. After about 20 minutes, you reach **Fragata**, with houses built on fantastic ledges and outcrops with sheer drops on either side. The track leads you round the head of the *ribeira* and then begins the descent towards **Ribeira da Prata**. From the saddle to the village is approximately a two-hour walk.

Crops here include sugar cane, cassava, bananas and maize, and coarse tobacco (*erva*). It is smoked in pipes by the old folk, who spurn cigarettes as a lightweight invention.

Ribeira Brava–Queimadas

Distance: approximately 5¹/₂km ; time: 1¹/₂ hours; difficulty: 2 (CW)
Follow the cobbled road out of town and up the right-hand side of the *ribeira*. After 30 minutes you reach the small village of **Talho**. At the village standpipe (on a small concrete platform with a telephone box next to it), turn right up a small cobbled track. Very soon the cobbles give way to dust and the path begins to look far less promising. Keep following it up the hillside, resisting the temptation to take an easier, wider path which heads left after a few minutes.

As you ascend, the path swings to the left and, 30 minutes from the phone box, you emerge on a saddle. Looking back over the *ribeira*, Monte Gordo is to the right – the massive hump-backed mountain surmounted by radio masts. Turning around and looking over into the next *ribeira* you can see **Queimadas** in the valley. Fajã is through a gap in the range above it.

It is a pleasant, though steep, descent to the village. It is well worth provoking any dog you see just to hear the extraordinary echo in this amphitheatre of a valley. At the T-junction by the old school turn left for Fajã to find transport back.

RASO AND BRANCO

Just 7km², Raso has sheer cliffs, which rise out of the water to a plateau no more than 164m high. It has the traditional stony plains but also grassy areas. To the south there are colonies of sea petrels and shearwaters, red-billed tropicbirds and brown boobies – but Raso's most celebrated occupant is the Raso lark (*Alauda razae*), one of the rarest birds in the world, which lives only here and is rated 'endangered' on the international Red List of threatened species. There are no more than 250 of these birds, known locally as *calhandra do Ilhéu Raso*; to the uninitiated, they can seem disappointingly small and brown.

Branco is even smaller than Raso – 3km². It is taller, at 327m, and has one, small water source. It is one of the most important sites in Cape Verde for breeding seabirds and is white from their guano deposits. Branco was the unlikely host to 30 inhabitants in 1833 – prisoners who were dumped there and left to survive or die.

The two islands were until 1940 the last outpost of the Cape Verde giant skink, a delightful lizard-like creature coloured a mottled white and brown and with a big, heavy tail. It was the second-largest skink in the world, reaching 65cm in length and lived among the rocks eating the seeds of plants and occasionally augmenting this diet with bird eggs. Their numbers began plummeting when the prisoners arrived. After that they were the sporadic victims of local fishermen who trapped them to eat – and their skins were popular as shoe material. The final blow was the series of droughts in the early 20th century.

A luckier creature is the giant gecko (*Tarentola gigas*). This lives in cliff holes and burrows on both islands.

Every October, according to Cornelis Hazevoet, one of the leading ornithology experts on the islands, local fishermen from Santo Antão and São Vicente visit the two islets to collect thousands of young Cape Verde shearwaters, whose numbers are threatened.

Appendix 1

LANGUAGE

If you are serious about learning a language before going to Cape Verde then the big decision is whether to choose Portuguese or Creole. Creole is virtually impossible to learn outside the islands unless you have access to a Cape Verdean community, one of whose members might give lessons. On the other hand, if you plan to spend some time there and need to win the confidence of people other than professionals and officials it will be essential to learn Creole – learning Portuguese may turn out to have been a confusing waste of time.

In the absence of Creole, having some Portuguese is of huge help – every new word you learn will give you a little more access to people and be invaluable simply in helping you to get around. Most people speak no other European language. Ten minutes a day for a few months will double the satisfaction you get from your holiday. Combined with a smattering of French, to make what we call 'Fraughtuguese', you'll get by.

Portuguese

The biggest barrier to the swift acquisition of some Portuguese is pronunciation – it really takes several weeks to master it before learning any words. After that, the rudiments are reasonably simple and English-speakers will recognise a large number of words, particularly when they are written down.

Pronunciation

The following are basic rules, although there are a lot of exceptions:
- If a word carries an acute (´) or circumflex (^) accent then stress the syllable that carries it. Otherwise stress the second last syllable.
- Vowels that carry a tilde (~) on the top, and vowels followed by 'm' are nasalised.
- Many vowels disappear, for example an 'e', 'a' or 'o' at the end of a word; and many 'e's at the beginning of words. Tone down unstressed vowels.
- Double vowels are pronounced as two separate vowels.

  s = 'sh' at the end of the word; 'z' in the middle; soft 'c' at the beginning
  z = 'sh' at the end of a word
  c = soft 'c' if there's a cedilla underneath or if it's before an 'i' or an 'e'
  g = soft 'j' if before an 'i' or an 'e'
  j = soft 'j'
  rr = rolled
  r = only rolled at the beginning of a word
  lh = 'ly'
  ch = 'sh'
  qu = 'kw', before an a; 'k' before an 'e' or an 'i'
  nh = 'ny'
  x = 'sh' or 's' – the rules are complicated – just take a chance
  a = as in 'father' when stressed; as in 'air' when unstressed

e = as in 'jet' when stressed; as in the second 'e' of 'general' when unstressed
i = as in 'seen' but shorter
o = as in 'not' or 'note' when stressed; as in 'root' when unstressed
u = usually as in 'root'
h = don't pronounce

Grammar

The most basic way of making something plural is by adding -s or -es to the end. The most basic verb endings are as follows:

I buy	*compr-o*	We buy	*compr-amos*
You buy	*compr-as*	You buy	*compr-ais*
You/he/she buys	*compr-a*	They buy	*compr-am*

Address all but intimates in the third person (literally: 'could he help me'). You don't need to bother with personal pronouns (I, you, he) unless you want to emphasise them (eg: *I* am talking to *you*)

Greetings

good morning	*bom dia*
good afternoon (after midday)	*boa tarde*
good evening (after 18.00)	*boa noite*
goodbye	*até logo* ('until later')
how are you?	*como esta?*
I am well/ everything's fine	*estou bem* ('shtoe beyng')

Questions, answers and useful phrases

What is your name?	*Como se chama?*
Do you speak English?	*Fale Inglês?*
Is it possible ... ?	*É possível ... ?*
How much does it cost?	*Quanto costa?*
What is this called?	*Como se chama isso?*
Can you help me?	*Pode me ajudar?*
Pardon?	*Como?*
Where?	*Onde?*
When?	*Quando?*
How?	*Como?*
Why?	*Porque?*
What?	*Que?*
Do you have a spare room?	*Tem um quarto vago?*
You're welcome	*De nada* ('it's nothing')
I am from London	*Sou de Londres*
My name is	*Me chamou*
Where is. . ?	*Onde fica. . . ?*
I don't know	*Não sei*
I don't understand	*Não compreendo*
Straight on	*Em frente*
On the right	*À direita*
On the left	*À esquerda*
More slowly	*Mais devagar*
I have to go	*Tenho de ir*
To have coffee	*Tomar café*
To have breakfast	*Tomar o café*

There is	Há
There is no...	Não há...
Too much	Demais
That's enough!	Basta
More or less	Mais ou menos

Menus

For basic words see the list below. This list is of common dishes:

cosido de peixe	fish steak
lula grelhada	grilled squid
arroz de marisco	shellfish cooked with rice
peixe serra	generally wahoo, a white, hard fish steak
bacalhau	dried cod
bacalhau a bràz	dried cod and chips fried together
cachupa rica	maize, beans, chicken, other meat
cachupa pobre	maize, beans
djagacida or jag	a chicken dish
conj	a soup
gufong	corn bread
pudim de leite	a milk pudding, rather like creme caramel
tarte de coco	sponge impregnated with coconut, like steamed pudding

Food and drink

bean	feijão	cheese	queijo
beef	carne de vaca	chicken (as food)	frango
beer	cerveja	chips	batatas fritas
bread	pão	coffee	café
cake	bolo	dessert	sobremesa
cassava	mandioca	eel	moreia
eggs	ovos	shrimp/prawn	camarão
haricot beans	congo	spirits	aguadente
lobster	lagosta	sweet potato	batata doce
maize	milho	tea	chá
meat	carne	tuna	atum
milk	leite	turkey	peru
octopus	polvo	veal	vitela
potato	batata	water	água
rice	arroz	wine	vinho
rum (local)	grogga		

Days and months

Sunday	domingo	Wednesday	quarta-feira
Monday	segunda-feira	Thursday	quinta-feira
	(second day)	Friday	sexta-feira
Tuesday	terça-feira	Saturday	sábado

January	janeiro	July	julho
February	fevereiro	August	agosto
March	março	September	setembro
April	abril	October	outubru
May	maio	November	novembro
June	junho	December	dezembro

SOCIAL INTERACTION
Steven Maddocks and Gabi Woolf

Greetings In social situations, men shake hands with men. Sometimes the handshake lasts for as long as the conversation, so a man may hold onto your hand while he's speaking to you. It takes some getting used to, especially for frigid, contact-shy Brits, but go with it. A man and a woman, or two women, generally shake hands plus a kiss on each cheek, even on first meeting.

Small talk This is the name of the game. Conversations tend to run round in circles. Each person will enquire about the other's wellbeing, the wellbeing of each member of the other's family, then their colleagues. Then the questions turn to life in general, work, health. Neither will actually answer any questions – they just keep asking each other. So the response to 'How are you?' is 'How are you?'

'Tudu bon?' There are about 50 variations on *'Tudu bon?'* (which means 'everything OK?') The *tudu* can be followed by *bon, ben, dretu, fixe, em forma*, OK, *sabi*, tranquil, cool, fine, nice, and a million others.

No The gesture for 'no' is a waggle of the index finger with a 'no' look on your face. It seems rude, but isn't.

Hissing If someone wants to get your attention, they will hiss at you. Sometimes this comes out as 'sss', sometimes more like 'psssssyeoh'! This can strike the newcomer as incredibly rude, but it's not meant to be, and it's a lot more effective than 'Ahem, excuse me... ahem... excuse me! Hello, excuse me?'

'Oi' This means 'Hi' and is very friendly.

Numbers

1	*um*	16	*dezasseis*
2	*dois*	17	*dezassete*
3	*três*	18	*dezoito*
4	*quatro*	19	*dezanove*
5	*cinco*	20	*vinte*
6	*seis* ('saysh')	30	*trinta*
7	*sete*	40	*quarenta*
8	*oito*	50	*cinquenta*
9	*nove*	60	*sessenta*
10	*dez* ('desh')	70	*setenta*
11	*onze*	80	*oitenta*
12	*doze*	90	*noventa*
13	*treze*	100	*cem*
14	*catorze*	1,000	*mil*
15	*quinze*	a million	*um milhão*

Common compound verbs

be	*ser* (I am: *sou*/he is: *é*/we are: *somos*/they are: *são*)
give	*dar* (I give: *dou*/you give, he gives: *dá*/they give: *dão*)
go	*ir* (I go: *vou*/you go, he goes: *vai*/let's go: *vamos*)
have	*ter* (I have: *tenho*/he has: *tem*/we have: *temos*/they have: *têm*)
like	*gostar de* (I like = *gostou de*)

Other common words

aeroplane	avião ('avi-ow')	father	pai
after	depois de	fever	febre
also	também	film	película
and	e	flight	vol
at	a	girl	rapariga
bad	mau, má	goat	cabra
baggage	bagagem	good	bom/boa
bakery	padaria	he	ele
bank	banco	heavy	pousado/a
bathroom	casa de banho	high	alto/a
battery	pilha	hill	colina
beach	praia	hospital	hospital
beautiful	lindo	hot	quente
bed	cama	hotel	hotel
before	antes de	house	casa
big	grande	hurt (to)	doer
boarding house	pensão	husband	marido
book	livro	I	eu
boy	rapaz	ill	doente
breakfast	pequeno almoço	in	em
	('pekaynalmoss')	key	chave
brother	irmão	lagoon	piscina
bus	autocarro	leave	partir
buy	comprar	letter	carta
candle	vela	light	luz (loosh)
car	carro	little	pouco
casualty department	banco de socorros	(as in 'not much')	
cat	gato	lorry	camião
change	troco	low	baixo/a (baysho)
cheap	barato	lunch	almoço
chicken	galinho	magazine	revista
church	igreja	man	homem
cinema	cinéma	market	mercado
city	cidade	matches	fósforos
closed	fechado	money	dinheiro
condom	camisinha	mosquito net	mosquiteiro
cow	vaca	mother	mãe
customs	alfândega	mountain	montanha
day	dia	much	muito
diarrhoea	diarréia	never	nunca
difficult	difícil	newspaper	jornal
dinner	jantar	night	noite
doctor	médico/a	nightclub	boite
dog	cão	no	não
drink (to)	beber	nothing	nada
drink	bebida	now	agora
early	cedo	of	de
eat	comer	old	velho
English	Inglês	open	aberto
enough	bastante	path	caminho
exchange (to)	trocar	pen	caneta

perhaps	*talvez*	thanks	*obrigado/a*
pharmacy	*farmácia*		('much obliged')
pillow	*almofada*	that	*esse*
please	*faz favor*	they	*eles/elas*
police	*polizia*	this	*este*
post office	*correio*	ticket	*bilhete*
rain	*chuva*	to	*para* ('*pra*')
rest	*descansar*	today	*hoje*
restaurant	*restaurante*	toilet	*sanitário*
road	*rua*	toilet paper	*papel higiênico*
room	*quarto*	tomorrow	*amanhã*
room for a couple	*quarto casal*	town	*vila*
room for one	*quarto individual*	town hall	*câmara*
room for two	*quarto duplo*	travel	*viajar*
salt	*sal*	travellers' cheques	*cheques de viagem*
school	*escola*	very	*muito*
sea	*mar*	village	*aldeia*
sell	*vender*	visa	*visto*
send	*enviar*	we	*nós*
she	*ela*	wind	*vento*
sheet	*lençol*	with	*com*
shop	*loja*	woman	*mulher*
shower	*chuveiro*	work	*trabalhar*
sister	*irmã*	yes	*sim*
small	*pequeno*	yesterday	*ontem*
sorry	*desculpe*	you (polite	*o senhor*
speak	*falar*	masculine)	
spouse	*esposo/a*	you (polite feminine)	*a senhora*
square (town)	*praça*	you (familiar)	*você*
sun	*sol*	you (polite	*os senhoros*
supermarket	*supermercado*	masculine plural)	
swim	*nadar*	you (polite	*as senhoras*
telephone	*telefone*	feminine plural)	

Creole

São Vicente Creole translations by 10th-grade pupils at the José Augusto Pinto School in Mindelo, São Vicente, with help from their teacher, Keith West. Santiago translations and introductory material by Steven Maddocks.

The Creole language varies widely across the archipelago, to the extent that people from São Vicente profess not to be able to understand their compatriots from Santiago. Although every island has its own version, the greatest difference is between the *Barlavento* Creole spoken in the north of Cape Verde and that spoken in the south (*Sotavento* Creole).

São Vicente Creole is slightly more Portuguese than Santiago, or *Badiu*, Creole – the latter contains more African words. Generally speaking, *Barlavento* Creole is more clipped and staccato, and *Sotavento* Creole is more open, with rounded vowels, and spoken more aggressively. There are differences in vocabulary, with each using its own slang. Among the biggest differences are subject pronouns, 'You' (singular) is *bu* in *Sotavento* Creole and *bo* in *Barlavento* Creole. 'You' (plural) is *nhos* and *bzot*, respectively.

An 'a' in *Sotavento* Creole often comes out as an 'o' in *Barlavento*, as in 'work' (*trabadju/trabodj*) or 'ill-mannered' (*malkriadu/malkriod*).

In Santiago they tend to pronounce the whole word. Consequently it is much easier for the beginner to understand what is being said. In São Vicente whole syllables – both in the middle and at the ends of words – may be left out. So for example the *-adu* at the end of words in *Sotavento* Creole becomes *-od* in *Barlavento* Creole – so *Kansadu* would be pronounced *Kansod*. In Santiago Creole, *v* changes to *b* and *lh* becomes *dj*, so the word for red – *vermelho* in the north – is pronounced *burmedju* in the south.

For more about the rivalries between Creole and Portuguese, see box page 24.

Below, the Santiago translation is given first, followed by the São Vicente version. The two different versions of Creole have been represented as simply as possible for a novice. All of the sounds correspond roughly to their English equivalents. Peculiarities are as follows:

tx represents the 'ch' in 'cherry'.
dj represents the 'j' in 'Jerry'.
x is the 'sh' of 'sham'.
j is the 'z' of 'pleasure'.
k is hard, as in 'kick'.
s is soft, as in 'sick'.

The only accents used here are to draw attention to stress. For verbs, in *Sotavento* Creole stress is always on the penultimate syllable, in *Barlavento* on the last syllable. This has been represented by an accented final a, e, or i.

Shopping

English	Sotavento Creole	Barlavento Creole
Excuse me, where is the shop?	*Undi ki e loja, pur favor?*	*Ondé k'e loja, d'favor?*
Do you have bottled water?	*Nhos tem agu di garafa?*	*Bzot tem agua d'garafa?*
How much does this cost?	*Keli e kantu?*	*Keli tonté?*
It's too expensive	*Kel e karu dimas*	*Kel e txeu kor*
I'm not paying that. It's a rip-off.	*N ka kre kumpra'l. Kel e robo!* (strong)	*N ka kre kompra'l. Bo ti ta ingana'm!*

Airport

English	Sotavento Creole	Barlavento Creole
What time will the flight leave?	*Ki ora ki avion ta sei?*	*Kazora k'aviau ta sei?*
Is there a telephone here?	*Li tem telefon?*	*Li tem t'lefon?*
I'm very upset because my baggage has not arrived	*N sta mutu xatiadu pa modi nha bagagem ka ben*	*N ta txeu xatiod mod nha bagagem ka ben*
I am in a hurry	*N sta ku presa*	*N ta k'pres*

Taxi

English	Sotavento Creole	Barlavento Creole
Please take me to Hotel X	*Pur favor, leba'm ti Hotel X*	*D'favor, leva'm té Hotel X*

Hotel

English	Sotavento Creole	Barlavento Creole
Do you have a vacant room?	*Nhos tem kuartu?*	*Bzot tem um kuart?*
May I see the room first?	*N kre odja kuartu purmeru*	*N ta gostá d'oia kel kuart primer*
What time is breakfast?	*Ki ora ki e ora di kafé?*	*Kazora k'e kafé?*

Bank

English	Sotavento Creole	Barlavento Creole
Where is the bank?	*Undi ki e banku?*	*Ondé k'e bonk?*
Can I cash travellers' cheques here?	*Nhos ta troka'm travelxek?*	*Bzot ta troká travelxek?*
What is the exchange rate?	*Kal ki e kambiu di oji?*	*Tonté k'e kambiu?*
When does the bank close/open?	*Ki ora ki banku ta fitxa/ta abri?*	*Kazora k'bonk t'f txá/t'abrí?*

	Sotavento Creole	Barlavento Creole
Hiking		
Where is the path to the peak?	*Undi ki e kaminhu pa piku?*	*Ondé k'e kamin pa piku?*
Is this the path to get there? (hiker points)	*Ekeli ki e kaminhu pa la?*	*Keli k'e kamin pa la?*
Where can I buy water?	*Undi ki N podi kumpra agu?*	*Ondé k'n podé kompra agua?*
How far is it to the valley floor?	*Falta txeu pa nu txiga fundu rubera?*	*Tont temp këgent t'levá pa txigá la na fund?*
How many hours to the road?	*Kantu tenpu falta pa nu txiga strada?*	*Tont temp k'falta'm pa'n txigá strada?*
Go left at the fork	*Na dizviu toma skerda*	*Na skina bo t'v'rá pa skerda*
Go right at the crossroads	*Na kruzamentu vira a direta*	*Na kruzament bo t'v'ra pa dreta*
Can you show me on the map?	*Bu podi mostra'm li na mapa?*	*Bo podé mostra'm li na mapa?*
I need a guide.	*N mesti um guia*	*N presiza d'um guia*
I want to go to the *grogue* distillery.	*N kre ba ti trapixe*	*N kre bai pa trapixe*
No more *grogue* or I'll get drunk.	*Si n toma mas grogu n ta fika moku*	*Se n tomá mas grog, n ta fuxká*
Is it possible to walk along that path? (point)	*N podi anda na kel kaminhu?*	*N podé anda la na kel kamin?*
I want to go to the crater	*N kre ba ti kratera*	*N kre bai pa kratera*
Is there public transport?	*Tem transport?*	*Tem transport?*
Restaurant		
Could you bring me the menu please?	*Traze'm ementa, pur favor*	*Traze'm imenta, d'favor*
We've been here a long time	*Dja dura ki nu txiga li*	*Diaza k'nu ta li*
Could I have the bill please?	*Traze'm konta, pur favor*	*Traze'm konta, d'favor*
Do you have any change?	*Bu tene troku?*	*Bo tem trok?*
Personal communication		
Hallo	*Oi/Ola*	*Oi*
Goodbye	*Txau*	*Txau*
Yes	*Sim*	*Sim*
No	*Nau*	*Nau*
Do you speak English?	*Bu ta papia ingles?*	*Bo t'falá ingles?*
Which island are you from?	*Bo e di ki ilha?*	*Bo e d'kual ilha?*
What is your name?	*Modi ki e bu nomi?*	*Mané k'e bo nom?*
My name is ...	*Nha nomi e …*	*Nha nom e …*
Can you help me?	*Bu podi djuda'm?*	*Bo podé isda'm?*
What is this called?	*Modi ki e nomi di kel kuza li?*	*Mané k'e nom d'es kosa?*
I don't understand	*N ka ta entendi*	*N ka ti ta entende'b*
Please speak more slowly	*Papia mas dibagar, pur favor*	*Falá mas d'vagar, d'favor*
I don't have any money	*N ka tene dinheru*	*N ka tem d'nher*
That's enough	*Dja txiga*	*Ta bom*

Miscellaneous

	Sotavento Creole	Barlavento Creole
If	*Si*	*Se*
Often	*Txeu bes*	*Txeu vez*
Already	*Dja*	*Ja*
Still	*Inda*	*Inda*
Now	*Gosi*	*Grinhasim*
Other	*Otu*	*Ot*
Sorry	*Diskulpa'm*	*Diskulpa'm*
How are you? ...	*Modi ki bu sta?*	*Manera bo ta?*
General greeting	*Tudu bon?*	*Tud dret?*
	Tudu dretu?	*Tud kul?*
Excuse me	*Kon lisensa*	*Ko l'sensa*
I'm here on holiday.	*N sta li di feria.*	*N ta d'feria*
I'm from London/England/	*Ami e di Londres/*	*Mi e d'Londres/*
America	*Inglatera/Merka*	*d'Inglater/d'Merka*
Collective *aluguer* (often a		
Toyota Hiace)	*Ias*	*Ias*
Bad/damaged/broken/ill/		
mistaken	*Mariadu*	no single word covers the same range
Good/excellent/cool/fine	*Fixe*	*Kul*
Good/tasty/delicious/fun	*Sabi*	*Sab*
That's not on	*Keli ka ta da*	*Keli ka ta dret*
There's a power cut	*Lus dju bui*	*Lus ju bui*
I don't eat meat	*N ka ta kumé karni*	*N ka ta k'mé karn*

Note:

You has familiar and polite, singular and plural forms, as well as gender. It would be rude to address an elderly stranger with the familiar form.

you (singular, familiar)	*bu* (except *bo e*, you are)	*bo*
you (singular, polite)	*nho* (masc), *nha* (fem)	*bosé* (masc & fem)
you (plural, familiar)	*nhos*	*bzot*
you (plural, polite)	*nhos*	*bosés*

Appendix 2

FURTHER READING

There is almost nothing about Cape Verde on the shelves of most British bookshops. Two exceptions are the Basil Davidson book listed below and Mitchell Serel's *The Jews of Cape Verde* (Sepher-Hermon Press, 1997). If you have a few months it is worth putting a request in to Waterstone's out-of-print-book search facility (✆ *020 7434 1195*). Alternatively, the British Library has many of the books below (membership is free but you need a letter, normally from an employer, explaining why no other library is suitable). Its catalogue can be searched on the internet (*www.bl.uk*). Also try the Travel Bookshop (*13 Blenheim Crescent, London W11;* ✆ *020 7229 5260*), which has some second-hand gems on its shelves. For the definitive digest of Cape Verdean literature in English consult the *World Bibliographical Series*, Volume 123, Cape Verde, by Caroline Shaw (Clio Press, 1991).

History

Berger Coli, Waltraud and Lobban, Richard A *The Cape Verdeans in Rhode Island: A Brief History*. On the same theme as Halter (see below).

Carreira, António *People of the Cape Verde Islands* (Hurst, 1982). A detailed analysis of one of the fundamental forces of Cape Verdean society: emigration, both forced and voluntary. It is an academic work by a respected Cape Verde historian.

Davidson, Basil *The Fortunate Isles* (Hutchinson, 1989). A one-volume history of the islands from start to finish by Britain's foremost historian of Africa. The book is a personal account of the emergence of a much-loved nation from the bonds of colonialism. There is a rather detailed analysis of Cape Verde's socialist policies in the last third of the book.

Davidson, Basil *No Fist is Big Enough to Hide the Sky: the Liberation of Guinea-Bissau and Cape Verde* (Zed Press, 1981). A lively account of the armed struggle in Guinea-Bissau.

Duncan, Bentley *Atlantic Islands: Madeira, the Azores and the Cape Verdes in 17th Century Commerce and Navigation* (University of Chicago Press, 1972). A formidable mass of information about the slave and other trades, spilling over into other centuries and with plenty of interesting titbits.

Halter, Marilyn *Between Race and Ethnicity: Cape Verdean American Immigrants 1860–1965* (University of Illinois Press, 1995). Written as part of a larger project to understand American immigrants from a variety of countries, this book is essential for a deeper understanding of Cape Verde, because emigration has played such a large part in moulding the country. As well as fascinating accounts of the lives of Cape Verdeans in the USA, it includes a lot of history of the land left behind.

Lobban, Richard *Cape Verde: Crioulo Colony to Independent Nation* (Westview Press, 1995), available from the publisher in Boulder, Colorado, is an excellent book with a broad sweep, by a seasoned Cape Verde-watcher. It is available from Westview Press (*5500 Central Avenue, Boulder, CO 80301-2877;* ✆ *(+1) 303 444 3541; www.westviewpress.com*) or for individual orders: Perseus Books Group Customer Service (*1094 Flex Drive, Jackson, TN 38301;* ✆ *+1 800 371 1669;* f *+1 800 453 2884;* e *perseus.orders@perseusbooks.com; www.westviewpress.com*).

Lobban, Richard *The Historical Dictionary of the Republic of Cape Verde* (Scarecrow Press, 1995). A very readable and up-to-date book. Ideal for answering many questions about the archipelago, it is less good as a straightforward history, which it doesn't claim to be.

Lyall, Archibald *Black and White Make Brown* (Heinemann, 1938). An intelligent and highly entertaining account of the journey this journalist made to Cape Verde and Portuguese Guinea.

It is worth an afternoon browsing through the library for the many accounts written by British sailors, civil servants and entrepreneurs who have passed through the archipelago. They include:

Burdon Ellis, Alfred *West African Islands* (Chapman and Hall, 1855). Entertaining and irritating by turns.

Dampier, William *A New Voyage Round the World* (Adam and Charles Black, 1937). This is an account of the sailor's visit in 1683, complete with pirates, bandits and a generally unfavourable impression of the Cape Verdean people.

Rendall, John *A Guide to the Cape Verde Islands* (C Wilson, 1856). Frustratingly lacking in detail given the promise of the title, but fascinating nevertheless.

Roberts, George *Account of a Voyage to the Islands of the Canaries, Cape de Verde and Barbadoes, in 1721* can be found within *A new general collection of voyages and travels, vol I*, collected by Thomas Astley (Frank Cass, 1968) – another lively set of adventures.

Valdez, Francisco Travassos *Six Years of a Traveller's Life in Western Africa, vol 1* (Hurst and Blackett, 1861) is an unusually positive account by a Portuguese sent to report on the islands for the government.

Portuguese titles

Carreira, António *Cabo Verde: Formaçao e Extinçao de uma Sociedade Escravocrata.*
Lopes, Jose Vicente *Cabo Verde: Os Bastidores da Independencia* (Spleen, 2002).

Both are available in Praia's Casa de Cultura.

Economy and politics

For factual information on the country's economy there are two reference books:

Africa South of the Sahara (Europa Publications). A reference book that is updated every year.
Europa World Year Book, by the same publisher, where it is covered less extensively.

In addition look for:

Foy, Colm *Cape Verde: Politics, Economics and Society* (Pinter, 1986). A penetrating guide to the working of government in post-independence Cape Verde.

Natural history

For birdwatchers, the perfect combination of books is:

Bannerman, David and Mary *History of the Birds of the Cape Verde Islands* (Oliver and Boyd, 1968). An entertaining book which combines distinguished ornithology with genial accounts of their times in Cape Verde.

Hazevoet, Cornelis *The Birds of the Cape Verde Islands* (British Ornithologists' Union, 1995). Order from the Natural History Book Service (*2–3 Wills Road, Totnes, Devon TQ9 5XN, UK;* ☏ *01803 865913;* f *01803 865280;* e *customer.services@nhbs.co.uk; www. nhbs.co.uk*).

Sargeant, Dave *A Birder's Guide to the Cape Verde Islands.* If you can afford it, this self-published account of a birding trip to the islands is full of hints on where to go interspersed with the palpable joys and frustrations of the hobby. It can be ordered from the Natural History Book Service.

Aves de Cabo Verde A cheaper option, if it is still in print, is this useful little orange booklet. It includes colour drawings of most of the birds, their local and Latin names and a short explanation in Portuguese. It was published by BirdLife International.

Plantas Endémicas A small guide to the country's vegetation, it may still be available on the islands.

Sailing

Hammick, Anne and Heath, Nicholas *Atlantic Islands: Azores, Madeira, Canary and Cape Verde Islands* (Imray, Laurie, Norie and Wilson, 1999). An essential practical guide for yachties.

Literature

Clew Parsons, Elsie *Folk Lore from the Cape Verde Islands* (American Folklore Society, 1923). In British libraries. A fascinating accumulation of tales she collected from American *emigrantes* in the early 1900s.

Hamilton, Russell *Voices from an Empire: A History of Afro-Portuguese Literature* (University of Minnesota Press, 1975). Includes an in-depth look at some of the leading Cape Verdean writers and poets.

Strathern, Oona *Traveller's Literary Companions* (In Print, 1994). Devoted to Cape Verdean poems, it is only worthwhile buying if you are interested more widely in African literature.

Donald Burness *Fire: Six Writers from Angola, Mozambique and Cape Verde* (Three Continents Press, 1977) This is of more substance and devotes some time to the exposition of Baltasar Lopes's novel *Chiquinho*.

Classic Cape Verde literature, which does not seem to be available in English, includes:

Lopes, Baltasar *Chiquinho* (1947). The seminal Cape Verdean novel and also a leader in the literature of Portuguese Africa. It is available in French translation.

Lopes, Manuel *Chuva Braba* (Wild Rain) and *Flagelados do Vente Leste* (Victims of the East Wind). The latter novel was the basis for the first Cape Verdean-produced feature-length motion picture, which has the same title and was shot on Santo Antão.

Health

Wilson-Howarth, Jane *Healthy Travel: Bites, Bugs and Bowels* (Cadogan, 2002).

Wilson-Howarth, Dr Jane and Ellis, Dr Matthew *Your Child Abroad: A travel health guide* (Bradt, 2005).

Activities

Although hiking is covered extensively in this book, there are many more walks which there is no space to cover.

Hirtle, Alex *Bemvindos A Assomada* (2001). Alex Hirtle was a Peace Corps volunteer in Santiago. His booklet has a map of Santa Catarina, the big hiking area of Santiago, depicting hiking and biking trails. There are also lists of artisans in the area (from whom visitors can buy crafts), cultural notes and information about the city of Assomada. The book is now very hard to find, but try at the town hall (*câmara municipal*) in Assomada, at Assomada's Museu de Tabanka, or various travel agencies and restaurants in Santiago.

Cabo Verde, Santo Antão, Guia dos Circuitos Turísticos. A beautifully produced guide to hikes in Santo Antão, each with a foldout, high-quality map to show the route. Although written in Portuguese, it is of great value even without the text. It might still be available on Santo Antão; otherwise try to get it from the agency Lux Development (*www.lux-development.lu*), which funded the project.

For more detail on where to surf, get hold of *The Surf Report*; try www.surfermag.com.

Miscellaneous

Germano Lima, António *Ilha de Capitães*. A Portuguese account of the history of Boavista.

Ludtke, Jean *Atlantic Peeks – an Ethnographic Guide to the Portuguese-Speaking Islands* (Christopher Publishing House, 1989). Recommended but hard to obtain in Britain.

Cimboa is a journal of historical, cultural and political articles, published by the Cape Verdean consulate in Boston.

Fragata, the in-flight magazine of the airline TACV, is worth picking up. The English translations of its articles are flawed, but the topics are interesting and there are good photographs.

Cape Verde library collections

The Cape Verdean Special Collection is in the James P Adams Library, Rhode Island College, 600 Mount Pleasant Av, Providence, RI 02908; ↘ (+1) 401 456 9653. In this collection you find books, newspapers, tapes of Cape Verdean television and radio programmes, photographs and various private Cape Verdean collections. There is about 40 linear feet of material.

The Arquivo Historico Nacional (*CP 321, Chã d'Areia, Praia, Santiago, Cape Verde*) was founded in 1988 and now comprises a large collection of historic and recent books as well as documents of the colonial administration concerning such issues as customs, emigration, and church matters among many other subjects.

Carreira, António *Cabo Verde: Formação e Extinção de uma Sociedade Escravocrata*. This is an important work on the Cape Verdean slave economy, and is available in Praia's Casa de Cultura for 2,000$.

Websites

There's a growing amount of information about Cape Verde on the internet. The biggest network of sites is hosted by the University of Massachusetts.

www.umassd.edu/specialprograms/caboverde This site will link you with everyone else.

www.capeverdeusembassy.org Cape Verde Eembassy in the United States.

www.caboverde.com The country's official website, with a mammoth collection of information of use to tourists.

www.allafrica.com Regular news about Cape Verde is published on .

www.eyeballs.net/verde Traudi Coli has scanned and launched part of her extensive collection of images of historical and contemporary Cape Verde.

www.parsimony.net For a forum for the discussion of Cape Verdean issues try forum 36456.

www.ccfpraia.com French cultural centre in Praia

www.mindelo.info Information about Mindelo

www.rootstravel.com Travel agency

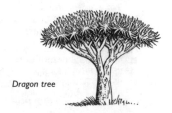

Dragon tree

Bradt Travel Guides

www.bradtguides.com

Africa

Africa Overland	£15.99
Benin	£14.99
Botswana: Okavango, Chobe, Northern Kalahari	£14.95
Burkina Faso	£14.99
Cape Verde Islands	£13.99
Canary Islands	£13.95
Cameroon	£13.95
Eritrea	£12.95
Ethiopia	£15.99
Gabon, São Tomé, Príncipe	£13.95
Gambia, The	£12.95
Georgia	£13.95
Ghana	£13.95
Kenya	£14.95
Madagascar	£14.95
Malawi	£12.95
Mali	£13.95
Mauritius, Rodrigues & Réunion	£12.95
Mozambique	£12.95
Namibia	£14.95
Niger	£14.99
Nigeria	£15.99
Rwanda	£13.95
Seychelles	£14.99
Sudan	£13.95
Tanzania, Northern	£13.99
Tanzania	£14.95
Uganda	£13.95
Zambia	£15.95
Zanzibar	£12.95

Britain and Europe

Albania	£13.99
Armenia, Nagorno Karabagh	£13.95
Azores	£12.95
Baltic Capitals: Tallinn, Riga, Vilnius, Kaliningrad	£12.99
Belgrade	£6.99
Bosnia & Herzegovina	£13.95
Bratislava	£6.99
Budapest	£7.95
Cork	£6.95
Croatia	£12.95
Cyprus see North Cyprus	
Czech Republic	£13.99
Dubrovnik	£6.95
Eccentric Britain	£13.99
Eccentric Edinburgh	£5.95
Eccentric France	£12.95
Eccentric London	£12.95
Eccentric Oxford	£5.95
Estonia	£12.95
Faroe Islands	£13.95
Hungary	£14.99
Kiev	£7.95
Latvia	£13.99
Lille	£6.99

Lithuania	£13.99
Ljubljana	£6.99
Macedonia	£13.95
Montenegro	£13.99
North Cyprus	£12.95
Paris, Lille & Brussels	£11.95
Riga	£6.95
River Thames, In the Footsteps of the Famous	£10.95
Serbia	£13.99
Slovenia	£12.99
Spitsbergen	£14.99
Switzerland: Rail, Road, Lake	£13.99
Tallinn	£6.95
Ukraine	£13.95
Vilnius	£6.99

Middle East, Asia and Australasia

Great Wall of China	£13.99
Iran	£14.99
Iraq	£14.95
Kabul	£9.95
Maldives	£13.99
Mongolia	£14.95
North Korea	£13.95
Palestine, Jerusalem	£12.95
Sri Lanka	£13.99
Syria	£13.99
Tasmania	£12.95
Tibet	£12.95
Turkmenistan	£14.99

The Americas and the Caribbean

Amazon, The	£14.95
Argentina	£15.99
Cayman Islands	£12.95
Costa Rica	£13.99
Chile	£16.95
Chile & Argentina: Trekking	£12.95
Eccentric America	£13.95
Eccentric California	£13.99
Falkland Islands	£13.95
Peru & Bolivia: Backpacking and Trekking	£12.95
Panama	£13.95
St Helena, Ascension, Tristan da Cunha	£14.95
USA by Rail	£13.99

Wildlife

Antarctica: Guide to the Wildlife	£14.95
Arctic: Guide to the Wildlife	£14.95
British Isles: Wildlife of Coastal Waters	£14.95
Galápagos Wildlife	£15.99
Madagascar Wildlife	£14.95
South African Wildlife	£18.95

Health

Your Child Abroad: A Travel Health Guide	£10.95

WIN £100 CASH!

READER QUESTIONNAIRE

Send in your completed questionnaire for the chance to win £100 cash in our regular draw

All respondents may order a Bradt guide at half the UK retail price – please complete the order form overleaf.

(Entries may be posted or faxed to us, or scanned and emailed.)

We are interested in getting feedback from our readers to help us plan future Bradt guides. Please answer ALL the questions below and return the form to us in order to qualify for an entry in our regular draw.

Have you used any other Bradt guides? If so, which titles? . . . .
. . . .

What other publishers' travel guides do you use regularly? . . . .
. . . .

Where did you buy this guidebook? . . . .

What was the main purpose of your trip to Cape Verde (or for what other reason did you read our guide)? eg. holiday/business/charity etc. . . . .
. . . .

What other destinations would you like to see covered by a Bradt guide?
. . . .

Would you like to receive our catalogue/newsletters?

YES / NO (If yes, please complete details on reverse)

If yes – by post or email? . . . .

Age (circle relevant category) 16–25   26–45   46–60   60+

Male/Female (delete as appropriate)

Home country . . . .

Please send us any comments about our guide to Cape Verde or other Bradt Travel Guides. . . . .
. . . .
. . . .
. . . .

Bradt Travel Guides

23 High Street, Chalfont St Peter, Bucks SL9 9QE, UK
☏ +44 (0)1753 893444 f +44 (0)1753 892333
e info@bradtguides.com
www.bradtguides.com

CLAIM YOUR HALF-PRICE BRADT GUIDE!

Order Form

To order your half-price copy of a Bradt guide, and to enter our prize draw to win £100 (see overleaf), please fill in the order form below, complete the questionnaire overleaf, and send it to Bradt Travel Guides by post, fax or email.

Please send me one copy of the following guide at half the UK retail price

Title	Retail price	Half price
. . . .	. . . .	. . . .

Please send the following additional guides at full UK retail price

No	Title	Retail price	Total
. . .	. . . .	. . . .	. . . .
. . .	. . . .	. . . .	. . . .
. . .	. . . .	. . . .	. . . .

	Sub total	. . . .
	Post & packing	. . . .
(£1 per book UK; £2 per book Europe; £3 per book rest of world)		
	Total	. . . .

Name . . . .

Address . . . .

Tel . . . .   Email . . . .

☐ I enclose a cheque for £ . . . . made payable to Bradt Travel Guides Ltd

☐ I would like to pay by credit card. Number: . . . .

    Expiry date: . . . / . . .   3-digit security code (on reverse of card) . . . . .

☐ Please add my name to your catalogue mailing list.

☐ I would be happy for you to use my name and comments in Bradt marketing material.

Send your order on this form, with the completed questionnaire, to:

Bradt Travel Guides/CAPV
23 High Street, Chalfont St Peter, Bucks SL9 9QE
✆ +44 (0)1753 893444   f +44 (0)1753 892333
e info@bradtguides.com   www.bradtguides.com

Index

Page references in bold indicate major entries; those in italics indicate maps.
Abbreviations: Boavista (Bv) Brava (Br) Fogo (Fg) Maio (Ma) Sal (Sl) Santiago (Sg)
Santo Antão (SA) São Nicolau (SN) São Vicente (SV)